Defining Corruption in the Ottoman Empire

Defining Corruption in the Ottoman Empire

Morality, Legality, and Abuse of Power in Premodern Governance

BOĞAÇ A. ERGENE

Great Clarendon Street, Oxford, OX2 6DP,
United Kingdom

Oxford University Press is a department of the University of Oxford.
It furthers the University's objective of excellence in research, scholarship,
and education by publishing worldwide. Oxford is a registered trade mark of
Oxford University Press in the UK and in certain other countries

© Boğaç A. Ergene 2024

The moral rights of the author have been asserted

All rights reserved. No part of this publication may be reproduced, stored in
a retrieval system, or transmitted, in any form or by any means, without the
prior permission in writing of Oxford University Press, or as expressly permitted
by law, by licence or under terms agreed with the appropriate reprographics
rights organization. Enquiries concerning reproduction outside the scope of the
above should be sent to the Rights Department, Oxford University Press, at the
address above

You must not circulate this work in any other form
and you must impose this same condition on any acquirer

Published in the United States of America by Oxford University Press
198 Madison Avenue, New York, NY 10016, United States of America

British Library Cataloguing in Publication Data

Data available

Library of Congress Control Number: 2023950620

ISBN 978–0–19–891621–5

DOI: 10.1093/oso/9780198916215.001.0001

Printed and bound by
CPI Group (UK) Ltd, Croydon, CR0 4YY

Links to third party websites are provided by Oxford in good faith and
for information only. Oxford disclaims any responsibility for the materials
contained in any third party website referenced in this work.

babama…

Acknowledgments

I would like to express my gratitude to the following colleagues (in alphabetical order) who generously shared with me insights and sources: Nurcan and Zeynep Abacı, Iris Agmon, Engin Akarlı, Jun Akiba, Abdurrahman Atçıl, Yavuz Aykan, Metin Coşgel, Beshara Doumani, Ayda Erbal, Huda Fakhreddine, Suraiya Faroqhi, Carter Findley, Nimrod Hurvitz, M. Asım Karaömerlioğlu, Cengiz Kırlı, Harun Küçük, Avi Rubin, Safa Saraçoğlu, Derin Terzioğlu, Ertuğrul Ahmet Tonak, Başak Tuğ, Maaike van Berkel, and Seçil Yılmaz. Coşkun Tuncer carefully read the entire text and made many useful suggestions. I also learned from the work of Elif Akçetin, Yasin Arslantaş, Marc Aymes, Heather Ferguson, Eda Güçlü, Gottfried Hagen, Joanna Innes, Toru Miura, Hedda Reindl-Kiel, and Claudia Römer, participants in a workshop that Cengiz Kırlı and I organized in Fall 2021 titled "Corruption in the Ottoman Empire." As my longtime mentors, Virginia Aksan, Şevket Pamuk, and David Powers advised me on various aspects of the project. Ginny, in particular, helped me to think about corruption in relation to broader trends and tendencies in Ottoman history.

I received editorial support from Pamela Haag, who was helpful in organizing my discussion. Christi Stanforth patiently and diligently read multiple versions of the manuscript, streamlined my often-convoluted writing (as much as possible), fixed the text's format, and offered valuable stylistic *and* substantive feedback. I feel very fortunate to have worked with her. Robin Fitch-McCullough and Tom Anderson-Monterosso at the University of Vermont and Kathryn Thornton at Brown University provided much-appreciated bibliographical help as my undergraduate research assistants. Gregory Woolston skillfully and meticulously prepared my diagrams.

The project was conducted, in part, with research support and funding by the History Department and the College of Arts and Sciences at the University of Vermont. I am grateful to Paul Deslandes, my former chair, and Bill Falls, my current dean, for allowing me to take a leave of absence in the middle of the COVID-19 pandemic to spend one semester in Turkey. In Turkey, the Economics Department at the Middle East Technical University (METU) hosted me in Spring 2021. I am appreciative of the hospitality that Meltem Dayıoğlu Tayfur and Şirin Saraçoğlu, successive chairs of the department, showed during my time there. The course I taught at METU, "The Political

Economy of the Ottoman Empire," allowed me to share some of the ideas in this book with a bright group of advanced economics and history students and receive their constructive criticisms.

In Vermont, I found much comfort in the personal and intellectual company of my friends and colleagues, Jonathan Huener, David Massell, and Sean Stilwell. I am privileged to be in the same department with them and other exemplary scholar-teachers, including Charlie Briggs, Dona Brown, Andy Buchanan, Felicia Kornbluh, Paul Deslandes, Sean Field, Melanie Gustafson, Abigail McGowan, Sarah Osten, Nicole Phelps, Susanna Schrafstetter, Alan Steinweis, and Steven Zdatny.

My thanks to Susan Ferber at Oxford University Press for her help in finding the right editor for this book, and to Thomas Stottor for being that person. With exemplary professionalism and good humor, Thomas guided the project through the various stages of the publishing process. I am also grateful to the anonymous reviewers for their valuable feedback and to Nadine Kolz, the book's title manager, and the production staff, including Kripadevi Prabhakar, Rachel H. Addison and Michael Hayes for their diligent work.

In those times when I needed personal support and encouragement, and there were a few occasions, I turned to my old friends Ali Berker, Mehmet Ali Çalışkan, Atabey Kaygun, Emre Sencer, and Ela Yazıcı İnan.

Finally, I would like to express my deepest gratitude to my dear sister, Simay Ergene Civelek, and my beloved wife, Febe Armanios, two of the most selfless, caring, and loyal individuals I know, on whom I continue to lean in every aspect of my life. Without the comfort they provided, it would have been very difficult, perhaps impossible, to write this book. A historian of the Ottoman Empire herself, Febe also read and commented on various drafts of the book.

I dedicate *Defining Corruption* to the memory of my father, Basri Cemil Güler Ergene (1932–2021), who passed away when I was working hard to complete its first draft. He was a passionate and prolific reader of Turkish, Ottoman, and religious history of all types. I used to joke that he might have read more books on these subjects since his retirement than I had since I received my doctorate. Born in the first decade of the modern Turkish Republic and proud of it, he was a man of different times and convictions from my own; we rarely, if ever, saw eye to eye on varied religious, historical, and political affairs. In fact, our arguments over such issues were frequent, passionate, at times bruising. Yet he never failed to listen when I talked with him, never gave less than his undivided attention when I asked him to reconsider an idea he inherently disagreed with. That was how he showed his love and devotion to me, among other ways. He might have been critical about much of what I claim in this book. But he was the best audience any historian could hope for.

Contents

List of Figures	xi
List of Tables	xiii
Glossary	xv
A Note on Transliteration	xix
Introduction: Conceptual Reflections	1
1. Corruption Based on Pre-Ottoman Jurisprudential Sources	29
2. Corruption in Ottoman Jurisprudence	50
3. Abuse and Predation in State Documents	81
4. Controlling Corruption	101
5. Corruption in Ottoman Political Literature	144
6. Corruption According to Accounts for Foreigners	192
7. Gifts as Bribes	225
8. On the Morality of Patronage: The Case of Ilmiye	239
Conclusion: Possible Rationalizations of Corruption and Other Afterthoughts	261
References	273
Index	309

List of Figures

1.1. Semantic Links among F-s-d, Z-l-m, and F-s-q in the Quran	31
3.1. Functional Tasks and Responsibilities According to the Circle	85
3.2. Rough Correspondence among Crime Categories	99
5.1. Causal Links in Corruption According to the Political Literature (Sixteenth to Eighteenth Centuries)	168

List of Tables

2.1.	Bribe Categories According to Ibn Nujaym (with Other Opinions)	58
3.1.	Corruption in Jurisprudential Works and State-Generated Texts	100
4.1.	Select Crimes and Punishments in the General Kanunname ("Kanunname-i Osmani") of Sultan Süleyman	113
4.2.	"The Punishment Scale for Salaried Persons...Convicted of Corruption" in Qinq China	115
4.3.	Mühimme and Şikayet Registers Explored	124
4.4.	Prevalence of Corruption Related Entries in the Registers	126
4.5.	Actors Involved in Corruption	128
4.6.	Acts of Corruption in Mühimme and Şikayet Registers	133
4.7.	Devr, Violence, and Imprisonment in Mühimme and Şikayet Registers	143
5.1.	Works Reflecting Pre-Sixteenth-Century Perspectives	148
5.2.	Works Reflecting Perspectives between the Sixteenth and Eighteenth Centuries	158
5.3.	Harmful Behavior in Government According to Political Texts	164
5.4.	Punishments and Other Measures to Control Corruption as Proposed by Ottoman Commentators	176
5.5.	Perspectives on Corruption in the Ottoman Political Literature	189
6.1.	Information about Foreign Accounts Cited in Chapter 6	196
6.2.	Litigation Fees According to Accounts for Foreigners	210

Glossary

Select foreign words that appear multiple times in the book.

adala (A.)/adalet (T.): justice

adaletname: rescript of justice

adil: just person; opposite of fasiq

adl: just-ness as a human quality

amir: ruler or prince

askeri: "military" or tax-exempt groups in the Ottoman Empire

avaid: a disbursement required for or following an appointment

beytülmal: public or state treasury

bidat: corrupt innovation

caize: a disbursement required for or following an appointment

danişmend: religious scholar or student

devr: illegal tour of inspection by provincial authorities

divan: imperial council

fasad (A.)/fesad (T.): mischief, disorder, or corruption

fasiq (A.)/fasık (T.): one who possesses the quality of fisq; opposite of adil

fatwa: legal opinion issued by a mufti

fiqh (A.)/fıkıh (T.): jurisprudential traditions

fisq (A.)/fısk (T.): disbelief, dishonesty, or immorality

ghaza: war in the name of religion

ghazi: one who fights ghaza

hadd: severe punishment for a crime identified in the Quran; pl. hudud

hadith: accounts of the Prophet Muhammad's and his companions' sayings and actions; pl. ahadith

hadiya (A.)/hediye or hedaye (T.): gift

Hanafi: the official legal school of the Ottoman polity

Hanbali: a Sunni legal school

ijma: jurists' opinions

ilmiye: religious establishment

iltizam: tax-farm

intisab (or intisap): personal or professional affiliation with a high-status person

irtikab (or irtikap): bad act, pilfering, dishonesty, extortion

kalebend defterleri: registers that contain particular types of punishments for criminals decided by imperial authorities

kanun: law

kanunname: law code comprised of kanuns

kazasker: a high-ranking judicial authority in the Ottoman polity

kufr: disbelief, infidelity

madrasa: school, often (but not always) of religious nature

mahsul: yield or earning

Maliki: a Sunni legal school

mazalim tribunal: tribunals that adjudicated corruption crimes (among others) in pre-Ottoman times

mevali: high-ranking qadis

miri: state owned

mollazade: son of a ranking ulema family

müderris: teacher

mufti: jurist authorized to issue legal opinions

mühimme defterleri: registers that contain correspondence pertaining to state affairs

muhtesib: market inspector

mülazemet: candidacy for an ilmiye position

mülazım: candidate for an ilmiye position

naib: deputy judge

paşa (or pasha): a military rank used for vezirs and governors

pişkeş: tribute; or a disbursement required for or following an appointment

qadhf: false allegation of zina

qadi: Islamic judge

rashwa (A.)/rüşvet (T.): bribe

reaya: "flock"; tax-paying groups in the Ottoman polity

şefaat: intercession

şeyhülislam: chief mufti

Shafii: a Sunni legal school

sharia: Islamic law

şikayet defterleri: registers that contain documentation related to complaints received by the imperial center

siyasa (A.)/siyaset (T.): government based on ruler's discretion often influenced by pre-Islamic traditions

sunna: practices of the Prophet and his companions that became accepted as normative by subsequent generations of Muslims

Tanzimat: era of reform between 1839–76

tazir: discretionary punishment for crimes not specifically mentioned in the Quran

teaddi: oppression

tımar: smaller prebendal grant of land or revenue to a military-administrative authority as compensation for his services

ulema: religious scholars, authorities, office-holders

ulemazade: son of a ranking ulema family

umma: Muslim community

vezir (or vizier): a member of the imperial divan; minister

voyvoda: a provincial military-administrative authority

waqf: charitable endowment

zakat (A.)/zekat (T.): obligatory alms

zeamet: medium-size prebendal grant of land or revenue to a military-administrative authority as compensation for his services

zina: illicit intercourse

zulm (A.)/zulüm (T.): oppression; injustice

A Note on Transliteration

For the sake of simplicity, in this book Arabic and Turkish names and terms are spelled using a modified version of the *IJMES* transliteration system that omits diacritical marks. The transliteration follows the Turkish version of the simplified system for the names and terms that appear primarily in Turkish sources and the Arabic version for those that appear primarily in Arabic sources and contexts. Terms that can be found in the main section of *Merriam-Webster's Collegiate Dictionary*, such as "sharia" and "hadith," are not italicized and follow *Merriam-Webster's* spellings. The original transliterations of the author names and titles cited in the bibliography are retained. I italicize foreign words when first introduced in the text (with the exceptions already mentioned) and when my discussion is focused on them.

Introduction

Conceptual Reflections

This book investigates how premodern Ottomans might have perceived acts that moderns might associate with "corruption." The wording in the previous sentence is unavoidably convoluted because there is no specific word for corruption in Ottoman Turkish as we typically understand it today: that is, as self-interested, fraudulent behavior by government officials abusing their positions, resources, and authority (cf. Nye 1967: 419).[1] The incompatibility between modern and premodern perceptions is not solely a matter of terminology. As a blanket term, "corruption" refers to misdeeds associated with one crime genus that encompasses bribery, extortion, embezzlement, favoritism, influence-peddling, graft, gratuities, sidelining, and perhaps a few others (Blundo and Olivier de Sardan 2006: 72–80). Yet it is doubtful that the Ottomans saw all these acts as related or even as crimes.[2] Indeed, while they might have been troubled by bribery, they appeared to be less concerned about

---

[1] For modern definitions of corruption as use of public sources for private gain, also see Johnston 1996; Holmes 2015; and Rose 2018.

[2] The second edition of *Redhouse's Turkish Dictionary*, published in 1880, translates "corruption" as بوزمقلق (*bozmaklık*; "to disturb" or "to disrupt") and چوروتمكلك (*çürütmeklik*; "to make it rot" or "to make it decay"). *Yolsuzluk* in modern Turkish, meaning the misuse of administrative and/or political authority, may be a twentieth-century usage, although references to it with the connotations of "improper" or "inappropriate" can be found in nineteenth-century official documents (Kırlı 2015: 63). And while *fasad* (Ottoman Turkish: *fesad*) is commonly utilized in modern Arabic to render the same meaning, it was used by Ottomans broadly to refer to acts that undermined social and gender hierarchies, security, and the dynasty's right and ability to govern what they regarded as their patrimonial realm. Many other related terms, such as *rüşvet* (bribery), *irtikab* (committing bad acts, pilfering, dishonesty), or *ihtilas* (embezzlement), had meanings that differ in their specificity. My impression based on modern dictionaries is that irtikab acquired the meaning of public office corruption in the late 1880s or early 1890s. These dictionaries include *Hazine-i Lugat* (1838), *Müntehab-ı Lugat-ı Osmaniyye* (1852–3), *Lehçe-i Osmani* (1876–82), *Lugat-ı Remzi* (1888), *Lugat-ı Ebuzziya* (1888), *A Turkish and English Lexicon* (1890), *Lugat-ı Naci* (1891–4), *Kamus-ı Osmani* (1895–1905), *Kamus-ı Türki* (1901), *Mükemmel Osmanlı Lugatı* (1902), *Resimli Kamus-ı Osmani* (1909–12), *Kamus-ı Fransevi* (1911), *Yeni Türkçe Lugat* (1912–27), and *Resimli Türkçe Kamus* (1928); they can be found at https://www.osmanlicasozlukler.com/ (accessed July 8, 2023). I should note, however, that the "Law Code to Prevent İrtikab" (*Men-i İrtikab Kanunnamesi*) of 1855 contains a set of laws about bribes, stealing (*sirkat*), and gifts (*hedaya*), which might suggest that the term had already begun to acquire a more comprehensive meaning somewhat earlier (Akgündüz 1987).

Defining Corruption in the Ottoman Empire: Morality, Legality, and Abuse of Power in Premodern Governance.
Boğaç A. Ergene, Oxford University Press. © Boğaç A. Ergene 2024. DOI: 10.1093/oso/9780198916215.003.0001

favoritism, for example, given the centrality of extended households in Ottoman politics, and not at all with after-the-fact gratuities. What's more, we should even expect variations in the premodern and modern definitions of particular transgressions.

This book takes these terminological and conceptual incongruities as starting points for its inquiry. If corruption, as moderns use the term, did not *precisely* exist in the Ottoman Empire before the nineteenth century, then what did? How should we conceive of its context-appropriate approximations? What specific acts were associated with them? How should we understand such acts individually and in relation to other transgressions? Given that the polity boasted an advanced judicial system and a sophisticated bureaucratic structure that helped the ruling elite govern according to well-established rules and regulations, we should expect concrete answers to such questions. Behavior that deviated from prescribed standards of conduct in legal and government affairs must have been as much a problem for the Ottomans as it has been for modern societies (cf. Akçetin 2023).

In this book, I contend that in the premodern era there were numerous discourses regarding acts (individually and as groups) that we would associate with corruption. One finds these discourses in a variety of archival and narrative genres of historical documents, including jurisprudential treatises, imperial orders and communication, chronicles, and travel and diplomatic accounts produced for foreign audiences. In large part, my research explores these sources to discern how Ottoman jurists, statesmen, political commentators, and foreign observers formulated their understanding of the relevant acts, including their causes and consequences, and how these perspectives reveal attitudes toward abuse by state officials that range from relatively moralistic to more pragmatic.

Two caveats before I delve into these tasks. First, the book is not about measuring corruption in the Ottoman context or making moralistic judgments about the nature of the polity and/or its agents based on such an effort. I do not attempt to determine how corrupt the premodern Ottoman polity was as compared to its contemporaries or modern standards, though I do explore the socioeconomic and political circumstances that might have justified certain types of behavior by state officials. While these questions have received some scholarly attention, I regard them either as inherently unanswerable or plainly anachronistic.[3] When concerns regarding the relative prevalence of

---

[3] Indeed, researchers frequently discuss the difficulty of accurately measuring corruption even in modern settings due to the lack of reliable data. See, for example, Banerjee, Hanna, and Mullainathan 2013: 1109; Ledeneva, Bratu, and Köker 2017: 4–5.

particular transgressions come up in my discussion, this is not because I find much value in these anxieties as measures of corruption, but because they appear in our sources. I engage with the question of the pervasiveness of corruption only indirectly in my efforts to represent various perspectives in Ottoman society and government.

The second caveat concerns terminology. Due to the potential discrepancy or incompatibility of the term's modern connotations with premodern Ottoman realities, I tried to avoid using "corruption" when I first began writing this book. Yet my initial inclination to replace that word with clunky expressions such as "predatory maladministration" or "acts of abuse by government officials" generated their own, mainly stylistic problems. Thus, after a while I allowed myself a broader scope, choosing to use the term "corruption" to make this book more readable based on the expectation that my audience will keep in mind my awareness of the term's historical instability. Therefore, I ask readers to assume that my use of the term in relation to acts and relationships in premodern Ottoman contexts is always implicitly in quotation marks, referring not *exactly* to the phenomenon associated with its modern definition, but to its premodern approximation(s). That said, I also believe that the following discussion justifies this choice conceptually.

Historiography of Corruption in Non-Ottoman and Ottoman Settings

This book is intended for serious students of Ottoman and Middle Eastern history, and readers broadly interested in the historical articulations of corruption from comparative and interdisciplinary perspectives. Thus, it engages with both non-Ottomanist and Ottomanist scholarships on the topic. In the present section, I survey these literatures to sketch their development and highlight their contributions to corruption research. I provide an outline of the book in the next section.

Corruption in Non-Ottomanist Scholarship

Modern, scholarly research on corruption outside of Ottoman history is extensive, encompassing multiple disciplines, from sociology, political science, and anthropology to economics and history. A comprehensive engagement with the entirety of this scholarship would be unwieldy, though such attempts do exist and a few of them are cited in the following discussion. Instead, I provide here a brief characterization of the prevalent concerns and tendencies in the relevant works, focusing on those that have influenced my work.

Since the decolonization of former colonies in Asia and Africa, corruption—political and public office corruption, in particular—has gained significant attention. According to the modernization theory, popularized in the 1950s and 1960s, social, economic, and political development requires the abandonment of traditional institutions and practices of government because they are inefficient and irrational according to modern standards. The associated literature also characterizes premodern societies or societies transitioning to modernity as venal, prone to bribery, and nepotistic due to the absence of well-established, Weberian bureaucracies and self-regulating market economies in these settings. Thus, higher stages of modernization imply lower levels of corruption (Wedel 2012: 458; Osrecki 2017: 106–7, *passim*; Kroeze, Vitoria, and Geltner 2018: 2–3; Mungiu-Pippidi and Hartmann 2019).[4]

The 1970s saw the emergence of scholarly perspectives that were critical of these expectations and challenged the effectiveness of Western- and market-oriented development models. Aside from the inherent Eurocentrism of such orientations, proponents of these positions also contended that policies consistent with the theses of modernization theory generated economic dependency on global capitalism, inequality, communal disintegration, and environmental decay in non-Western nations. In this context, we notice novel approaches to corruption in the disciplines of sociology, anthropology, political science, and history, including efforts to resist universalistic definitions. Instead of making assertions about the broader causes and consequences of corruption in "traditional" societies, researchers began to focus on the contextually shaped meanings of the notion and to micro-analyze particular practices, looking at how they were performed and legitimized (Osrecki 2017: 109–14).

As corruption lost its appeal as a universal category of analysis in many disciplines, economists "discovered" it (Osrecki 2017: 115). Methodologically, economic approaches to corruption ignored the terminological and definitional

---

[4] This short description does not do justice to the contributions of specific researchers often linked to the modernization theory. According to Samuel Huntington, for example, corruption is a by-product of the transition to modernity. Huntington (1968: 59–60) argued that corruption perceived as predatory behavior by public officials for private considerations was possible only in settings where there was a recognition of difference between public versus private interests, a condition he associated with modernization. This position is reminiscent of what we observe in later historical literature that resists any comparison between premodern and modern settings. Huntington also argued that corruption in the process of modernization might have helped new groups to challenge the privileges of the traditional elite and influence government; ibid.: 59–71.

complexities associated with the term. Economists also invested heavily in developing quantitative methods to measure corruption across nations in order to calculate the impact of the associated practices on economic performance and development (Bardhan 1997; Hindess 2012). These tendencies resonated with the "global corruption paradigm," which gained steam in the 1990s with the end of the Cold War and the collapse of communist regimes that featured top-down, centrally planned economic models (Ledeneva 2013; Mungiu-Pippidi and Hartmann 2019). At this time when liberal economic policies were popular around the globe, a technocratic engagement with corruption—an effort promoted by international and non-governmental organizations such as the World Bank, the International Monetary Fund, the Organization for Economic Cooperation and Development, and Transparency International—came to dominate the "corruption talk" outside academia (Ledeneva, Bratu, and Köker 2017: 5–6; Engels 2018: 167–8).

In academia, objections to universalistic and technocratic characterizations of corruption have been especially prominent in anthropology and history. Until the 1990s, anthropologists were reticent to engage with the issue of corruption because they did not want to reproduce "clichéd images of political dysfunction, especially in postcolonial and other contexts that routinely bear the brunt of transnational governance" (Muir and Gupta 2018: 84). But their work has explored directly related themes since the early to mid-twentieth century, including patron-client relations, kinship and social networks, and formal and informal systems of exchange, such as gift giving (Sahlins 1972; Parry 1986; Carrier 1990 and 1991; Mauss 1990; Smart 1993; Xin and Pearce 1996; Smart and Hsu 2007; and Yan 2009 and 2010, among many others). Anthropological research that focuses on corruption has been more visible in the past two or three decades. Overall, the discipline's prominent (though not exclusive; see Pardo 2013) concern with non-Western, colonial, and postcolonial settings, often viewed through comparative lenses, has sensitized researchers to the plurality of potentially conflicting perceptions of social interactions (Olivier de Sardan 1999; Blundo and Olivier de Sardan 2006). Instead of characterizing particular types of behavior, such as bribery, nepotism, and kickbacks, as pathologies that should be remedied, anthropologists have engaged with them holistically—that is, in relation to other (including structural) aspects of the contexts where they are found, including their moral and/or political economies (Gregory 1982; Pierce 2016). Also, both the hybridity present in social settings and the blurred boundaries that separate various conceptual spaces (such as "public" vs. "private") often feature in anthropological research as topics of curiosity, not problems that require resolution for economic or political advancement. The discipline's strong desire to explore meanings and practices as phenomena negotiated (and renegotiated) "on the ground" has promoted locally engaged approaches to corruption (cf. Pardo 2013). The attention paid in a few publications to various "discourses of corruption" (Gupta 1995, 2005) further distinguishes this scholarship for my purposes in this book.

The historical study of corruption is generally limited to Europe, where most attention has been paid to the British, German, French, and Dutch cases. The notion has also been studied in the contexts of ancient Greece and Rome, often in relation to theories of state and good government. References to the ideas of specific philosophers, religious thinkers, and political figures such as Aristotle, Cicero, St. Augustine, and Machiavelli are common in this literature. More recently, historians have also begun to explore the notion in relation to European colonial institutions and practices (Kroeze, Dalmau, and Monier 2021).

Since the 1970s, most historical studies of corruption have emphasized the notion's contextual nature and attributes, and how its meaning changed over time, especially between the seventeenth and nineteenth centuries and during state formation and other forms of political transformation. Consequently, many historians have been hesitant to interpret the relevant practices and articulations in the past based on modern standards and have tended to be critical (even if implicitly so) of earlier scholarship that offered judgmental or moralistic characterizations of premodern governmental practices (Hurstfield 1967; Aylmer 1973: 139–40; Harding 1981: 47–9; Kettering 1986: 192–206; Sawyer 1988; Peck 1993: 5, 7–9; Prest 1991: 69–70; Kerkhoff 2012: 33; Lindeman 2012: 582–5; Engels 2018; Engels and Monier 2021: 339–41).[5]

If there is a historiographical tension in this recent literature, it might be about what proper contextualization means in regard to specific connotations of corruption. For Peter Bratsis (2003a, 2003b), for example, contextualization requires a sharp detachment of the premodern and modern conceptions of corruption. In premodern understandings of the notion, "there was a strong imagery of decay and regression, of something becoming less and less capable, potent, or virtuous. This understanding contained the idea that through disease, old age, the influence of vice, or any other reason, the ability to seek the good and virtuous is decreased and possibly destroyed" (Bratsis 2003b: 15). However, "political corruption is an *exclusively* modern phenomenon made

---

[5] See also the vast literatures cited in these works. For rare instances of pushback to this inclination, see Harding 1981; Rubinstein 1983; and Sawyer 1988.

possible only after the rise of the public/private split and the concept of interests" (ibid.: 14; emphasis mine). With reference to the well-known work of Mark Philp (1997), Bratsis also questioned the possibility of "public office or trust" in the premodern era and, thus, the very existence of public office corruption (ibid.: 12).

Such categorical articulations of the unrelatability of premodern and modern notions are rare, yet we find resembling interpretations in many influential works. For example, according to Sharon Kettering (1986: 192), "traditional political clientelism" did not possess "an inherent tendency to produce political corruption" or "encourage bribery and graft, malversation and peculation, nepotism and favoritism... if early modern standards are applied." And while the premodern patronage practices may be inherently corrupt according to modern standards, they were not considered so in the premodern era (ibid.). In her works on patronage and family networks in early modern Europe, Julia Adams (1994, 2005a, 2005b) also resists associating nepotism with corruption, a term she avoids almost completely. As I will demonstrate shortly, similar understandings of contextualization have also been noticeable in the Ottomanist scholarship.

Another way to contextualize corruption is to identify gradual shifts in the broader connotations of the concept rather than major ruptures that generate incompatible notions in different eras. We find traces of this tendency in the writings of Linda Levy Peck (1993), Barry Hindess (2012: 8), and Jens Ivo Engels (2018: 175), among others. But it might be most clearly expressed in Bruce Buchan and Lisa Hill's survey of corruption in European history. According to Buchan and Hill (2014), one can identify multiple concurrent connotations of the notion in most historical settings, including a "degenerative" conception associated with moral and spiritual decay and "public office corruption" that refers to an abuse of public trust for private gain (ibid.: 7). While "these two loosely connected, but nevertheless distinct, conceptions existed in parallel for centuries" since ancient Greece, from "the mid-to-late eighteenth century... the public office conception began to displace the degenerative conception" (ibid.: 8).[6] Elsewhere, Buchan (2012: 83) described

---

[6] Buchan and Hill (2014: 15) acknowledge the tension between their and Bratsis's characterizations of long-term change in the meaning of corruption as follows: "Peter Bratsis challenges the assumption that there is 'an unbroken line in the concept of corruption' (understood as abuse of office) and that it is a 'concept common to nearly all political forms and historical epochs'; the 'ancient understanding of corruption' he suggests 'is far removed from the modern one'... We are somewhat skeptical of these kinds of claims and argue... that both degenerative and public office conceptions characterised discourse on political corruption until comparatively recently."

this process as a "narrowing definition of corruption," implying again the premodern relevance of public office corruption, though the word "narrowing" also implies a gradual fading of other meanings of the term.

For the purposes of this book, it is significant that Buchan and Hill recognize the potential plurality of perspectives on corruption in any given context (premodern or modern), which is consistent with findings in recent anthropological studies on the topic (cf. Blundo and Olivier de Sardan 2006: 97). Toon Kerkhoff (2013: 91) makes the same point when he describes the premodern Dutch polity as one that was based on "different and sometimes competing value systems" with corresponding perspectives of corruption. This was an environment that boasted a "value pluralism," comprising "face-to-face values on the shop floor," "legal-bureaucratic values," and patrimonial sensitivities, perhaps among others (ibid.).[7]

Outside of European history, corruption research might be most prominent in the historiography of imperial China. Although Chinese historians have occasionally expressed interest in identifying the broader connotations of corruption (cf. Park 1997: 698), they have largely focused on exploring the causes and consequences of corruption in various realms of government and identifying the ways that imperial authorities policed and disciplined these transgressions (Zelin 1984; Kiser and Tong 1992; Park 1997; Will 2004; Thornton 2007; Akçetin 2021). One also notices in Bradly Reed's (1995, 2000) research a quasi-ethnographic interest in the relevant practices of low-level provincial functionaries.

Unfortunately, historical scholarship on corruption and associated transgressions is very limited in Islamic and Middle Eastern settings, even though the subfield has generated sophisticated scholarships on political, legal, and economic topics. Works by Maaike van Berkel (2011, 2018) and Mathieu Tillier (2009, 2017, 2018) explore legal and administrative corruption in early Islamic history and provide clues about how various polities in the medieval era addressed this concern institutionally and in practice. References to corruption also exist in publications on *mazalim* courts (Nielsen 1985, 1990; Hurvitz 2013). In the Mamluk context, there are relevant publications by Toru Miura (1997), John Meloy (2004), and Jo van Steenbergen (2006), and perhaps a few others, but in this area too the topic has yet to receive sustained, systematic interest. The limited state of Ottoman historiography on corruption is thus

---

[7] Jens Ivo Engels (2018: 170–2) uses the phrase "competing norm systems" to refer to the same phenomenon. Kerkhoff's and Engels's ideas have been shaped by Hillard von Thiessen's earlier scholarship in German, a language I cannot read.

generally consistent with what we find in other subfields of Islamic and Middle Eastern history.

This discussion of the state of corruption research on non-Ottoman settings provides a streamlined orientation to the field and helps situate my work within broader scholarship. Inevitably, it has overlooked many topics that received some attention in individual works. My exploration of various aspects of the Ottoman corruption in the following pages will give me additional opportunities to reflect on a few of these topics and engage with specific examples of the non-Ottomanist research in a more direct manner.

Corruption in Ottomanist Scholarship

Before considering the Ottomanist literature on corruption, let me briefly highlight some fundamental aspects of premodern Ottoman society and history to help the uninitiated reader better appreciate the ensuing discussion.

The Ottoman polity was founded at the turn of the fourteenth century in northwestern Anatolia by Turkic-speaking nomadic populations.[8] It would continue to exist under the leadership of a single dynastic line, the descendants of the state's eponymous founder (Osman), until after World War I. Initially the polity was geared toward conquest and acquisition of loot, and it spread rapidly to the Balkans and central Anatolia. In short order, the Ottomans acquired the territories of the former Byzantine Empire, including its capital, Constantinople (modern-day Istanbul). After the fifteenth century the polity began to prioritize sociopolitical stability, effective government, and efficient exploitation of its resources. At its peak, this vast land-based empire connected Asia, Europe, and Africa and was home to many cultures, languages, and religions, including Turkish-, Kurdish-, and Arabic-speaking Muslims; Greek-, Armenian-, and Arabic-speaking Christians of many denominations; and Jews.

The Ottomans developed a centralized and sophisticated administrative system after the fifteenth century. From this point onward, we note the emergence of a unified leadership with absolutist and patrimonial claims to power, though these were occasionally challenged by various political interests both at the empire's center and in the provinces. The ruler was supported

---

[8] Here as elsewhere in the book, I often use the term "polity" when I feel uncomfortable with specific connotations associated with alternative terminology, including "principality," "state," "dynasty," and "empire." "Polity" can also be used as a broader abstraction (as compared to "state," for example) comprising both the government and the subjects or citizens. On the latter issue, see Collins and Lawford-Smith 2021.

by a large and powerful military and an increasingly complex bureaucratic apparatus that ran the state. The imperial government had relatively direct control over the empire's lands in the Balkans and Western and Central Anatolia; elsewhere, it exerted influence over local power holders by indirect means and arrangements.

At the top of the state's bureaucratic-administrative setup was the imperial council or *divan-ı hümayun*, where important state matters were discussed and decided by the highest military and judicial officials and ministers (viziers) responsible for specific functions. The grand vizier presided over the divan in the absence of the sultans, who gradually stopped attending the meetings. The government apparatuses also included a sophisticated provincial administration under local governors and a court system where judicial appointees administered justice and conveyed to the center information about the affairs of their jurisdictions and petitions by provincial communities.

Islam was one of the major building blocks of the Ottoman polity. Muslims constituted the majority of the population since very early times. After the sixteenth century, the empire defined itself as the foremost protector of the Sunni Muslims against the Shiite Safavid threat in the east and Christian Europe in the west. The dynasty applied itself to the adornment of important Muslim sites within its domains, including the holy cities of Mecca and Medina, and the protection of pilgrimage routes. The legal system was built largely on the sharia, or holy law, supplemented by dynastic laws (sing. *kanun*), which often reflected the polity's discretionary priorities and local customs. The system derived legitimacy both from its Islamic credentials and from pre- and non-Islamic traditions of good government inherited from older polities in the region.

The Ottoman fiscal structures, too, were shaped by practices and institutions of earlier states, and not only Islamic ones. The prebendal (*tımar*) system—the primary mode of revenue extraction until perhaps the seventeenth century—finds its roots in both the Byzantine and Abbasid Empires. In this setup, the state owned the agrarian lands and assigned the revenues due from them to local military and administrative authorities in return for service, such as participation in military expeditions. The tımar holders were required to extract revenues from cultivators, which they used to meet their and their retinues' needs and to maintain peace and order in their jurisdictions. After the sixteenth century, due to the rapid monetization of the economy and intense financial requirements of the polity, short and longer-term tax-farming came to replace the tımar system and ultimately became the prevalent form of public finance.

The empire was primarily an agrarian state sustained by the peasants. merchants, craftsmen, and urban laborers also shouldered the financial needs of the polity. The fiscal system depended on consistent and sustainable revenue extraction from productive classes via a variety of taxes and fees. The system's concern with revenue extraction is obvious in the way official documents distinguish various components of the society primarily as *askeri* (military), who claimed connection to a branch of the state apparatus and were exempt from taxation, and *reaya* (flock), who were subject to taxation. While the boundaries between askeri and reaya status became increasingly vague in later periods, concerns with effective and efficient revenue collection remained central to the state's policies until its end.

In the highly heterogenous context of the Ottoman order, religious distinctions influenced social life and inter-/intra-communal relationships. Most faith communities had their own leadership structures and religious, legal, and educational institutions and were responsible for assessing and collecting their members' taxes. Non-Muslims had inferior positions in the premodern Ottoman society, at least in legal and political terms. And while interfaith interactions might have been common in certain realms of life, such as commerce and financial interactions, non-Muslims tended to live isolated lives in terms of communal matters.

Ottoman historians used to divide the history of the polity into periods of rise, decline, and collapse. According to this older historiography, the Ottoman Empire began to experience increasingly frequent and serious problems from the seventeenth century onward that culminated in the polity's downfall in the nineteenth and twentieth centuries. These problems included military reversals against the empire's European adversaries; economic and fiscal crises; social unrest both at the center and in the provinces; the rise of powerful households and political groups that challenged the dynasty's political authority and legitimacy; and failures in leadership. Various historians have also cited the increasing prevalence of corruption as one symptom of Ottoman decline during this period.

Since the late 1980s, such attempts at periodization have been largely discredited. Many historians have pointed out the absurd nature of the claim of a centuries-long, uninterrupted decay. Others have stressed that the declinist characterizations of Ottoman history privileged the perspective of the state or dynasty and ignored others. Broader trends in the realms of economics, social life, political relationships, and even diplomatic and military affairs cannot be described in such an overarching manner. A few historians have described the seventeenth and eighteenth centuries as an era of temporary crises often followed by periods of improvement; fiscal improvisation and evolution; political pluralism; individualism; cultural and artistic efflorescence; and, overall, adaptation to novel circumstances at regional and global scales. Some have argued that a few of these developments should be perceived as aspects of Ottoman "early modernity," a label that has recently become popular in the field, but it is difficult to detect a consensus among colleagues on the precise meaning of this phrase (Aksan, Ergene, and Hadjikyriacou 2020). This vagueness has led me to opt for "premodern" to describe the temporal focus of this book, though I also acknowledge the occasional difficulty of making broad generalizations about the premodern state and society (cf. Ergene 2020).

In the Ottoman context, it is common to characterize the nineteenth century as an era of attempted reform and modernization, which lies beyond the purview of this book, except in those brief instances when I discuss how the historians of this period have characterized corruption (later in this introduction) and when I make very provisional claims about the ways that perceptions of corruption might have changed during the Ottoman transition to modernity (in the conclusion).

References to corruption abound in the scholarly literature on premodern Ottoman history, that is from the polity's beginnings until the nineteenth century.[9] Yet systematic, contextually sensitive research on practices associated with the notion is limited.[10] This section will survey scholarly work on the topic, but my intentions here are strictly methodological, which has limited my selection of works: I primarily discuss works that pertain to the question of how Ottoman corruption has been characterized.

Any historiographical look at the modern scholarship on Ottoman corruption should perhaps begin with Ahmet Mumcu's *Tarih İçinde Genel Gelişimiyle Birlikte Osmanlı Devleti'nde Rüşvet (Özellikle Adli Rüşvet)* (*Bribery [Specifically, Judicial Bribery] in the Ottoman Empire along with Its General Development in History*). This is the earliest and still the only book-length work dedicated to the study of corruption in the premodern Ottoman Empire, though it focuses on only one specific type of transgression. Originally written as the author's 1968 habilitation thesis for the Faculty of Law at Ankara University, the book was first published in 1969. Its scholarly impact has

---

[9] Notable examples include, among many others, Halil İnalcık 1965, 1988a, 1988b; Suraiya Faroqhi 1992; Linda Darling 1996, 2013; Heather Ferguson 2018; Pal Fodor 2018; Marinos Sariyannis 2019; and Samy Ayoub 2020.
[10] See Kroeze, Dalmau, and Monier (2021: 2) for a critique of treating corruption "more as a symptom... than as a specific subject of enquiry" in various areas of historical research.

been limited outside of Turkey because it has not been translated into major European or Middle Eastern languages. Yet in Turkey it has generated considerable interest: the book was republished twice, first in 1985 and again in 2005 (with no revisions in either case), which underscores its enduring influence on Turkish scholarship on Ottoman history.

Osmanlı Devleti'nde Rüşvet (Mumcu 2005), which is based on archival documents produced by government functionaries, Ottoman chronicles, court records, fatwas issued by Ottoman jurists, and reports of European travelers and diplomats in the empire, aims to provide a panorama of bribery up until the Tanzimat period (1839–76). The book's main argument is that while bribery is known to have existed in the Ottoman lands since the polity's founding, it became endemic from the second half of the sixteenth century. Mumcu mentions, with varying degrees of persuasiveness, a few reasons for this development, including the growing numbers of government officials with low moral standards (2005: 270–3, 293–4); the central government's inability to protect judicial authorities who might have resisted crimes by abusive officials (2005: 273–4); deteriorating economic circumstances (2005: 292–4), compounded by a "feudal" vanity among officials looking to demonstrate status by displaying wealth (2005: 291–2); and the spread of the sales of offices at exorbitant prices, shorter tenures, and longer wait times spent between appointments; all of which motivated officials to abuse their positions while in office (2005: 295–303).

As its full title makes clear, *Osmanlı Devleti'nde Rüşvet* focuses on the judicial realm and processes. While Mumcu also gives examples of bribery in the realms of finance, military, infrastructural developments, and charity work, he makes a special effort to identify how bribes were offered to and accepted by legal actors, how bribery affected various judicial processes, how such acts were policed and punished by government authorities, and how various Ottoman rulers and administrators struggled to limit bribe-induced judicial abuse. According to the author, judicial bribery was the "gravest [*en vahim*] form of bribery" (2005: 17) because it both weakened the system's ability to fight abuse and maladministration in other realms of government and undermined the government's ideological legitimacy.

The fact that the book explores a topic that can be perceived as unflattering to the Ottoman polity differentiates it from a prominent tendency in the scholarship on Ottoman law and legal administration since the mid-twentieth century. Ideologically, Mumcu's work made a critical contribution because it shifts attention away from the ideals and institutions of government, and toward practices and ensuing conflicts on the ground.

With more than fifty years of hindsight, however, one can easily point out a few problems in the book. For one, Mumcu's treatment of the topic reveals an attachment to a now largely discredited periodization in which the sixteenth century divides an era of relative grandeur from an era of decay, evident in his treatment of bribery as both a symptom and a cause of the Ottoman decline. Also important for my discussion is that the author makes next to no attempt to contextualize the meaning and morality of bribery. Mumcu states at the beginning of the book that while bribery can be defined in several ways, he is interested in a narrow, "legal" (*hukuken*) meaning, whereby a state representative "accrues benefits for himself in ways that are unacceptable in the social order by performing or refusing to perform certain acts" (2005: 1). The book does not explore how this definition compares to premodern Islamic jurisprudential characterizations or whether it was congruent with contemporary Ottoman views. Nor does the author discuss how the notion might have changed over time or how various groups within the Ottoman realm might have characterized it. In the text, bribery is treated as a concept without history, bearing the same constant meaning to everyone at all times, and based primarily on the "universal human inclination to prioritize private interests" (ibid.).

Mumcu's focus on bribery as a topic worthy of investigation distinguishes his book for the purposes of the present study. But a few issues he raises in the work epitomize broader trends in his era. In particular, his claim about the prevalence of bribery (and, by implication, corruption) after the sixteenth century is common in earlier scholarship.[11] And while I am unaware of any deliberate engagement with Mumcu's book until the 2000s, in the 1990s a few historians critically tackled the tendency to view bribery/corruption as symptomatic of Ottoman decline.

For example, Rifa'at Abou-El-Haj, in his *Formation of the Modern State* (1991), stressed the need to properly situate corruption in the Ottoman context, in the same way that European historians writing about the topic after the 1970s did in response to earlier, more critical historical assessments of the premodern polities (cf. Kerkhoff 2012: 33). Without naming any names or citing any works, Abou-El-Haj criticized the older scholarship for treating corruption anachronistically—that is, for using "modern sociological standards" such as "merit, public service, equity, and rationalized practices"

---

[11] See, for example, Lewis 1958 and 1961; Berkes 1964; Shaw 1976; Shaw and Shaw 1977. For various criticisms of the declinist tendencies in these works, see Howard 1988; Hathaway 1996; Kafadar 1997; Quataert 2003.

(1991: 8–9).[12] Central to Abou-El-Haj's criticism is the claim that the ruling elite in the premodern Ottoman polity "made no distinction between personal patrimony and property on the one hand, and the public treasury on the other. Those members of the ruling class who were in power appropriated whatever wealth they could, without any sense of corruption or greed, but rather out of a sense of entitlement" (ibid.: 56). Consequently, Ottoman elites "took nepotism and personal influence (intisap) for granted. To obtain public office for family members or for members of one's household, or to arrogate to oneself and to members of one's household great and somewhat fabulous wealth, were considered legitimate practices as long as one belonged to the ruling class" (ibid.: 55–6). Thus, Abou-El-Haj argued, "a different attitude toward practices which by the standards of the nation-state would be regarded as corrupt must be attributed in part to the way the Ottoman ruling class viewed public trust" (ibid.: 108n13).

Although Abou-El-Haj's call for proper contextualization is welcome, there are a few problems in how he engages with the topic. In the course of rejecting other scholars' treatment of corruption, Abou-El-Haj treats some of their sources dismissively. For example, he insists that frequent complaints by contemporary commentators (such as Mustafa Ali and Koçi Bey) about government abuse and misconduct that modern historians took as evidence of widespread corruption should instead be seen as self-interested denunciations of broader socioeconomic and political transformations that had left them behind.[13] More important, perhaps, Abou-El-Haj never provides an alternative conceptualization of corruption that might be appropriate for a premodern setting, assuming that he believed analogous notion(s) did exist.[14] I believe these two problems are connected: an effort to devise a contextually

---

[12] "*Nearly all the scholarly literature that I have reviewed* is premised on the unspoken, perhaps even unconscious, assumption that the modern standards of the nation-state constitute the unchallenged norm by which to assess early modern political life" (Abou-El-Haj 1991: 8; emphasis mine). Yet Abou-El-Haj's historicism has found an appeal among a few critiques of the decline theory whose targets of criticism are well known (see note 11). See, for example, Quataert 2003: 3, 7n8.

[13] Elsewhere, Abou-El-Haj criticized Metin Kunt and "his predecessors," including Colin Imber, for reading "Ottoman political commentators without reconstructing their context" (Abu-el-Haj [sic] 1986: 222–3). See Howard (1988: 54) for a mild criticism of Abou-El-Haj's reductionism. The changes that Abou-El-Haj (1991) identifies during the sixteenth and seventeenth centuries include the erosion of the ruler's patrimonial authority; the economic and political rise of the vizier and *paşa* households; the gradual collapse of the *miri* system and the proliferation of privately controlled agrarian lands; the decline of merit as a criterion in government appointments; and enhanced obstacles to peasants' mobility.

[14] Linda Peck's (1993: 5) criticism of the European historiography on corruption applies well to both Mumcu's and Abou-El-Haj's positions: "Most historians' attitudes toward corruption have tended either to be moralistic, thereby placing themselves in the position of condemning behavior without concern for context, or dismissive, arguing that the charge of corruption was simply the tool of 'outs'

appropriate corollary to corruption might have led to a more nuanced treatment of the sources.

Haim Gerber is another influential scholar who rejected the claim of intensifying corruption after the sixteenth century, but for very different reasons. Whereas Abou-El-Haj would question any argument that corruption existed in a premodern polity if the analysis was based on "modern sociological standards" (including rationality, efficiency, and the separation of public and private interests), Gerber used precisely those standards to argue that the Ottoman polity *cannot* be considered corrupt. According to Gerber, by the seventeenth century the Ottoman government had developed a sophisticated judicial-administrative system that was able to combat its officials' abuses and misconducts.[15] The effectiveness of this system, Gerber maintained, is evident in the thousands of complaints against corrupt officials in the Ottoman archives. Earlier historians had taken these complaints as evidence of the ubiquity of corruption, but Gerber interprets them as evidence of an effective anticorruption regime:

> So many complaints of harsh abuses might give the impression that the Ottoman Empire in its entirety should have collapsed as a consequence. That this did not happen should give us reason to ask, "Why not?" In fact, in the book of complaints itself [the complaint register that Gerber examines in this study], there is evidence of processes and people that worked against the abuse and deprivation of rights. (Gerber 2018: 9)

According to Gerber, complaints against government officials should be perceived as evidence that maladministration was addressed and managed quite effectively through the system of provincial courts and highly institutionalized reporting mechanisms (ibid.). Worth highlighting in Gerber's work is his inclination to take state-generated documents at face value and treat them as inherently objective, transparent, and comprehensive sources. Indeed,

---

versus 'ins.' Unable to accept the testimony of complaint literature about venality that stretches from the Middle Ages to the present, unwilling to apply modern conceptions of corruption to early modern government, most historians have dealt with the issue by avoiding it."

[15] One could argue that Gerber's treatment of the topic represents a Weberian defense of the Ottoman polity against its Weberian characterizations of irrationality and arbitrariness. According to Gerber (2018: 28), Weber "provided the most fruitful historical model for studying [Ottoman law], even though it was deficient in empirical accuracy." Gerber (1994, 1999) thus tried to defend the Ottoman legal system against those characterizations that reproduced specific claims he associated with Weberian characterizations of Islamic law, not by rejecting the categories intrinsic to Weber's sociology for being reductionist or Eurocentric, but by affirming the positive qualities of Ottoman law according to these categories and in line with the Western European experience.

Gerber's scholarship tends not to critically engage with these sources by, for example, highlighting their biases, agendas, or knowledge gaps. Gerber also overlooks conflicting perspectives from non-state sources, including foreign accounts.

Two article-length studies that appeared in Turkish more than thirty years after the initial publication of Mumcu's book (Doğan 2002; Çelik 2006) were the first to directly engage conceptually with his work, and ultimately they demonstrate its enduring influence. These well-researched and empirically rich studies are not comprehensive critiques of Mumcu's book; rather, Muzaffer Doğan (2002: 38n7) and Yüksel Çelik (2006: 27–8, 32n19) specifically address Mumcu's arguments pertaining to monetary or in-kind payments that accompanied appointments to government posts, and they criticize Mumcu for conflating such disbursements with bribes.[16] They insist that these payments—including *pişkeş, caize,* and *avaid,* among others—constituted legally sanctioned forms of entitlement for higher authorities that were duly and unambiguously recorded in the state's archives and served ceremonial, symbolic, and political purposes.[17]

Doğan's and Çelik's criticisms apply largely to Mumcu's arguments regarding bribes for government posts, not to any other type of transgressions in the judicial-administrative system—for example, bribes extended to the qadis (Islamic judges) in litigations or payments made to tax collectors for favorable tax assessments. But whether intentionally or not, Doğan's and Çelik's critique

---

[16] According to Doğan (2002: 38n7), "Mumcu, after he mentions the ranking officials' rights to collect in-kind and cash payments based on the appointments that they make/authorize, presents all such payments as examples of bribes" (Mumcu, Osmanlı'da devlet ricalinin yaptıkları atamalar karşılığında bir miktar para veya mal alma hakları olduğunu zikrettikten sonra alınan bütün para ve malları rüşvet örneği olarak nakletmeye devam ediyor). Çelik (2006: 32n19) posited that Mumcu "identifies all in-kind and cash payments to the ruler, grand vizier and ranking state officials as bribes and improper behavior, which is not accurate" (padişah, sadrazam ve daha alt mevkilerdeki devlet ricali ve memurlara sunulan nakdi ve ayni hediyelerin tamamını rüşvet ile usulsüzlük kapsamında değerlendirmektedir ki, bunun doğru olmadığı açıktır).

[17] Doğan suggested that the Ottoman state instituted these payments (particularly caize or avaid) when it felt the financial need, perhaps in the second half of the sixteenth century, and recognized their legal status from the time they appeared. According to Doğan, they find their roots in customary offerings (pişkeş) to the ruler by his subjects, symbolizing their allegiance and subservience. Furthermore, he insisted, such payments were mentioned in some *kanunname*s, or legal codes, and their payment records were kept among official documents (Doğan 2002, 35–45, 68). Çelik (2006: 27–33) stressed that legitimate payments for (or following) government appointments, which included not only pişkeş, caize, or avaid, but also disbursements made under other names (such as *destaviz, boğça/bohça hediyesi/bohça baha, tekaddüme, tuhfe-i hicazi, hediye-i hicazi,* and *kır hediyesi*) to middle-level state officials, were regular (*ber mutad*), customary, and legally recognized payments. However, Doğan's and Çelik's subsequent analyses diverge. For Doğan, such arrangements were *generally* (though there were exceptions) legal, legitimate, and understandable ways to raise funds. Çelik argued that before the mid-nineteenth century the Ottoman government failed to adequately differentiate between legal/customary gifts and bribes (2006: 45–6, *passim*).

of Mumcu's assumptions concerning payments for appointments also calls into question Mumcu's other interpretations. Doğan and Çelik both argue that Mumcu's claims were based on selective and careless reading of archival sources and that he was influenced by hypercritical observations made either by exaggeration-prone Ottoman commentators or by foreign observers of the empire (Doğan 2002: 38–9; Çelik 2006: 27). Many in the latter group lacked the knowledge, experience, or linguistic skills to comprehend the subtleties of Ottoman institutions and practices, relied excessively on hearsay and unverified reports by others, or were ideologically opposed to the Ottomans (Doğan 2002: 38n7; Çelik 2006: 32, 39).

Doğan's and Çelik's criticisms overlap with my own view that Mumcu's research, while useful in many ways, inadequately contextualizes bribery in the Ottoman setting. However, their treatment of the topic also raises some concerns. First, they tend to dismiss contemporary Ottoman and non-Ottoman reports that contradict their opinions.[18] Second, and more specifically, Mumcu's main criticism of payment-for-appointment arrangements, including routine outlays of pişkeş, caize, avaid, and the like, is not that these constituted bribes. It was that, *in practice*, if such payments were utilized primarily to raise revenue, which was often true during times of financial difficulty, then they could enable incompetent and inexperienced candidates to attain important posts solely by giving the largest amounts to those with the power to appoint them. Furthermore, such payments often put financial pressures on appointees, which forced them to engage in abusive practices to raise revenue during their tenures in office, such as seeking bribes from or extorting the subjects in their jurisdictions.[19] Mumcu also observes that those who had to pay exorbitant sums for their offices, even if as legal tributes or compulsory gifts, had fewer qualms about selling offices that they controlled to undeserving individuals.

---

[18] Doğan's and Çelik's views on the claims of contemporary Ottomans that contradict their opinions are reminiscent of Abou-El-Haj's inclinations, which I discussed above. On the other hand, a rejection of contemporary European sources in favor of state-generated documentation is parallel to what I noted in Gerber's work.

[19] Actually, it is possible to find in Mumcu's book attempts to distinguish bribes from legally required payments upon appointments while, at the same time, emphasizing the possible connections between these. He writes (2005: 296), for example, that "it was legitimate to make pişkeş or caize payments upon appointments to official posts. These were undoubtedly followed by bribes. Bribes were hidden and illegitimate means to complement caize [and pişkeş?] payments; it was natural to offer them within this mechanism [of offering gifts in return for appointments]" (Osmanlı Devleti'nde makam almak için caize ya da pişkeş verilmesi meşru idi. Bunun arkasından şüphesiz rüşvet gelirdi. Rüşvet, caizenin meşru olmayan ve gizli tamamlayıcısı idi; ancak bu mekanizma içinde verilmesi tabii hale geliyordu).

In fact, the tendency to differentiate payments for appointments from bribes in categorical terms could be just as problematic as Mumcu's alleged conflation of the two, given that all such payments—monetary or in-kind outlays accompanied by office grants—are based on a sense of reciprocity. While the logical continuum between sanctioned payments and their unsanctioned counterparts is clear in Mumcu's work, Doğan and Çelik appear to treat these as if they were ontologically separate, even though sanctioned payments were often negotiable and existing appointments could be canceled for the sole purpose of collecting more such payments that accompanied reappointments (Doğan 2002: 45–6; Çelik 2006: 28–9, 38).[20] That the system lacked well-defined criteria to distinguish tributes and compulsory gifts from bribes indicates murky boundaries between them, at least in terms of their functions, a point that Çelik (2006: 26–7) also acknowledges.

Interestingly, Doğan and Çelik did not disagree with Mumcu about the most basic features of and trends in Ottoman sociopolitical and economic history. All three scholars concurred that in a patrimonial regime it was natural for the ruler to expect compensation for delegating his authority to rule and his right to extract resources from his subjects (Doğan 2002: 68; Mumcu 2005: 295–6). They also agreed that the Ottoman polity faced major financial pressures beginning in the late sixteenth century and that these pressures forced the system's operatives to improvise possible remedies.

What they disagreed on was how to view the legitimacy of some of these remedies. Doğan's critique of Mumcu's work, in particular, can be read as a defense of the Ottoman polity by a historian who claims to understand it on its own terms—that is, with reference to its own documents, terminology, traditions, and self-justifications—and is inclined to sympathize with its actors and their choices:

> Assigning government offices for money is a practice that emerged in the second half of the sixteenth century and one that matured over time. It would be very wrong to associate it only with the grand viziers' and other higher authorities' [moral] degeneration based on their greed for wealth. This is because the time in question is a critical period and one that corresponds to a number of developments that influenced the subsequent centuries. The most important of these developments was the [relative] loss of income by fixed-income groups, whether dependent on state allocations

---

[20] Implicit here is that payments for appointments, whether in sanctioned or unsanctioned forms, had contingent features subject to the circumstances and self-serving calculations (Doğan 2002: 46).

or stipends, due to high inflation. Such losses were experienced by the sultan's and grand vizier's treasuries and high-level officials as well as lower-level state appointees. In addition to such losses, there also were other developments in this period that further amplified the expenses... Thus, [new] expenses required [new] appropriations. (Doğan 2002: 46–7)[21]

What is not clear in this quotation is why the historian should feel compelled to affirm the inherent morality of any form of extraction that stemmed from the state's or its agents' needs, especially if these negatively affected other segments of the society.[22]

Fortunately, scholarly attempts to differentiate gifts and bribes in the Ottoman context have moved beyond approaching the question from a political perspective centering on the state's (or its agents') virtues or flaws. In recent research on gift-giving in the Ottoman era (Reindl-Kiel 2012; Açıkgöz 2018), we find more ethnographically informed and comparatively inclined analyses that seek to understand these exchanges in terms of the social and cultural functions they served in the Ottoman context. Clearly, more work needs to be done in this area, but I see as suggestive Hedda Reindl-Kiel's emphasis on the importance of gift exchanges as a form of communication with important social functions, not excluding immediate considerations of transactionality.

Although this book does not focus on the modern era, a perusal of the scholarship on the nineteenth century offers important and directly relevant insights. Once again, Mumcu's work is a good starting point for appreciating how Ottomanists have treated the topic of corruption in the modern era, even though the nineteenth century appears to be an afterthought for him and

---

[21] "Netice olarak devlet görevlerinin para karşılığı verilmesi XVI. yy. ikinci yarısından itibaren ortaya çıkan ve gittikçe olgunlaştırılan bir uygulamadır. Sebeplerini de sırf sadrazamların veya üst yönetim birimlerinin servet hırslarından kaynaklanan yozlaşmaya bağlamak son derece yanlıştır. Çünkü sözü edilen tarihler çok önemli ve sonraki yüzyılları büyük oranda etkileyen bazı gelişmelerle çakışan bir dönemdir. Bunlardan en başta geleni, ister tahsisat, ister maaş usulü olsun sabit gelirli kesimlerin yüksek enflasyon sebebi ile uğradıkları önemli gelir kayıplarıdır. Bu kayıplar alt kademedeki görevliler için olduğu kadar padişah hazinesi, sadrazam hazinesi ve diğer üst ricalin gelirleri için de geçerliydi. Bu kayıplara karşılık masraflarının artışını icab ettirne başka gelişmeler de bu dönemden itibaren karşılarına çıkmaktadır.... Bir diğer ifadeyle masraflar yeni tahsisatları gerektirmektedir."

[22] Describing an act as a crime from the vantage point of the state is not uncommon in Ottoman history-writing. For example, Halil İnalcık (1965: 52) defined bribery as "things that an official accepts for his own benefit though [the act] is against the [state's] law codes and defies the state's interests" (Rüşvet, kanuna ve devlet menfaatine aykırı olarak yetkilinin özel çıkarı için kabul ettiği şeydir). I hope to show in the following pages that variable considerations of bribery existed in the Ottoman context. At the same time, I should note that İnalcık recognizes in the same place the very fluid boundaries between bribery and many legitimate and illegitimate forms of extraction.

INTRODUCTION 21

comprises a very small portion of his discussion (fifteen pages; 2005: 274–89). According to Mumcu, during the reigns of Selim III (d. 1808) and Mahmud II (d. 1839) and the Tanzimat era (1839–76), the Ottoman government made substantial attempts to curb the bribery that had plagued the polity for so long, primarily by better defining those acts deemed unacceptable and better delineating through legislation how they should be punished. The government also made efforts to improve enforcement of the new codes. Important in this regard is Mumcu's emphasis on the hybridity of codification efforts: while he highlights the European influence on these attempts, various codes enacted in the reform movement also displayed continuities with premodern Islamic jurisprudential traditions and Ottoman precedents. Ultimately, Mumcu also argues (2005: 286–9), the effort to eradicate bribery was partially successful at best, since enthusiasm for transforming the system waned in the latter part of the nineteenth century and old habits remained entrenched among government officials.[23]

One sees a somewhat different conceptual approach in Cengiz Kırlı's *Yolsuzluğun İcadı: 1840 Ceza Kanunu, İktidar ve Bürokrasi* (*Invention of Corruption: The 1840 Penal Code, Government, and Bureaucracy*), which explores three high-profile adjudications involving ranking members of the Ottoman government accused of venality and self-interested abusive behavior in the 1840s.[24] The main contention of Kırlı's book is that the notion of corruption is a modern one, as articulated in the judicial and administrative transformation that the Ottoman polity and society experienced during the Tanzimat era. Thus, Kırlı argues that what we moderns view as corruption may not exist in any premodern setting where personalized, reciprocal exchanges involving government officials, often referred to as "gifts," constituted regular, "structural" mechanisms of wealth extraction and distribution and were thus "completely legitimate according to legal and social norms" (2006: 48). Only in the modern period did such interactions come to be regarded as condemnable, and this modern view is based on newer constructions of governance that aimed to replace the networks where officials were connected based on mutual interests with networks where officials were loyal only to the state (2015: 109). Implicitly, then, the Ottoman government's efforts to address issues pertaining to corruption should be seen not as

---

[23] See Çelik 2006 for a consistent discussion of the Tanzimat era.
[24] The book appeared in 2015 but is based primarily on an article that was originally published in 2006 in the journal *Tarih ve Toplum*.

attempts to fix age-old problems, as Mumcu argued, but as attempts to instill a novel governmental and administrative *Weltanschauung*.

There is much to admire in Kırlı's call for contextually sensitive analysis (2015: 9–18), which echoes Abou-El-Haj's refusal to use modern categories to describe premodern realities. Yet I am less inclined to follow his distinctions between pre-Tanzimat (that is, "premodern") and Tanzimat (that is, "modern") conceptions of administrative abuse and misconduct in absolute, black-and-white terms primarily by discounting the plurality of the relevant characterizations on both sides of the temporal threshold, a point that came up earlier in my discussion of the non-Ottomanist scholarship on corruption. As I will elaborate, one can see these multiple formulations in several genres of narratives and documents. This abundance of articulations about corruption forces us to consider the possibility that pre-nineteenth-century characterizations of the notion may not be a distinct formulation, but may instead constitute a spectrum of conceptualizations that are sometimes in tension with each other in just the same way Kerkhoff (2013) and Engels (2018) proposed for particular European settings. I suspect that post-Tanzimat characterizations of corruption might have some degree of continuity with *a few* of these pre-Tanzimat formulations in the same fashion that Buchan and Hill (2014) have suggested.

This issue has broader implications, as is clear from the disagreement between Avi Rubin and Timur Kuran regarding Islamic/Middle Eastern corruption and underdevelopment. Kuran (2011: 295) blames the relative backwardness of Muslim societies in the modern era at least partially on their "norms of state-subject interaction involving nepotism, bribery and rule bending as a matter of course." Echoing Kırlı's treatment of the topic, Rubin (2018: 39) objects to this characterization and suggests that Kuran has conflated plain gift-giving with bribery and corruption: "What many European observers interpreted as corruption was actually a practice of gift giving defined by the norms of a society composed of complex social networks of patronage."

Regardless of how one might feel more generally about Kuran's explanations of Ottoman backwardness compared to Western standards, one should note that Ottomans themselves were aware of the blurred boundaries between gift exchanges and bribery and did not hesitate to complain about transactions that masqueraded as gift-giving.[25] This does not mean that we should make no

---

[25] In this regard, see Susan Rose-Ackerman's (2010: 140) criticism of the anthropological literature on non-Western settings for subscribing to the "simplistic claim" that "corruption is a Western concept

effort to differentiate these acts, but it does mean that such endeavors are not guaranteed to generate clear-cut distinctions (see Chapter 7). What's more, I am concerned that any attempt to propose strict, inviolable conceptual boundaries between such interactions runs the risk of characterizing the nineteenth-century transformation—erroneously—as a process without any direct, organic links to pre-nineteenth-century conceptions of government (cf. Tezcan 2010; Ayoub 2020).

Recently, Iris Agmon offered a sophisticated articulation of Kırlı's and Rubin's positions and noted,

> The meaning of corruption has varied from one culture to another. Moreover, these different cultural meanings have changed substantially throughout history, or, rather, across histories. Originally, the term corruption was rooted in the history of Western Europe, in association with an ideal conception of the state and its operation. Hence in addition to the inherent analytic vagueness of the term, it is predisposed to be used in a Eurocentric, Orientalist manner. (2017: 254)

It is useful that Agmon strives to properly contextualize corruption, but I have hesitations about amplifying the distinctions between premodern versus modern and European versus Ottoman conceptions to the extent that any overlap between them is lost. As unique as the conceptual worlds, governmental ideals, and juristic-administrative practices associated with these realms might have been, it may be an exaggeration to suggest that they existed in isolation and thus that the one cannot be translated to the other, at least partially (cf. Schull 2014: 143–4). In fact, I would argue that the Ottomans' adoption of "modern" and/or "European" categories and institutions to some degree involved transliterating older concepts and institutions in novel forms, adapting the imported ideas to the existing ones. Hence, while it might be true that corruption as we define the term today did not exist precisely in Ottoman lands before the nineteenth century, the Ottomans already possessed notions and perspectives that helped them to develop or adopt newer characterizations of corruption, including those derived from Western sources.

Beyond concerns about source use, empirical facts, and historical continuity between premodern and modern eras, my doubts about the positions discussed

---

used to belittle or to undermine cherished cultural traditions," which signifies a "deeply conservative respect for tradition." In fact, native moralistic denunciations of many relevant practices that might be linked to local cultures are common in many non-Western societies (ibid.: 130).

thus far are also based on an important theoretical disagreement. If we define corruption as the (mis)use of public roles, authority, and resources for personal gain, a rejection of the analytical utility of the notion in a premodern setting can be justified only if we assume that the notion of "public" and everything that goes with it, including conceptions of civic order, communal welfare, and particular types of state-society relations, is strictly limited to the modern era.[26] I disagree with this supposition.

The association of the public with European modernity is most prominently articulated in Jürgen Habermas's work *The Structural Transformation of the Public Sphere* (1991). There Habermas argues that the emergence of bourgeois civil society in Western Europe in the eighteenth century generated a deliberative space where notions associated with common good, separate from the interests of both political authority and private individuals, were formulated in democratic, inclusive, and disinterested fashions.[27] While this thesis appealed to many scholars, it also generated many critical responses, especially from historians, who tested its empirical validity in particular settings. Specifically, some historians questioned Habermas's claim that bourgeois civil society as it emerged in various early modern contexts was uniformly democratic, inclusive, or committed to the promotion of common good. Others argued that there might have existed not one public but multiple publics that embodied competing perspectives on the common good, comprising both bourgeois and non-bourgeois actors: women, peasants, the working classes, the urban poor, and so on. A few also insisted that sophisticated articulations of public interest, such as those embodied in various Christian traditions, predated bourgeois capitalism.[28]

These critiques have influenced Islamic studies. Shmuel Eisenstadt (2002, 2006a, 2006b), for example, after objecting to the conflation of the (European)

---

[26] According to Peter Bratsis (2003a: 7), "what we understand as corruption only comes into being with modernity and the corresponding organization of social life and interests by way of the categories of the public and private." See also Bratsis 2003b: 12–15. In a yet-to-be-published coauthored essay, Rubin and Agmon (2021: 9–10) make the very same point, arguing that "the public-private chasm is a modern notion" and that "its meaning in contemporary contexts is far from self-evident.... In the Ottoman empire of the late nineteenth century, the reformers took measures to indoctrinate this new distinction among the expanding officialdom. However, even when considering the specific dynamics of the modernizing Ottoman state, the applicability of present-day definitions of corruption to the late-Ottoman period is questionable, let alone to earlier periods." I look forward to fully engaging with this essay after its publication.

[27] For an argument that held the absence of "civil society" responsible for Ottoman underdevelopment, see Mardin 1969.

[28] See Mah 2000 for a comprehensive review of the critical historical literature focused on European lands that emerged in response to Habermas's thesis. Regarding the specific objections distilled in the above paragraph, see the responses by Nancy Fraser, Geoff Eley, Mary Ryan, and David Zaret in Calhoun 1996.

bourgeois civil society and the public sphere,[29] points to premodern Islamic legal traditions as a realm in which deliberations about the common good abounded.[30] Armando Salvatore and Dale Eickelman (2004: 5) insist that "the public sphere is...not limited to 'modern' societies" and that various Islamic societies, historical and contemporary, have boasted "sites(s) where contests take place over the definition of the 'common good,' and also of the virtues, obligations, and rights that members of society require for the common good to be realized. This emergent sense of public goes hand-in-hand with the sharing of norms that define ideas of community and the responsibilities of those who belong to it." While we can identify a prominent concern with communal welfare in Islamic jurisprudential traditions, Salvatore and Eickelman (2004: xii) also recognize other discursive realms—including popular, political, and mystical ones—where ideas about civic order and conduct were articulated (cf. Frierson 2004: 122).

Given that the Ottoman Empire was a long-enduring and highly bureaucratic polity, it is no surprise that its notions of political legitimacy were based at least partially on concerns about commonweal (cf. İnalcık 1992 and 1993; see also Chapter 3).[31] Aslıhan Gürbüzel (2023) has recently made a strong effort to demonstrate the existence of numerous publics in the seventeenth-century Ottoman polity, composed of the janissaries, artisans, and members of the religious hierarchy and sufi orders. These groups collectively constituted a "public sphere" where various political ideals competed independent of the political visions and ideological frameworks imposed by the palace and the imperial bureaucracy (ibid.: 2–3, 17).

If we are willing to concede the possibility of premodern and non-European public spheres (Eickelman and Salvatore 2004: 6; Gürbüzel 2023: 3), with their own concepts of communal welfare, then it would not seem anachronistic to differentiate between public and private in the pre-nineteenth-century Ottoman Empire, even if the boundaries between the two might have been

---

[29] Eisenstadt (2006a: 144) argued that in the Western European context, "civil society entails direct participation in the political process of corporate bodies or a more or less restricted body of citizens in which private interests play a very important role. Such society entails a public sphere, but not every public sphere entails a civil society, as defined in the contemporary discourse. In every civilization, especially in contemporary ones with some complexity and literacy, a public sphere—but not necessarily a civil society type—will emerge." Later he added that "public spheres develop and are constituted also in 'premodern' societies—and while they do indeed have far-reaching impact on the political dynamics of their respective societies, such developments are not necessarily tantamount to civil society in the modern sense" (ibid.; cf. Eisenstadt 2002: 141).
[30] In this regard, see Zaman 2004, where the author investigates various characterizations of "common good" in Islamic legal traditions with specific reference to notions of *maslaha*.
[31] For references to expressions in fifteenth-century Ottoman official documents that might be translated as "common good" or "collective benefit," see Selçuk 2021: 361.

different, even less precise than those in the modern era.³² This premise justifies my interest in what Buchan and Hill (2014: 8) called public office corruption, which, as we have seen, they trace all the way back to antiquity in European history. Corruption as a distinct, overarching crime genus might not have existed in the premodern Ottoman polity. But corrupt acts defined as self-interested abuses of power by actors with communal functions or in positions of authority, whose responsibility it was to protect the wellbeing of God's and the ruler's subjects, did exist.³³ In what follows, I seek to contextualize such acts not by rejecting the possibility that they existed, but by exploring how premodern Ottomans perceived them, which other types of transgressions they associated them with and why, and whether they thought such clusters corresponded to broader categories of crimes.

This task is a significant component of our broader efforts to understand Ottoman state-society relations and governmental practices. As Akhil Gupta stated in the context of modern India (1995: 376), "The discourse of corruption [is] a key arena through which the state, citizens, and other organizations and aggregations came to be imagined. Instead of treating corruption as a dysfunctional aspect of state organizations, I see it as a mechanism through which 'the state' itself is discursively constituted."

A Note on the Book's Organization

In this book, to understand how premodern Ottomans might have perceived corrupt acts, I survey various genres of texts representing particular discursive fields.³⁴ According to Gavin Kendall and Gary Wickham (1999: 41), a discursive field "delimit(s) what can be said while providing the spaces—the

---

[32] A comparison of the public versus private realms in the premodern and modern eras is beyond the scope of the book both thematically and temporally, though it does deserve dedicated research.

[33] Karen Barkey (2016: 115) defines "corruption" in the Ottoman context as "departure from specified rules of conduct." Compared to what I propose above, this definition appears somewhat broad.

[34] The notion of a discursive space or field finds its roots in Michel Foucault's work, particularly *The Archeology of Knowledge* (2002). It is directly related to what he calls a "discursive formation" and defines as a "regularity," referring to "an order, correlations, positions and functionings, transformations," among "objects, types of statement, concepts, or thematic choices" that constitute the formation (41). The regularity in question does not imply a "unity" among those objects, statements, concepts, and so on. Rather, a discursive formation is constituted by a "system of dispersion" that articulates differences as well as uniformities among these; it makes particular differences/uniformities (and not others) perceivable. For example, in fiqh traditions, conflicting opinions among jurists from various legal schools on the causes and consequences of divorce belong to the same discursive formation because their justifications are based on a largely consistent methodology. For Foucault's specific thoughts on the discursive attributes of texts from different genres, see Foucault 1981.

concepts, metaphors, models, analogies—for making new statements." Thus, by identifying what was "said" about abuse by government officials and their predatory practices in my sources, I also make inferences about what was "sayable" in the discursive spaces associated with them.[35]

Chapters 1 and 2 survey jurisprudential formulations on corruption composed in pre-Ottoman and Ottoman times, respectively. The first chapter considers the notions and terminology related to corruption and associated behavior as found in the scriptural sources of Islam and as discussed in the scholarship on early Islamic history, and the second explores jurisprudential sources popular in the Ottoman era to identify how they characterized notions and practices associated with corruption. Likewise, Chapter 3 and, in part, Chapter 4 examine relevant articulations in state-generated documents, such as the Ottoman law codes, rescripts of justice, and imperial orders. As I observe in these chapters, the discursive realms associated with the jurisprudential and state-generated texts diverge not only in terms of their ideological orientations, but also in their attention to specific acts and actors pertaining to corruption.

Chapter 5 explores how corruption is treated in the premodern Ottoman political literature. This genre includes commentaries on political ethics; advice literature intended for the ruler and high-level government officials; chronicles; and reform treaties, among others. My consideration of the relevant texts is structured chronologically: I distinguish writings composed before the early sixteenth century from later ones, a temporal threshold that corresponds to a major political-bureaucratic transformation, based on the assumption that these groups would illustrate different perspectives on corruption.

---

[35] An earlier model in the Ottoman historiography for my analysis can be found in Dror Ze'evi's *Producing Desire: Changing Sexual Discourse in the Ottoman Middle East, 1500–1900* (2006: 1–15). See also Selim Kuru's (2008) perceptive and in-depth review of Ze'evi's book, where the author observes that "the use of discourse, and the 'discursive' [in *Producing Desire*], is...elusive, since...they seemingly refer not to the production of bodies of knowledge and the institutional frameworks that develop around it, but rather, to topics found in a variety of texts analyzed, without necessarily referring to a particular discourse. In the context of Ze'evi's analysis[,] texts appear as fragments reflecting sexual mores rather than as elements of a discursive totality" (677). While I do not believe that the analysis in the present book is susceptible to these criticisms, one can also point out in response to Kuru that (1) methodologically, the term "discourse analysis" can refer to a wide variety of approaches in a plurality of fields (ranging from literary studies to anthropology, sociology, political science, and to folklore), many of which lack consistent or even fully articulated sets of procedures (Johnson and McLean 2020), and (2) in history, our sources tend to delimit the scope of our analyses, often rendering them incomplete and provisional. For the latter reason, a more reasonable expectation might be to consider individual studies as contributions to a cumulative research endeavor that might mature over time with the contributions of multiple researchers who share parallel objectives. See Ferguson 2018 for a more recent example in the Ottoman context with a comparable methodological approach. For examples of research on modern corruption discourses, see Gupta 1995 and 2005.

Chapter 6 surveys twenty or so accounts composed between the late sixteenth and early nineteenth centuries primarily for Western audiences by authors who were often (though not always) from Europe. The chapter describes how these authors evaluated odd, abusive, or predatory practices in the Ottoman polity and reflected on their broader implications in relation to their backgrounds, audiences, political worldviews, and genre-specific conventions. The chapter also highlights the quasi-ethnographic material in the accounts pertaining to legal and bureaucratic processes not well-represented in the "native" sources.

I complement my exploration of different textual genres and discourses with chapters that elaborate specific issues raised in particular points of my discussion. Chapter 4 discusses Ottoman attempts to monitor, police, and punish acts associated with corruption and how various economic, political, and institutional factors might have influenced such efforts. Chapter 7 explores the vague relationship between gifts and bribes in terms of their functional and performative qualities. Chapter 8 tackles the morality of patronage and favoritism, a topic that has received little scholarly attention. The discussion focuses on the *ilmiye* establishment primarily because of the considerable secondary scholarship on this sector of the Ottoman society and the large number of available primary sources on the education and career paths of the qadis and *müderris*es. The conclusion contemplates the perspectives of those guilty of corruption and ties the findings and arguments presented in specific chapters to broader issues raised in this introduction.

1
Corruption Based on Pre-Ottoman Jurisprudential Sources

This chapter considers the notions and terminology related to corruption and its constituents as found in the primary sources of Islam and as discussed in the scholarship on early Islamic legal history. Its primary objective is to generate preliminary insights that offer a starting point for my discussion in Chapter 2 and help me better understand the Ottoman material.

The Quran and prophetic traditions put some emphasis on communal unity and wellbeing. One can also identify in these texts and later jurisprudential interpretations built upon them an obvious concern with self-regarding acts by religious and administrative authorities. The chapter initially identifies how related issues are articulated in these sources and then surveys subsequent institutional developments and governmental-administrative practices in the pre-Ottoman era, but with broader temporal influence.

Corruption in the Quran and Hadith Traditions

Corruption as many moderns define this term—the abuse of political, military, or administrative authority for personal benefit through a set of specifically defined acts (such as bribery, nepotism, extortion, and collusion)—has no equivalent in the Quran.[1] That being said, the scripture does provide terminology that encompasses a variety of relevant notions. Perhaps the most obvious and frequently cited are the words derived from the root *f-s-d*, which is directly related to the noun commonly used for corruption in modern Arabic, *fasad* (cf. Arafa 2012: 196, 197, and *passim*). According to one source, fasad is used eleven times in the Quran to mean "mischief," "destruction," "oppression," "disorder," and "disbelief." *Fasada*, a verb that appears in the holy text three times, could mean "to spoil" or "to fall into disorder." *Afsada*,

---

[1] This definition of corruption is inspired by Joseph Nye (1967: 419). For a comprehensive discussion of many other definitions, see Heidenheimer and Johnston 2002.

another verb that appears in the scripture fifteen times, can mean "to ruin," "to play havoc," and "to cause damage." Finally, *mufsid* and *mufsidun*, which appear in the Quran twenty-one times, refer to cruel, mischievous, destructive, and divisive people (Badawi and Abdel Haleem 2008: 709–10).[2] According to 30:40, "Allah created the humans, provided for them, will cause them to die, and then will give them life," but the next verse (30:41) suggests that fasad "appeared on land and sea because of people's actions." Among those who cause fasad according to the Quran are those kings who, "whenever they enter the city, despoil it and humiliate the noblest of its people" (27:34); likewise, the Pharaoh caused fasad by dividing his people into factions, oppressing some groups, and killing their young sons (28:4).

Another root with a general set of meanings associated with corruption is *f-s-q*. Words linked to this root, such as *fasaqa* (Ottoman Turkish [hereafter "OT"]: *feseka*), *fisq* (OT: *fısk*), and *fasiq* (OT: *fasık*), appear fifty-four times in the Quran, and their meanings range from disbelief, disobedience to God's law and orders, apostasy, and rebellion by breaking the law, transgressing, fomenting trouble, acting immorally, cheating, lying, making false accusations, and being untrustworthy (Badawi and Abdel Haleem 2008: 710–12).

A third set of words is derived from the root *z-l-m*. Various generations of Muslims—including the Ottomans, as we will see—often utilized *zulm* (OT: *zulüm*), in particular, to refer to various acts linked to governmental abuse and predatory maladministration.[3] The term is often translated as "injustice" but also has a host of related meanings. Terms derived from *z-l-m* occur hundreds of times in the Quran and could mean "darkness, disbelief, tyranny, oppression," "putting something in the wrong place, acting improperly," and "causing someone to suffer a loss" (ibid.: 585–7). In 38:24, 18:13, and 10:44, the Quran uses the term *zalama* to mean, respectively, "to treat unfairly," "to not give full measure," and "to deny someone something due to them," usages that call to mind modern definitions of corruption.[4] Quran 4:10 uses *zulman* to refer to the deceitful appropriation of orphans' property. A *zalim* could be a person who wrongly seizes someone else's belongings.[5]

---

[2] Arafa (2012: 197) suggests that according to various Muslim jurists and lexicographers, fasad might refer to "mischief, abuse, rottenness, spoiledness, decay, decomposition, putrefaction, depravity, wickedness, viciousness, iniquity, dishonesty, and pervertedness."

[3] In the Ottoman context, see Mumcu 1985.

[4] *Quran* 38:24: "Indeed he has treated you unfairly by asking for your ewe [to add] to his ewes"; 18:13: "Both gardens produced their [proper] yield and did not hold back any [due part] of it"; 10:44: "God does not suffer people any [injustice]—it is they who wrong themselves."

[5] *Quran* 12:79: "God forbid that we should take other than the one with whom we found our property: for if we did so, we would be zalim"; see Badawi and Abdel Haleem 2008: 586.

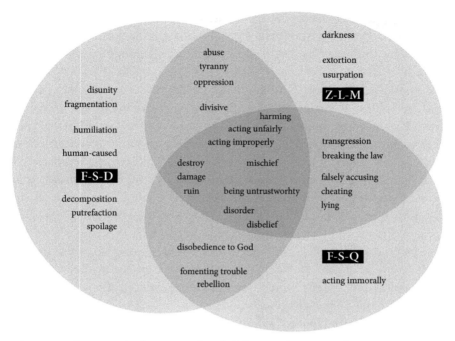

Figure 1.1 Semantic Links among F-s-d, Z-l-m, and F-s-q in the Quran

The web of meanings identified in Figure 1.1 might indicate how the scripture infers the broader connotations of these terms. Some of these meanings, such as tyranny, disbelief, mischief, disorder, lying, and their close cognates, are shared by two or all three roots. These overlaps make it possible to imagine the associations between more specific connotations of individual roots, such as biological putrefaction (f-s-d), darkness (z-l-m), and immoral actions (f-s-q), through their connections to the roots' shared meanings. The result is what Izutsu (1964: 35–41) calls a "semantic field" that contains combined meanings. Hence, crimes and misdemeanors such as lying, extortion, and usurpation are transgressions related to rebellion, tyranny, even apostasy and godlessness, and thus suggest connections between particular acts of greed and abuse, religious impropriety, communal disharmony, and disrespect for God's law. Historians have noted a similar semantic range associated with corruption in ancient Greece, Rome, and medieval Christendom. In these contexts the word has connotations that range from bodily decomposition, loss of physical form, loss of moral integrity, loss of virtue, godlessness, sin, greed, political decrepitude, tyranny, and loss of liberty to what Buchan and Hill (2014: 27) have called "public office corruption."

To be sure, attempts to associate Quranic terms with particular types of crime, behaviors, or relationships are often based on ex post facto readings of the text, informed by the desire to find in the scripture clues, if not prescriptions, that could resolve problems in later periods. This approach is common in Islamic jurisprudential traditions and makes it possible to argue that the holy book condemns a specific act (say, extortion or embezzlement) even if it does not explicitly reference it if the interpreter can reasonably demonstrate that this act generates fasad or zulm. In other words, while the Quran does not contain vocabulary that might effortlessly get translated as "abuse of power," "predatory administration," or "corruption" as these terms would be defined in subsequent eras, it could offer religious justifications to denounce them as transgressions based on their possible effects on the Muslim community.

Beyond a terminology with relatively general connotations and broad applications, exegetes have identified in the scripture verses they associate with specific acts of abuse often linked with corruption. For example, the Quran states that one should "not consume one another's wealth unjustly or send it to rulers or judges [al-ḥukkam] so that they can aid you to consume parts of other people's property" (2:188). Although the verse is vague, many exegetes have read it as an injunction against bribing officials, presumably with the intention to claim others' wealth or property (Rosenthal 1964: 136; Köse 2008: 142–3, 145; Arafa 2012: 213). Elsewhere (5:42), the Quran disapproves of consuming what is unlawful (suht), and scholars have associated this term, too, with bribery (Köse 2008: 146–50; Arafa 2012: 198).[6] But if suht could indeed refer to bribery, it would also connect the notion to an entirely distinct set of meanings. According to Franz Rosenthal (1964: 136), suht might refer to consuming unclean food (such as pork and alcohol), taking interest, telling untruths, and slandering.[7] Based on his research in early jurisprudential

---

[6] The Quran uses the term suht in this verse to condemn the sinful behaviors attributed to the Jews: "They [Israelites] are listeners of falsehood, devourers of suht" (5:42). According to Rosenthal (1964: 136), suht may be etymologically related to the Hebrew and Aramaic word for "bribe," or shuhd. Yet Joseph Lowry (2003: 174) provides a different etymological connection: "In Leviticus 22:25, a Hebrew cognate, mashḥat, refers to inherent 'corruption' or 'mutilation' which renders certain ritual offerings unfit (see consecration of animals; corruption) but the more usual sense of the biblical Hebrew cognate is 'destruction,' which is how a related Arabic word is used at Q 20:61." Lowry (ibid.) also notes the possibility that the term might have originated from suhta, which means "depravity" or "corruption" in Syriac. In their discussion of the topic, Arafa and Köse cite hadiths attributed to the Prophet and Ali ibn Talib where they are reported to have stated that suht corresponds to bribery (Köse 2008: 146; Arafa 2012: 203).

[7] Rosenthal suggested that the precise meaning of the term in the Quran cannot be established with certainty: "The 'eating' of suht admits of many possibilities.... The corresponding verbal root also is too general in its meaning of corruption or destruction and is not of much help in determining the meaning of the noun" (ibid.).

sources, Saffet Köse (2008: 148) suggested that suht could be associated with greed and gluttony and could refer to gains derived from extortion, plunder, gambling, soothsaying, and prostitution, "embarrassing, shameful acts, ones that generate repulsiveness and ones for those who are responsible would do anything possible to hide from the general public." What's more, since acts such as gambling, soothsaying, and consuming of impure substances are among behaviors explicitly forbidden in the scripture, bribery (as suht) implies a lack of divine guidance and/or godlessness. These meanings are also connoted by terms derived from f-s-d and z-l-m.

Other scholars (for example, Iqbal and Lewis 2014: 17) have also identified verses in the scripture that they regard as condemnations of nepotism and embezzlement of communal property. For example, 4:135 urges believers to "stand firmly for justice, witnesses for God, even as against yourselves, or your parents, or your relatives; and whether it be (against) rich or poor."[8] Verse 3:161, which might have been revealed to protect the Prophet from accusations of embezzlement of the war loot that was supposed to be divided among Muslims, states, "It is not for any prophet to defraud [*yaghulla*, the war loot]. Whoever does so will bring what he wrongly took [*ghalla*] with him on the Day of Resurrection. Then every soul will be paid in full what it hath earned, and they will not be wronged."[9]

The verses quoted above might not constitute a comprehensive list of references in the scripture to behaviors relevant to modern understandings of corruption.[10] Moreover, the scholarship on the Quran does not provide much systematic guidance on how we should understand Quranic statements regarding such acts in relation to others that might have motivated them or certified their legitimacy—statements involving, for example, the merits of gift exchange or favoring kin and family members.[11] Nevertheless, limited and imprecise references (from a modern perspective) to behavior related to

---

[8] The exegetes of the Quran consider this verse especially relevant for witnessing in commercial transactions, transfer of wealth to orphans on maturity, and disputes involving crimes against individuals and property. To uphold justice, testimonies should not be swayed by considerations beyond what was actually observed, including kinship, personal connections, sympathy, or "hatred for a people"; see Nasr et al. 2015: 253. See also Quran 5:8.
[9] On the various meanings of the words derived from *gh-l-l*, see Badawi and Abdel Haleem 2008: 673–4. According to *The Study Quran* (Nasr et al. 2015: 175), this verse might relate to various incidents in the context of the battle of Badr, involving valuable objects Muhammad did or did not claim as his share from the war loot, actions pertaining to the distribution of spoils, or the actions and consequences of Muslim archers who left their spots during the battle seeking personal wealth.
[10] See, for example, 74:6, where the scripture warns against "conferring favors in order to acquire more."
[11] See, for example, 27:35–56 for gifts and 17:24, 2:177, 4:36, 8:41, and 16:90 for kin and family. Cf. Guo 2002; and Giladi 2002.

corruption in the scripture should not distract from the fact that the Quran does stress the need for an ethical and socially responsible communal order, whereby Muslims are urged to live virtuous, god-fearing lives and to be respectful of each other's interests and wellbeing. The Quranic ideal is a unified and harmonious community of believers (*umma*), whose members are urged to avoid moral transgressions and collectively instructed to "enjoin the good and forbid the evil" (3:104, 3:110). Overall, the scripture idealizes and emphasizes justice (as, among other things, intracommunal fairness and equity), goodness, integrity, and honesty as social virtues. So, while the scripture is less inclined to precisely define many of these categories, it does urge its readers to be cognizant of God's expectations based on what Khaled Abou El Fadl (2002: 14; see also Abou El Fadl 2003) has called their "lived realit[ies]."[12]

As another foundational source for Islamic law and ethics, second only to the Quran in terms of its importance, the *ahadith* (plural of hadith) contain more direct references to specific acts that moderns associate with corruption—bribery, in particular—and clues about how Muslims should regard and sanction them.[13] For example, according to one widely cited account, the Prophet "cursed the one who gives a bribe (*al-rashi*; that is, bribe-giver) and the one who takes it (*al-murtashi*; bribe-taker)" (Arafa 2012: 204–5; Iqbal and Lewis 2014: 9; Abu Dawud 2008: 4:3580).[14] Various versions of this report through different chains of transmission also include among the cursed intermediaries (*raish*) in bribe exchanges. Parallelly, it has been reported that the Prophet said "both the briber and the bribee will be in hell" (Arafa 2012: 204).

But what did it mean to offer and accept a bribe at the time of the Prophet? Based on medieval lexicographical sources, Franz Rosenthal (1964: 140)

---

[12] According to Kevin Reinhart (2002: 60), "A general feature of qur'ānic ethical terminology is that it typically commends the good far more than it stipulates what the good is; the Qur'ān assumes that much of the good and its opposite is known or recognizable" to contemporary Muslims. In this sense, "the Qur'ān takes for granted the vices, virtues and modes of human organization present at the time of revelation" (55–6; cf. Abou El Fadl 2002).

[13] Obviously, ahadith are accounts of what the Prophet said or did, or his approval of or lack of objection to something said or done in his presence. As such they contain perspectives and/or attitudes that Muslims associate with the Messenger of God.

[14] A common term used for bribery in ahadith is *al-rashwa* (adopted to Persian as *rishwat* and to Turkish as *rüşvet*), derived possibly from the Arabic *rasha*, a verb supposedly denoting a chick's extending its neck toward its mother with the expectation of being fed (Sahillioğlu 1966: 692; Köse 2008: 139). Ibn Nujaym, a sixteenth-century Egyptian mufti, suggested that the word originally referred to the act of secretly drawing water from a well by a bucket attached to a string (1966: 692). Other terms used to refer to bribery also include, in addition to suht in the Quran, *itawa* and *bakhshish*, but Rosenthal (1995: 466) suggested that none of them "became as unambiguous and forceful as ra<u>sh</u>wa."

defined bribery as "achieving something one needs through trying to get into someone's good graces," presumably by making monetary payments and other types of offers or extending favors. Thus, the act might not have been inherently or unequivocally illegitimate: "If the bribe is given to achieve an improper purpose, it falls into the forbidden category. However, if the purpose in offering a bribe is to obtain a right or to repulse an injustice, it does not fall under the curse contained in the aforementioned tradition of the Prophet" (ibid.; but cf. Rosenthal 1995: 466). This interpretation, though ostensibly influenced by technical distinctions among various types of bribes that subsequent generations of jurists identified (see Chapter 2), contradicts the clear statement in the above hadith that bribe exchanges are categorically condemned, regardless of objectives. More recently, Saffet Köse (2008) argued that while one can indeed attribute a neutral meaning to the term in early lexicological traditions,[15] classical Hanafi jurists were more likely to use it specifically for compensations or payments made for legally dubious or impermissible transactions. According to Köse, these included rights, benefits, or privileges inappropriate for contractual transactions. Thus, for example, the term "bribe" is used in the Hanafi works for payments or compensations made between co-wives in return for a transfer of their rights to spend the night with their husband; payments made to wives for not exercising their rights in their marriage contracts that would lead to the annulment of the marriage; disbursements made for transferring to third parties the right of preemption (*shufa*); and compensations made in return for accepting the designation of surety (*kafala*) for an outstanding debt (2008: 140–1).

Hadith reports further elucidate how the Prophet and an early generation of Muslims might have perceived the relevant acts. These accounts reproach the abuse of trust by representatives of the religious-political authority who were motivated by self-interest. For example, a few variations of the hadith that reports the Prophet's condemnation of bribe-givers and bribe-takers contain the expression "in matters of governance or judgment" (*fi'l-ḥukm*), which limits the Prophet's admonition to those involved in legal and/or administrative schemes (Rosenthal 1995: 466; Iqbal and Lewis 2014: 9; Arafa 2012: 205). According to another, albeit weaker, hadith, a judge's acceptance of a bribe amounts to infidelity (*kufr*) (an-Nasa'i 2007: 6:5668). A particularly well-cited hadith reveals the Prophet's concern about how government functionaries

---

[15] "Rüşvet, istenilen menfaate ulaştıran vasıta olduğu için" (Köse 2008" 139); "Rüşvetin sözlükteki bir başka anlamı da yapılan iş karşılığında verilen ücret/bahşiştir" (140).

might illegitimately benefit from their positions.[16] According to this report, the Prophet sends a man named Ibn Lutbiyya to collect payments from Muslims made to the government. When Ibn Lutbiyya returns from his assignment with his collections, he says to the Prophet:

> "This is for your wealth and this is a gift (for me)." The Messenger of Allah... said: "Why don't you sit in the house of your father and mother so that the gift may come to you, if you are telling the truth.... By Allah, no one of you takes something from [what is entrusted to you] unlawfully, but he will meet Allah, exalted is He, on the Day of Resurrection carrying it, and I will recognize one of you who meets Allah carrying a groaning camel, or lowing cow, or bleating sheep." (Muslim 2007: 5:4740)[17]

Although the hadith is not specifically about bribery, it does highlight the significant concern in early Muslim polity with the potential conflict of interest between those who represent the religious-political authority and their representatives, which indicates that what modern economists might call a "principal-agent conflict" was a well-known problem in Islamic history. Indeed, a parallel tension between the same parties over revenue sources can be found in reports of Umar ibn al-Khattab's words and deeds. Umar (d. 644 CE), the second caliph after Muhammad and one of the most celebrated rulers in early Islamic history, is said to have recorded "the possessions of his officials at the time of their appointment and confiscated partly or wholly whatsoever they added whilst in office on suspicion of benefiting from public appointment" (Iqbal and Lewis 2014: 9). He also required his representatives to keep records of their revenues and expenses for inspection (ibid.).

The account of Ibn Lutbiyya's actions points toward another relevant tendency in hadith reports: a degree of anxiety regarding gifts. We know about the importance of gift exchange in societies where reciprocity among individuals, families, kin groups, or tribes is a dominant "form of integration," in Karl Polanyi's terms (2001: Ch. 4).[18] In all likelihood, Arabia during the Prophet's time was one such setting. Indeed, gift exchange is generally praised

---

[16] See, for example, "Rüşvet: Alan da Veren de Yanacaktır!" (2013: 195).
[17] For different versions of the same report, see Muslim 5:4738 and 5:4739; also cf. Köse 2008: 149; and "Rüşvet: Alan da Veren de Yanacaktır!" 2013: 195. While the report does not contain a direct reference to bribery, in some studies it is brought up in relation to the latter. See Köse 2008: 149; "Rüşvet: Alan da Veren de Yanacaktır!" 2013: 195.
[18] According to Polanyi (2001), three distinct "mechanisms of structural integration" (reciprocity, redistribution, and exchange) have historically shaped the main aspects of all economic systems, often in combinations where one of these remained dominant. "Substantivist" in nature, Polanyi's

in many hadith accounts. For example, it is widely reported that the Prophet "would accept gifts and he would give something in return" (at-Tirmidhi 2007: 4:1953). "When something [food] was brought to him," another report states, "the Messenger of Allah would ask: 'is this charity (*asadaqa*) or a gift (*hadiya*)?' If they said: 'Charity,' he would not eat it [but distribute it among Muslims]. And if they said, 'a gift' he would eat it" (at-Tirmidhi 2007: 2:656).[19] The Prophet is also reported to have emphasized the symbolic importance of the gift when he said, "O Muslim women, no woman should look down on a gift given by her neighbor even if it is the meat from a sheep's hoof" (Muslim 2007: 3:2379).[20]

It is the gift's importance in facilitating and reproducing reciprocity that makes it such a potent conceptual tool for legitimizing various forms of economic appropriation, including some that might otherwise be deemed unacceptable. In Ibn Lutbiyya's case, it is notable that he does not hide that he accepted offerings, a point that receives little attention in the literature about this account. Indeed, it appears that the Prophet doubts the legitimacy of gift exchanges because of Ibn Lutbiyya's reliance on their presumably sacrosanct nature to justify them.[21] Here it is significant that the Prophet does not question the *concept* of gift exchange as a prevalent socioeconomic practice; instead, he demonstrates, even if implicitly, his displeasure with its unduly flexible connotations.

The Prophet's sensitivity to the manipulable meaning of the gift is evident in other hadiths as well. For example, in one instance we find Muhammad advising Umar ibn al-Khattab to accept gifts when he is "not hoping for it or asking for it," but not to "hanker after it" (Muslim 2007: 3:2406). Another hadith, in which the Prophet is reported to have urged Muslims to accept presents so long as they remain presents but to reject them when they become bribes (Abu Dawud 2008: 3:2958 and 3:2959), demonstrates the uncertainty of

---

contributions to economic history insist on the "embeddedness" of economic choices and behavior (including the production and circulation of things) in wider social, cultural, and political institutions and practices (Elardo and Campbell 2006; Bălan 2012).

[19] Perhaps the distinction between charity and gift was that the former was intended for communal purposes, including but not limited to the wellbeing of the poor, and the latter was for the personal consumption of the Prophet.

[20] For the importance of gifts that are not bribes in hadith reports, see "Rüşvet: Alan da Veren de Yanacaktır!" 2013: 195–6.

[21] In their study of the history of corruption in Western settings, Buchan and Hill (2014: 39–40) identify an almost identical incident in the context of ancient Rome, in which the gifts a high-ranking state official received while he was on duty came under a very similar type of scrutiny: "Take the case of Julius Bassus, a former governor charged by the Senate with having 'naively and unguardedly accepted things from the provincials as a friend of theirs.' His accusers described these tributes as 'thefts and plunder' whereas Bassus himself referred to them as 'gifts.' Tellingly, Bassus had never attempted to conceal his so-called 'crimes' and had even mentioned them to the emperor."

the purposes of these exchanges. This very ambiguity is also clear in another hadith, where Muhammed is reported to have said, "If a judge (qadi) accepts a gift (hadiya), he has consumed something unlawful, and if he accepts a bribe (rashwa), that takes him to the level of disbelief (kufr)" (an-Nasa'i 2007: 6:5668). Thus, for judges, accepting gifts and bribes have comparable, though not exactly identical, consequences. While the former leads to sin, the latter is tantamount to losing one's afterlife.

The concern about the status of gifts received by state appointees continued after the passing of the Prophet. Umar ibn al-Khattab, the second caliph, is reported to have urged state appointees "not to accept gifts [while on duty], since these constitute bribes" ("Rüşvet: Alan da Veren de Yanacaktır!" 2013: 199). He is also said to have established rules and precedents regarding gifts presented to officials, focusing particularly on how to differentiate them from taxes and how to control the financial burden that such offerings put on the populace (Iqbal and Lewis 2014: 9, 15). Nevertheless, anxiety about how to differentiate gifts from bribes remained prevalent among subsequent generations of Muslims (see Chapter 2).

The hadith literature also contains references to and condemnations of embezzlement and favoritism, again specifically in the context of legal and administrative matters. The hadith regarding Ibn Lutbiyya may be taken as an example of the first concern. In regard to favoritism, the Prophet urged his followers to "carry out the legal punishments on relatives and strangers [just the same], and do not let the fear of [being] blame[d by them] to stop you from carrying the command of Allah" (Ibn Majah 2007: 3:2540). He also chastised those who asked for leniency for a Qurayshi woman found guilty of theft: "O people, those who came before you were doomed because if a nobleman among them stole, they let him off. But if a lowly person stole, they carried out the punishment on him. By Allah, if Fatima the daughter of Muhammad were to steal, I would cut off her hand" (Muslim 2007: 4:4410). Finally, the Prophet stated that the Day of Judgment would be close when trust (or honesty; *amanah*) is lost, and trust (or honesty) is lost "when [political] authority is given to those who do not deserve it" (al-Bukhari 1997: 8:6496). As is well known, after the Prophet's passing, accusations of favoritism directed at Uthman ibn Affan (d. 656 CE) and his kin justified and motivated a widespread rebellion against him, which ultimately led to the Sunni-Shiite split.

Islam emerged in an environment where tribal affiliations and connections based on kinship were the main bases of social identity. In this sense, the emphasis found in the Quran and the Prophet's traditions on a unified Muslim community has been recognized, correctly, as revolutionary. However, the course of Islamic history after the Prophet's death also demonstrates that in practice allegiance to one's family, kin, clan, and tribe at the expense of other Muslims did not disappear. According to Frederick Denny (2001: 370), "Even though Islam could claim larger authority than the traditional tribal system for the ordering and regulation of community life, the old system was by no means simply abandoned. Rather it was incorporated into the larger complex of Muslim community life." This could perhaps best be seen in the development of genealogy as a discipline of knowledge in the post-Quranic times. Following Frederick Donner, Denny sees this development as a way for Arabs to preserve their dominance over other peoples in the early Islamic empire: "Arab tribal legitimation became stronger, not weaker, as other peoples embraced Islam and questioned the Arab suzerainty" (ibid.). In this context, Maaike van Berkel's (2018) observation that nepotism at this time received less critical attention in comparison to bribery and embezzlement in medieval Islamic sources might be relevant.

Overall, it would not be wrong to claim that Prophetic traditions contain more information than the Quran about various acts plausibly associated with corruption, including perceptions of them in the early Muslim community, and the reasons they were disconcerting. Nevertheless, these sources give us an unsteady basis for defining acts that we now link to corruption, or understanding how they might relate to each other. In later times, generations of Muslim jurists would make efforts to better articulate the boundaries and consequences of such acts, which led to the emergence of more nuanced and elaborate considerations in numerous volumes on jurisprudence and political philosophy.

Jurisprudential Considerations of Corruption

With the gradual development of Islamic jurisprudence (*fiqh*; OT: *fıkıh*) from the second/eighth century onward, we observe attempts made by Muslim jurists to compile and define various types of venality and consider them in the realms of politics and government. In these articulations a somewhat coherent perspective on the topic emerges. It is not my objective to comprehensively survey how these jurisprudential articulations emerged and evolved over time. That would be an overly ambitious project for the solo historian, and one that others with more appropriate qualifications have only partially achieved.[22] Instead, I intend to make some initial observations based on the secondary literature to form preliminary opinions about prominent tendencies in the jurisprudential scholarship.

Based on what we find in the works of modern researchers who have published on the topic, most premodern jurisprudential considerations related to corruption are unambiguously focused on the office of the qadi, though sporadic references to other judicial actors also exist (see Chapter 2 for more on these actors). This attention indicates that most premodern jurists regarded corruption involving the qadis as a particularly serious concern, since the presumption of impartiality in the enforcement of God's law was critical for the stability of the community and/or legitimacy of the political and administrative order (Köse 2008; Arafa 2012: 206). According to Johansen (2002: 1570), jurists

> place qadis at the heart of their considerations, as they represent the norms of sacred law and, through their application, guarantee justice for their subjects. In the words of jurists, they are "the representatives of the Prophet" and thus the custodians of the ethical and religious character of public service. Their office has a religious dimension, akin to "service to God." (Original in French)

Johansen (ibid.) also argued that the qadis' judgments require more scrutiny because they represent acts of performative speech ("actes de parole performatifs [inšā]"), unlike the pronouncements of other legal actors (including the muftis), which depict observations ("actes de parole constatatifs [akhbâr]"). A parallel difference exists between qadis and non-judicial authorities (ibid.).

Further, a quick glance at the works of influential Hanafi jurists such as Burhan al-Din Marghinani (Merginani 1986), Molla Hüsrev (1980), and Ibrahim al-Halabi (Halebi n.d.) would reveal that the qadi's bribery receives a particular emphasis in premodern jurisprudential works. The relevant discussions include deliberations pertaining to the functions of different types of bribes—for example, those offered in order to obtain government appointments, receive verdicts in the court, and protect oneself and one's relatives and

---

[22] See, for example, Rosenthal 1964; Johansen 2002; Köse 2008; and Arafa 2012. Their accounts, though immensely useful, are all too brief and incomplete in terms of their source-bases to provide a truly comprehensive historical survey.

property from oppression and extortion—and the degrees of culpability of those involved in bribe-induced transactions based on their personal circumstances and motivations (cf. Rosenthal 1964; Köse 2008; "Rüşvet: Alan da Veren de Yanacaktır!" 2013; Iqbal and Lewis 2014). This preoccupation with bribery might indicate the term's potentially expansive meaning. As I will explain further in my discussion of the Ottoman political texts, the word could be utilized to describe payments or favors that could be associated with office sales, extortion, or kickbacks, suggesting that the lexicographical boundaries separating these notions were more ambiguous for premodern Muslims than they are for moderns. It is also possible that the emphasis on bribery compared to other transgressions, such as excessive extraction or embezzlement by tax collectors, is related to which areas of human interactions have customarily been emphasized and neglected in fiqh (see below and Chapters 3 and 4).

Most jurists regard any decision by qadis that is demonstrably based on bribery as null and non-binding, although jurists disagree about how this proscription could be implemented (Johansen 2002: 1587; Köse 2008: 153-4). The qadis whose guilt is proven or acknowledged by their own admission (*ikrar*) could also be subject to punishment, including (but not limited to) public chastisement, expulsion from office, and payment for damages caused by their actions (Köse 2008: 151-3).

The punishments prescribed for the qadi's corruption are classified as *tazir* (or "discretionary") punishments (Arafa 2012: 227-34), which involve retributions for crimes and misdemeanors not specifically mentioned in the Quran. These punishments, at the discretion of those who enforce the law, range from simple warnings and stern reprimands to fines, banishment, imprisonment, and even corporal punishment, often in the form of beatings or flagellations. The sentence depended on the status of the offender, the severity of the crime, the religious-political authorities' desire to set an example, and other considerations of society's interests and values. In the case of corrupt qadis, corporal punishment was generally considered less effective than the threat of public reproach and shaming associated with dismissal from one's position (ibid.).

In the context of this discussion, one question that deserves some attention is how jurisprudential traditions dealt with the *suspicion* of corruption in the qadi's work. In other words, what about decisions by the qadi that are so unorthodox, extraordinary, or even plainly erroneous that they generate suspicions of illegitimate motivations, without definitive proof of the same? In a rare study on qadis' errors, Ulrich Rebstock (1999: 18) stated that the qadi is secure from accusations of error (*halat*) and claims of liability (*daman*) in his judgments "by virtue of his office," unless he explicitly contradicts the "primary sources" of law (that is, the Quran, sunna, and scholarly consensus, that is, *ijma*) or his judgment is based on an explicit intention to misrepresent jurisprudential principles. Thus, Islamic jurisprudential traditions allow individual qadis considerable latitude for judicial interpretation, even in ambiguous and uncertain contexts. There is no process for judicial review of the qadis' decisions in most instances, and the law establishes no judicial hierarchy among the qadis, which makes equally valid their varying opinions on specific issues.[23] Even judgments based on evidence that is later proven faulty—for example, testimonies by false witnesses—can neither be nullified nor subsequently reversed.[24] The costs and liabilities caused by such judgments may afterward be redistributed among the judicial actors responsible for them, but the judgments themselves remain valid.[25]

The qadi's immunity from error and liability for damages caused by his faulty decisions has important implications for corruption. Although this principle might have helped qadis protect their independence against external influences, at times it might also have allowed them to willfully ignore precedents set by earlier jurists, or procedural consistency. Since the unorthodox nature of the decisions themselves could not be regarded as a prima facie indicator of the qadi's unjustifiable motivations, any allegation of corruption had to be proven by the testimony of witnesses who personally observed inappropriate interactions between the qadi and his clients and possessed the stature, courage, and protections to publicly accuse him of corruption. Even if litigation against a corrupt qadi could be pursued, and succeed, the dismissed qadi could regain his position later if he was judged to be

---

[23] According to the classical doctrine, David Powers explains (2007), "a decision may be reversed if the pronouncing judge was not legally competent to pass judgment, e.g., if he was a sinner, had been punished for unlawful slander, or did not possess the requisite qualities of moral uprightness.... Second, a judicial decision also may be reversed if a judge who is legally competent nevertheless engages in the improper use of independent reasoning (ijtihād), as, for example, if his judgment contradicts a Qur'ānic text about whose plain meaning there is universal agreement, if it contradicts a widely transmitted ḥadīth, or if it opposes the consensus of Muslim jurists" (see also Powers 1992). Jurists considered it necessary to allow qadis a wide interpretative scope and level of protection in their judicial operations to shield them from outside pressures and ensure their independence (Rebstock 1999: 14, *passim*).

[24] However, there may have been conflicting opinions in the Ottoman context. See Chapter 2.

[25] The qadi is protected from the liability caused by his erroneous judgment in almost all cases. When erroneous judgments are based on false witnesses, the liability for the damages belongs to the witnesses. If the judge's error violates a "claim of God" (*haqq allah*), the "public treasury" (*bayt al-mal*; OT: *beytülmal*) is liable for damages. If a claim of man (*haqq al-ibad*) is violated, the damage may or may not be replaceable. If it is replaceable (and if the error is not due to false witnesses), the beneficiary of the erroneous judgment is liable for the damage by restitution of the object or restoration of the claim. If it is not, the beneficiary must make a compensatory payment to the victim (Rebstock 1999: 24). In Chapter 2, I engage with the issue of false witnessing in more detail.

rehabilitated (Köse 2008: 153). Furthermore, not all damages caused by the qadi's corruption required full or partial compensation, or *could* be compensated (Rebstock 1999: 22–5, 31, 32).

Classical jurists also considered pre-emptive measures, in addition to reactive ones, to limit judicial venality. Indeed, one of the main personal qualities of the ideal qadi, according to jurisprudential expectations, is *adala* (OT: *adalet*),[26] which is often translated as "justice" but which Emiel Tyan (1960: 209–10) defined thus:

> As an adjective, the word ʿ*adl* expresses more particularly a juridical conception, and has numerous applications. However, agreement has never been reached on a definition of the term, as the Mālikite jurist Ibn Rushd observes. Furthermore, the various definitions that have been formulated are too comprehensive and imprecise. In al-Māwardī's definition, ʿ*adāla*, the quality of ʿ*adl*, is described as a state of moral and religious perfection. For Ibn Rushd it consists in not committing major sins, and also avoiding minor ones. But another author observes that such a state can be found only very exceptionally, in the saints; that ʿ*adāla* simply describes the state of a person who in general obeys the moral and religious law. This last conception is the one that came to be finally accepted. In the latest stage of Muslim law, as it appears in the codification undertaken in the Ottoman empire about the middle of the 19th century, the following definition is given: "The ʿ*adl* person is one in whom good impulses prevail over bad [ones]" (*Madjalla* art. 1705). In short, one can translate ʿ*adl* by "person of good morals," with the essentially religious sense that this has in Islam.... The antonym of ʿ*adl* is *fāsiḳ*.

In theory, choosing the right person for the job might be a good way to avoid corruption. But Tyan's discussion indicates that (1) there might have been no universal agreement on the meaning of the term, which would make it difficult to use it as an effective standard for recruitment, and (2) the adala of the qadi did not necessarily guarantee complete imperviousness to all immoral acts. One could technically be considered just, or *adil, overall* if he was *mostly* adil. As long as a person's specific misdemeanors did not overwhelm his overall appearance of integrity, he could still be considered

---

[26] Jurisprudential manuals all emphasize that one must be just (adil), in addition to being a free Muslim male, knowledgeable in law, and authorized to perform *ijtihad*, to be considered for the qadiship.

deserving of qadiship. Furthermore, one's demonstrable "fisq," or immorality, did not uniformly disqualify him from being appointed as a qadi, or lead to dismissal from this position.

Policing Corruption and the Need for Institutional Development

Perhaps because jurisprudential measures inadequately protected against corruption, stringent administrative measures for this purpose were developed and became increasingly prevalent. Many such measures, which later became part of *amal*,[27] date back to very early Islamic history. From the eighth century onward, for example, qadis in Egypt were sent to their jurisdictions from distant locations (Tillier 2017: 135–6). While this might have had more to do with the central government's intention to assert its power over the peripheries, it also helped to displace local qadis from established networks and tribal affiliations, and thus reduced their influence on judicial practice (ibid.). Additionally, the institution of notary-witnesses (*shuhud udul*) in the same period, possibly related to the appointment of non-local qadis to provincial jurisdictions, put the qadis' operations under the direct scrutiny of a local body of judicially experienced observers (Peters 1997). Such scrutiny could help the qadi with legally uncertain matters. For example, decisions based on local customs or minority opinions required the complicity of notary-witnesses (Serrano Ruano 2007). More importantly, however, the institution may have direct relevance to the idea of controlling corruption. According to İnalcık (1986: 4), "The use of shuhūd [in the Ottoman context]...was designed to check the ḳāḍī and to ensure that a decision was reached in the presence of an unbiased and expert body."

Furthermore, various Islamic regimes made efforts to audit the activities of their judicial and, especially, non-judicial officials, often by establishing specific appeal procedures and creating departments dedicated to this purpose

---

[27] Serrano Ruano (2007) defines *amal* as practices that, "while not intrinsically legal, acquire legal relevance in certain circumstances." They may not find their roots in jurisprudential sources and cannot be considered as "intrinsically legal," but for various reasons they became incorporated into legal considerations and practice. "Over time, the concept of ʿamal has allowed for the recognition of customary practices that stand in clear contradiction to the letter of the sacred texts or that supplement areas in which the law is silent. Once a legal practice acquires the status of ʿamal, muftīs and qāḍīs are required to follow it, with the result that the ʿamal may become a source of law, even if its authoritativeness has been an open question among Muslim jurists" (ibid.).

(van Berkel 2011, 2018).[28] Perhaps the best-known administrative anticorruption measure was what van Berkel describes as "the petition and response procedure, generally, but inconsistently, referred to as *mazalim* in the chronicles and administrative manuals" (2018: 72). The mazalim, which varied significantly in terms of their setups and operations from one setting to another, were tribunals "through which the temporal authorities took direct responsibility for dispensing justice" (Nielsen 1990: 933; see also Nielsen 1985). In other words, "temporal authorities," initially the caliphs and regional rulers but more often their representatives, heard grievances from subjects, resolved disputes, and punished perpetrators in ways not specifically elaborated in jurisprudential treatises.

The mazalim tribunals differed from sharia courts in two fundamental ways, both of which are directly related to corruption. The first difference concerns the types of cases: mazalim tribunals regularly adjudicated financial-administrative disputes, including issues pertaining to tax levies and land-grant distributions; looked into problems regarding the overall security of the public; and, occasionally, functioned as a court of appeal for cases decided in sharia courts. The tribunals also investigated complaints involving corruption by government functionaries. In fact, according to Nimrud Hurvitz (2013: 140), the mazalim tribunal's "main purpose was to enable ordinary subjects to complain about the administrative elite of the empire. The mazalim was a means by which the rulers addressed the abuse of power perpetrated by powerful state officials."

The way al-Mawardi (d. 1058) outlined the responsibilities of the mazalim tribunals in his *al-Ahkam al-Sultaniyya* (Māwardī n.d.) confirms Hurvitz's description.[29] Of the ten specific functions thus outlined, five concern issues directly related to abuse of power by state functionaries, including the prevention of "oppression and maltreatment of the public," which al-Mawardi considers "an essential duty" of the office; "remuneration due to public officers for the taxes collected," during which "just practices need to be observed" (90–1); "monitoring the records prepared by government" to prevent forgery

---

[28] According to van Berkel (2018: 74), the audit offices (often called *diwan* or *majlis al-zimam*), possibly borrowed from Byzantine models, are known to have existed since the Umayyad times. Subsequently, the Abbasids, Buyids, and Seljuks instituted departments with the same function, albeit under slightly different names.

[29] Scholars agree that al-Mawardi's *al-Ahkam al-Sultaniyya* represents the first and most comprehensive depiction of the mazalim tribunal and its functions before the emergence of modern scholarship on the topic. Another contemporary depiction is the homonymous work by Abu Yala Muḥammad ibn al-Husayn ibn al-Farra (d. 1066), which overlaps with al-Mawardi's observations to a significant extent (Hurvitz 2007).

and falsification (91–2); "restoration of usurped property" by the state; and monitoring the affairs of charitable endowments (92).[30]

The second major difference between the mazalim tribunals and the sharia court involves their procedures and the limits to their authority. According to al-Mawardi, those who presided over the mazalim tribunals had wider discretion and freedom of action than the qadis with regard to evidentiary and interrogative processes. The tribunals could physically coerce those under investigation, accept evidence below the standards required by sharia courts, subpoena witnesses, and postpone hearings to allow judicial investigation (Nielsen 1990: 934). Thus, they were better suited to fight corruption than the sharia court. Hurvitz (2013: 150) makes this point clear when discussing these institutions' different overall attitudes toward crime:

> The contrasting approaches of *shari'a* courts and *mazalim* tribunals stem from two different value systems and social visions. The underlying value that guided *shari'a* courts was to do justice and therefore to defend the rights of the suspects. This implies that they demand high standards of proof. Conviction of a suspect is made on the basis of solid evidence arrived at through stringent investigative procedures. These requirements protected suspects from potentially abusive courts of law. The main advantage of this approach is that it reduces the likelihood of convicting innocent individuals.... The procedures of the *mazalim* tribunals and police were based on a very different social vision. Their main priority was to prevent crimes that were perpetrated by common criminals or the corruption of state officials. To facilitate these goals, they needed to round up and convict as many criminals as possible. As a consequence, their procedures of interrogation enabled them to utilize harsh measures of investigation, threaten suspects and resort to other acts that disregarded suspects' rights.

For the purposes of our discussion, I should stress that the mazalim jurisdiction finds its historical roots not in Islamic jurisprudential traditions, but in pre-Islamic traditions of governance, particularly the Persian ones (Hurvitz 2013: 140, 152–3; van Berkel 2018). This is an important point because the two traditions idealize different sociopolitical orders. And since what they propose

---

[30] Nielsen and van Berkel's limited attempts to catalogue the subject matters of individual mazalim cases in their sources confirm this impression. Van Berkel (2011: 714) points out that of the eighteen cases mentioned in *The History of Viziers* by Hilal Ṣabi (d. 1055), nine deal with "official abuse." Twenty-two of the eighty-nine cases Nielsen (1985: 139–58) lists in the appendix of his book can be classified broadly as related to corruption.

as society's normative functioning differs, what they consequently perceive as threats to the "normal" also differ. In other words, we find in these traditions alternative models of political and administrative ethics.

Generally, classical Islamic jurisprudence pays minimal attention to issues of what moderns have called "constitutional" or "public law"—that is, matters pertaining to state-society relations. Instead, fiqh is more concerned with humans' relationship to God and with human-to-human interactions. In the latter regard, the law's main purpose is to manage relationships between and among members of the community of believers and to prevent those relationships from breaking down. As Wael Hallaq has suggested (2009: 84), the law is designed not to control or discipline, but to promote peace within umma, primarily by delineating the divinely sanctioned boundaries of personal rights and rules of social interactions. This is why the classical works of jurisprudence contain a plethora of contracts designed to regulate every aspect of human life, from commercial transactions to marriage and divorce; from charitable giving to compensation for murder and bodily injury. This is consistent with how Lawrence Rosen (2000) has described the primary function of Islamic law as the "regulation of reciprocity" among Muslims, who are expected to treat each other if not as equals in the modern sense of the term (since the law elevates men over women and free individuals over the enslaved),[31] then at least as comparable legal entities, or, in Brinkley Messick's (2003) words, as "sharia-subjects." While some Muslims might be subservient to others, all Muslims are subservient to God by constitution, and "the law was perfectly clear that the lives, property and internal relations of the subjects were sacrosanct as long as they observed the law themselves" (Crone 2004: 282).[32]

---

[31] According to Rosen (2000: 163), Islamic law may not treat individuals as equals even though it "equates" them. In issues pertaining to justice, "'equating' is more appropriate than 'equality' or 'equalizing' because Islam and contemporary Arab culture stress the notion of balancing things by finding something of equivalent weight or import, not something identical in nature or overall worth." For example, while men and women are not legally equal, they share inviolable, God-given rights and privileges of identical nature, which the law functions to protect from external meddling. In this sense, the "idea of justice as equating" means "putting on a scale that reflects difference, as sticking to the straight course by balancing things that are different through the calibration of proper place and weight" (ibid.; see also, more generally, 158–67).

[32] This interpretation of the philosophy of Islamic jurisprudence is consistent with how other historians have characterized the nature of early Islamic community. For example, according to Ann Lambton, in the first Islamic polity the legitimacy of government required as much devotion to the wellbeing of the Muslim community as commitment to the fulfillment of the requirements of God's law (Lambton 2013: Ch. 2). Consistent with this general orientation, the religious-political authority was held in trust and had to be accountable to the umma. Lambton (2013: 14) suggested that "the civil wars of the first two centuries, the political controversies over Umayyad rule, and the attacks on the personal piety and behavior of the caliphs are illustrations of the extent to which this principle [that is, ruler's subservience to God and accountability to the umma] found adherence."

From this perspective, an act disrupts the social order if it threatens the ties that constitute the umma, and its gravity is directly proportional to the disruption it causes. If the function of the law is to maintain peace among Muslims, and if it seeks to accomplish this task by establishing a level playing field on which differences are resolved in a way that does not disturb communal coexistence, then corruption might be perceived as an act that menaces this order. This is why the jurisprudential literature pays so much attention to how the qadis conduct themselves, specifically in their treatment of litigants. If the former are not honest brokers of the law, then peaceful coexistence becomes difficult.[33]

Because the main concern of Islamic jurisprudence is to regulate interactions between private persons, Muslims' attempts to develop "public law" were significantly influenced by ancient Persian traditions of governance, which focus on "dealings between... private people and the state" (Crone 2004: 282). Ancient Persian traditions of government are based on a vision of sociopolitical order that is considerably different from the jurisprudential conception of umma. Rather than defining the rights and privileges of common Muslims in relation to other "sharia-subjects," the political literature outlining Persian traditions of government is composed from the vantage point of the ruler and depicts a sociopolitical order that justifies his authority and elevated status. According to Patricia Crone (2004: 146), Persian traditions of governance "glorified the very kingship that the early Muslims regarded as offensive to God" and took pride "in their deeply inegalitarian socio-political organization." The Persian political literature regarded earthly rulers "as belonging to a special class of human beings" who were singled out by God with "divine effulgence" and whom he put "in charge of the rest of the mankind" (53). This literature also emphasizes that subjects have a duty to obey their rulers (155). *Siyasa* (OT: *siyaset*)—government, or "the art of staying in the saddle" (156)—requires the ruler to ensure, among other things, that his underlings do not conspire against or steal from him.[34] In this context, corruption might be

---

[33] According to Baber Johansen (2002: 1571 and *passim*), qadiship, as characterized in classical works of jurisprudence, is a "public" office; qadis serve the interests of the community of believers. Any self-serving, that is, "private," consideration that jeopardizes this responsibility represents corruption.

[34] Relevant here is Rosen's definition of the Islamic state in the premodern era as "*un*reciprocity incarnate" in the sense that "the state has legitimacy inasmuch as it manages tasks that are necessarily hierarchically arrayed, such as leadership in war and oversight of various criminal laws. The state also has the ability to support the vertically arrayed layers of the society in such a way as to keep alive the capacity of individuals to form ties to others that may yield important networks of their own" (Rosen 2000: 161–2, 172; emphasis in the original). This view plainly contradicts the jurisprudential principle that "an executive power of the law of God is vested in each and every Muslim," a principle Michael Cook has associated with the Quranic maxim that Muslims are required to "command right and forbid wrong" in every phase of law, including the political sphere: "Under this conception the individual

associated with acts that would undermine the political and financial bases of the regime headed by the ruler.[35]

* * *

This chapter's survey of Islamic scriptural sources has identified several loosely associated terms and verses in the Quran and a multitude of hadith reports relevant to particular aspects of corruption. As suggestive as this material may be in terms of its emphasis on the communal wellbeing of the Muslim umma, it may not constitute a coherent articulation of the notion in a fashion that resembles how we understand it today. Yet later jurists relied on scriptural pronouncements to generate a discursive space where we do, indeed, find more systematic formulations and prescriptions. In general, the classical judicial discourse on corruption is focused largely on the office of the qadi and on his acts that can loosely be characterized as bribery. Other state and legal authorities and many types of transgressions that moderns associate with corruption are not as well represented in them. Also, this discourse provides only a limited basis for condemning and punishing predatory, self-interested behavior by officeholders. This is why Muslim polities early on adopted practices and institutions, largely borrowed from pre-Islamic settings, to effectively monitor and control corruption. The hierarchical nature of the idealized sociopolitical order that these new practices infused into Muslim administrative traditions existed in tension with those implicit in the classical works of jurisprudence. These divergent approaches also imply multiple, conflicting perspectives on corruption. In the next few chapters, I trace these perspectives and their broader implications in the Ottoman context.

---

believer as such has not only the right, but also the duty, to issue orders pursuant to God's law, and to do what he can to see that they are obeyed. What is more, he may be issuing these orders to people who conspicuously outrank him in the prevailing hierarchy of social and political power" (Cook 2000: 9–10). Unlike those who bear the collective and individual responsibility to "command right and forbid wrong," subjects in the Persian-inspired advice literature have only partial agency, limited to pleading for the ruler's mercy and protection when they faced oppression by lesser power holders.

[35] Here I should stress that various premodern Islamic legal systems (as opposed to fiqh traditions), including the Ottoman, demonstrated the flexibility to accommodate the two perspectives on social order despite the inherent tensions between them. Relevant to this discussion is the fact that the classical jurists explicitly recognized the legislative privileges of the political authority to draw from local customs, non-Islamic legal systems, and non-Muslim imperial traditions as long as their interpretations did not conflict with clear Quranic and hadith-based injunctions. Over time, most jurists came to recognize legislation based on these non-fiqh-based sources as sharia-compliant. See Ergene 2014: 114–17.

2
Corruption in Ottoman Jurisprudence

This chapter delves into Ottoman jurisprudential works to identify how Ottoman jurists characterized the notions and practices associated with corruption. As we have seen, the primary sources of Islam highlight the importance of communal unity and welfare. Also, bribery and associated issues are standard topics in classical jurisprudential interpretations as threats to this objective, especially in passages that discuss the work of the qadi. Finally, little can be found in this pre-Ottoman jurisprudence about self-regarding, predatory acts by non-judicial actors. In the Ottoman context, those jurists who commented on topics related to corrupt acts tended to replicate these general tendencies, albeit in ways that suggest there were diverse opinions on specific matters. In the preceding chapter, I took a broader perspective to identify the rough outlines of the discursive field; in this one I look more closely at specific formulations of corrupt acts in the Ottoman context, consider their implications, and identify their variations with respect to other contemporary opinions when possible.

The following discussion focuses largely, though not exclusively, on the corruption-related insights of two jurists: Zayn al-Abidin ibn Nujaym al-Misri, known as Ibn Nujaym (1520–63), and Muhammad Amin ibn Abidin, or Ibn Abidin (1784–1836), who were among the most prominent representatives of the Hanafi *maddhab*, the official legal school of the Ottoman polity. Ibn Nujaym lived in Egypt during the early period of Ottoman rule. According to Samy Ayoub (2020: 62), Ibn Nujaym's "legal works were the principal point of reference for seventeenth- to nineteenth-century Ḥanafi jurists, and they profoundly shaped debates and opinions among Ḥanafis in this later period." What distinguishes the scholarship of Ibn Nujaym, as a first-generation legal scholar from Ottoman Egypt, is his ability to engage with the opinions of the Anatolian jurists and accommodate, if at times in a strained fashion, the legal authority of the Ottoman sultan. His formulation of the legal maxims (*qawaid*) of the Hanafi school garnered much interest among later jurists and was regarded as a precedent for the nineteenth-century codification efforts (Ayoub 2020: 52; Bayder 2022). Ibn Nujaym also wrote extensively on major practical concerns of his era, particularly the administration of waqfs, taxation, and litigation, in the context of which he negotiated imperial regulations and

Egyptian customs (Ayoub 2020: 46, *passim*; Atik 2021: 237). Ibn Nujaym stressed the need to limit the authority of government functionaries, called for greater oversight on their actions, and alluded to their corruption (Ayoub 2020: 55, 58–62). In what follows, I will focus on a treatise (*risale*) that he composed specifically on bribery; this treatise was well known and celebrated in Ottoman lands, as evidenced by Katib Çelebi's (d. 1657) reference to it in his *Mizan al-Hakk fi Ihtiyar al-Ahakk*.[1]

Ibn Abidin (1784–1836), a jurist and mufti from Damascus, was a much-respected Hanafi scholar in the nineteenth century, "a synthesizer of the late Hanafi tradition in the late Ottoman Empire" who built on his encyclopedic knowledge of the Hanafi scholarship from the earliest times (Ayoub 2020: 95–6). His jurisprudence was influenced by major social, economic, and political transformations at the turn of the nineteenth century, when the government elites in Istanbul and Cairo were pursuing military and administrative reform, large segments of the Ottoman society were encountering global capitalism and Western modernity, and various reactionary groups (such as the Wahhabis) were articulating radical criticisms against mainstream Islamic practices and institutions (Hallaq 2002: 44; Ahmad 2009: Ch. 2). In this context, Ibn Abidin stressed the importance of local customs as a source of law in jurisprudential attempts to accommodate diversity across Muslim communities (Hallaq 2002; Ahmad 2009: 48; Ayoub 2020: 104, 110, *passim*). His interpretations also demonstrated his strong inclination to respond to changing circumstances by utilizing the legal notion of "necessity" (*darura* in Arabic) (Ayoub 2020: 96, 110). Wael Hallaq (2002: 55) sees Ibn Abidin's work as "a first step, paving the way to modern legal reform" that would follow in the nineteenth and twentieth centuries. At the same time, Ayoub (2020: 28–9, 109) insists that Ibn Abidin continued to appeal to the Hanafi school's eponym and founders and remained within the school's methodological boundaries. In this chapter, I engage with his *Radd al-Muhtar ala al-Durr al-Mukhtar*, a commentary on al-Haskafi's (d. 1677) *Durr al-Mukhtar*, which has been celebrated as an authoritative work that offers novel solutions to modern-day problems.[2]

---

[1] The treatise I will discuss, *Risala fi Bayan al-Rishwa wa Ahkamiha* (n.d.), is included in a compilation of forty-one treatises by Ibn Nujaym titled *Majmuat al Rasail Ibn Nujaym*, all based on the questions directed to him about various issues and collected by his son, Ahmad, after his death. See Özel 1999; Ryad 2015; Ibn Nujaym 1966 and 2004. In this chapter, I rely on Sahillioğlu's (Ibn Nujaym 1966) and Pekcan's (Ibn Nujaym 2004) translations of the treatise.

[2] *Radd al-Muhtar* is particularly admired in the subsequent jurisprudential scholarship because of Ibn Abidin's determination to survey and engage the opinions of many different scholars on almost every legal issue, which helps to explain the text's great length. In the following discussion, I rely on Davudoğlu et al.'s translation of the work (Ibn Abidin 1982–94).

I focus on Ibn Nujaym and Ibn Abidin not only because they were among the giants of the late Hanafi maddhab, but also for two other reasons. First, they commented extensively on topics associated with corruption. Second, they wrote in very different time periods, so their works may reveal interpretive variations over time.[3] I will also complement Ibn Nujaym's and Ibn Abidin's insights with the opinions of other Ottoman and non-Ottoman jurists to demonstrate variations in jurisprudential positions.

Jurisprudential Articulations about Qadis and Their Corruption

Ibn Nujaym (1966: 691–2, 2004: 258) writes that his treatise on "bribery (*rishwa* or rashwa) and its components" aims to "identify what the qadi is allowed to accept from others and what he is not, distinguish the types of bribes that may be halal, or permissible, and the ones that may not be, and make clear how bribes are different from gifts." As in earlier jurisprudential treatments of the topic, Ibn Nujaym emphasizes the qadi's office. Also, the jurist seems to recognize here, at least implicitly, that the term rishwa could have a neutral, non-pejorative meaning. In fact, Ibn Nujaym makes this very point early in his discussion, when one of the lexicological meanings he offers for rishwa is *jul*, which could simply mean "reward, fee, or tip." Then again, the term in its technical-jurisprudential (*istilahi*) sense refers to property or things of value "that one offers to a judge or someone else in order to facilitate a judgement in his favor or to influence the latter to do something he desires" (1966: 691, 2004: 258). Ibn Nujaym points out that rishwa in this category is forbidden according to the Quran, the sunna, and jurists' opinions (ijma), but his later discussion, as we shall see, qualifies this assertion. Incidentally, Ibn Abidin (1982–94: 12:124), writing in the early nineteenth century, defined bribery in the same way: "Bribery is what a person gives to a judge or any other person to decide in his favor, or to compel him to do what he wants."[4]

---

[3] While Ibn Nujaym's treatise focuses specifically on bribery, Ibn Abidin's comments on bribery and other relevant issues are sprinkled throughout his multivolume commentary.

[4] That said, in some Ottoman jurisprudential sources the term finds common use more broadly, to denote fees for service or compensation in return for benefits, specifically when such transactions were considered suspect or illegitimate (cf. Köse 2008: 139–40). For example, in Ebussuud Efendi's (d. 1574) fatwas, it could refer to payments that facilitate marriage contracts: "Question: If Zeyd allows his daughter Hind to get married to Amr only after Amr

The impetus for Ibn Nujaym's treatise was a fatwa that, he stated, erroneously claimed that some Hanafi authorities did not distinguish bribes to qadis from those offered to non-judicial officials, including rulers and, presumably, their representatives (sing. *amir*; OT: *emir*) (1966: 691, 2004: 258). Unfortunately, I could not locate the fatwa in question and do not know its specifics. According to Rosenthal (1964: 137), there is a long history of disagreements about whether bribes or gifts offered to judicial and political or administrative officials should be seen as equivalent.[5] But because Ibn Nujaym does not cite the objectionable fatwa, his own opinion about the difference between bribes to judicial and non-judicial authorities is unclear. Since his "technical" definition concedes that a bribe might be extended

---

pays him three hundred akças as 'gift' (*ağırlık*; literally, 'load' or 'weight'), would Amr be able to claim this sum from Zeyd after the marriage (contract) is enacted? Answer: Yes. If marriage is conditional upon payment, the latter would not be a 'gift' but a bribe." (Mesele: Zeyd kızı Hind'i, Amr'ın üç yüz akça ağırlığın almayınca Amr'a tezvic eylemese, Amr ba'd-et-tezvic üç yüzü Zeyd'den almağa kadir olur mu? Cevab: Olur. Vermediği takdirce tezvic etmemek mukarrer olucak, ağırlık olmaz rüşvet olur). (Düzdağ 1972: 37) "Question: If at the time of their marriage, Hind gives Zeyd as a gift [*ergenlik*] an orchard and Zeyd gifts Hind in return a caftan, can Hind claim that orchard back from Zeyd when they separate a year later? Answer: Yes. [Those are] bribes. She [is required to] return [the caftan] to Zeyd." (Mesele: Hind hin-i tezevvücde Zeyd'e ergenlik bir bağ verip, Zeyd dahi ivaz bir kaftan vermiş olsa, bir yıldan sonra mufarakat ettikte Hind Zeyd'den ol bağı almağa kadire olur mu? Cevab: Olur, rüşvettir. İvazın Zeyde verir). (Ibid.)

Making payments as a condition for marriage was legally impermissible, so such payments had to be returned to the payee on request, which is consistent with the fatwas above. According to Colin Imber (1997b: 89–90), "The custom whereby the husband and the wife exchanged gifts on marriage had, in the sixteenth century, the Turkish name, *ergenlik*. The *ergenlik* itself was a gift from the wife to the husband, for which she received a gift in return. Since the custom was not part of the Islamic contract of marriage, the law did not explicitly assign ownership to the property exchanged in this way, and this inevitably gave rise to litigation on divorce, when both parties reclaimed their gifts." Comparable uses of "bribery," particularly in relation to marriage contracts, can also be found in Ibn Abidin's work, where he discusses the status of payments made to the relatives of the prospective brides in order to gain their consent to or support for the arrangement. Like Ebussuud, Ibn Abidin (1982–94: 5:569–70) considered such payments unlawful and said that in cases where the marriage contract ended, on request they should be returned to the party who had made them. Sixteenth-century Ottoman jurist Birgivi Mehmed Efendi (d. 1573) regarded the *tapu* fees that taxpayers paid to prebendal authorities to cultivate state-owned lands as illegal, which is why he called them "bribes" (Ivanyi 2020: 228–9).

[5] "Already at an early date, the view that a distinction should be made between the two groups [viz. judges and administrative officials] was implicitly indicated by those scholars who inserted, into the aforementioned tradition concerning God's curse resting upon those involved in bribery, the words 'in judgment,' thereby more or less restricting the application of the tradition to the judiciary. In the ninth century, the Mâlikite Ibn Ḥabîb stated flatly that legal scholars considered it equally reprehensible to give gifts to the central government (*as-sulṭân al-akbar*), judges, provincial officials ('*ummâl*), or tax collectors—a statement which presupposes the existence of other authorities who did make a distinction between the different categories" (ibid.). Rosenthal (137–8) also indicates that in fourteenth-century Egypt, the legality of gifts extended to political and judicial authorities generated disagreements among leading legal scholars associated with the Shafii school.

both to judicial and non-judicial officials,[6] whatever distinction he had in mind must involve the legal repercussions of the consequent acts or the variable nature of associated punishments.

Ibn Nujaym's exploration of the topic commences in earnest with references to two relevant and well-known Quranic verses (4:29 and 2:188), along with the commentaries of a few medieval jurists, including Halwani (d. 1056), Baydawi (d. 1286), and Biqai (d. 1480), and a number of relevant hadiths.[7] He then summarizes the four jurisprudentially defined "components" of bribery (*rüşvetin kısımları*), based on Qadikhan's (d. 1196) *Fatawa* and Ibn Humam's (d. 1457) *Fath al-Qadir*, a commentary on Marghinani's (d. 1197) *Hidaya*. The "components" in question actually refer to the types or scenarios of bribery involving judicial and administrative authorities.

Consistent with earlier jurisprudential articulations (cf. Rosenthal 1964; Johansen 2002; Köse 2008; "Rüşvet: Alan da Veren de Yanacaktır!" 2013; Iqbal and Lewis 2014), Ibn Nujaym (1966: 693, 2004: 259) points out that while some bribes are prohibited (*haram*) for both those who offer and those who accept them, others are prohibited only for those who accept them. These are the (two) types prohibited for all parties:

1. *Bribe offered to get appointed to the position of the qadi.* This was a widely accepted rule, as indicated by consistent opinions in fatwas by many Ottoman muftis.[8] In Ibn Nujaym's treatment of the topic it is unclear whether this rule was also valid for many other positions. Ibn Nujaym discusses this type of bribery twice in the treatise. His first reference to it, exclusively based on Qadikhan's *Fatawa*, does not mention other possibilities. Yet according to *Fath al-Qadir*, which Ibn Nujaym brings up toward the end of the text, "bribes extended to obtain qadiship and amirship" are prohibited for both givers and takers. But Ibn Nujaym makes no reference to rulership when he immediately adds, "Thus, those who offer bribes to be appointed as qadis are not permitted to become qadis" (1966: 694, 2004: 261).

---

[6] This possibility is consistent with the hadith pertaining to the incident involving Ibn Lutbiyya discussed in the previous chapter.

[7] Quran 4:29: "O you who have believed, do not consume one another's wealth unjustly but only [in lawful] business by mutual consent"; 2:188: "And do not consume one another's wealth unjustly or send it [in bribery] to the rulers in order that [they might aid] you [to] consume a portion of the wealth of the people in sin, while you know [it is unlawful]." The three commentators see these verses as applicable only to processes associated with the qadi's responsibilities.

[8] For example, according to Ibn Kemal (İnanır 2011: 117), the appointments of the qadis who attain their positions by paying bribes are invalid and their judgments null (Mesele: Rüşvetle kadı olanların şeran kazası caiz ve hükümleri nafiz olur mu? Cevap: Olmaz). One exception to the rule was proposed by Ibn Abidin (1982-94: 12:137), who suggested that a qadiship attained by bribes should hold if the briber is the only qualified person in the community who can serve as the qadi.

2. *Bribe offered by litigants and accepted by qadis in litigations for favorable judgments.* This type is also haram for both parties, whether or not the judgment in question is legally justifiable.[9]

The third and fourth types of bribery are those not equally prohibited for the givers and takers:

3. *Bribe given to protect one's life and property from a threat or danger.* This type of bribe is still impermissible for the person who accepts it, but not for the person who offers it. The law prohibits the acceptance of bribes offered in such cases because Muslims are ethically obligated to protect other Muslims' lives and property (cf. Köse 2008: 151).
4. *Bribe given to an intermediary to "intercede with the ruler" to obtain a favor from him or to prevent a potential harm.* In this case, too, accepting the bribe is prohibited, though offering it is not. On the other hand, if the person promises no compensation to the intermediary for his service but rewards him with what Ibn Nujaym calls a "bribe" after he receives the assistance, the payment would be halal to the person who accepts it according to the established opinion, if the purpose of the intercession is legitimate (cf. Rosenthal 1964: 148). Thus, according to Ibn Nujaym, a bribe can be a previously unpromised reward in return for assistance. Alternatively, the person seeking intercession might "hire" the intermediary for a short period (perhaps for a day) and pay him for his services. In this case, the "salary" offered to the intermediary would legally be different from a bribe, and legitimate (Ibn Nujaym 1966: 695, 2004: 259).

Since all four types of bribes are illegal at least to accept, any payment or offer that counts as a bribe should be returned to the person who offers it.[10] Yet because offering bribes is permissible in some circumstances, generations of

---

[9] Ottoman fatwa compilations contain many relevant opinions from various authorities. Consider the following examples by Ebussuud Efendi and Erzurumlu Hacı Feyzullah Efendi, respectively: "Question: If it is legally established that a qadi named Zeyd had accepted bribes, what would be status of his judgments? Answer: Judgments acquired by bribes, even if consistent with the law, are invalid" (Mesele: Zeyd-i kadının rüşvet ekl eylediği şer'le sabit ve zahir olsa, şer'an hükmü nafiz olur mu? Cevab: Olmaz. Rüşvetle hüküm şer'a muvafık olsa dahi nafiz olmaz) (Düzdağ 1972: 134). "Question: In a litigation between Zeyd and Amr, if the qadi named Bekir accepts a sum of money as bribe from Zeyd and decides in Zeyd's favor, would his judgment be valid? Answer: It would not" (Mesele: Zeyd, Amr ile bir hususa muteallika davasında Bekir-i kadıya mürafaa oldukta Bekir ol hususu hüküm etmek için Zeyd'den şu kadar akça rüşvet alıp Zeyd'e hükm eylese hükmü nafiz olur mu? Cevap: Olmaz) (Ünal 2015: 88). Notice that these fatwas do not consider the legality of offering and accepting the bribes. Instead, they focus on the validity of judgments based on the bribes.

[10] Various Ottoman fatwas make this point explicitly. For example: "Question: If Zeyd receives a certain sum from Amr as a bribe to assist the latter in a certain matter, can Amr [later] claim the sum

Ottoman muftis frequently found themselves resolving issues around how such bribes might be returned. Such complications include questions related to the forms (including currency) in which bribes could be returned, the responsibilities of the intermediaries in the process, whether bribes could be demanded from the heirs of the deceased bribees, how the alleged bribees could reject such claims, and many other matters.[11]

In his own writings three centuries later, Ibn Abidin (1982–94: 12:123–5) replicates almost exactly the classification we find in Ibn Nujaym's work, one that itself is based on older formulations. If we had to distill certain tendencies out of these rules, we might note the emphasis placed on the need to protect one's life and property against unfair treatment by authorities, which could turn bribery into a justifiable action by the threatened parties. Thus, the jurisprudential concern with the act is primarily linked to its broader consequence: whether it harms or protects specific individuals. The clear focus in these rules on the qadi's work and appointment must be related to the fact that each qadi, in addition to enforcing God's law, served a particularly important role in protecting communal (umma) solidarity.

At the same time, unresolved questions remain. One such question is related to ambiguity regarding the status of bribes meant to facilitate the acquisition of other offices. Ibn Nujaym does not comment on the legal status of bribery to obtain non-judicial positions besides amirship. In his discussion based

---

back from Zeyd? Answer: He can" (Mesele: Zeyd bir hususun temsiyeti için rüşvet tarikiyle Amr'ın şu kadar akçesini alsa Amr meblağ-ı mezburu Zeyd'den istirdada kadir olur mu? El-Cevab: Olur) (Ahmed Efendi and Hafız Mehmed el Gedusi 2014: 367).

[11] Consider the following fatwas from various compilations: "Question: If Zeyd gives a sum of money as a bribe to Amr via the latter's servant Bekir and if Zeyd [later] claims back that sum from Bekir, may Bekir say that he 'gave that amount to Amr; claim it from him'? Answer: He may not" (Mesele: Zeyd, Amr'in ademi Bekr'e bir husus için bir mikdar akçe rüşvet verse hala Zeyd meblağ-ı mezburı Bekr'den taleb eylediğinde Bekr mücerred "ben onu Amr'a verdim var ondan al" deyüb vermemeğe kadir olur mu? El-Cevab: Olmaz) (Ünal 2015: 42). "Question: If Zeyd were to claim a sum of money as a bribe from Amr in return for assisting the latter in a matter and if Zeyd orders his servant Bekir to receive the sum [bribe] from Amr, after which Bekir receives the sum and delivers it to Zeyd, from whom would Amr claim back the sum? Answer: from Bekir" (Mesele: Zeyd bir hususun temşiyeti için rüşvet tarikiyle şu kadar akçe Amr'dan alacak oldukda hizmetinde olan Bekir'e "Amr'dan ol kadar akçeyi al" deyü emretmekle Bekir dahi Amr'dan ol kadar akçe alıp Zeyd'e verse hala Amr meblağ-ı mezburu istirdad murad ettikde Zeyd ve Bekir'den hangisinden alır? el-Cevab: Bekir'den alır) (Kaya, Algın, Trabzonlu, and Erkan. 2011: 534). "Question: [Assume that] Zeyd, Amr, and Bekir offer a sum of money as a bribe to Beşir to receive his help in a matter and [that] Beşir subsequently spends that sum. If Zeyd [later] claims that amount from Beşir in its entirety, may Amr and Bekir claim their shares from Zeyd? Answer: They may" (Mesele: Zeyd ve Amr ve Bekir bir maslahatlarını itmam icin Beşir'e cümlesi maan rüşvet tarikiyle şu kadar akçe verip Beşir meblağ-ı mezburu istihlak ettikden sonra Zeyd ol kadar akçeyi tamamen Beşir'den alsa Amr ve Bekir meblağ-ı mezburdan hisselerini Zeyd'den almağa kadir olurlar mı? el-Cevab: Olurlar) (228). "Question: If Zeyd gives his slave Amr to Bekir as a bribe and if Bekir frees Amr without Zeyd's permission, is Zeyd permitted to disregard Amr's freedom and claim back Amr as his slave? Answer: Yes" (Mesele: Zeyd kulu Amr'ı bir hususun temşiyeti için rüşvet tarikiyle Bekir'e verdikden sonra Bekir Amr'ı Zeyd'in izninsiz itak eylese Zeyd ıtkı muciz olmayıp Amr'ı istirkaka kadir olur mu? el-Cevab: Olur) (Kaya 2009: 99).

on pre-Ottoman Hanafi jurists, Baber Johansen (2002: 1580) restricts this type of bribery strictly to qadiship. According to Köse (2008: 150), whose insights are also based on pre-Ottoman sources, the restriction applies to all official positions, although he also notes that premodern jurists discuss this form of bribery specifically with reference to qadiship. In his summary of Ibn Nujaym's analysis of bribery, Katib Çelebi (Kâtip Çelebi 2016: 118)—a seventeenth-century Ottoman intellectual—mentions that this prohibition covers amirship and qadiship, indicating how at least some Ottomans interpreted it at that time.[12] But the fatwas I am familiar with from the Ottoman period tend to limit the discussion to the acquisition of qadiship. Ibn Abidin (1982–94: 12:125), in contrast, claims that the rule applies not only to rulership, but also to governorship.[13]

Also, in his discussion of the third type of bribery (to protect one's life and property), which is permissible for the briber, Ibn Nujaym does not specify the types of circumstances in which the rule might be applicable. What if the danger to one's life and property was caused by the judgments of a qadi in a litigation? In such a situation, wouldn't a bribe offered to a qadi in order to defend one's life and property override stipulations pertaining to the second type of bribery involving qadis' bribe-induced judgments, which is impermissible to both parties?[14] Table 2.1 presents clues regarding Ibn Nujaym's opinions regarding bribery and indicates how they diverge from a few other interpretations.

In addition to these unanswered questions, one scenario that Ibn Nujaym does not address can be found in relevant Ottoman fatwas: bribing third-party interceders to obtain their support for one's appointment to a qadiship. Although many classical jurists considered such bribery morally unpalatable, there is no established rule against seeking qadiship. And given the potentially licit nature of this desire, might paying intermediaries (rather than those

---

[12] G. L. Lewis (Kātib Chelebi 1957: 125) translates "taklîd-i każâ ve emârete..." as "[to secure] a judicial and other office."

[13] Ibn Abidin also considers the rules related to gifts to qadis (see below) applicable to most other government authorities.

[14] According to Johansen (2002: 1575), "The Hanafi doctrine strictly forbids the official [*fonctionnaire*] to accept bribes offered in such cases, because religious ethics oblige every Muslim to protect his brothers and sisters in religion against injustice and despotism. It is not justifiable to ask for payment as a precondition for such service. Yet, bribery, in this scenario, is considered a legitimate, permissible, and morally licit means of defense because one has the right and even the moral duty to protect oneself, one's wealth, and one's reputation against injustice and despotism" (original in French). Since Johansen identifies the bribee in this category as an "official" (*fonctionnaire* and, earlier, *agent public*; ibid.), which presumably includes the qadi, this would make bribing a qadi legally acceptable at least for those threatened by his actions. Similarly, Rosenthal (1964: 142) suggests that "while a person is forbidden to offer a bribe to a judge for sponsoring an unjust cause, he is fully within his rights when offering one in the interests of justice, in order to protect his life and property."

Table 2.1 Bribe Categories According to Ibn Nujaym (with Other Opinions)

	In litigations (to qadis) 1		In appointments 2		To non-qadis, seeking licit favors or to save life/property 3		Seeking illicit favors 4
	If lit. are fair a	If lit. are unfair; to save life/property b	To qadiship/amirship a	To other positions b	Direct payments a	To intermediaries b	
To offer	No	?[i]	No	?[ii]	Yes	Yes	No
To accept	No	No	No	?[ii]	No	*Possible*	No

[i] Maybe permissible according to other sources; see the text.
[ii] Maybe permissible according to Johansen (2002: 1576–7). Not permissible according to Köse (2008: 150) or Ibn Abidin (1982–94: 12:125).
Italic: Via a legal ruse or by previously unannounced, after-the-favor payment.

Source: Ibn Nujaym 1966 and 2004.

who decide on the appointments) for this purpose likewise be regarded as permissible? The possibility combines two types of bribery that Ibn Nujaym treats separately, corresponding to columns 2a and 3b in Table 2.1. Remarkably, according to a fatwa by Ibn Kemal (d. 1534), a sixteenth-century Ottoman *şeyhülislam*, appointment to qadiship through paid intercession of third parties might be permissible.

Question: If (prospective) qadis bribed a *kazasker* or (specific) *paşa*s to have their names to be submitted to the ruler (*hüdavendigar*) and if the ruler remains unaware of the bribes nor receives these bribes [himself], would the appointments and subsequent judgments of these qadis be valid?

Answer: If his appointment is based on bribery, that qadis' judgments are void. (However), if the appointment is based on intercession and the bribe is received by the intercessor, [the qadi's judgments] would be valid. His appointment cannot be considered to be attained by bribes. (İnanır 2011: 119)[15]

The fatwa identifies three actor categories involved in such arrangements for the qadis. The first is the ruler, to whom the names of the prospective qadis are submitted and who technically makes the appointments. The second is those who seek qadiship and therefore bribe influential officials (that is, the kazaskers and the paşas) in order to be recommended to the ruler. The third is those influential officials who recommend nominees to the ruler in return for payments from the former. The fatwa concerns the legality of a specific type of relationship between officials and nominees and the legal consequences of their interactions, while bracketing interactions between the ruler and nominees, and between the ruler and officials.[16] While confirming the illegitimacy of appointments based on bribes *in principle*, the opinion also affirms the legality of appointments obtained through bribes to interceders (*şefi*) so long as the ruler does not benefit from such payments and remains unaware of their existence. Thus, only bribes to formal decision-makers would disqualify one

---

[15] "Mesele: Kadılar kadıaskere veya paşalara rüşvet verip kendilerini kadılık icin Hüdavendigara arz ettirseler ama rüşvet aldıklarını Hüdavendigar bilmese, rüşvet Hüdavendigara vasıl olmasa, şer'an kazaları caiz olur mu, hükümleri nafiz olur mu? Cevab: Hüküm nafiz olmaz, rüşvetle kadı olduysa. Şefaetle olup rüşveti şefia verdiyse nafiz olur, taklid-i kaza rüşvetle olmuş olmaz."

[16] The fatwa implicitly distinguishes the ruler's role in the appointment, which is consistent with how Yasemin Beyazıt (2009: 437) describes the process as one that requires the ruler's formal acceptance and authorization of the recommendations submitted to him. Thus, the appointment decisions, even if pro forma, belong solely to the ruler, which is why it is important to explicitly point out in the question that he neither benefits from nor is informed of any payments.

from qadiship and would render invalid the judgments by qadis appointed in this fashion.

Assuming that the term paşas refers to grand viziers, it is noteworthy that Ibn Kemal's fatwa trivializes the consequences of bribes to very high-level judicial and administrative officials, who played critical roles in the qadis' appointment processes. As is well known, the kazaskers of Rumelia and Anatolia, who occupied the second- and third-highest-ranked positions in the judicial hierarchy, just beneath the şeyhülislam, were responsible for making appointment recommendations for lower-level qadiships, which got routinely confirmed by the ruler (Uzunçarşılı 1988: 87).[17] The grand viziers were not only involved in the appointment decisions of higher-level qadis at some point in time (ibid.), they were also responsible for conveying the judicial authorities' recommendations to the ruler and securing his approval (Beyazıt 2009: 437).

To gauge how representative Ibn Kemal's fatwa was, consider the following fatwa by the renowned Ottoman jurist Ebussuud Efendi (d. 1574), who served as the şeyhülislam of the empire between 1545 and 1574, slightly after Ibn Kemal:

Question: If a qadi named Zeyd acquires his qadiship by the intercession of someone other than the ruler whom he had paid or as a result of someone's favor, would his judgments be legally valid?

Answer: (If he acquires the position) through bribery, his judgments would not be valid. This is the accepted opinion (among jurists). His qadiship would be void. And even though attainment of the position by favor is also impermissible, the judgments (of those who had acquired their positions in this way) that are consistent with the law cannot be reversed. (Düzdağ 1972: 133)[18]

Ebussuud's opinion, like Ibn Kemal's fatwa, identifies three separate actors involved in the appointment of the qadis: the qadi, the ruler, and parties who played intermediary roles between the two. Likewise, the issue of concern here

---

[17] Until the mid-sixteenth century, the kazaskers nominated the candidates for lower-level jurisdictions for the ruler's approval. The nominations for higher-level, *mevali* jurisdictions also required the endorsement of the grand vizier. After the mid-sixteenth century, nominations for lower-level posts came to require the şeyhülislam's endorsement. Around the same time, the şeyhülislam also took over the responsibility of making nominations for higher-level qadiships. See Uzunçarşılı 1988: 87–90; and Beyazıt 2009: 437.

[18] "Mesele: Zeyd- kadı, Padişah-ı din-penah hazretlerinden gayriye akçe verip vesateti ile, ya bir kimse şefaati ile kadılık alsa, şer'an hükmü nafiz olur mu? Cevap: Rüşvetle alınacak nafiz olmaz, kavl-i müftabih budur. Kadı olmaz, ma'zul-i mahzdır. Şefaatle almak eğerçi haramdır, amma şer'a muvafık edicek hükmü döndürülmez."

is the legal status of qadi appointments obtained through influence exerted by third parties on the appointment decision. The latter fatwa does not specify whom the questioner had in mind as third parties. They could be anyone other than the ruler whose support could be obtained in some fashion. The fact that the fatwa differentiates between the ruler and everyone else involved in appointment decisions confirms our suspicion, based on Ibn Kemal's fatwa, that contemporary Ottoman jurists differentiated legally between the formal approval of appointments (by the ruler) and everything that preceded this approval. Without such a distinction, there would have been no need for Ebussuud's or Ibn Kemal's fatwas. But unlike Ibn Kemal's fatwa, Ebussuud's opinion further differentiates among those categorized as (intermediary) others: those whose facilitation was obtained by money, and those whose favors were not. In Ebussuud's fatwa, the term şefaat appears to be used specifically to describe the latter group's actions. In Ibn Kemal's fatwa, şefaat could be obtained by bribes. Yet in his opinion, Ebussuud calls paid intercession vesatet, which might or might not have had a more transactional meaning than şefaat.

Ebussuud's interpretation regarding the status of qadiships obtained through paid and unpaid intercession of the third parties is not entirely consistent with Ibn Kemal's opinion, at least on the surface. Ebussuud interprets that if the intercession leading to the appointment is obtained by bribe, then the position is illegitimate and void. And while Ebussuud's fatwa describes intercession not obtained by payments as haram, it also resists disqualifying the action. In other words, the qadiship remains valid. This is why, unlike the judgments by qadis who secured their positions by bribe-induced intercessions, judgments by qadis who benefited from non-bribe-induced intercessions remain valid so long as they were also consistent with the law. The prevalence of this interpretation among jurists is confirmed in Ibn Abidin's work (1982–94: 12:123, 126): "According to the work titled *Fetih*,[19] the status of the one who obtains his [qadiship] through intercession is similar to the one who desires to obtain qadiship for the purpose of serving the community, not like the one who obtains qadiship through bribes. Bezzaziye[20] makes the same point slightly differently: 'While it may not be halal to acquire the position via intermediaries [the appointment is still valid]'" (also see 12:128).[21]

---

[19] Presumably, Ibn Humam's *Fath al-Qadir*.
[20] Presumably, *Fatawa al-Bazzaziya* by Muhammad al-Bazzazi (d. 1424).
[21] Ibn Abidin also equates the consequences of bribes to the sultan and bribes to his "extensions" (*haşiyesi olan kişilere*; possibly his family members or representatives) with the sultan's knowledge: qadiships acquired in these ways are null, and the judgments of such qadis non-binding (12:123).

Ibn Nujaym's treatise includes a formulation that might speak to the seeming inconsistency between Ibn Kemal's and Ebussuud's fatwas. Ibn Nujaym (1966: 693, 2004: 259) indicates that it is permissible to accept a bribe that is not explicitly promised to an interceder for his assistance in an endeavor involving the sultan's decision that is offered to him after the successful completion of the task.[22] Could Ibn Kemal have had in mind these types of (not overtly promised) payments when he described as permissible bribes to interceders in qadiship appointments? If so, then perhaps the apparent contradiction between the two fatwas is the result of an incongruity in terminology: Ebussuud's definition of a bribe might have differed from Ibn Kemal's use of the term as something perhaps more analogous to a gift. I will return to this issue below.

In addition to defining the types of bribes, Ibn Nujaym devoted a specific section to the status of gifts and how they differed from bribes.[23] Ibn Nujaym, identified three types of gifts:[24] The first type is halal both to offer and to accept. "Gifts based on love and friendship" fall in this category. The second type is haram both to offer and accept. This category comprises gifts aimed at unjustly obtaining something. The third type is permissible to offer but impermissible to accept. This category includes gifts offered to prevent injustice (or zulüm). As with bribes extended in comparable circumstances, one way to accept a gift offered for this purpose is to fictitiously "hire" the recipient for a short period of time, in which case the "gift" is effectively transformed into compensation for service. Gifts not promised before the service but offered after the fulfillment of the favor are also regarded by the majority of jurists as permissible to accept.

Like many other pre-Ottoman jurists (cf. Rosenthal 1964; Johansen 2002; Köse 2008), Ibn Nujaym seems to presume that gifts and bribes are meant to serve different purposes: while gifts are expressions of affection, bribes are forms of compensation. This is why he asserts (1966: 694) that a gift, unlike a

---

[22] "Eğer, Sultan nezdinde düşen işimi yap diye ricada bulunulmuş olup hiçbir surette rüşvet söz konusu yapılmamış, fakat o iş görüldükten sonra o işi yapana rüşvet verilirse, bazılarına göre bunu almak helâl sayılmaz, diğer bazılarına göre ise helal sayılır ki doğrusu da budur" (Ibn Nujaym 1966: 693).

[23] According to Sahillioğlu (Ibn Nujaym 1966: 694), this section is based on a work that Sahillioğlu ambiguously calls "Akziyye." Pekcan (Ibn Nujaym 2004: 260) suggests that Ibn Nujaym's reference is to the section called "Akdiye" (or "judgments") in Abd al-Rashid al-Buhari's (d. 1142) *Hulasa al-Fatava*.

[24] Ibn Nujaym's formulations are broadly consistent with those of jurists highly regarded in Ottoman times, including Halabi (Halebi n.d., 196), Hüsrev (1980: 312), and Marghinani (Merginani 1986: 179).

bribe, is not conditional.[25] However, Ibn Nujaym fails to instruct his readers on how to differentiate such payments when they often do not know the exact relationship between the giver and the recipient. Presumably because of this difficulty he concludes "gifts extended to qadis are indistinguishable from bribes, (thus they are) impermissible for those who offer them and those who accept them" (1966: 695, 2004: 261; cf. Hüsrev 1980: 312).[26]

Hence, despite his recognition of a distinction between gifts and bribes in principle, Ibn Nujaym's discussion obscures the difference between the two in practice. Indeed, his characterization of the second and third types of gifts[27] raises an obvious question: can an offering in pursuit of a specific result be a true gift if a gift, by definition, has no conditions attached? Indeed, the jurist's obfuscation of gifts and bribes in daily interactions can be read as an implicit acknowledgment that "true gifts," as Marcel Mauss called them, are few and far between and that the meaning of the term "gift" could vary based on context (see Chapter 7).

Despite the general popularity of the dictum that gifts extended to qadis were indistinguishable from bribes, premodern jurists also considered a few possible exceptions. For example, qadis were allowed to accept gifts from close relatives[28] and from friends in the habit of presenting gifts before the qadi assumed his office.[29] In the latter case, post-appointment gifts should not increase in value or frequency, and gift-givers should not appear in court as litigants (Rosenthal 1964: 141; Johansen 2002: 1582–3; Köse 2008: 159).[30] It may be that only these types of gifts can reasonably be based on love and affection. However, Rosenthal (1964: 142–3) reports that according to Ibn Aqil, a twelfth-century Hanbali jurist, gifts that qadis began to receive after

---

[25] Rosenthal (1964: 136n8) attributes Ibn Nujaym's interpretation to "a commentary by Abū Naṣr al-Baghdādī (apparently, Aḥmad b. Muḥammad b. al-Aqtaʿ, who lived in the eleventh century) on a famous work by al-Qudūrī (d. 428/1037)."

[26] According to Ebussuud (Düzdağ 1972: 133), a qadi cannot judge the case of a litigant whose food he ate ("Mesele: Zeyd-i kadı, hükm-i şerif ile ahar kadılığa vardıkta, davacıların sofraya getirdikleri yemeği yese hükmü nafiz olur mu? Cevap: Yemeğin yediğine hükmü nafiz olmaz"). Ibn Abidin (1982–94: 12:158) insists that the qadis are required not to participate in any transactions, presumably involving litigants or potential litigants, that unduly benefit them or generate windfalls for them. According to most jurists, the requirement about gifts to the qadis also applies to the qadi's sons and other members of his household (Rosenthal 1964).

[27] This is also why the maneuver he suggests to make the third type of gift permissible is identical with the one that he earlier recommends to render the fourth type of bribe legal.

[28] Parents and children, according to most jurists. A few other jurists include maternal and paternal aunts and the daughters of the qadis' brothers among "close relatives." Ibn Abidin (1982–94: 12:162) does not regard the children of brothers as close relatives.

[29] For a consistent fatwa from Şeyhülislam Zenbilli (or Zembilli) Ali Efendi (d. 1526), see Ural and Sarı 1996: 91.

[30] Ibn Abidin (1982–94: 12:162) suggests that according to one opinion, the value of the gift from friends may be allowed to increase in proportion to the wealth of the friend.

their appointments, though they were "disapproved," were not strictly forbidden so long as they were given by those not involved in a lawsuit before the qadi in question. Some jurists also considered it permissible for qadis to accept gifts from the ruler, the governor of their jurisdictions, and the chief justice, none of whom are under their jurisdiction (Ibn Abidin 1982–94: 12:161–2).[31]

Ibn Nujaym does not indicate whether the functional equivalence of gifts and bribes for the qadis also holds for non-judicial officials. In fact, there are many different opinions on this issue. For example, according to al-Sarakhsi (d. 1090), qadis and governors were supposed to observe identical standards pertaining to gifts (Johansen 2002: 1582). For Jamal al-Din al-Qazwini (d. ?), whose twelfth-century *Kitab Mufid al-Ulum wa-Mubid al-Humum* was popular in Mamluk Egypt, gifts to "lower-level officials" are permissible if they are reciprocated in licit ways (Rosenthal 1964: 139).[32] On the other hand, Ibn Abidin (1982–94: 12:159), writing in the nineteenth century, extends the rule of impermissibility of gifts to other officials when he writes, "The status of gifts to state functionaries who serve the Muslims is similar to gifts offered to the qadis." In Ibn Abidin's discussion (12:159–60) these officials include tax collectors, market inspectors, and officials involved in waqf administration, in addition to the governors. He also includes the muftis in this group, at least in relation to their interactions with those seeking fatwas from them.

Based on this discussion, we can perhaps reconsider the legality of payments associated with intercessions in qadi appointments. As noted earlier, Ebussuud recognized the legality of intercessions leading to qadiships if they were obtained without bribes. But what if payments to intercessors were gifts in the form of previously unannounced, after-the-favor offerings? Unfortunately, we do not find among Ebussuud's fatwas an opinion addressing this contingency. Yet both Ibn Nujaym and Ibn Abidin acknowledge that it was permissible for intercessors to accept gifts following successful attempts to assist

---

[31] Jun Akiba (2021: 6; cf. Akgündüz 1990–6: 11, 124, 220) has recently suggested based on the lawcode (that is, *kanunname*) of 1673 ("New Kanun" or *Kanun-ı Cedid*) that the qadis and other court personnel may accept unsolicited "gifts" for their scribal services, such as preparing legal deeds.

[32] According to Rosenthal, this interpretation became influential in Mamluk Egypt because it legitimized the prevailing practices (ibid.). Indeed, in al-Qazwini's treatment of the topic we find a justification of gifts *while* acknowledging the expectations of reciprocity that they signify. Because true gifts are unlikely, and given that it is hopeless to ban such exchanges, al-Qazwini seems to differentiate between appropriate and inappropriate gift exchanges by considering whether the reciprocities that these gifts generated were licit or illicit. In fact, licit reciprocation might be the best way to limit the danger of impropriety associated with gifts, because reciprocated gift exchanges are known quantities: they can be properly identified and assessed to grasp the exact nature of the relationship between the transacting parties. And because reciprocated gifts do not constitute unfulfilled obligations that will have to be redeemed in the future, they do not generate the potential dangers of illicit favors. For more on al-Qazwini and his work, see Van Gelder 2001.

friends and clients. According to Ibn Nujaym (1966: 694), "Gifts do not have conditions. Yet our sheikhs [viz. legal scholars] consider gifts that are well-known to be offered to [influential people] in return for their [indirect] help in endeavors involving the Sultan as permissible to accept. There is no obstacle to accepting gifts from parties after fulfilling their desires, as long as these offerings were not conditional for assistance."[33] Ibn Abidin (1982-94: 12:125) expresses the same sentiment: "A gift to an interceder for providing indirect assistance in an affair involving the ruler's decision is considered to be acceptable by our *ulema*, even if the gift's connection to the interceder's assistance is well known, so long as the gift is not conditional for the assistance. If the interceder assists the person seeking help without demanding a payment and if the latter subsequently offers a gift to the interceder, it would be permissible to accept that gift."[34]

This explanation supports the theory that the apparent inconsistency between Ibn Kemal's and Ebussuud's fatwas on the topic is merely terminological. In Ibn Kemal's fatwa, a bribe might be an unpromised, after-the-favor reward, the payment that Baber Johansen (2002: 1577) calls "a bonus (Fr. *Prime*) for success, not like rent or the price of a service" (original in French). For Ebussuud such unpromised, unconditional offerings to intercessors should presumably be called gifts, not bribes. Given that Ibn Nujaym uses these terms interchangeably when describing the very same type of transaction in his treatise,[35] we can perhaps surmise that an uncertainty pertaining to these terms was common, at least in the sixteenth century.

---

[33] "Hediye vermek şartsız olup fakat hediyeyi alan bunun kesinlikle Sultan nezdinde bir şefaat için verildiğini biliyorsa, üstadlar (meşayih)imiz bu durumda hediyeyi almakta bir beis olmadığını söylemektedirler. Birisinin işini gördükten sonra, koşulmuş bir şart yoksa veya beklenen birşey olmadığı halde hediye verildiğinde kabul etmekte herhangi bir beis yoktur."

[34] A consistent opinion can also be found in Şeyhülislam Yenişehirli Abdullah Efendi's (Kaya, Algın, Trabzonlu, and Erkan 2011: 540) fatwas:

Question: If Zeyd, who is a government official, assists Amr in a matter, without a [promise of a] bribe, and if Amr subsequently gives Zeyd a horse, though the latter makes no demand for it [viz. as a gift], and Zeyd subsequently exhausts/wastes this horse [because of harsh use?], can Amr's heirs claim the horse's value from Zeyd after Amr's passing? Answer: They cannot.

(Mesele: Erbab-ı devletten Zeyd Amr'in bir maslahatına rüşvet kavlinsiz sa'y ve itmam edip ba'dehu Amr sıhhatinde Zeyd'e bila-taleb bir bargir ihda ettikden sonra Zeyd bargiri istihlak edip ba'dehu Amr fevt olsa veresesi bargiri Zeyd'e tazmine kadir olurlar mı? el-Cevab: Olmazlar).

[35] Compare Ibn Nujaym's statement that I cited in the previous paragraph to the following one also in his text: "According to some (scholars), if someone requests for assistance from an interceder in an endeavor involving the sultan without making a prior promise of a bribe, but offers a bribe after the assistance is provided, the payment would not be halal to accept. According to others [viz. other scholars], the payment would be halal, which is the correct opinion" (Sultan nezdinde düşen işimi yap diye ricada bulunulmuş olup hiçbir surette rüşvet söz konusu yapılmamış, fakat o iş görüldükten sonra o işi yapana rüşvet verilirse, bazılarına göre bunu almak helâl sayılmaz, diğer bazılarına göre ise helal sayılır ki doğrusu da budur) (1966: 693).

66   DEFINING CORRUPTION IN THE OTTOMAN EMPIRE

Ibn Nujaym mentions only tangentially the important issue of consequences of bribes to qadis. In this regard, he agrees with the prevalent jurisprudential traditions that bribe-induced judgments are null and non-binding (1966: 695, 2004: 261; cf. Johansen 2002: 1587, *passim*), which is consistent with the opinions of many Ottoman muftis cited earlier.[36]

Despite Ibn Nujaym's reticence on the issue, there seems to be a consensus among Hanafi jurists that qadis who accepted bribes *deserve* dismissal from their positions.[37] But jurists have disagreed on whether a bribe-accepting qadi should be considered automatically dismissed at the moment when he accepted the bribe (or once such an allegation is proven) or whether his expulsion should be based on an ensuing decision by the political authority. According to Johansen (2002: 1579; cf. Ibn Abidin 1982–94: 12:128–9), while the former position was prevalent among the Hanafi jurists of Iraq before the eleventh century, the latter became influential among Hanafis in subsequent centuries, based on the opinions of jurists from Transoxania.

In the Ottoman context, I found one opinion by Şeyhülislam Menteşezade Abdürrahim Efendi (d. 1716) that aligns with the first position:

Question: If a qadi named Zeyd accepts a sum of money from Amr as a bribe in a litigation involving Amr and Bekir and decides in Amr's favor, what should be done to Zeyd?

Answer: The money should be returned to Amr and Zeyd is dismissed in punishment.[38]

Other şeyhülislams appear hesitant about stating that qadis who engage in dishonest acts (including but not limited to bribery) are automatically dismissed from their posts. Consider, for example, the following opinion by Minkarizade Yahya Efendi (d. 1678):

---

[36] But see Ibn Abidin's discussion of the issue later in this chapter.

[37] This is a discretionary punishment, or tazir, meaning that because the primary sources of Islamic law (that is, the scripture and the prophetic sunna) contain no fixed prescriptions for the offense, it is decided by legal officials on a case-by-case basis (Chapter 1). It was common for the classical and post-classical jurists to recommend relatively lenient tazir punishments for offenders with high status, all other factors being equal. Jurists explain this tendency with reference to the tazir's corrective and rehabilitative function: while a simple warning or rebuke could be adequate to reform those who are religiously informed and socially aware and can be easily reminded of the broader consequences of their actions, harsher prescriptions would be required for those who lack refinement, education, and a sense of social-communal responsibility (Ibn Abidin 1982–94: 8:283; Midilli 2019: 128).

[38] Quoted in Mumcu (2005: 224n177): "Mesele: Bir beldede kadı olan Zeyd, Amr'ın Bekir ile bir hususa müteallik davalarını istima eder oldukta Amr'in rüşvet [sic] bir mikdar akçesini alıb hususu mezburu Amr'a hükmeylese Zeyd'e ne lazım olur? Cevab: Aldığı akçe Amr'a red olunub azil ile tazir olunur."

Question: Is a qadi named Zeyd allowed to perform [unjustified] inspections in the countryside during which he forces the subjects to pay him [illegal] fines for not preforming daily prayers and compels them to host him in their houses and demands to be fed by them?
Answer: He is not. If (these are allegations are) true, he is deserving of dismissal.[39]

The opinion by Feyzullah Efendi (d. 1703):

Question: If the qadi named Bekir accepts a bribe from Zeyd in a litigation involving the latter and Amr and decides against Amr, would his verdict be valid?
Answer: No. Bekir would be deserving of dismissal.[40]

Finally, the opinion by Akmahmudzade Mehmed Zeyni Efendi (d. 1751):

Question: What should be done to the qadi named Bekir if he favors Amr in a litigation against Zeyd and delays pronouncing a judgment (against Amr) by saying "I would not make a judgment regarding this issue" while it was legally established that Zeyd is in the right?
Answer: He becomes a sinner and he is deserving of dismissal.[41]

The question surrounding the fate of a bribe-taking qadi raises an important concern: if the qadi was not immediately removed from his office, then what was the status of the judgments he made after his bribe-induced decision but before he received the judgment of the political authority? This is an issue that Ibn Nujaym does not discuss. Fortunately, we find a detailed treatment of the topic in Ibn Abidin's discussion. Ibn Abidin (1982–94: 12:126–8) identifies three opinions in the jurisprudential literature regarding the verdicts of bribe-accepting qadis. According to the first opinion, the qadis' verdicts in trials for

---

[39] Cited in Mumcu (2005: 222n163): "Mesele: Bir kasabada kadı olan Zeyd reayanın üzerine çıkıp elbette bana bi-namaz akçesini vermek ve beni evinizde kondurup ziyafet edin deyip mezburların bi gayri hakkın bir nesnesini almağa kadir olur mu? Cevab: Olmaz. Vaki ise azle müstehak olur."
[40] "Mesele: Zeyd Amr ile bir hususa müteallika davasında Bekir-i kadıya murafaa oldukda Bekir husus-ı mezburu hükmetmek icin Zeyd'den şu kadar akçe rüşvet alıp hükmeylese hükmü nafiz olur mu? el-Cevab: Olmaz, Bekir azle müstehak olur" (Kaya 2009: 233).
[41] "Zeyd Amr ile bir hususa müteallika davasında Bekir-i kadıya murafaa olub hak Zeyd'in yedinde olduğu sabit olmuş iken kadı Amr'ı himaye edip 'ben bu hususu hükm etmem' deyüp hükmü tehir eylese kadıya ne lazım olur? Cevab: Asim olup azle müstehak olur" (Ünal 2015: 111). Mumcu (2005: 222n165) attributes the same fatwa to Çatalcalı Ali Efendi (d. 1692).

which they accepted bribes and other (including subsequent) trials are all valid. According to the second opinion, while the bribe-induced verdicts are null, the qadis' decisions in other trials are valid. In the third opinion, qadis' bribe-induced and other verdicts are all null and non-binding. Significantly, Ibn Abidin's ensuing discussion completely ignores the last option, presumably because the qadi's immediate dismissal at the instance of accepting a bribe (which would have made his subsequent verdicts null) was not a prevalent jurisprudential opinion in the nineteenth century.

It is fascinating that Ibn Abidin is inclined to side with the first opinion— the one that affirms the validity of both the bribe-induced judgment and all other verdicts of the depraved (fasiq) qadi.[42] To justify this opinion, the jurist first acknowledges that most earlier authorities subscribed to the second position, according to which the immoral qadi's bribe-induced judgments are unenforceable, but all other verdicts by the same qadi, if not influenced by illegitimate means, are valid and binding.

Yet Ibn Abidin also concedes that there is no consensus among jurists on this issue. And following the views of al-Bazdawī (d. 1089 or 1100) and Ibn Humam, he suggests that if bribe-induced verdicts were considered null, then every single verdict by every single qadi in his time should be considered null, since it had become customary for the qadis to collect payments from litigants (perhaps tantamount to litigation fees, presumably from those who win their cases, separate from other scribal and notarial fees) under the name *mahsul* (yield or proceeds). According to him, a mahsul is indistinguishable from a bribe.[43]

---

[42] Fasiq is a "person with fisq," or an immoral person. As discussed in Chapter 1, one condition of holding qadiship is the quality of justice as a personal trait. And historically speaking, jurists considered how one might demonstrate his justice in his acts and his general demeanor. Most jurists define one's justice as the inclination "to avoid great sins, and not to insist on lesser ones." The opposite of justice is fisq, which corresponds to "committing great sins [if incidentally] and insisting on lesser ones [habitually]." Other evidence of fisq, jurists wrote, included one's tendency to abandon the compulsory requirements of religion (such as prayer and fasting during Ramadan) (Yavuz 1995; Uludağ 2010). According to the dominant opinions in the Maliki, Hanbali, and Shafii schools, one whose fisq is evident should not be appointed as qadi. And if he does become a qadi, his decisions are null and non-binding. Some prominent Hanafi jurists, including Abu Hanifa (d. 767), Abu Yusuf (d. 798), and Muhammad al-Shaybani (d. 805), might have shared this opinion as well. But the dominant Hanafi inclination is more lenient: while it sees the appointment of a fasiq as a qadi deplorable, it does not consider such an appointment illegal or non-binding if the person's fisq is known by the decision-maker before the appointment (cf. Hüsrev 1980: 248, 307; and Merginani 1986: 173). Nevertheless, the Hanafis do generally regard the revelation of a qadi's fisq *during* his tenure as a reason for his dismissal. Also, see below.

[43] Defterdar Sarı Mehmed Paşa (d. 1717) associated the qadis' mahsul intakes with bribes even more unequivocally than Ibn Abidin did: "At the present time some among the judges also give bribes the title of 'income' [maḥṣūl] and do not execute the laws of God. They decide... in favor of whichever side shows the greater bribe. If they wish, the debtor comes off creditor and his bankruptcy becomes as the wealth of Korah" (Defterdar 1935: 91). Nevertheless, Defterdar's association of the term with bribery is not entirely consistent with Ibn Abidin's.

Later, Ibn Abidin identifies the common practices of tax farming or subcontracting qadiships to qadis and *naibs*—called *muqataa*s and *iltizams*—as one reason that litigants are forced to make mahsul payments (1982-94: 12:128).[44] The parties in these transactions, Ibn Abidin points out disapprovingly, view payments from litigants as halal, and the sultan himself habitually sells judgeships and allows judges to charge the litigants, presumably so that they, in turn, can make payments to him. Finally, Ibn Abidin mentions that some qadis even allege—falsely, he insists—that Ebussuud issued a fatwa that permits charging mahsul (ibid.).

To be clear, Ibn Abidin remains deeply unconvinced of the legtimacy of mahsul payments and subcontracting qadiships. In his discussion, he also does not refute the argument that involvement in such practices would render the qadis fasiq, although he does point out another prevalent opinion that judgments by qadis known to have poor characters are not always null. But his inclination to identify with the most lenient option is based on his pragmatism and inclination to accommodate the prevalent practices of his day. According to Ibn Abidin, enforcing the established jurisprudential position on the question would lead to absolute chaos and anarchy and render the legal system completely dysfunctional. Given that mahsul payments had been almost universal in his opinion, nullifying bribe-induced judgments would create havoc by opening all past disputes to new adjudication (Ibn Abidin 1982-94: 12:127-8).[45]

But why might Ibn Abidin see mahsul payments, if they indeed corresponded to litigation fees, as tantamount to bribes? For one thing, such payments, like bribes, would conflict with the essence of qadiship: *mahsul* refers broadly to the product of one's labor and economic endeavors (12:127) and if qadis administer justice because they receive payments from litigants, then that would subvert the widely established jurisprudential principle that the qadis' primary responsibility should be to enforce God's law, without any expectation of material reward for their work (Atar 2001; cf. Tyan and Káldy-Nagy 1978). This perspective holds that qadiship is a religious service, not a revenue source; its reward comes in the afterlife, not in this one. Further, God's law is not an instrument for making money. Also, technically, both mahsul payments and bribes imply a transactional relationship between litigants and the qadi, often with blurred boundaries; indeed, a mahsul payment to a qadi

---

[44] On farming out of qadiships, see Akiba 2023.
[45] Ibn Abidin also considered payments made for other types of religious service, such as reciting the Quran, permissible based on necessity, though this is contrary to the dominant opinion among earlier jurists (Ayoub 2020: 112-13; cf. Ivanyi 2020: 214-17).

before or after a judgment by a litigant (presumably by the winning side) comes close to a payment-for-judgment that bribery represents. And while one might point out that, unlike bribes, mahsul payments did not *in theory* compel judges to side with specific parties, there are reasons to doubt the validity of this assumption *in practice*.[46] One relevant angle here is the distinct possibility that fees paid for adjudications might have generated a pro-plaintiff bias in the court's operations. In the context of early modern English legal history, Daniel Klerman (2007) argued that since the English common law courts received fees on a per-case basis, judges had incentives to attract plaintiffs to court in order to hear more cases and, consequently, tried to please plaintiffs to some extent, at times interpreting the law in their favor and making it more difficult for defendants to prevail. If the Ottoman courts also charged litigants (cf. Dörtok Abacı and Ergene 2022), this might have generated incentives to adjudicate more disputes, leading to a similar pro-plaintiff bias.[47]

Ironically, Ibn Abidin's disillusionment with legal practice during his time led to his begrudging acknowledgment of the legality of bribe-induced verdicts, as a way to prevent a complete institutional collapse. Stuck between the choices of remaining faithful to prevalent jurisprudential opinions and what he considered the only logical option to maintain a degree of socio-legal stability, he chose the one he regarded as based on necessity (*darura*) for the benefit of the society (*maslaha*)—and his choice here exemplifies a common tendency among jurists, according to Wael Hallaq (2002).

Other than dismissal from office, specific references to other types of punishments for bribe-accepting qadis are lacking in Ottoman jurisprudential texts. In this regard, the decision must have been left to the discretion of the administrative authorities and made on a case-by-case basis (see Chapter 4).

Bribes and gifts were not the only threats to the judge's impartiality. And although Ibn Nujaym does not specifically comment on these additional

---

[46] Ibn Nujaym too argued that a qadi should not accept fees for serving a function that was expected of his position and that there was no difference between payments made to qadis before or after their verdicts, whether or not the latter are consistent with law (1966: 694, 695, 2004: 260, 261). In this regard, also see Ivanyi's (2020: 215–17) discussion of Birgivi Mehmed Efendi's opinions, who too condemned the fees collected by the judges, muftis, and teachers in exchange for performing their duties. Yet, Birgivi also argued that these individuals were permitted to receive gifts or donations from the treasury or charitable endowments so long as the funds used for such purposes were not tainted by unsanctioned revenue sources and the gifts or donations extended to them were made to please God.

[47] The fact that litigation fees were not technically considered as lawful might be evident in the fact that they are not listed in Ottoman kanunnames or archival documents as legitimate sources of revenue along with other types of charges for scribal and notarial services, at least until the nineteenth century. However, there is some evidence that they were common in practice, especially after the sixteenth century. See Akiba 2021; Dörtok Abacı and Ergene 2022; and Chapter 6 below.

threats, other jurisprudential sources composed or popular during the Ottoman times do, and thereby hint at contemporary expectations of fairness in litigation. Perceptions of favoritism emerge as one area of concern. Qadis may not attend gatherings in their honor or appear in public in ways that might generate an impression of affection toward specific individuals or groups (Hüsrev 1980: 313; Merginani 1986: 179). According to Halabi (Halebi n.d.: 197), the qadi may not even shop in the locale where he adjudicates disputes, presumably in or close to a public market. Generally, the court should be held in a public venue or the qadi's residence (ibid.: 196).

Concerns about favoritism also determined how the qadi was expected to conduct himself in court. The qadi was not supposed to adjudicate disputes involving himself, his relatives, or his enemies. Furthermore, he was required to interact with litigants and witnesses in particular ways. For example, he was to treat litigants equally. If he conversed with one, he was required to talk with the other as well. If he smiled at one, he could not frown at the other. If he asked one to sit while in his presence, he was also required to allow the other party to do so. He was not permitted to ask one litigant to leave the courtroom and remain there alone with the other one. He was not allowed to secretly communicate with any of the parties. He was forbidden to advise litigants about how they could formulate their complaints or respond to their opponents' accusations. And he was not to ask witnesses leading questions or instruct them on how to testify (Halebi n.d.: 196–7; Hüsrev 1980: 313–14; Merginani 1986: 177–80).

While these expectations are paralleled in most jurisprudential works from different eras, it is not clear in the literature how they were enforced before or during the Ottoman era; nor are the legal consequences for deliberate or unintentional violations of these expectations. Nor do we observe in the works of Ottoman jurists, including the fatwa collections, the volume of discussion or the range of opinions on the topic of favoritism that we observe on bribes and gifts to the qadis. Thus, while impressions of favoritism must have certainly compromised the qadi's putative independence, such might not have been taken as seriously as bribery, and probably did not generate comparable judicial or punitive consequences.[48]

---

[48] Chapter 8 provides a broader treatment of favoritism as a possible source of corruption in the Ottoman context.

Corruption of Other Judicial Actors: Witnesses and the Mufti

While the qadi's position and work are the focal point in classical works of jurisprudence, scholars also considered the corruption of court witnesses and, to a lesser extent, the mufti.

Witnesses who testified in litigations were not necessarily government officials or religious functionaries. Yet, their service to the court had a direct bearing on social peace and harmony. This is why their honesty and disinterested participation in legal processes receive some attention in jurisprudential discussions. Premodern jurisprudential works regard witness testimonies almost as the default type of evidence in litigation, an impression largely confirmed by historical treatments of premodern legal practice. Indeed, litigants supported their claims or rejected those of their opponents in premodern courts, when they could, more by witness testimonies than by any other form of evidence (Peters 1997). The value attributed to witness testimonies in legal doctrine and practice must have put a premium on false witnessing as a means to obtain the desired results for those litigants, at least for those who possessed the means and skills to use it for their purposes.

But another aspect of Islamic legal practice might have also rendered false witnessing relatively practicable, if indirectly so: evidentiary procedures made it difficult for disputing parties to challenge the *substance* of the claims made by their opponents' evidence that the court deemed appropriate to consider. According to premodern court procedures, litigants possessed different evidentiary responsibilities based on the nature of their claims. The law places the proof of responsibility on the party whose contention is deemed contrary to the initial legal presumption (Coşgel and Ergene 2016: Ch. 8, 2014: 135–7). For example, in a debt dispute, the qadi would first hear the claim by the plaintiff (the alleged creditor) and then demand a response from the defendant (the alleged debtor). If the defendant denied the debt allegation, the qadi would require the plaintiff to provide evidence to support his claim, since the legal presumption in this case is that the alleged debtor is free from debt. However, if the defendant acknowledged the original debt transaction but also contended that the debt had been paid before the trial, then the court would require him to prove it, since in this situation the defendant had made a (counter) claim that demanded proof.

Technically, the qadi decided which party should bear the burden of proof. He might assign this responsibility either to the plaintiff or the defendant depending on their claims in court. And by doing so he implicitly denied the opposing party the opportunity to submit evidence in support of their position. In other words, the opposing party lacked the ability to challenge the claims made against them by providing their own evidence. In the debt-dispute example, if the qadi had granted the proof of responsibility to the plaintiff and the latter had submitted false testimonies, indicating that the defendant had borrowed from him but never paid back a specific sum, then the defendant would not be allowed to challenge the (false) claim by providing his own rebuttal evidence (for example, an alibi).

Jurists fought witness corruption by pre-emptively attempting to ensure their good character. They insisted that a witness, just like a qadi, should ideally be someone who is just or adil, and not a fasiq—one prone to committing small sins, and not particularly inclined to avoid the big ones either (Ibn Abidin 1982–94: 12:456, 477, 482–3; cf. Tyan 1960: 209; and Peters 1997: 297). A fasiq is also characterized as someone whose malicious inclinations prevail over his good behavior (Tyan 1960: 209). More specifically, jurists suggested that individuals with particular habits should be avoided as witnesses. For example, those who: drink alcohol; sing, dance, and play music; gamble and play backgammon; play with birds; enter the bathhouse naked; eat, urinate, or defecate in public; and those who, if men, act like women and, if women, presumably vice versa (Peters 1997: 297; cf. Halebi n.d.: 232–5; Hüsrev 1980: 261–5; Ibn Abidin 1982–94: 12:504-16; and Merginani 1986: 217–18). Individuals not concerned about acting in such ways and developing bad reputations would have no qualms about lying, either. Also, while a repentant fasiq might be allowed to act as a witness, someone who has committed a *qadhf* offense (false accusation of illicit intercourse or *zina*) is barred from doing so, even after they repent (Aktan 2002; cf. Hüsrev 1980: 260; Ibn Abidin 1982–94: 12:458, 489–90; and Merginani 1986: 215).[49] In other words, a person who acts in such a callous way, bending the truth with deadly consequences, should never be trusted to make accurate statements in court.[50] And according to Ibn Abidin (1982–94: 12:490, 500), those who provided false testimonies in the past should be treated similarly unless they later repented.

Other measures accompanied efforts to pre-empt false witnessing. In particular, litigants' assertions that questioned the opposing witnesses' honesty

---

[49] Zina is punishable by death or severe flogging, depending on the offender's marital status. Qadhf, if proven, is punishable by flogging of up to eighty strokes. According to ibn Abidin (1982–94: 12:490, 500), some jurists allowed the slanderers to testify if they sincerely repented.

[50] According to the Ottoman jurist Çatalcalı Ali Efendi (Demirtaş 2014: 1:601), the testimonies of habitual liars are unacceptable ("Kizb ile maruf olan Zeyd'in şehadeti makbul olur mu? El-Cevab: Olmaz").

could trigger a formal process to investigate witnesses' justice based on their reputations (*tadil ve tezkiye*) that could lead to their dismissal (Ibn Abidin 1982–94: 12:450; Doğan 2017).[51] The procedure appears to have focused on investigating the reputations of witnesses rather than specific incidents that might have impugned their testimony. The jurisprudential sources I have consulted do not indicate how the qadi might have chosen the individuals who confirmed witnesses' reputations.[52]

It is possible that concerns about communal peace and harmony made litigants or qadis hesitant to sully the names of specific individuals. This is precisely why some jurists recommended private investigation of reputations in tadil (Hüsrev 1980, 249; Ibn Abidin 1982–94: 12:450; Merginani 1986: 209), even though a public inquiry would have made it relatively difficult for disreputable witnesses to testify in subsequent litigations.[53] A nineteenth-century source, the Ottoman Civil Code or *Majallah al-Ahkam al-Adliyya* (Berki 1986: 385), advised that if the reputation of a witness was challenged in court, the qadi should simply ask the litigant to supply an alternative witness, without making any public pronouncement about the rejected witness or the reason(s) for their disqualification. Finally, again according to the Ottoman Civil Code (386), "if the justice of the witnesses has been demonstrated in relation to one particular case, the judge does not need to inquire into the credibility of the same witnesses within six months," no matter the kinds of objections against them in subsequent litigations (cf. Aydın 2020: 178).

Notably, witnesses' bad reputations did not automatically disqualify their testimonies. In fact, most jurists agreed that qadis could pronounce judgments based on testimonies made by a fasiq, since according to Hüsrev (1980: 248), while "justice is required for a (legal) action based on witnessing, it is not a

---

[51] The term tadil, originally defined in the science of hadith verification, refers to the confirmation of the adl or justice of those who testify in court by others who know them. It carries overlapping connotations with tezkiye, another technical term that denotes the judge's corroboration of the qualifications of the witnesses (Doğan 2017: 13–14). The two terms often appear simultaneously in jurisprudential texts and court documentation. According to Çatalcalı Ali Efendi (Demirtaş 2014: 1:602), testimonies acquired through "bribes" (or payments) are not acceptable ("Zeyd Amr'ın müddeasına şahadet etmek icin Amr'dan şu kadar akçe rüşvet alub şahadet eylese makbul olur mu? El-Cevab: Olmaz"). While Ibn Abidin agrees with this opinion (1982–94: 12:439–440, 444), he also mentions (12:445) another interpretation that supports the idea of compensating the witnesses for their troubles, when there are others who could take on the responsibility of witnessing.

[52] Doğan (2017: 15) suggests that such people should not include individuals who might bear grudges or hostile intentions against the witnesses. They might include neighbors, colleagues, or longtime acquaintances. Cf. Aydın 2020: 172–3.

[53] On the other hand, occasional lists of habitual false witnesses exist in a few court registers from Istanbul, which must have been compiled to prevent these individuals from testifying in litigations. See, for example, the entry dated 2 Zilhicce 1165/October 11, 1752 in Havas-ı Refia (Eyüp) Court Records, Vol. 190, 3. I am grateful to Zeynep Dörtok Abacı for bringing this information to my attention.

requirement for being qualified as a witness. An immoral person (fasiq) is qualified for guardianship, judgeship, rulership, and imamate. We believe that he is also qualified to be a witness" (cf. Merginani 1986: 207-8; Halebi n.d.: 195).[54] According to Ibn Abidin (1982-94: 12:105, 448, 456, 479), the Hanafis generally treated verdicts based on testimonies from witnesses of ill repute as binding (cf. Aydın 2020: 183).[55] Other Ottoman jurists' opinions about verdicts based, specifically, on false testimonies are inconsistent. According to Zenbilli (or Zembilli) Ali Efendi (d. 1526), based on Abu Hanifa's opinion, such verdicts might have remained valid even after the discovery of the witnesses' lies (Ural and Sarı 1996: 91).[56] According to Çatalcalı Ali Efendi (Demirtaş 2014: 1:570), however, they were null.[57]

The consequences of false witnessing might include compensation for damages caused by inaccurate testimonies and tazir punishment.[58] The former required litigation by those who suffered damages against the witnesses, not the party who benefited from their testimonies in the original litigation. And the damages sought were proportional to the witnesses' role in the judgment. For example, if only one of the two male witnesses subsequently confessed that his testimony was deceptive, then he would be forced to pay half of the damages incurred by the verdict. If the original verdict was based on testimonies by more than three male witnesses and only one of these was subsequently deemed untrue, no damages could be sought, since the statements of the other

---

[54] On this issue, Ibn Abidin's treatment of the topic indicates varying opinions among jurists who influenced him, at least in terms of the nuances of their considerations. At one point, the jurist confirms that ill reputation is not an impediment to witnessing, though the qadis are not required to pronounce verdicts based on these (1982-94: 12:448). At a different point, however, Ibn Abidin suggests that corrupt witnesses should not be allowed to testify in court, even if they repent, unless some time (six months to one year) has passed after their repentance (12:483). For other jurists, repentance makes the testimony of a fasiq acceptable immediately (12:483-4), unless, presumably, the fasiq has slandered others with accusations of zina.

[55] Imam Shafii disagreed with this opinion (ibid.).

[56] This point is indirectly reported by the editor of the volume, as follows: "Yalan şahidin şahidliğine dayanarak hüküm veren kadının verdiği hüküm iki imamın aksine Imam Ebu Hanife'ye göre zahiren ve batınen geçerli olur" (ibid.). See Merginani 1986: 235, for a consistent opinion.

[57] "Mesele: Zeyd, Amr'dan bir hususu dava ve Amr inkar edip Zeyd'in müddeasına Bekir ve Beşir şahadet itdiklerinde kadı şahadetlerini kabul edip mucibi ile hükm etdikten sonra Amr, Zeyd'den: 'Sen ba'de hükm Bekir ve Beşir yalan şahidler olup husus-ı mezbura yalan yere şahadet etdiklerini ikrar etmişdin' deyü dava ve Zeyd'in ikrar-ı meşruhuna ikamet-i beyyine eylese hükm-ü mezbur münkaz olur mu? El-Cevab: Olur." But also see a contrary opinion by the same jurist in the case of two witnesses who merely retract their testimonies without admitting an intention of deliberate falsification (ibid.: 1:637-8; cf. Aydın: 291). Yavuz Aykan (2016: 152-60) identified a case in the court records of eighteenth-century Amid in which the qadi revoked a previous verdict because the winning side confessed in a subsequent court hearing that their witnesses had lied in the first trial. The revocation was justified by a fatwa issued by the local mufti of Amid, based on earlier opinions by prominent Hanafi jurists Şeyh Bedreddin (d. 1420) and Khayr al-Din al-Ramli (d. 1671).

[58] False testimonies do not generate compensation if they do not lead to a judgment by the court (Hüsrev 1980: 282; Merginani 1986: 235).

witnesses were adequate to justify the initial verdict (Hüsrev 1980: 282–3; Merginani 1986: 236).[59] Also, in cases where false witnessing led to execution or corporal punishment, while only monetary compensation could be sought from witnesses according to the Hanafi position (Hüsrev 1980: 285; Merginani 1986: 239), other legal schools called for *qisas* or identical retaliation (Aydın 2020: 272).[60]

All jurists called for tazir punishment for false witnessing, but they disagreed on what that punishment should be. While Abu Yusuf and Shaybani suggested that false witnesses should be publicly shamed and beaten, Abu Hanifa and Shafii prescribed shaming the offenders but not administering corporal punishment (Halebi n.d.: 248; Merginani 1986: 232–3). The latter prescription assumes that false witnessing is often revealed by the perpetrator's confession and that a threat of physical punishment would discourage those who might otherwise be inclined to confess. Ibn Nujaym (1966: 695–7, 2004: 261–3) stated that while some scholars considered beating and imprisonment appropriate punishments for individuals paid to witness falsely, others, including Abu Hanifa, considered public shaming a more severe punishment. Ibn Nujaym also suggested that the qadi might justifiably allow the perpetrator's head to be shaved, or dirt or mud to be smeared on his face, or his turban to be knocked down during public shaming.[61] Generally, while Ottoman jurists articulate both positions, there might be some preference for the latter one in later periods.[62] According to Ibn Abidin (1982–94: 8:284), the proper punishments for false witnessing include public shaming: officials could blacken the faces of the culprits and/or force them to ride asses through the town's streets while facing backward.

We do not know the prevalence of false witnessing in various Ottoman contexts. While there are several reports about the practice—both by premodern

---

[59] In a case where one male and two female witnesses testify and the testimony of one of the female witnesses is subsequently retracted, that female witness would be required to pay a quarter of the damages (Hüsrev 1980: 282).

[60] This is the case for deliberately false testimonies. In testimonies that are inaccurate but not deliberately so, all jurists call for material compensation for lost life or limbs (ibid.). False witnessing supportive of zina claims might have been treated as qadhf or false allegations of illicit sexual intercourse (ibid.: 275).

[61] Ibn Nujaym also suggested that the qadi might punish those who offered bribes to the qadis in the same manner (ibid.)

[62] According to Necati Demirtaş (2011–12: 2:611–12), while Ebussuud prescribed a vague discretionary punishment, Şeyhülislam Yahya Efendi (d. 1644) recommended both public shaming and corporal punishment. The prescribed punishment in Çatalcalı Ali Efendi's (Demirtaş 2014: 1:253) and Yenişehirli Abdullah Efendi's (Kaya, Algın, Trabzonlu, and Erkan 2011: 163) opinions is "tar by public shaming." According to a fatwa by Şeyhülislam Feyzullah Efendi (Kaya 2009: 10), a qadi can dismiss a prayer leader (imam) from his position if he habitually provides false testimonies in court.

Ottomans and Western observers of the Ottoman judicial system (Chapter 6)—it would be imprudent to make any assessment of its pervasiveness based solely on those reports. That being said, the importance of witness testimonies in evidentiary processes and litigants' relative inability to challenge the substance of false testimonies creates the impression that false witnessing was a potentially effective way to win litigations. I should note that these impressions are based on jurisprudential considerations. I discuss in Chapter 4 how premodern Ottomans attempted to control false witnessing in practice, along with a few other corruption crimes.

As a legal actor, the mufti receives minimum attention in premodern jurisprudential works. Both Marghinani (Merginani 1986: 174) and Hüsrev (1980: 309) briefly mention jurisprudential debates on his expected qualities. Jurists considered whether a fasiq might be allowed to serve in this role. Although there appear to be disagreements on the issue, most jurists opined that he could not (cf. Ibn Abidin 1982–94: 12:112–5).

Ibn Abidin describes the standards of qadiship and muftiship in an analogous fashion, at least with respect to the nature and limitations of their compensation. As in the case of the qadi, it was inappropriate for the mufti to accept compensation from those who asked him legal questions or sought his opinions involving their disputes with others because the service of providing legal guidance is religious and thus should not require material compensation (12:444, *passim*).[63] In addition, Ibn Abidin (12:160) argued that the mufti's legal opinions, non-binding yet often critical in the court's verdicts, should be insulated from influence by litigants. One might infer from this discussion that the practice of accepting fees for fatwas might have led some muftis to issue opinions influenced by selfish considerations.

According to Ibn Abidin, gifts to muftis from those who seek favorable opinions should not be accepted, but gifts as signs of love, respect, and appreciation for the mufti's wisdom and learning, presumably by those not immediately seeking fatwas from them, are legitimate and acceptable (ibid.). Nevertheless, the jurist also acknowledges that despite the relative similarity between the qadi and the mufti in relation to payments for their work, jurisprudential opinions regarding the qadi are better established and more widely acknowledged than those pertaining to the mufti (ibid.).

---

[63] The mufti may receive a salary from the public treasury (8:510).

Corruption of Nonjudicial Government Officials in Ibn Abidin's Work

Recently, Yavuz Aykan (2021) identified a fatwa by Şeyhülislam Sunullah Efendi (d. 1612), in which the mufti called for the seizure of monies and property that belonged to the public treasury (*beytülmal*) from those who had embezzled them. Parallel fatwas on the same issue can also be found among Şeyhülislam Feyzullah Efendi's (d. 1703) opinions, one of which specifically concerns the actions of a non-judicial official:

Question: If Zeyd, a state official and military commander, keeps for himself a portion of his soldiers' salaries that originated from beytülmal and also seizes other property by using his official position, can the ruler legally appropriate these [from Zeyd] and transfer them to beytülmal?

Answer: He can. (Kaya 2009: 132–3)[64]

Aside from such instances, jurisprudential considerations of corruption by military or administrative authorities are limited in the premodern era. In Ibn Abidin's work, however, we find some relevant discussion, which might be indicative of his inclination to engage with the problems of his age. According to the jurist, for example, a fasiq governor, just like a fasiq qadi, deserves dismissal (Ibn Abidin 1982–94: 12:130), an argument that follows established jurisprudential traditions to associate the two offices in bribery-related matters. Ibn Abidin also notes other legal experts who argued that bribe-accepting officials with extractive functions should be removed from service and that their property should be seized and returned to those they abused (12:34–5). Elsewhere the jurist insists that testimonies of government officials who act tyrannically or unjustly should not be accepted by law (12:488, 506). He considers collecting unfair taxes as one of many tyrannical acts, and his list of figures who might commit such transgressions includes not only the qadi, but also village and community heads, local tax assessors and their informers, and court officials (12:488). In his discussion of gifts to non-judicial authorities, including tax collectors, market inspectors, and members of the police

---

[64] "Rical-i devletten olup tavâif-i askeriyeden bir taifenin reisi olan Zeyd taife-i mezbüreye ulüfeleri için beytülmalden verilen malın bir mikdarını mezburlara vermeyip nefsi için alıkoyup ve sair cah-ı devlet ile şu kadar mal kesb ve cem eylese seyyidü's-selâtin imamü'l-müslimin padişahımız hazretleri ol malı bilcümle ahzedip beytülmale vaz etmeğe şer'an kadir olur mu? el-Cevab: Olur." The fatwa is reminiscent of the hadith pertaining to the incident involving Ibn Lutbiyya discussed in the previous chapter.

force, Ibn Abidin states that "their [legal] status resembles those extended to the qadis" (12:159). In particular, forced payments under the aegis of gifts to government officials, from village heads and crafts elders, are forbidden (12:159–60).

While Ibn Abidin's treatment of the corruption of non-judicial actors is a rare example in jurisprudential works, it is also sporadic and unsystematic. In general, his remarks are based on isolated statements and suggestions found in a small number of earlier texts. More broadly, Ibn Abidin stays within the boundaries of traditional jurisprudential coverage when, for example, he discusses topics related to taxation and other forms of wealth extraction (under the subtitles *ushr, jizya, zakat*; OT: *öşür, cizye, zekat*) usually included in classical texts. Consequently, questions such as what or who can be taxed are treated in some detail, but much less attention is paid to issues around potentially conflicting relationships between the ruler and agents responsible for wealth extraction in his name, various types or methods of illegitimate wealth extraction, or how claims of unfair extraction should be investigated or adjudicated. It does not seem that Ibn Abidin is especially concerned about corruption in other contexts such as taxation, or what we moderns might call public policy. In this sense, Ibn Abidin's discussion, while rich in comparison to earlier texts, does not significantly broaden the scope of the jurisprudential attention he inherited from his predecessors.

* * *

One sees a considerable degree of continuity between pre-Ottoman and Ottoman jurisprudential treatments of corruption, which is not surprising given the self-referentiality of fiqh traditions. Like their classical counterparts, Ottoman jurists remained focused on judicial actors, in particular the qadi and to a lesser extent witnesses and the mufti, and the various types of bribe exchanges in which they were often involved. The relative lack of jurisprudential prescriptions for non-judicial actors generates the impression that expectations for this group might have been articulated in different discursive fields, and this will be a topic for the next chapter.

Jurisprudential treatments of corruption evince some anxiety about how to categorically differentiate legitimate and illegitimate forms of reciprocity and, at times, a relative failure to do so. This problem is particularly evident in Ibn Nujaym's work, where the author often used the terms "gifts" and "bribes" interchangeably and did not sharply distinguish one from the other. Concerns about judicial appointments facilitated by payments to ranking officials also received attention by the judicial authorities. Occasionally, Ottoman jurists attempted to accommodate certain morally questionable practices based largely on pragmatic considerations, as we observed in Ibn Abidin's discussion of the financial aspects of the Islamic court's operations.

Given the imprecise boundaries separating legitimate and illegitimate actions, and the many divergent opinions on the legality of a large number of practices, it makes sense that many premodern jurists considered the anticipatory measure of bringing people with good character to important positions as an effective prophylactic for corruption. The task of distinguishing good and bad behavior in such a confusing terrain must be easier, the theory held, if undertaken by honest, God-fearing Muslims who would not be inclined to take advantage of the complexity and diversity of considerations addressed in the jurisprudential discourse. The jurisprudential traditions also implemented measures to monitor and punish corruption by judicial actors, but it is not clear how effective these might have been.

3
Abuse and Predation in State Documents

Kanunnames, adaletnames, yasaknames, and other government-issued legal documentation, including imperial orders, comprise another category of sources relevant to the topic of corruption, though their objectives, ideology, and contents diverge from those of jurisprudential works and align more directly with pre-Islamic traditions of government (Chapter 1).[1] Authored by the ruler (or, rather, in his name by his representatives) and directed at his subjects and those who govern them on issues including those that moderns associate with corruption, these documents are intended to prove the ruler's commitment to the welfare of his subjects. One good articulation of this goal is in the preamble of the Niğbolu (or Nicopolis) District Kanunname, promulgated in 1516 (Akgündüz 1990–6: 3:413):[2]

> Our endless praises and gratitude are due to Allah and our prayers and greetings are for [the Prophet] Muhammad Mustafa. Sultan Selim Şah son of Bayezıd Han ... has worn the crown of God's shadow (*zill-i ilahi*) and sat in the throne of rulership. His intention is to implement the divine law, augment the right religion, aid those who are infirm and weak, and enforce the rights of the flock (*reaya*) so that, because of his justice, people of religion and inhabitants of this world are prosperous and happy. It is with this intention that he desired to be informed about the country's important issues and affairs related to the people's property, to distinguish the right from the wrong, and to save the dominated from the fear caused by the

---

[1] The Ottoman kanunname, a compilation of kanuns, was a legal code that contained state directives on criminal penalties, urban and rural taxation, land use, market organization, manufacturing and artisanal production, and military matters. According to İnalcık, the term yasakname, popular in the earlier periods, had an overlapping meaning and uses with kanunname. Adaletname, or "edicts of justice," were sultanic proclamations that identified and proscribed specific acts of abuse and injustice against the sultan's subjects. For more extensive information on these terms, see İnalcık 1965, 1978a, 1978b, 1988a, 1988b, and 2001; Howard 1995/6; and Ergene 2014.

[2] Niğbolu/Nicopolis, located in modern Bulgaria, was captured by the Ottomans in 1396. In the sixteenth century, the locale was part of an eponymous *sancak* (or district) in the Rumeli province. The Niğbolu Kanunname was among the more extensive kanunnames issued during the reign of Yavuz Sultan Selim (1512–20), composed of more than 130 clauses on a wide variety of issues, including taxation, military service, customs fees and regulations, fines, and others (ibid.). The text is an abridged translation into Turkish by Ahmed Akgündüz from its Persian original.

dominant, the oppressed from the tyranny of the oppressor, the weak from the burden of the powerful, the subordinates from the oppression of their superiors, the trustworthy from the usurpations by the dishonest, and [common] people from the reproach of their leaders. So that tyranny and bribery would be eradicated, [under his rule] innovation (*bidat*) is removed and extractions that cause oppression and torment are banned. So that all dues and taxes due to the state, whether they are market fees or tolls from non-Muslims, or levies based on [agrarian and other sorts of] production, [and everything else] are consistent with the divine law and in accordance with old, established rules (*kanun-ı kadim*) in their essence and in their details/implementation. Whatever revenues these [extractions] generate are to be used to enrich my treasury (*hazine-i amire*)[3] for the benefit of the military, and for the expenses of the cavalry and the army.

In this idealized depiction, the Ottoman society is composed of elements that are potentially irreconcilable, and the ruler must maintain social order and prevent those beneath him from falling into anarchy. Good government, the preamble indicates, requires a devotion not only to the implementation of the divine law, but also, and perhaps primarily, to a commitment to establish justice. This commitment depends on the ruler's determination to manage or even eliminate the tensions between mutually antagonistic binaries (for example, weak and infirm versus strong and powerful; dominated versus dominant; oppressed versus oppressor; common people versus leaders) that constitute the realm.[4]

Such hierarchical characterizations of the social order and rulership differ from jurisprudential works premised on the equivalence, if not equality, of "sharia-subjects." And the association of "bribery" with the oppressors' "tyranny" in the preamble is not a prevalent articulation in fiqh discourses. In this chapter, I explore perspectives in state-generated documents, focusing specifically on various forms of self-regarding abuse of power by state officials that threaten the subjects' welfare. For this purpose, I first consider the polity's broader ideological claims and bases of legitimacy that find their roots outside the jurisprudential traditions, which I perceive as central to its characterizations of good government. Later in the chapter, I look into how imperial documents specified predatory conduct by government officials and how

---

[3] Ariel Salzmann (2003: 84) defines "hazine-i amire" as "operational treasury...devoted to the running of the state, war, and the management of the empire's vast latifundia."
[4] On alternative, not necessarily consistent formulations of justice in premodern Islamic political contexts, see Mottahedeh 1980: 179; Ergene 2001; Khadduri 2002; and Sariyannis 2019: 438–41.

particular notions in these documents might correspond, or not, to modern characterizations of corruption.

Kanunnames, adaletnames, and yasaknames comprise only one set of state-generated documents relevant to corruption in the Ottoman context. However, I focus on these documents because we find in them the most revealing aspects of the state's discourse on corruption. I discuss other types of official documents in the next chapter.

The Circle of Justice and Its Political Economy

The preamble of the Niğbolu Kanunname, like many other imperial documents, describes the Ottoman sociopolitical order as a complex system of entities with distinct ranks, roles, and privileges. At the very bottom of this hierarchy are the common folk, who seemingly lack the ability to defend themselves against oppression. In the middle are the dominant and powerful people the preamble calls "superiors" and "leaders." They are strong enough to exploit commoners and lack the nature or discipline to resist that urge. At the very top is the ruler, whose claim to political legitimacy derives from the shortcomings of the entities beneath him: the combined weakness of the commoners and evil disposition of the superiors. The preamble holds that only the holy law and the ruler's absolutist rule can protect the former against oppression by the latter.[5]

This representation of social divisions is consistent with what we find in various formulations of the "Circle of Justice" or "Circle of Equity," one of the most enduring and powerful articulations of the idealized social order in the Ottoman context that attributes particular positions and functions to all social entities.[6] While various formulations of this notion can also be found in many

---

[5] According to İnalcık (1965: 49), "The ruler's absolute authority, above and beyond all other rules, laws, and bases of authority, is ultimate remedy against injustice. [In this depiction of] Middle-Eastern state...a link is assumed between absolute authority and justice. The state is based on the ruler's strength and power and the state's function is to enhance his ability." For a very similar formulation by the same author, see İnalcık 1993: 71–2. Elsewhere, İnalcık (1988b: 33) characterized the Ottoman ruler as "one authority that is not secondary to any other, except for that of God. He is above all others who represent his authority and it is only him who could eradicate their abuse of their power." According to Linda Darling (2013: 3), "In the Near Eastern concept of state, the ruler with divine blessing or even divine appointment, protected the realm from external and internal enemies." On a different note, Tezcan (2010) discusses how the ruler's absolutist claims to power were resisted by "constitutionalist" parties during the seventeenth and eighteenth centuries.

[6] I agree with Darling (2013: 4) when she states that in many premodern settings, including the Ottoman Empire, "the Circle was more than a literary curiosity; it was a description of real political relations in an agrarian empire, an understanding in capsule form of the political and economic interdependence between rulers and ruled that Middle Eastern governments and peoples had arrived at."

pre-Ottoman settings,[7] Ottomans often referred to the Circle, implicitly or explicitly, as a normative model for socioeconomic relationships and as a reference point in their criticisms of major social transgressions.[8] Indeed, references to the Circle are particularly prevalent in discussions on surplus extraction and various types of exploitation, so we must pay special attention to it as we investigate Ottoman formulations of corruption. In the rest of this section, I will review aspects of this construct and tease out its implications for notions of abusive, predatory administration.[9]

There are numerous characterizations of the Circle by both Ottoman and pre-Ottoman authors. For the purposes of this discussion, however, two relatively concise accounts should suffice:

Hasan Kafi Akhisari (d. 1615): Rulership is possible only by (the support of) the military. The military requires wealth. Wealth accumulation is possible only when the realm prospers. And the realm prospers only by justice and good government. (Akhisari 1979–80: 254)[10]

Koçi Bey (mid-seventeenth c.): The might and strength of the dynasty increases by means of the military. The military requires [wealth in] the treasury. The treasury['s prosperity] depends on the flock. The flock's welfare is based on justice. (Koçi Bey 1972: 50, 1994: 65)[11]

---

[7] According to Darling, who has published the most authoritative and comprehensively researched work on the topic, the conceptions of the social order one observes in the Circle go back to the third millennium BCE. Thus, while the scholarship on the topic generally associates the Circle with ancient Persian traditions of government, Darling (2013: 6) has insisted that "the ideas contained in the Circle of Justice... were already articulated in the political ideology of the Sumerian city-states around 2500 BCE." Although the Persians themselves were slow to adopt it after conquest of Mesopotamia in the sixth century BCE, "by the time of the rise of Islam... the Circle formed a secure part of Persian political culture and was expressed in writings that survived into Islamic times" (11).

[8] In the Ottoman context, the earliest references to the Circle appear in the sixteenth century (Darling 1996: Ch. 9, and 2013: Ch. 8), though similar notions of social order and hierarchy can be identified in Ottoman political literature earlier, perhaps in the first half of the fifteenth century (Sariyannis 2019: 440; Darling 2014: 61). In general, Kınalızade Ali Çelebi (d. 1572) is credited with coining the term "Circle of Justice" (Darling 2013: 2), which remained popular in Ottoman political commentaries until the nineteenth century (Sariyannis 2019: 440).

[9] It is common in the scholarly literature to cite the Circle, or consistent characterizations of justice, as the ideological foundation of the Ottoman state ideology. See, for example, İnalcık 1965, 1988b, and 1993; İslamoğlu-İnan 1994: 5–6; Darling 1996: 283–99; Barkey 1994: 27–8, and 2008: 100–1. Recently, Heather Ferguson (2018: 258) suggested that "justice [as formulated in the Circle] was both a strategy of the petitioner and an assertion of imperial authority. It was therefore not merely a theoretical or philosophical principle but an administrative and political strategy that inscribed a grammar of rule shared between the Ottoman establishment and the diverse inhabitants of the realm."

[10] "Padişahlık ve sultanlık olmaz, illa erler ile olur; asker ise olmaz, illa mal ile olur; mal ise olmaz, illa vilayet mamur olmak ile olur; vilayet ise olmaz, illa adalet ile dahi hüsn-i siyaset ile ma'mur olur."

[11] "Velhâsıl saltanat-ı âliyyenin şevket ve kuvveti asker ile, askerin ayakta durması hazine iledir, Hazinenin geliri reâyâ iledir. Reâyânın ayakta durması adâlet iledir."

Like the Niğbolu Kanunname, the formulations of the Circle by Akhisari and Koçi Bey presume a society composed of entities with specific functions: the ruler, the "military," and the "flock," or, alternatively, the "realm" (*vilayet*) minus the ruler and the "military."[12] In very general terms, the "military" consists of agents or representatives of the ruler who are exempt from taxation, and the flock consists of tax-paying subjects. In this setup, the ruler provides "justice" in return for wealth generated by the flock. The military provides service to the ruler in return for the flock's wealth. The flock provides wealth to the military in return for the ruler's justice (see Figure 3.1).[13]

Following the insights of many previous scholars, including Halil İnalcık (1965) and Linda Darling (2013: Ch. 1), I should immediately point out that the notion of justice intrinsic to the Circle has a very specific meaning: the

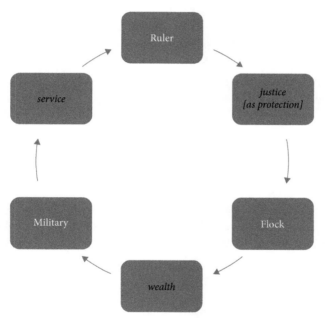

Figure 3.1 Functional Tasks and Responsibilities According to the Circle

---

[12] Various other formulations of the Circle further differentiate the military and the subjects by, for example, distinguishing the soldiers from the bureaucrats in the military and the townsfolk from the peasants in the flock (Darling 2013: Ch. 8).

[13] The Circle's conception of a social order composed of mutually exclusive constituent entities is of course not unique. Parallel characterizations can be found in Platonic and Aristotelian political philosophy, which was introduced to Middle Eastern audiences by the works of al-Farabi (d. 950), al-Miskawayh (d. 1030), Ibn Sina (d. 1037), and Ibn Rushd (d. 1198). See Lambton 1980; and Marlow 1997.

ruler's protection of the flock from oppression and exploitation.[14] Further (and as already implied), the Circle attributes different levels of agency to the constituents of the social order. The ruler is the active party who enforces justice; the military possesses some agency as well and is capable of pursuing its own interests at the expense of other groups; the flock, on the other hand, is the passive beneficiary of the ruler's justice, lacking the ability (if not the will) to defend itself against oppression. Also, justice according to the Circle is supposed to be the basis of the relationship between the ruler and the flock, but not the relationship between the flock and the military or the military and the ruler. Thus, the Circle's justice does not delineate relationships that involve all groups in the society.

The ruler's justice is strictly instrumental: it is a wealth-extraction strategy (Ergene 2001: 66–9; Darling 2013: 3–4) premised on ideas about how to most persuasively justify this objective in a precapitalist setting.[15] Indeed, the relationships presumed in the Circle are consistent with the "tributary mode of production" as defined in Marxist-inclined literature, whereby productive classes are "allowed access to the means of production while tribute is exacted from [them] by political or military means" (Wolf 1982: 79–80).[16] In this setting, wealth extraction from producers takes place primarily outside the realms of production and commerce (that is, in extra-economic ways), often but not exclusively through taxation and compulsory labor demands, agrarian and otherwise. The Circle's tributary character is evident in its association of the flock, and no other group, with wealth generation.

In the tributary relationship the economic resources available to non-productive groups and the social order's financial ability to maintain and reproduce itself are based on the flock's capacity to generate wealth and the dominant groups' ability to extract it, all else being equal (including demographic, environmental, and technological factors). As we can imagine,

---

[14] The Ottoman political lexicon contained alternative definitions for justice, of course, such as "balance" and "equilibrium" among classes, or "putting things in places where they belong" (Ergene 2001 75; Sariyannis 2019: 438–41). As I stated, my interest in the Circle and the definition of "justice" intrinsic to it stems from the notion's prevalent position in official discourses on corruption.

[15] See Anastasopoulos 2013: 279, for a consistent interpretation: "If... justice in the context of the 'circle of justice'... meant protection of the subjects from the fiscal and other abuses of state officials and the powerful, then from the state's perspective the notion of justice had a particular meaning, and served specific practical purposes, namely order, stability, and the proper and uninterrupted functioning of the fiscal mechanism. Thus, justice was a medium rather than a goal... which may explain why sometimes the Ottoman state was willing to condone arrangements not fully in accordance with the law as long as they secured its tax income." For another parallel representation of the Circle's political economic implications, see Ferguson 2018: 6.

[16] For a comprehensive and up-to-date discussion of the materialist, Marxist-inclined literature on the Ottoman state's extractive efforts, see Kaya 2022.

however, all else was often *not* equal. For example, military expeditions with favorable results could generate financial rewards and also expand the tax base through the acquisition of new lands and populations. During such times, the pressure on the flock to generate wealth and on nonproductive groups to extract it might diminish. By the same logic, times of military crisis and territorial contraction would increase those pressures. Likewise, regional and interregional commercial trends, climactic factors, and demographic patterns also must have affected the economic foundation of the social structure. Setting aside these contingencies, however, implicit in the Circle's functional division of society is the inherently conflictual relationship between wealth producers and wealth extractors.

For successful and sustainable wealth extraction in any tributary setting, extractors must convince producers that revenue extraction will also somehow benefit them. Indeed, while the Circle affirms the tributary social structure by associating wealth production with the flock, it also provides a justification for tributary extraction. The reward for acquiescing to surplus extraction for the flock is protection from excessive (that is, devastating) exploitation. The Circle assigns the task of protecting the flock to a specific actor, the ruler, and represents him as a neutral figure, one with no explicit interest in the surplus generated by the flock. Obviously, the flock requires protection from external enemies and criminal elements within the polity. Also, during natural disasters, the flock might require support from the ruler's private coffers. But given society's tripartite nature, the alliance between the ruler and the flock cannot be against anyone but the remaining entity represented in the Circle—the military—whom the Circle identifies as the *direct* beneficiaries of wealth extraction. Implicitly, then, the Circle designates the military as the only structural threat to the flock's wellbeing.

The Ottoman political literature often attributes the ruler's inclination to protect the flock to his cognizance of divine law and ancient customs,[17] his

---

[17] See, for example, 'Aziz Efendi's (1985: 8) *Book of Sultanic Laws and Regulations*, where an exemplary hypothetical ruler explains his charge as follows: "Up until now, through neglect and unawareness, our subjects have been reduced to such poverty and helplessness that, no longer able to meet their tax obligations they...have been forced to leave their land and homes and opt to serve as laborers in a distant place... My subjects however being sacred charges granted by the Lord of mankind (Praises to be God, the Lord, the Pardoner) the all protecting God to show his favor to me has awakened me from the sleep of unawareness, and I have realized that when on a day as full of reproach and remorse as the final day of judgment, a special council of the king of kings is convened and I am questioned in the presence of the Almighty, master of vengeance, about the good and evil I have accomplished. I intend to have an answer for the Lord God and to be in possession of the pride of being able to look into the face of God's beloved, the Prophet."

personal qualities,[18] or both. But these factors are superfluous to the Circle's functional logic. The protection of the flock is, instead, construed as a requirement for the stability of the tributary system. And assuming that the ruler's connection to the realm is patrimonial—in other words, that he claims the realm's economic resources as his own—his reasons for protecting the flock from excessive, suboptimal forms of exploitation would be self-serving.[19] If the military is allowed to over-extract producers' wealth, that might eventually ruin the tax base and make future extractions difficult, even impossible.

The materialist literature on precapitalist societies (cf. Haldon 1993) identifies two moments of conflict in any tributary setting: first, at the instance of surplus extraction, based on the tension between the producers and extractors; and second, at the instance of surplus distribution, among extractors as they clash over their relative shares. The Circle acknowledges the first instance when it requires the flock's protection from threats to their wellbeing by the military. Regarding the conflict over distribution, however, the Circle is silent, due to its characterization of the ruler as an actor personally disinterested in wealth accumulation. Yet if the ruler's commitment to protect the flock is based on a determination to ensure his long-term interests, we may regard the tension between the ruler and the military (also) as a distributive conflict: wealth not extracted by the military *now* corresponds to the promise of wealth that the ruler will need in the *future*.

Why would the military not be just as concerned with the long-term stability of the polity as the ruler? Perhaps because it is assumed that these agents' predatory inclinations will always overcome their medium- and long-

---

[18] İdris Bitlisi (1991: 21–4), a prominent member of the sixteenth-century Ottoman literati, explicitly identifies justice as one of those innate, God-given virtues, alongside wisdom, courage, and temperance, that the ruler has to possess. These personal qualities can provide a justification for an autonomous, even arbitrary rule, which is occasionally praised in some sources. The anonymous author of Hırzü'l Mülük (1994: 35), for example, argues that because of their superior personal qualities, the Ottoman sultans are not bound by the Ottoman laws (kanun-ı Osmani), and "whatever they choose to do, becomes Law."

[19] According to Carter Findley (1980a: 227), "The Ottoman Empire was, in Weberian terms, a patrimonial state...Theirs was in a real sense an image of the State as household, with the dynasty figuring as the family proper, the Ruling Class as the slaves of the head of the family and the staff of his household, the Subject Classes as 'flocks' entrusted by God to the care of the family head, and the territory of the State, with theoretically limited exceptions, as the dynastic patrimony. The values and ideals of the imperial tradition provided the State with its means of legitimation and thus with an imperial counterpart to those conceptions of honor...These values and ideals gave the State its distinctive identity; hereditary succession within the dynasty provided the means by which to maintain this identity over time; and a variety of relationships extending beyond the limits of kinship but still characteristic of the archetypal patriarchal household—the status of the Ruling Class as slaves and of the Subjects as 'flocks'—provided the mechanisms by which to link millions of people to the dynasty and all it represented." For more on the patrimonial nature of the Ottoman polity, see Findley 1989; İnalcık 1992 and 2018; Barkey 1994 and 2016; Kobas 2019; and Chapter 8.

term needs; in other words, they lack the wisdom that the best rulers possess. Or perhaps because the military was assumed to have incentives to prioritize their short-term interests over the needs of the flock, which would make sense given the military's awareness of their instant disposability. The transient nature of their service, then, would lie at the root of the danger they pose to the social order.

Then again, the ruler's alliance with the flock against the military should be understood within the bounds of the patrimonial order. It is true that the Circle puts a premium on the flock's ability to sustain and reproduce itself for the long-term stability of the order. Yet one cannot regard the ruler's concern with the flock's wellbeing as altruistic. Indeed, the Circle does not propose an upper limit to the ruler's exploitation: any form and amount of extraction beyond what is necessary for the flock to reproduce itself might be legitimate. And since the flock's survival is important only for the ruler's inherently self-serving reasons, it could be sacrificed, if temporarily, when circumstances of expediency require over-exploitation—that is, exploitation even beyond the limits of the flock's survival.

Moreover, the ruler's protection of the flock is conditional on the flock's continuous compliance and existence *as* a flock. Any attempt by the flock to change its status would destabilize the system and should not be allowed. Socioeconomic mobility—for example, when members of the reaya try to enter the military—would erode the fiscal base and thus would pose a threat to the system's long-term stability. Similarly, the flock is expected to accept the authority of the ruler and remain subservient to him; refusal to pay taxes would threaten the system. Overall, the flock does not have a say in their relationship with the ruler: that relationship is not contractual, and wealth producers have no legitimate right to withdraw their services in the patrimonial framework of the Circle. In principle, they are indeed the flock of sheep, and what they produce belongs to the ruler.

Admittedly, there is a way to characterize the ruler's relationship with the military as reciprocal, based on interdependence, and this could be used as a justification for demanding rewards (for example, a right to extract wealth) in return for their loyalty and service (Ergene 2001: 70–8). From the ruler's perspective, however, it is not clear that the military can justifiably refuse service or extract wealth from the flock beyond what is permissible absent compensation. It is in fact possible to characterize the mutual dependency of the ruler and the military as non-contractual (cf. Darling 2013: 7–8): while the ruler is expected to be generous to the military within limits, the latter are required to continue service whether or not the former rewards them. The absolutist character of the ruler's claims to power and the terminology used to refer to his slaves and servants in various examples of Ottoman political literature make the latter interpretation likely among the primary audiences of the Circle in the Ottoman context.[20]

Finally, the Circle is silent on how exactly the ruler is supposed to protect the flock against over-exploitation. Since the relationship between the extractors and producers tends to be direct in prebendal forms of wealth extraction, the military is in the position to take what they need from the flock without the involvement of a third party, including the ruler. Because the ruler cannot control the flow of resources from the flock to the military, his ability to influence the military's exploitative inclinations must be based on external factors or mechanisms. The Circle may assume that the military has an unconditional sense of loyalty to the ruler and abides by his wishes regardless of the consequences; and if that were true, there would be an even lower likelihood of a contractual relationship between the two entities. Alternatively, the Circle takes for granted the ruler's ability to detect and punish any transgression against his (that is, the realm's) broader interests, thus attributing to him qualities of omnipresence and omnipotence.[21]

Here one might point out that this characterization of the Circle's functional logic is broadly consistent with how Mehmet Genç famously characterized the "guiding principles" of Ottoman economic life from its beginning to the late eighteenth century. According to Genç (2009: 192), Ottoman economics "was motivated by... three main principles, provisionism, fiscalism, and traditionalism." Provisionism meant the state's dedication to fulfilling the material needs of the populace and guaranteeing their welfare. Fiscalism meant its commitment, first and foremost, to fulfilling the state's needs for finances. Traditionalism meant the state's inclination to maintain existing socioeconomic practices, relationships, and institutions and thus its resistance to any form of social change or mobility (Genç 2007: 525–6, 2009: 192–3). Genç (2007: 526–7, 2009: 193) also suggested that these priorities required

---

[20] I use the terms "absolutist" and "patrimonial" in my discussion as aspects of the ideological and discursive claims of the imperial government. Recent scholarship has demonstrated the limitations of these claims in practice, especially after the sixteenth century. In the latter regard, see Tezcan 2010; Yaycıoğlu 2012, 2016; and Gürbüzel 2023, among other publications.
[21] In its various formulations, the Circle also overlooks the possibility of intragroup competition and conflicts among the military over wealth sources. Indeed, the Circle disregards the possibility that a moderate level of extraction from producers might be inadequate for *all* extractors. This may be because it assumes that in a well-ordered and properly governed order, the needs of the military should never surpass what can be safely and justifiably extracted from the productive classes. In such an environment, the extraction levels of the military would be stable, and the numbers of the military would remain constant unless the productive capacity of the flock could be augmented.

the government to remain vigilant in its attempts to control all "factors of production" in the economic sector: land, labor, and capital. Importantly, Genç (2009: 194) recognized the possibility of conflict among the "guiding principles" of Ottoman economy and suggested that fiscalism, which served the state's interests, trumped all other considerations in such instances.[22]

As in jurisprudential works (but perhaps more pointedly), the concern with self-regarding, predatory acts by those in positions of power—the military—that might threaten the welfare of those under their authority—the flock—is central to the Circle's functional logic, though this is not because upholding the collective interests of the "sharia-subjects" (Chapter 1) is an objective on its own, but because the flock's prosperity is assumed to be instrumental to the fiscal stability of the social order and, thus, the longevity of the dynasty. Corrupt acts defined as such constitute a threat to society as well as a betrayal of the ruler.

Such acts obviously concern wealth extraction, the legitimacy of which is based on an economic calculation. According to the Circle, the wealth extracted from the flock should have upper and lower limits. Extraction cannot be "excessive"—that is, so burdensome that it would jeopardize the flock's ability to reproduce itself—yet it must suffice to cover the financial needs of the military. Thus, if

t = **total** wealth produced by the flock;
r = the amount required by the flock to **reproduce** itself;
f = amount needed to **feed** the military; and
e = amount of wealth **extracted** from the flock,

the boundaries for optimal surplus extraction would be

(1) $t - r \geq e \geq f$

Per the Circle's logic, it should not matter whether the various *forms* of surplus extraction are religiously sanctioned, grounded in long-established

---

[22] "The economic policy of the state, however, was not always wholly consistent. The official Ottoman purchase regime (*miri mübayaa*), for instance, driven more by fiscalism than provisionism, worked to limit the costs of the state at the expense of its subjects. This policy imposed a tax-like levy to facilitate the provision of goods and services for the state at a price usually lower than the market prices (and sometimes even below production costs). During times of peace, this purchase regime had little effect on the people, but in times of war and during economic crises, larger-scale craftsmen and tradesmen would be vulnerable to the ever-increasing demands of the state" (Genç 2009: 194).

customary practice, or based on the whims of the ruler, so long as their overall yields remain within certain limits: the legitimacy of extraction is determined by the levels of the surplus generated by producers and extracted by the military. Implicitly, then, it is immaterial whether wealth is extracted through regular taxation, irregular levies, or methods that might resemble extortion or bribery, so long as the amount extracted stays within certain limits and does not threaten the system's long-term stability.[23]

The preamble of the Niğbolu Kanunname distinguishes two overarching types of extractions, based exclusively on their impact on the reaya's welfare and the state's fisc. On the one hand, the preamble identifies some extractions as "usurpations," "oppressive extractions," and payments associated with "tyranny and bribery." On the other hand, it lists "taxes due to the state," "levies based on [agrarian and other sorts] production," and revenues "for the benefit of the military." While the text establishes the ruler's intention to eradicate the first group, it also highlights the need to finance the necessary expenses of his government. The distributive conflict over wealth extracted from the flock, which is only implicit in the Circle, is clear in the preamble: given the infeasibility of expanding the flock's productive capacity, limiting the extractive tendencies of those who rely on the surplus the flock generates is the only way the ruler can guarantee the stability of his regime.

Ideas intrinsic to the Circle are well represented in the preamble, but the text does not lack jurisprudential references.[24] Indeed, while "extractions that cause oppression and torment" are based on unsanctioned "innovation" (bidat), all taxes due to the state and the ruler's treasury comport with the "divine law" and "old established rules."[25] It would be rash to assume that references to Islamic jurisprudence were nothing more than rhetoric; however, it is good to recall that the Ottomans did experiment with many methods of

---

[23] Again, while in the long run it is the levels (but not the form) of the wealth generated and extracted that determine its legitimacy, in the short run, when the circumstances demand it—for example, at times of military crises—even this requirement may be relaxed. In other words, the patrimonial nature of the regime makes it justifiable for the ruler to extract more than what is required for the flock to reproduce itself and to pass that on to the military to feed them, when the survival of the polity depends on this.

[24] More generally, I do not claim that state-generated documents were impervious to jurisprudential concerns or formulations. For example, kanunnames contain systematic (if implicit) references to jurisprudential sensitivities in their engagement with particular types of crimes and their punishments (see Chapter 4). I assume a less categorical position in this regard: while it is possible to run into plenty of jurisprudential material in these documents, this genre of sources also makes it possible to explore discursive and ideological articulations based on siyasa traditions.

[25] İnalcık (1965: 53) defines the term bidat according to the "Ottoman legislator" ("Osmanlı kanun koyucusuna göre"; that is, the ruler) as "things (şeyler) that contradict the holy law, customs (örf), commands of the ruler, age-old/established rules (kanûn-i kadîm) and the [imperial] registers (defter)," without providing a source for this definition.

surplus extraction, and some of them were incompatible with inherited jurisprudential traditions or custom (cf. Bilge 2015: 56–7).[26] Thus, I am inclined to read the preamble's differentiation between extractions based on bidat versus divine law or established traditions as an attempt to enhance the regime's claim to legitimacy without undercutting its claim to a share of producers' labor. In fact, one could argue that extractions that cause otherwise avoidable suffering for the flock or jeopardize the long-term stability of the social order are, by definition, contrary to divine law.[27]

Here, it is worth emphasizing that the preamble uses the term "bribery" in a way we did not encounter in the last chapter's discussion of Islamic-Ottoman jurisprudence. Though the kanunname is also a legal document, it does not appear to be concerned with the technical attributes of the word as we see in jurisprudential discussions. Instead, this text, which conveys the ruler's perspective, casually links the term bribery to other extractions that burden subjects, regardless of form. From the ruler's point of view, bribery belonged to a category of offenses that undermined legitimate patterns of surplus extraction and distribution, and it was objectionable precisely for this reason.

Corruption in Ottoman State Documents

Taking my cue from the Niğbolu Kanunname, which associates the crime of bribery primarily with the exploitation of the reaya, I explore in this section the types of abuse of office mentioned in state-generated documents that sacrificed the taxpayers' (and thus the state's) interests to those of state

---

[26] A good example of such improvisations might be observed in the significant shift in early modern Hanafi jurisprudence on land possession, ownership, and, most importantly for the concerns of our discussion, taxation. This shift was based largely, though not exclusively, on the efforts of prominent Ottoman jurists such as Ibn Kemal (d. 1536) and Ebussuud Efendi (d. 1574). See Johansen 1988; Moutafchieva 1988: Ch. 1; Cin 1986: 19–39; Akgündüz 1990–6: 1:135–94; Imber 1997a: 115–38; and Mundy and Smith 2007: Chs 1–2 for different takes on the topic that reflect the authors' distinct ideological positions. Ottoman historians have also raised questions about the compatibility of Ottoman criminal prescriptions in general, and fines in particular, with established Hanafi traditions. On this topic see Barkan 1943, 1952; Heyd 1967, 1973; Imber 1997a: Ch. 9; Peters 2005: 71–5, 92–3; and Ze'evi 2006: Ch. 2, among others. On a very interesting and informative discussion of the sharia compliance of a number of taxes in the Ottoman context, including *avarız* and *resm-i hınzır* (that is, tax on swine), see İnalcık 1995.

[27] Relevant here as well are the varying levels of abstraction pertaining to the socioeconomic relationships in the Circle compared to what we observe in state-generated documents. The latter are obviously more concerned with specifying the exact ways in which the government authorities exploited the taxpayers. Further, in many settings, new forms of extraction, attempts that can technically be categorized as bidat, must have been responsible for making the overall extraction excessive. In such circumstances, the elimination of any unsanctioned form of extraction must have been an effective way to limit excessive overall extraction.

authorities.[28] This effort also aims to identify a conceptual category in one Ottoman discursive space—that of the premodern state—that might be analogous to modern characterizations of corruption insofar as it grouped a specific set of transgressions based on shared attribute(s).

In kanunnames of various types issued between the fifteenth and seventeenth centuries, examples, broadly defined, of such crimes include the following:

- Excessive taxation and acquisition of compulsory labor by subject populations premised on (otherwise) legitimate forms of cash, material, and labor extraction by military, administrative, and judicial actors.[29]
- Usurpation of economic resources—such as money, food, animals, and firewood—*not* based on legitimate forms of extraction by military, administrative, and judicial actors.[30]
- Excessive and redundant fee and fine collection for notarial and administrative services. For example, the orders issued by the imperial center include:
  o frequent references to inappropriate fees charged by judicial authorities for dividing estates, registering marriage contracts and slave manumissions, and issuing notarial documents of various sorts;[31]
  o complaints about punishments and fine extractions not based on prior investigation and/or judgment by the qadis;[32] instances of illegal fine extraction from criminals or their relatives subsequent to punishments by *hadd* penalties or involving limb-severance;[33] and illegal or redundant fine extraction by those, including some authorities, who were not permitted to extract such fines;[34] and

---

[28] One could suppose that the paternalistic, protective language implicit in the state's ideological formulations was also central to a moral economy that shaped taxpayers' expectations of a just social order, which remains largely invisible in our sources and unexplored in the modern scholarship. However, we should be careful not to reduce one to the other since the interests of the state and its subjects were not aligned.

[29] For examples of instructions involving excessive taxation, see Akgündüz 1990–6: 3:458–9, 4:392–3, and 5:509, 514, *passim*.

[30] See, for example, Akgündüz 1990–6: 3:416, 458–61, 4:390, 400, 683, 5:510, 514–16, and 6:135, 316–17.

[31] The courts' involvement in estate divisions was compulsory only when estate divisions led to disputes among heirs or when the latter included non-adults. Imperial documents contain repeated references to incidents in which the court officials redivided already divided estates, or divided them against the wishes of the heirs even when this was not necessary. In some cases, court officials were also accused of interjecting themselves in the divisions of non-Muslim-owned estates or forcing non-Muslims to pay them before they were allowed to bury their dead; see Akgündüz 1990–6: 1:586, 5:53–4, 514, 540–1.

[32] For example, see Akgündüz 1990–6: 3:94, 414, 459, and 4:304–5, 400–1.

[33] Akgündüz 1990–6: 3:377.   [34] Akgündüz 1990–6: 3:377, 4:400, 5:517.

o complaints about market inspectors' (sing. *muhtesib*) excessive and inappropriately frequent punishment of marketplace people; and their negligence.[35]
- Falsification of documents, false witnessing, and striking out entries in the court registers to hide previous offenses.[36]
- Vague references to bribes offered to court officials in court processes, including litigations.[37]

A few of these acts appear to have received more frequent mention than others in the kanunnames. These include excessive or illegal extraction of resources and utilization of forced labor by military-administrative officials and their representatives (cf. Faroqhi 1992: 13, 17). References to other varieties of abuse, including bribery in judicial and administrative processes, and especially litigations, are rarer. This might be due to the relative prevalence of such concerns in the jurisprudential documents (as observed in Chapter 2) or the fact that their immediate impact on common people or the political authority's coffers was negligible compared to other forms of predatory malpractice by government officials.

One notices in state-generated documents the use of a few loosely associated terms in relation to such crimes: primarily, zulüm and *teaddi*, which could both mean "oppression" or "maltreatment," often of the common folk, but also fesad and bidat, among others. This terminological tendency led Ahmet Mumcu (1985: 7–9) to suggest that the Ottomans saw these acts as constitutive of a specific, if not particularly well defined, crime category. And although frequent references to such acts exist in various types of state-issued documents (especially kanunnames) in the context of other concerns (such as the methods and logistics of tax collection, military mobilization, and transportation of supplies from rural to urban locales), the polity used a specific subgenre of decrees, called adaletnames, or "rescripts of justice," to communicate orders concerning these acts, at least until the mid-seventeenth century.[38] This bureaucratic-scribal specialization supports Mumcu's inclination to consider zulüm crimes as a distinct (if semi-legal) crime typology.

---

[35] Akgündüz 1990–6: 2:191–4, 4:400, 5:514–15, 9:525.
[36] Akgündüz 1990–6: 3:93, 6:470, 9:502, 529.
[37] Akgündüz 1990–6: 6:134. Cf. Faroqhi 1992: 19.
[38] Suraiya Faroqhi (1992: 10) suggested that "promulgating [adaletnames] in order to rectify specific abuses goes back at least to the reign of Sultan Selim [d. 1520]. But such rescripts multiplied during the troubled years of the Celali uprisings [at the turn of the seventeenth century]."

Which specific transgressions are mentioned in the adaletnames and in what manner? And if they constituted a specific typology as Mumcu suggested, how should we distinguish it from a modern characterization of corruption? A close examination of an example of this subgenre of documents should provide some answers to these questions. In an early seventeenth-century (1018 AH/1609 CE) adaletname (Akgündüz 1990–6: 9:562–9) addressed to administrative and judicial officials in the Anatolia Province, provincial authorities are linked to the following crimes, in the rough order as listed in the document:[39]

- The governors, sub-governors, and their agents conduct raids over the populace and extract resources with many illegitimate excuses. Such acts include
    o descending on villages in their jurisdictions with many men in their retinues;
    o forcing villages and rural communities to host them and their retinues for days at a time;
    o appropriating people's animals, food, and firewood without making any payments to them;
    o illegally charging fines and imposing levies (*kan cürmü ve öşrü*) in these locations for individuals whose death was no one's fault.
- The governors and sub-governors also assign their own revenue sources to their own men as tax farms. The tax farmers exploit the peoples in their jurisdictions by over-extracting legitimate revenue sources or demanding illegal payments and by allowing bribe-paying bandits in their jurisdictions to prey on local populations.
- Because of these acts, the taxpayers leave their homes and plots, which are then seized by officials and provincial strongmen, including tımar-holders and the slaves of the sultan (that is, *kapıkulus*), who convert them to privately owned farms. This behavior prevents the original residents from returning to their homes and, thus, erodes the tax base.

---

[39] See İnalcık (1965: 90–1) for an extensive discussion of the contents of this document. In the same article (123–33), İnalcık also provides the full text of the adaletname in its original script (in print). According to Faroqhi (1992: 10), this particular rescript "became especially famous, possibly at least in part due to the rhetorical elaboration with which the text described the abuses of governors, kadis and other officials in immediate contact with the subject population." Incidentally, while the adaletname rhetorically connects the need to protect the taxpayers to the claims that God entrusted them to the ruler and that their happiness and wellbeing should be ensured in the "justice-filled reign of the ruler" (Akgündüz 1990–6: 9:562), it also stresses that acts that jeopardize the taxpayers' welfare lead to the erosion of the tax-base (9:563) and that the protected flock are responsible for fulfilling their obligations and paying their taxes in full and on time (9:567–8).

- The governors and sub-governors neglect their duties to chase, catch, and punish the bandits. It is their duty to apprehend and punish the criminals in their jurisdictions, but
  - while chasing them they should resist the temptation of descending on rural communities and seizing their property;
  - any supplies obtained from the taxpayers during the chase should be paid for according to current official pieces (*narh-ı cari*);
  - the chasing parties should not include excessive numbers of riders.
- The qadis or their naibs, who often obtain their offices through subcontracts,
  - frequently visit villages, forcing people to host them for long periods of time and claiming their food, animals, and firewood;
  - count the graves in these villages and inquire about who has died. Then they accuse people of interring their dead without permission, though permission is not needed. They also force non-Muslims to pay them to be allowed to bury their dead;
  - interject themselves in the division of estates, even when this is not legally required, and seek compensation for their service;
  - overvalue property in estate evaluations so that they can obtain higher fees;
  - redivide already divided estates, claiming that previous divisions were inaccurate;
  - claim valuable property from the estates in lieu of their scribal and notarial fees;
  - accept bribes to assign prebendal plots and tax farms to those who lack imperial orders and certificates, and reject the claims of those who do possess such orders and certificates;
  - associate with local administrative officials (*voyvodalar*) to extort payments from well-off individuals with unfounded accusations;
  - accept bribes from well-off individuals to strike out incriminating entries in the court ledgers;
  - accept bribes from indebted or bankrupt tax farmers to falsely register well-off individuals, without their knowledge, as their sureties;
  - charge fees for preparing and recording unneeded documents, for unneeded notarizations; and overcharge for notarial and scribal services;
  - falsely report individuals as people who resisted imperial orders, blackmail them, and extort their money and property in cooperation with local administrative officials;

- o "and many such acts of injustice and oppression" (*bunun emsali enva-ı zulm ü teaddi*).
- The document also orders the local authorities to apprehend and punish without negligence
  - o moneylenders who charge interest rates higher than 15 percent and abuse those who cannot repay their loans by forcing them into compulsory labor or having them imprisoned for long periods of time; as a result, the victims flee their lands;
  - o "oppressors" (*zaleme*), who force common people into unfair, exploitative transactions;
  - o "profiteers" (*muhtekirler*), who use force to buy goods cheaply, store them, and sell them at exorbitant prices at times of need;
  - o "money-changers," who disregard the official rates in currency exchanges.

The transgressions listed in the adaletname largely overlap with the extractive abuses cited individually or in small clusters in various kanunnames. The document is clearly intended to compile crimes against the taxpayers, for most of which the government officials are held responsible. The adaletname provides significant details about such transgressions (and their variations) that were common at one point in time, more so than what we find in most kanunnames. The order in which the transgressions are listed in the document indicates that the imperial center put the greatest emphasis on extractive improprieties by the highest-level military-administrative authorities, just as I observed in the kanunnames. While illegal or excessive revenue extraction by the judicial actors also receive attention, adjudicative transgressions are not specifically mentioned. The qadis' and naibs' bribery is cited multiple times, but not in the context of litigations.

Modern conceptualizations of corruption consider bribery, collusion, scribal and notarial fraud, and illegal or excessive taxation as prominent examples of the misuse of public office for personal gain (cf. Nye 1967; Blundo and Olivier de Sardan 2006: 72–80). In the adaletname, such acts are counted among crimes that involve the abuse of taxpayers, or zulüm.[40] The document also links these acts to particular delinquencies, including negligence in pursuing and punishing bandits, profiteering, trading on the black market, and charging excessive rates in credit transactions and currency exchanges—behaviors that moderns do not often associate with public office

---

[40] The reader should note that the term zulüm must have had broader connotations in daily use. My discussion in this chapter pertains to its more technical connotations as found in state-generated documents.

corruption.[41] Nevertheless, the latter constitute a relatively marginal group in the adaletname, whose focus is clearly elsewhere. On the other hand, the document appears disinclined to link with zulüm other acts often associated with corruption in modern contexts. Indeed, particular forms of favoritism are not mentioned (see Chapter 8). Neither are embezzling tax revenues or skimming resources that belong to higher officials: though the Ottomans regarded such acts as transgressions against the state's fiscal interests, they do not appear to have been viewed as crimes that harmed the common folk.[42]

Based on these considerations, Figure 3.2 demonstrates the overlaps and incongruities between two broad notions, zulüm and a modern conception of corruption, in terms of their coverages of specific crime types.

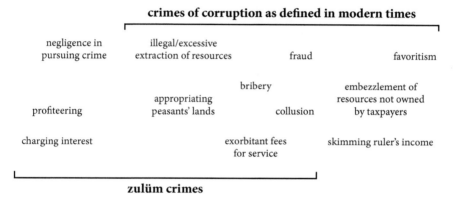

Figure 3.2 Rough Correspondence among Crime Categories
Note: Crimes identified in this figure are intended to be representative, not comprehensive.

* * *

This chapter has identified a framework on corruption distinguishable from jurisprudential perspectives delineated in Chapter 2. Ideologically, the framework was based on pre-Islamic traditions of government as encapsulated in the Circle of Justice, which presupposed a hierarchical social order of functionally disparate constituents. The Circle puts a premium on the welfare of the productive classes, but only because they were instrumental to the viability

---

[41] İnalcık's (1965) survey of other adaletnames from slightly earlier and later periods reveals very similar compilations of crimes.

[42] In addition to the frequent orders by the imperial center directed at its provincial representatives to collect in full and transmit on time the tax yields due to the state coffers, such anxieties also become explicit, for example, in the center's warnings against the local authorities' appropriation of estates without heirs for their own use, instead of transferring them to the treasury (beytülmal), and their seizure of the portions of customs revenues. See, for example, Akgündüz 1990–6: 1:575, 6:130–1.

Table 3.1 Corruption in Jurisprudential Works and State-Generated Texts

	Jurisprudential	State-Generated
Source	Scriptural sources; jurisprudential elaborations based on these	Pre-Islamic traditions as articulated in state documents (often complemented by jurisprudential considerations)
Ideological Objective	Maintain the egalitarian ethos of the community of believers (umma)	Wealth extraction and distribution; tributary concerns
Conceptions of Social Order	Unified, egalitarian, composed of sharia-subjects	Patrimonial, hierarchical, composed of unequal entities
Conceptions of Corruption	Self-regarding acts by religious authorities that threaten the unity and wellbeing of the community of believers and potentially generate fissures among sharia-subjects	Self-regarding acts by sultan's servants that threaten the taxpayers' and, ultimately, the ruler's interests and disturb the idealized patterns of wealth extraction and distribution
Specific Coverage	Bribery by qadis in appointment and court processes; secondarily, acts of other court officials and judicial functionaries	All state actors and all means of wealth extraction; judicial actors in non-litigational tasks

of the ruler's patrimony. According to the tributary logic of the Circle, the legitimacy of a particular form of extraction was based less on what it *was* than on how it impacted the fiscal base of the realm.

The state-generated documents are also uniquely concerned with a broader spectrum of transgressions associated with corruption; specifically, extractive crimes by non-judicial actors and misconducts by judicial actors in non-litigation tasks. These transgressions might have constituted a particular crime genus, zulüm, which partially overlaps with types of offenses that modern people associate with corruption. This coverage filled extensive gaps in the jurisprudential literature pertaining to abuse and predation by government officials (see Table 3.1). The next chapter considers how this representation is manifested in the polity's attempts to manage corruption, as revealed in a broader selection of official texts and records.

4
Controlling Corruption

The Ottoman polity made efforts to limit crimes against taxpayers' and the state's financial interests. These included, most famously, making appointments to government positions and rewarding officials based on merit; granting select government officials short tenures and frequently rotating them to reduce their chances of establishing prominent ties in their jurisdictions; and supporting judicial-administrative institutions, including a provincial court system and direct petition channels to the imperial center that allowed it to keep in check the abusive inclinations of local authorities (Faroqhi 1992: 18).

The overall effectiveness and consistency of these measures, however, surely varied based on many variables. Economically, the most important factor was presumably the cost of anticrime measures relative to the returns they generated. Gary Becker (1978: Ch. 4) suggests that from the government's perspective it makes sense to pursue anticrime measures only when they generate tangible benefits, including fiscal gains though not exclusively so. More recently, Edgar Kiser and Xiaoxi Tong (1992) proposed an economic model to examine the costs of controlling corruption in Qing China (1644–1912) that considers various institutional variables that shaped anticorruption efforts in one premodern, highly bureaucratized setting.

In the first part of this chapter, I apply Kiser and Tong's analysis to the Ottoman context to think systemically about the polity's ability and incentives to fight against corruption in the pre-Tanzimat era, an approach that is lacking in extant scholarship. Later, I survey the types of complaints submitted and responses by the imperial center, as found in eight mühimme and şikayet registers,[1] in an effort to empirically substantiate the range of issues targeted by Ottoman anticorruption efforts. In the same section, I also provide impressions about the punishment of corruption crimes based on evidence from *kalebend defterleri*, or "registers of those confined to fortresses."

---

[1] As I discuss in more detail later in this chapter, these registers contain documentation and correspondence produced by the divan-ı hümayun (or imperial council), composed of the highest-ranking judicial and administrative officials in Istanbul. It is common to translate "mühimme registers" as "registers of important affairs." The term "şikayet register" can be unambiguously translated as "complaint register."

The discussion in this chapter is built on the conceptual insights introduced in Chapter 3 as they relate to the topic of controlling corruption, based on a wider selection of state-generated documents.

Measuring, Monitoring, and Sanctioning Corruption in the Ottoman Context

In this section I introduce a conceptual model to consider the Ottoman polity's ability to control corruption based on a few key variables. While aspects of this analysis are hypothetical, the suppositions that it features are also historically plausible since they are based on the relevant scholarships in premodern Ottoman and non-Ottoman contexts. The discussion intends to provide a bird's-eye view of the broader issues concerning the fight against corruption and help us consider them in a systematic and comprehensive manner. Before I proceed, I should point out that a few considerations below are also relevant for many other premodern settings. Thus, the analysis might be applicable more broadly than just to the Ottoman polity and should not be regarded simply as a way to gauge the effectiveness of Ottoman efforts to control corruption in comparison to those of its contemporaries.

According to Kiser and Tong (1992: 303), "All rulers will weigh the costs of corruption and the costs of control, and will invest in control only when it provides a net benefit.... This implies that the greater the costs of control, the higher the level of corruption. Moreover, some corruption will exist in any fiscal bureaucracy, and the minimum level of corruption will be a function of the minimum cost of effective control." Specifically, a polity's ability to control corruption is determined by its ability to measure its taxable assets and other sources of revenue, to monitor the activities of its agents and their interactions with taxpayers, and to sanction good and bad behavior in government practices at acceptable costs for each purpose (304–5). The "costs" in question can be both economic and non-economic.

Measurement

In the Ottoman context, possibly the best-explored measurement tool was the fiscal surveys (*tahrirs*) conducted by the imperial center between the fifteenth and seventeenth centuries: the tahrirs assessed the polity's tax-paying subjects and taxable resources to determine their capacity to generate revenue.[2] The information generated in province- and district-level surveys was recorded in official registers called tahrir defterleri. Usually conducted immediately after the conquest of a region and updated thereafter, these records were critical in deciding how much to extract in specific locales, in what form and fashion (based on persons, input, output, or activity), from which groups. They also helped assess the activities of government functionaries responsible for extraction (Coşgel 2004; Öz 2010).[3]

For the purposes of measuring the tax base, however, the tahrirs had certain limitations. For one, they provided estimates of the potential yield rather than actual revenues extracted in a locale (Alexander 1999; Kolovos 2007). Moreover, they were not regularly revised, or were revised only infrequently, to reflect the constantly changing circumstances on the ground (Öz 2010: 426).[4] Scholars have also identified surveys that were incomplete, failing to encompass all taxable resources and activities in a given administrative unit (Lowry 1992: Ch. 1; Coşgel 2004: 89). Quite a few of these problems are directly related to the high cost of producing and updating the surveys. The task involved assembling and mobilizing officials from the center, largely at the expense of local populations (Öz 2010: 426–7). Their work entailed intensive and time-consuming cooperation with local officials and representatives of the taxpayers. The process must have carried a social price as well, as it often generated tensions locally. In several instances negotiations between inspectors and taxpayers led to quarrels, threats of violence, and even local uprisings (Faroqhi 1986: 29; Öz 2010: 427).[5] These factors (or "costs") must have limited the overall effectiveness of tahrirs as precise tools of measurement.

Tahrir surveys largely disappeared beginning in the late sixteenth century (Öz 2010: 428–9; cf. Kolovos 2007) for reasons that may be related to broader socioeconomic and fiscal changes, including the progressive monetization of the economy and, more immediately, the imperial government's increasing need for direct, in-cash forms of revenue extraction to finance its expanding

---

[2] For a more general discussion of measurement in the Ottoman fiscal system, see Coşgel 2005, 2015.

[3] For detailed, useful discussions on how tahrirs were conducted in particular locales and how the relevant practices might have varied over time, also see Alexander 1999 and Kolovos 2007.

[4] According to Mehmet Öz (2010), the Ottomans often disregarded their own requirements about how frequently the tahrirs should be updated. As a rule, the registers were supposed to be revised every thirty years. But in reality, some tahrirs were updated more frequently based on need and others much less so.

[5] Indeed, mühimme registers contain plenty of examples of local resistance, sometimes "rebellion" (isyan), to the imperial center's attempts to conduct surveys. See entries 78, 277, 326, 432, 435, and 455 in 7 Numaralı Mühimme Defteri (1998).

military and peacetime expenses (Salzmann 1993: 398–400). In this context, short- and longer-term farming of the revenue sources (iltizam and *malikane*, respectively) increasingly replaced prebendal allotments and extraction, which made tahrir surveys somewhat irrelevant for tax assessments. Instead, the potential yields of revenue sources were now measured in auctions, where those sources were granted to the highest bidders. What makes this development pertinent to our discussion is that in this new arrangement, compared to the preceding prebendal system, there was potentially a sharper contrast between the interests of the ruler and those of the taxpayer because aggressive bids by potential investors in the revenue sources, which directly and immediately benefited the ruler, implied more intense extractive pressures exerted on taxpayers. Thus, the ruler might have faced more pronounced short-term disincentives to protect the taxpayer against abusive extractive practices (more on this in Chapter 5).

Monitoring

Accurate measurement of the tax base was obviously not a viable anticorruption tool in non-fiscal realms of government. Monitoring of the government officials' functions was, in principle, more broadly applicable to all realms of the administration. Scholars have long recognized the existence of separate executive and judicial structures as an institutional arrangement that kept local authorities in check, limiting the potential excesses in their interactions with common people under their jurisdictions. This may well be true for many provincial contexts, but the archival sources also indicate instances of failure by judicial and military-administrative authorities to contain each other's crimes, unless they received support from the imperial center.[6] This factor made petitions to the capital, both by local officials and taxpayers, a viable option for monitoring the activities of government functionaries.

According to Halil İnalcık (1988b: 33), the Ottoman inclination to use petitioning to seek help from the imperial center against crime was aligned with the "Middle Eastern system of state and government." Indeed, Ottoman historians have seen petitioning as a popular way to control the abusive activities of those who preyed on the common folk (Faroqhi 1986, 1992;

---

[6] See, for example, among many others, entries 121 and 943 in *3 Numaralı Mühimme Defteri* (1993); 107, 527, and 858 in *7 Numaralı Mühimme Defteri* (1998); 82, 114, and 173 in *82 Numaralı Mühimme Defteri* (2000); 501 in *85 Numaralı Mühimme Defteri* (2002); and 260 and 340 in *91 Numaralı Mühimme Defteri* (2015).

İnalcık 1988b; Zarinebaf 2010: 148–52). According to Linda Darling (2013: 143–4),

> All subjects of the sultan—men, women, Muslims, non-Muslims, rich, poor—had the right to petition the ruler directly, and thousands and thousands of petition records survive to show that they exercised that right regularly. People from all walks of life brought their petitions to the sultan's court and presented them, orally or in writing, to the assembled viziers and chief scribes. Governmental and military personnel, judges, townspeople, villagers, and nomads also sent petitions to the capital through the post system.[7] Women, including Christians and peasants, often petitioned the sultan, and some journeyed from distant provinces to attend the sultan's court in person and receive justice from the ruler. Those who could not travel to the sultan's palace presented petitions in the shariah court and had them forwarded to the capital, or they got judges to write petitions for them.[8]

The imperial center's response to these petitions could take multiple forms. In most cases, orders were sent to provincial authorities to behave themselves, act according to the law, and investigate and, if necessary, punish those responsible for abusing the taxpayers. In others, inspectors accompanied these orders to make sure that the local officials carried them out. In serious allegations of crime, inspectors were ordered to capture those accused of wrongdoing and take them to the capital for trial and punishment (Mumcu 1985: 25–7; Acun and Acun 2007: 137–9, 144–5).

The sheer volume of petitions against government officials, many of which contained allegations of what we might perceive as acts of public office corruption (Zarinebaf-Shahr 1996: 86–9; Acun and Acun 2007: 141–2; Zarinebaf 2010: 151), has led many Ottomanists to believe that petitions and complaints to the imperial center were an effective control mechanism against abuse and predatory administration (İnalcık 1965, 1988b).[9] According to

---

[7] According to a statistical analysis of the information found in an early sixteenth-century Register of Commands (*Ahkam Defteri*), petitions composed by taxpayers outnumbered those generated by local authorities more than threefold (Acun and Acun 2007: 133–5). Suraiya Faroqhi (1986: 31) observed in a complaint register dated 1675 that those linked to "private individuals" made up a large portion, "if not the majority," of the petitions. The shares of the settlements, guilds of tradesmen, and tribal units were not insignificant either. But see my observations in the next section, which draw a more context-dependent picture.

[8] According to Faroqhi (1986), petitioning to the ruler should be seen in the Ottoman context as a political act "from the bottom up," since it involved a declaration by the taxpayers, or those who represented them, of their rights and demand for justice.

[9] According to Darling (2013: 144), over time, perhaps from the second half of the sixteenth century, "the hearing of petitions became not just the personal act of rulers who wished to be seen as just, but the

Darling (2013: 144), the "increase of complaints after the mid-sixteenth century" stems, among other factors, from taxpayers' "expectations of favorable response." Suraiya Faroqhi (1992: 35), who is reliably cautious about interpreting the historical record,[10] notes that the large number of petitions in the imperial archives indicates the system's success (1986: 30–1), and she favorably compares the Ottoman rulers' responses to petitions of justice to those of their European counterparts.[11]

This may well be. But the problem with judging the effectiveness of a control mechanism based on what is found in the archive is that we lack information on what is missing. In the absence of complaints that never turned into petitions and petitions that never made their way to the imperial center, it is difficult to empirically assess how well the Ottoman state monitored the actions of government functionaries. Since we cannot count what might never have existed, any effort to weigh the effectiveness of petitioning would require us to speculate about factors that disincentivized the reporting of abuse.

One critical aspect of petitioning as a way to monitor abuse is that it is reactive,[12] which forces us to consider the financial and non-financial costs of communicating with the imperial center or high-level provincial authorities. As many historians have pointed out (İnalcık 1988b: 35; Acun and Acun 2007: 128; Darling 2013: 143–4), one could report abuse in many different ways. It was common for individuals and groups to complain about provincial authorities either in person or by sending petitions. It was also possible for these parties to obtain letters by sympathetic local authorities in support of their grievances (Taş 2007: 191–2; Tuğluca 2010: 55–60; Yörük 2019: 85–9).

---

perennial administrative function of a bureaucratic state that enacted justice on a daily basis." This is consistent with İnalcık's (1988b: 38) emphasis on the systematic, consistent, and rule-following nature of Ottoman judicial bureaucracy, which pursued petitions even against the ruler's associates.

[10] This is what Faroqhi states in the conclusion of her important study on petitions (1992: 35): "At the present stage, it is important to maintain a critical distance from our source materials, which were always written by Ottoman officials. The latter, however, cannot be regarded as impartial recorders. To the contrary, they were the indirect addressees of the taxpayers' petitions, as parties with a stake in the game. Officials were themselves the cause of many collective protests. Certainly, the officials drafting the rescripts contained in the mühimme registers had interests which did not always coincide with those of the provincial administrators against whom most protests were directed. But even so, there were interests common to Ottoman officialdom as a whole, and caution is in order."

[11] "The assumption that the ruler was willing to aid the poor taxpaying subjects, and was not party to the exactions of his officials, is familiar both from Ottoman and from early modern European contexts. However, while such assumptions were totally unrealistic where rulers such as Louis XIII and Louis XIV were concerned, Murad III's experiments in the conduct of local administration do make it comprehensible that Ottoman provincials should have believed that the Sultan was on their side" (Faroqhi 1986: 30–1).

[12] With regard to taxation, the prevalence of prebendal extraction in the "classical" period must have limited the possibility of monitoring in more direct fashions. A setup that involved direct, unmediated interaction between the tax collectors and the taxpayers must have made excessive or illegitimate extraction likely (İnalcık 1965: 52).

Naturally, all these endeavors must have incurred expenses. The financial burden of reporting abuse must have included the costs associated with composing the complaint letters, particularly when they required the involvement of local qadis and naibs, who charged for scribal and notarial services. In addition, the complainants or their representatives had to travel long distances and stay for extended periods in the imperial and provincial capitals to establish contacts with the relevant authority.[13] And in these locations they must have sought help from various authorities to deliver their petitions to the right offices and individuals, so the expense calculation should include any tips, gifts, and bribes required to those officials (Faroqhi 1992: 2).[14]

Thus, there might have existed contextually specific monetary and non-monetary thresholds for reporting of abuse, and it is likely that when the expenses associated with reporting the abuse exceeded its damages, the abuse often went unreported.[15] In principle, a strategically oriented official could have minimized the chances of investigation and punishment by keeping the burden of his abusive activities under this threshold, in monetary terms and otherwise.[16] Modest infractions that persisted over long periods of time at bearable levels must have generated fewer risks for abusers.[17] The threshold must have remained lower for petitions that did not involve the local qadi's or

---

[13] According to Hülya Taş (2007: 201-2), a trip between Ankara and Istanbul in the seventeenth century, which contained eleven stop-points (*menzil*) at the time, might have taken about eleven or twelve days.

[14] Unfortunately, I know of no systematic study that has explored the financial burden of petitioning in any pre-Tanzimat context. Faroqhi (1986: 30) suggested that a group of petitioners from Ankara paid their representative in Istanbul 200-300 guruş, a significant sum at the time, to submit their petition to the imperial council in the late sixteenth or early seventeenth century. However, she also insisted that "the expenses involved were not prohibitive, as villages and tribal communities also made use of this mechanism. Moreover[,] the frequency of these complaints to the Divan [imperial council] indicates that they were not ineffective, even though certain cases might apparently be pushed back and forth between a local court and the authorities in Istanbul. For if the opposite had been true, it is probable that many of the provincials flocking to Istanbul in person or by proxy would have found better ways of using their money" (30-1).

[15] This consideration would explain the relative preponderance of petitions that contain scores of serious accusations and ones that describe exorbitantly excessive extractions from the early seventeenth century onward. For example, according to my observations in the mühimme and şikayet registers, the petitions against qadis and naibs accusing them of charging 10-50 guruş for scribal fees (compared to the officially prescribed 8-12 akçes) are considerably more numerous than those who blamed them for charging less excessive, but still significant, fees. On court fees in the Ottoman Empire, see Dörtok Abacı and Ergene 2022.

[16] Of course, the ability of the local authorities or their representatives to keep their abuse under a certain threshold might have been limited when they purchased their positions through competitive bidding, which required them to invest in considerable sums to acquire their extractive entitlements. The mühimme and şikayet registers contain clear references to this tendency. See, for example, entries 480 and 541 in *7 Numaralı Mühimme Defteri* (1998), which indicate that some provincial positions were acquired as tax farms in the late 1560s and that this practice led those in office to overcharge for their services. I return to the connection between office sales and corruption in Chapter 5.

[17] For a partial impression of the substantial amounts of resources (monetary and otherwise) devoted to the investigation of what might only be called "grand corruption" allegations involving

naib's support, but these petitions probably yielded satisfactory results less frequently. The threshold of abuse must also have varied according to a location's distance from imperial and provincial capitals, due to the relative costs of travel and accommodation.[18] Finally, the cost factor must have made the abuse complaints of individuals or small parties and poorer groups less likely to be reported than those that involved larger groups and wealthier parties.[19]

The non-financial costs of reporting must also have significantly influenced petitioning behavior. In particular, potential petitioners must have contemplated the consequences of their complaints (for example, reprisals by their abusers), which could well have made people hesitant to speak up against acts of injustice.[20] This factor might have made it even less likely that individual parties or small groups, who lacked the protection that large corporate bodies might have garnered for their members, would vocally protest predatory acts. Also, local judicial authorities might often have been pressured to ignore local grievances or even attracted reprisals for conveying them to the imperial center (Mumcu 1985: 27; Faroqhi 1992: 2).[21]

Another factor might have been concerns about the effectiveness of petitioning. A report by chronicler Naima (2007: 2:720) attributed to the qadis during the reign of Murad IV (r. 1623–40) indicates the qadis'

---

two subsequent governors of Egypt (Süleyman Paşa [d. 1548] and Hüsrev Paşa [d. 1544]), see Bacqué-Grammont 1979; and İpşirli 2015. In this case, the funds alleged to be embezzled, extorted, and appropriated in other illegal ways justified the sums and effort invested in the investigation.

[18] According to Acun and Acun's (2007: 132) research on an early sixteenth-century "register of commands" (*Ahkam Defteri*), petitions arrived to the capital more frequently from nearby places than from distant locales. This register contained references to one petitioner arriving from as far as Trabzon (138), located on the eastern Black Sea coast in Anatolia (a distance of more than 1,000 kilometers on land). Tuğluca's (2010: 48) survey in four late seventeenth-century şikayet registers indicates that a majority of the petitions to the imperial council originated from Istanbul (13 percent) and nearby provinces of Rumelia (31 percent) and Anatolia (19 percent). Yörük (2019: 68–9) too made a similar observation based on an early eighteenth-century şikayet register.

[19] Petitions filed by larger parties might have been less costly than petitions by individuals or smaller groups on a per capita basis, all else being equal. Yet such petitions must have also required a greater organizational effort, involving intragroup deliberations and negotiations. In other words, what made such petitions financially affordable might have generated more formidable logistical obstacles than petitions by individuals or small groups did.

[20] There is evidence for such reprisals in official documents, which often took the form of physical attacks against individuals accused of filing complaints against specific authorities, their imprisonment, and appropriation of their property. See, for example, entries 858 in *7 Numaralı Mühimme Defteri* (1998); 114 in *82 Numaralı Mühimme Defteri* (2000); and 297 in *4 Numaralı Atik Şikayet Defteri* (Tataroğlu 2015).

[21] Mumcu (1985: 27) mentions plenty of instances of attacks against local courts perpetuated by alleged abusers to discourage reporting or prevent post-reporting investigations. In one report I encountered, a group of villagers who complained about the abusive acts of their tımar-holder mention that their qadis (plural) chose not to report their situation to the imperial center because of the qadis' fear of the tımar-holder; see entry 310 in *4 Numaralı Atik Şikayet Defteri* (Tataroğlu 2015). Another entry reports the existence of qadis bribed by local officials to quash reports against them; see entry 202 in *85 Numaralı Mühimme Defteri* (2015).

frustrations with the ineffectiveness of their petitions against oppressive government functionaries. In this regard, we should note that counter-reporting also played a role in thwarting complaints against provincial authorities. Frequently, those who had been accused of abuse sent their own petitions or representatives to the capital to respond to their accusers, proclaim their honesty and trustworthiness, and make counteraccusations.[22] In fact, if abuse complaints were perceived as discredited in subsequent investigations, initial complainants might eventually be punished (Mumcu 1985: 26–7).[23] It must have been important as well to have connections and support at the imperial center to blunt the impact of petitions, and even to get them dismissed. If petitions did result in investigations against allegedly abusive authorities, bribes extended to inspectors sent from the imperial center could tempt them to protect the abusers (Erdem 2017: entry 589). According to Naima (2007: 4:1784), even when petitions succeeded in generating orders to punish oppressors, such decisions could be reversed by payments to higher-ups.[24]

Ironically, expectations regarding the consequences of a successful petition might have further disincentivized reporting abuse. The danger that the current abusive authorities might be replaced with equally (or potentially more) abusive new ones could have somewhat tempered individuals' eagerness to seek justice against oppression—particularly during times of economic or military difficulty, when many local officials were under significant financial pressures of their own.

Sanctions

Finally, we should consider the impact of *sanctions* on how government representatives behaved in their interactions with the ruler and taxpayers. In

---

[22] For examples of such defensive counterpetitions, see entries 169 in *82 Numaralı Mühimme Defteri* (2000); and 317 and 519 in *14 Numaralı Atik Şikayet Defteri* (Erdem 2017).

[23] The same qadis quoted by Naima (2007: 2:720) bring up the dangers of reporting the abuse of local officials as follows: "When we try to end the oppression of a certain voyvoda or cizye-collector in our jurisdictions (either ourselves or by petitioning to the capital), the latter accuse us of obstructing the collection of the ruler's property, accepting bribes [from the taxpayers], [unnecessarily] protecting the flock, and preventing our service. They would have us dismissed from our positions by such lies and slanders." For a consistent mühimme entry from about the same period (1630/1), see entry 146 in *85 Numaralı Mühimme Defteri* (2002), where the qadis of Bosnia are accused of unduly interfering with the extractive efforts of the local tımar- and zeamet-holders and ordered to cease their involvements and petitions against them. Aşık Çelebi (2018: 203–4) identified parallel anxieties among the qadis about a century earlier.

[24] This is why, according to Faroqhi (1992: 2), "even after the complainants had received a rescript in their favour, it was probably in most cases impossible to get it implemented without further activities that in our system of categorization would be considered political."

their modeling based on Qing China, Kiser and Tong (1992: 304–5) suggest that the ruler might employ a combination of positive and negative sanctions in his attempts to influence his agents' behavior. The positive sanctions might include rewards in the form of salaries or other sources of revenue, official recognitions, and promotions.[25] Negative sanctions could take the form of punishments such as public shaming, temporary or permanent dismissal from office, seizure of assets, exile, imprisonment, and corporal (including capital) punishment.

In the Ottoman context, we should expect to observe that competence, experience, and dedication to good government generally corresponded to material rewards and high positions in government service. In fact, the representation of the polity as a meritocracy that rewarded good service was common in late medieval and early modern Europe (Busbequius 1744: 75; Meeker 2001: 110–14; Lockman 2004: 44–5). However, it is not clear whether positive sanctions were consistently used to promote moral government. First, the literature on the emergence and proliferation of oligarchic networks involving the vizier and paşa households and powerful provincial families, at least after the sixteenth century, suggests that factors other than loyalty to the ruler or dedication to public good must have influenced appointment and promotion patterns in government service (see Chapter 8). Second, in those times when the state's short-term interests might conflict with the interests of the taxpayers, the enforcement of sanctions that advanced the former might mean curbing those intended to encourage good government. During periods of economic difficulty, for example, the need to sell high-level offices and auction lucrative revenue sources to the highest bidders in order to generate short-term windfalls might close off measures that advanced the careers or enhanced the incomes of non-corrupt government representatives. In such instances, simply put, the cost of allocating government positions and revenue sources based solely on good service or character might have been high.

---

[25] Scholars of corruption generally agree that the abuse of taxpayers tends to intensify when the government officials' incomes are low compared to their expenses (Hurstfield 1967: 26–7; Zelin 1984: 37–45; Prest 1991: 77, 93, and *passim*; Ni and Van 2006: 318–23), which might have been the case in the Ottoman context as well (see Chapter 5). However, according to Kiser and Tong (1992: 305), "the effect of salary increases on compliance is not linear. It will be greatest at the lowest levels, but will suffer from diminishing returns at higher levels.... At the lowest levels, salary increases can keep corruption low by making officials dependent on rulers, but only if monitoring is good enough that rulers can detect and dismiss corrupt officials.... Because these conditions are often not present, we predict that increasing salaries of lower officials will decrease corruption more than increasing salaries of higher officials." Jakob Svensson (2005: 33) suggested that in modern settings, "paying higher wages can deter corruption under certain circumstances."

To gauge the effectiveness of negative sanctions against corruption, on the other hand, one should start with surveying the types of punishments inflicted on abusive behavior. I will return to the implications of Kiser and Tong's modeling in this regard after I complete this task. As I discussed earlier (Chapter 1), Islamic jurisprudential sources prescribe tazir, or discretionary, punishments for a limited number of offenses that can be associated with corruption. These prescriptions are "discretionary" in the sense that those authorized to enforce the law punish offenders on a case-by-case basis, depending on the nature of the crime, the damage it caused, the status and previous history of the perpetrator(s), and the identity of the victim(s). According to jurisprudential traditions, tazir punishments can range from a simple (even non-verbal) chastisement to public shaming, imprisonment for a period of time, or bodily beatings.[26] In general, it was common for premodern jurists to recommend relatively lenient tazir punishments for offenders with high status, all else being equal (Peters 2005: 66; Midilli 2019: 128). In the Ottoman context, the most popular jurisprudential prescription for qadis who accept bribes is dismissal from their positions, although jurists disagree about whether this was supposed to be automatic or based on the political authority's decision (Chapter 2). This tendency does not necessarily mean that harsher punishments were never imposed on dishonest Ottoman qadis, as we will see later in this chapter. On the other hand, fiqh-based punitive prescriptions for deliberate false witnessing ranged from public shaming to corporal punishment. The more lenient options, those that excluded beating and long terms of imprisonment, seem to be popular among Ottoman jurists, at least before the seventeenth and eighteenth centuries.

As I observed in Chapter 3, state-issued commands, directives, and correspondence contain more comprehensive references to abuse and predatory maladministration by non-judicial actors than jurisprudential sources. This is why we might also expect them to include specific punitive prescriptions for such acts. Generally, kanunnames contain broad lists of crimes. Based on twenty-two kanunnames with general (empire-wide) and more limited (provincial or sub-provincial) coverage from the fifteenth and sixteenth centuries, I counted more than eighty different crime specifications (including sexual, moral/religious, against persons, against property, and so on), each of which

---

[26] According to jurisprudential traditions, the harshest tazir cannot exceed in severity the most lenient hadd punishment, or penalties with fixed prescriptions based on scriptural or prophetic sources, which is commonly identified as forty (sometimes eighty) lashes for the public consumption of alcohol. Thus, various jurists identified the most severe tazir punishment as thirty-nine (or seventy-nine or seventy-five) lashes (Peters 2005: 53–67).

prescribed punishments, including variations according to the identities of the culprits (men, women, slaves, non-Muslims, married adults, adolescents). The lists even contain demonstrably obscure sub-variations of crimes and their punishments, such as "demanding bread and yogurt from travelers"; "parenting sons who allow themselves to be penetrated by others"; "having intercourse with animals"; "Muslims selling alcohol"; and "intentionally abandoning daily prayers" (Akgündüz 1990–6: 3:89–93). Table 4.1 provides a selection of crimes and punitive prescriptions based on the General Kanunname of Süleyman (d. 1566) for demonstrative purposes.

Despite this level of specificity, however, the kanunnames list almost no punishments for unsanctioned extraction or other types of abuse by government authorities, including many acts that we moderns perceive as crimes of corruption.[27] The significance of this observation becomes obvious if we consider the clear and detailed punitive prescriptions in the criminal code of Qing China, another highly bureaucratic imperial entity. This point is highlighted by the remarkably precise information in Table 4.2 based on the Qing code (Park 1997: 972).[28]

No comparable categorization is possible for the Ottoman polity in the pre-Tanzimat era. How do we explain this discrepancy and what does it say about Ottoman strategies to punish predatory maladministration? According to Leslie Peirce (2003: 117), kanunnames are "blueprint[s] for organizing and administrating the vast agrarian and commercially based domain that was the Ottoman Empire."[29] As such, they are codes that contain state directives on a variety of issues, including urban and rural taxation, land use, market organization, manufacturing, and artisanal production. This may explain why the

---

[27] In the 120 or so specific clauses that Heyd regards as the "Ottoman Criminal Code" in the General Kanunname of Süleyman, only three contain references to crimes committed by government appointees, and none prescribes a specific punishment for those crimes. One of these clauses indicates that tımar-holders identified as thieves should be apprehended and reported to the capital (Heyd 1973: 118; cf. Akgündüz 1990–6: 4:302). The second and third merely forbid the local authorities from punishing and collecting fines from common folk without qadis' verdicts against them (Heyd 1973: 127). Among those acts that might be associated with corruption, punishments are prescribed only for false witnessing and forging documents, crimes not specific to government functionaries. According to the Kanunname of Süleyman, false witnesses should be chastised and publicly shamed. Those who forge documents should also be chastised and subjected to corporal punishment. The hands of those who habitually falsify documents should be amputated (Akgündüz 1990–6: 4:303; cf. Heyd 1973: 121).

[28] For institutional and philosophical bases of the Qing efforts to control corruption, see Akçetin 2021.

[29] Colin Imber (1997a: Ch. 1) suggests that kanunnames were shaped by local, "feudal" customs and practices in tax collection, land use, and administrative matters that Ottomans encountered in conquered territories. Codes for specific locations and communities could vary significantly; see also Barkan 1943: xxi–xxxiv; Heyd 1973: 38–40; and İnalcık 1978b: 562.

Table 4.1 Select Crimes and Punishments in the General Kanunname ("Kanunname-i Osmani") of Sultan Süleyman

Crime	Punishment
Illicit intercourse by a married man	If not death by stoning (*recm*), a fine of 400 akçes from the wealthy; 50 akçes from middle-income and poor individuals
Illicit intercourse by an adolescent/unmarried male	A fine of 100 akçes from the well-off; 50 akçes from the middle-income; 30 akçes from the poor
Illicit intercourse by a (married) woman	Same as the punishment for the (married) man; let her husband pay her fine
Illicit intercourse by an unmarried female	Same as the punishment for the adolescent male
If a woman commits fornication and her husband keeps her	A fine of 100 akçes from the well-off (husband); 50 akçes from the middle-income; 40 or 30 akçes from the poor
Pimping by a female	Tazir, including chastisement and public shaming; corporal punishment can be converted to a fine at the rate of an akçe for a stroke
Illicit intercourse, perpetuated by slaves	Same as the punishments for free persons
If someone approaches another's wife, or kisses her, or licks her, or touches/rubs against her	Tazir; can be converted to a fine at the rate of an akçe for a stroke
If someone kidnaps a virgin or enters in the house of another with the intention to commit illicit intercourse	Castration of the perpetrator
If someone rips the collar of another during a fight	Tazir in the form of chastisement; no fines necessary
If someone pulls and tears someone's else's moustache or beard during a fight	Tazir, presumably including chastisement; corporal punishment can be converted to a fine of 20 akçes for the well-off and 10 akçes for the poor
If someone injures and bleeds another's head during a fight	Tazir, including chastisement; corporal punishment can be converted to a fine of 30 akçes
If someone ambushes and shoots arrows at someone	The perpetrator's arrows should be stuck to him and he should be publicly displayed ("oku sancub gezdireler")
If someone ambushes and displays his knife to someone (as a threat)	Tazir, including chastisement; a fine of 50 akçes

Continued

Table 4.1 *Continued*

Crime	Punishment
If someone intentionally dislocates another's eye or tooth	Retaliation in kind (*kısas*); no fines; if retaliation is not pursued or necessary, a fine of 200 akçes
If women fight	If they are not among honorable women (*muhadderattan*), a tazir punishment of maximum forty strokes, which could be converted to a fine at the rate of 1 akçe for three strokes
Murder	Retaliation in kind; if retaliation is not pursued or possible, a fine of 400 akçes
If a Muslim drinks, produces, or sells wine	Tazir, including chastisement; corporal punishment can be converted to a fine at the rate of 1 akçe for two strokes
If someone steals geese or duck	Tazir, including chastisement; corporal punishment can be converted to a fine at the rate of 1 akçe for two strokes
If someone steals a beehive, sheep, or lamb	If the act causes significant financial damage, the thief's hand should be amputated; if not, the punishment is tazir, including chastisement; corporal punishment can be converted to a fine at the rate of an akçe for a stroke
If someone steals a horse or mule or donkey, or head of cattle	Corporal punishment (*siyaset edeler*): amputation of his hand
If someone enters a garden and steals fruit	Tazir, including chastisement; corporal punishment can be converted to a fine at the rate of 1 akçe for two strokes
If someone intentionally abandons prayer	Tazir, including chastisement; corporal punishment can be converted to a fine at a rate of 1 akçe for two strokes

Source: Akgündüz 1990–6: 4:296–305; cf. Heyd 1973: 93–131.

kanunnames outline specific prescriptions for some types of crime but not others.[30]

In regard to the administration of justice, kanunnames appear to function as handy guides to help local authorities implement a generally sharia-consistent enforcement without having to go through volumes of fiqh treaties accumulated by generations of jurists.[31] Indeed, the punitive prescriptions listed in

---

[30] Midilli (2019: 275–6) confirms my impression regarding the types of punitive prescriptions in the kanunnames: "[Classical Ottoman penal laws] generally concern the affairs of the reaya...They tend not to include penalties based on the siyasa,...inflicted on the askeri class due to their faults and errors while in office. The Ottoman law codes contain very few prescriptions regarding the official responsibilities of the askeri class."

[31] Thus, various historians regarded kanunnames as evidence of a high degree of standardization and bureaucratization in Ottoman administrative apparatus; see Akgündüz 1990–6: 1:78–135; and Midilli 2019: 58–60. For an alternative view, see Heyd 1973: 180–3. For a broader look at this topic, see Ergene 2014.

Table 4.2 "The Punishment Scale for Salaried Persons...Convicted of Corruption" in Qinq China

Punishment	Value of the Spoils		
	Bribes for Unlawful Favors	Bribes for Lawful Favors	Influence Peddling
Light Bamboo			
20 blows			under 1 tael
30 blows			1–10 taels
40 blows			20 taels
50 blows			30 taels
Heavy Bamboo			
60 blows		under 1 tael	40 taels
70 blows	under 1 tael	1–10 taels	50 taels
80 blows	1–5 taels	20 taels	60 taels
90 blows	10 taels	30 taels	70 taels
100 blows	15 taels	40 taels	80 taels
Penal Servitude			
1 yr and 60 blows	20 taels	50 taels	100 taels
1.5 yrs and 70 blows	25 taels	60 taels	200 taels
2 yrs and 80 blows	30 taels	70 taels	300 taels
2.5 yrs and 90 blows	35 taels	80 taels	400 taels
3 yrs and 100 blows	40 taels	90 taels	500 taels
Exile			
2,000 li and 100 blows	45 taels	100 taels	N/A
2,500 li and 100 blows	50 taels	110 taels	
3,000 li and 100 blows	55 taels	120 taels	
Capital Punishment			
Strangulation after the Assizes	over 80 taels	over 120 taels	N/A

Note: Adopted from Park 1997: 972, in simplified form.

Süleyman's kanunname demonstrate an intimate relationship with established jurisprudential traditions: they appear to be based on the types of crimes extensively discussed in the works of jurisprudence, and they prescribe fiqh-based punishment categories (qisas and tazir, in particular) in their treatment. The kanunname also reveals the distinctive approach in fiqh traditions of differentiating punishments based on the identity of the culprits (including, for example, whether one is married/adult or unmarried/adolescent; male or female; free or slave; Muslim or non-Muslim).[32]

---

[32] Despite the close link with jurisprudential traditions, Ottoman kanunnames also function to convert the implementation of Islamic law into a revenue stream. When, for example, a crime calls for a tazir punishment, the texts often allow it to be converted to a fine, that is, a monetary reward for local officials (Heyd 1973: 181–3, 275–98). Thus, the texts' relationship with jurisprudential traditions does not signal the political authority's passivity in its role as the implementer of justice. Rather, those in

The lack of references to punishments for extractive transgressions by government officials might be due to the fact that (a) the inherited fiqh traditions lack specificity in the realms of government and fiscal affairs in general and offenses committed by state authorities in their positions of power in particular, which makes it impossible to compile, organize, and present them and their associated punishments in a format consistent with other types of crimes; and/or (b) the relationship between the ruler and his servants followed a different logic and was managed according to an alternate set of principles associated with siyasa, ones less bounded by fiqh traditions for sharia-subjects and thus more cognizant of the sociopolitical hierarchy and its power differentials.

Let me elaborate on the latter point. As indicated earlier, the relationship between the ruler and his agents in many premodern Islamic contexts was significantly influenced by political and philosophical sources other than fiqh traditions. Although siyasa might represent a realm within the Islamic legal system, just as fiqh is, it is based largely on extra-divine traditions of government. Notions and issues pertaining to the ruler's authority and his relationship to his servants, including his expectations from them and how they might be disciplined when these go unfulfilled, are part of the siyasa's concern.[33]

Following this train of thought, it is worth stressing that the rationales for punishment in fiqh and siyasa traditions diverge. In fiqh, punishments for crimes against one another are decided through assessments of "what was done" (murder, illicit intercourse, robbery, etc.) and "by whom" (man or women, free or slave, Muslim or non-Muslim, wealthy or poor), largely in a gradated prescriptive framework, which associates certain types of punishment with specific types of crime. The actual consequences of a crime do sometimes matter in determining its punishments—for example, when a

---

power seek to benefit from this role financially in a way many Hanafi scholars considered inappropriate or flat-out illegal. In Hanafi traditions, while a handful of jurists (including Abu Yusuf) acknowledged the propriety of claiming criminals' assets, this was supposed to be a temporary measure until the latter redeemed or rehabilitated themselves, after which their assets were supposed to be returned to them. Financial penalties claimed by the political authority appear to have gained their first support by some Transoxianian jurists after the twelfth century (Köksal 2016: 128–9).

[33] This is consistent with how most researchers define siyasa in the Ottoman context—that is, as the ruler's legislative authority in those areas where jurisprudential traditions provide inadequate guidance. There are wide-ranging opinions among Ottomanists about the extent to which the siyasa challenged pretexting jurisprudential opinions; on this issue, see Ergene 2014; and Köksal 2016: 111–16, and *passim*. The claim that fiqh- and siyasa-based legal interpretations originate from separate conceptions of social order does not necessarily mean that they collectively constituted an inherently unstable legal system or that the siyasa legislation rendered the Ottoman legal traditions "secular," as some historians have argued in the past. Rather, I would generally agree with the (now prevalent) position that siyasa legislation filled in the jurisprudential gaps in a fashion that did not explicitly contradict jurisprudential rulings, although tensions did exist between the two.

fistfight leads to a ripped collar or a broken bone. But this consideration is one of many factors used to determine the punishment, and often not the primary one.

In siyasa traditions, however—and consistent with the Circle's functional logic, which prioritizes the long-term wellbeing of the ruler's patrimony—the question of consequence might be the critical factor in determining the punishment for a criminal act based on the damage it might inflict on the tax base. Thus, acts of a certain nature that would not cause as much damage in some situations as in others should accordingly receive different forms and degrees of punishment.[34] Also relevant in determining how to punish crimes against the ruler's interests would be the *consequences of the punishment*. Types of punishment that might incur high costs by the ruler's calculations might be avoided, postponed, or treated leniently. In general, scholars emphasize the considerable discretionary privileges of those in power in both the adjudication (Heyd 1973: 192–5)[35] and the punishment (Peters 2005: 67–8)[36] of crimes under siyasa jurisdiction—certainly broader than in fiqh-based processes involving sharia-subjects.

Therefore, it would make sense for the kanunnames and other state-issued documents *not* to prescribe specific punishments for abusive and predatory behavior by government officials. This situation would also explain the inconsistency that Ahmet Mumcu (1985: 26–33) noted in the imperial government's

---

[34] In siyasa traditions, punishments do not necessarily require specific acts of crime but can be imposed based on a perception of threat to the order and the political authority's control over it. See Köksal 2016: 35, 50, and *passim*. According to Peters (2005: 67-8), whereas fiqh-based *"ta'zīr"* punishment can only be imposed for acts that are forbidden by the Shari'a, *siyāsa* punishment may be administered for *any* act threatening public order, regardless of whether or not the perpetrator is blamed for it." Also, "for *ta'zīr* [the aim for punishment] is in the first place [to] reform the offender and in the second place deterrence. *Siyāsa* justice, on the other hand, is administered in the public interest, to protect society from persons whose acts constitute a danger to law and order (*fitna*)." In the Ottoman context, the ruler or his representatives were often the people who defined what constituted "public interest" and "danger to law and order."

[35] According to Heyd (1973: 193), in such adjudications, suspects were frequently "punished (and more particularly executed) siyâseten without having been tried in a cadi's mahkeme or in another court of law (such as a divân). This was done especially when the accused was caught *flagrante delicto* or when nothing could be legally proved against him. In many cases the Sultan or the Grand Vizier first asked for a fetvâ legalizing such punishment, but they often considered it unnecessary to obtain the consent of the ulemâ."

[36] Both fiqh and siyasa traditions allow those in power to impose discretionary punishments, but in fiqh-based punishments there are certain standards that must be observed. For example, tazir punishments in fiqh should not be as severe as the punishments for hadd crimes or murder with intent. Thus, they cannot include execution or amputation of limbs. They should also not involve torture, excessively long terms of imprisonment, fines, or punitive seizure of one's property. Furthermore, in tazir-based beatings, there are certain expectations regarding the nature and length of the staff that can be used for inflicting pain, how the staff should be held, where on the body the offender can be struck, and what he or she is allowed to wear. No such limitations exist for siyasa punishments. See Başoğlu 2011; and Midilli 2019: 86–99.

efforts to punish specific zulüm crimes by state authorities (cf. Koç 2017: 273–306).[37] In such cases, punishments could range from chastising culprits and requiring them to return what they obtained through abuse to expulsion from office, corporal punishment, imprisonment, banishment, penal servitude (in the galleys), confiscation of property, and execution.[38]

Clearly, the Ottoman legal system gave those in power the ability and tools to effectively punish corruption; there seems to be little disagreement on this issue in the scholarship. However, the relative effectiveness of these punishments and the limits on the ruler's prerogative to punish those who committed crimes against his or the taxpayers' interests, or both, have received less systematic attention. Based on Kiser and Tong's insights, the following considerations might be relevant in this regard.

Among possible punishments for corruption, chastising perpetrators and forcing them to return misappropriated goods to victims might have been relatively weak sanctions, since they "amounted to little more than restoring the precorruption status quo" (Kiser and Tong 1992: 315). But the same factor must have also made them relatively "inexpensive" from the ruler's perspective, and thus incentivized their frequent employment. While sanctions that involved expulsion from office and more severe punishments might have generated stronger disincentives against corruption, they must have also come with higher costs. According to Kiser and Tong (1992: 305), the cost of removing officials from their posts might be considerable if the "reserve army" of replacement officials is in short supply or "competence is gained only on the job." In the Ottoman context, the government might have had reasons to disregard this problem for extended periods after the sixteenth century, when growing numbers of government officials were competing for limited numbers of administrative and judicial posts (see Chapter 5).

At the same time, sanctions that led to government authorities' removal from their offices might also have meant the elimination of good extractors; that is, officials who were competent and reliable in collecting and conveying the revenues vital to the polity. This might have been less of a problem if the ruler's interests perfectly aligned with those of the common people: in such

---

[37] Mumcu (1985: 47) also notes that the zulüm crimes were often treated on a case-by-case basis based on a multitude of factors, including (but not limited to), the imperial center's temperamental and strategic priorities; its ability to enforce its authority in different provincial settings; the pressures it received from various centers of influence; and the abusers' own power and connections. Thus, various attempts to punish the relevant crimes generated very dissimilar repercussions for the culprits.

[38] On confiscation of property (müsadere), see Arslantaş 2017. According to the author (94), this punishment was used for serious bribery and embezzlement crimes between 1750 and 1839. In many cases, it could accompany dismissal from position, banishment, and execution (96).

cases the potential short-term disruptions to extraction might have been a reasonable trade-off for the long-term wellbeing of the tax base. But in cases where they did not—again, for example, in times of economic difficulties—the ruler's heightened concern for unimpeded revenue flow must have raised the cost of punishing state agents who prioritized the ruler's interests along with their own over those of the taxpayers.[39]

Particularly severe punishments could have "expensive" political consequences (Arslantaş 2017: 46, 98, 115–17, *passim*). The banishment, imprisonment, seizure of the property, or execution of officials who were well connected in the capital or enjoyed the support of influential provincial networks, or those who had developed independent political and military bases of power, might have generated debilitating tensions, even threats of violence, that would have required significant resources to defuse.[40] The substantial cost of eliminating such power brokers might have forced the center to be lenient. As many researchers have observed (for example, İnalcık 1965: 88; Heyd 1973: 263; Darling 2013: 144), Ottoman state directives and communications (including adaletnames) contain frequent threats of very harsh punishment against both military-administrative and religious-judicial officials who abuse their authority in their jurisdictions, including penal servitude in the galleys, being "pound[ed] in stone mortars" (*dibekte döğülmek*), being subjected to "brutal pain" (*eşedd-i azab*), and "severe corporal and capital punishment" (*salb ve siyaset*). In the context of our discussion, while we might acknowledge that the severity of the potential sanctions might have lowered the crime rates (Kiser and Tong 1992: 308), scholars have also considered that emphatic or frequent *threats* of such severe punishments might imply that they were infrequently enforced. In other words, the promise of harsh penalties might have been used to compensate for the fact that such punishments were costly and rare.[41]

---

[39] In fact, it might have been a safer bet for the corrupt officers to enhance their own intakes at the expense of the taxpayers rather than the state. Here we should note Mumcu's (1985: 31, 47) observation that the imperial center could forgive and reappoint previously dismissed officials, often when the latter could provide financial compensation in return for such actions. In such cases, payment-for-reappointment schemes would amount to generating additional disincentives for the government to keep the corrupt agents out of service.

[40] Yasin Arslantaş's (2017: 142–3 and 244–5) research on the confiscation of property for crimes including (but not limited to) corruption in the late eighteenth and early nineteenth centuries demonstrates that this sanction was indeed sensitive to considerations of costs and benefits. Factors that influenced the latter included the distance of the property subject to seizure from the center, the bargaining powers of the individuals subject to the sanction, and the composition of their wealth that determined its "confiscability."

[41] See Park 1997 and Ni and Van 2006 for studies of corruption in imperial China, where severe punitive prescriptions for corruption were only rarely accompanied by enforcement. According to Ni and Van (2006: 322), the probability of a Chinese official being punished for corruption might have been less than one tenth of 1 percent in the eighteenth century.

Here, then, is a simple conceptual template that highlights a few important factors relevant to the fight against corruption. Research on this topic in the Ottoman context is inherently prone to certain methodological shortcomings. It tends to be anecdotal because it often relies on inductive generalizations based on a few historical cases. And it disregards the fact that successful acts of corruption rarely left any trace in the archive. A model like the one presented above is useful not because it captures the past in all its complexity, but because it might allow us to form historically informed, realistic expectations about the topic.

The Ottoman polity had possessed tools and mechanisms to limit abusive behavior by government officials. In particular, I noted how the imperial center might have measured the tax base, monitored the activities of provincial authorities, and sanctioned good and bad behavior. But the polity also lacked the ability or willingness to eliminate all predatory behavior and instead strived simply to keep it under a certain level—a situation that was surely not unique to the Ottomans. Based on the discussion thus far, the following are some of the more important considerations that influenced the state's efforts to control corruption:

1. The tahrir surveys allowed the imperial center to assess the burden placed on productive groups by local officials, but they were imprecise and infrequently updated because of the costs associated with such endeavors. In the seventeenth century they would disappear entirely, further reducing the polity's ability to accurately measure the revenue sources.
2. Monitoring and sanctioning corruption in distant locales must have been especially costly and therefore difficult.
3. Corruption by low-level officials that affected relatively limited numbers of taxpayers or did not exceed a certain threshold (monetary or otherwise) in terms of the harm it caused might have been regarded as not worth pursuing. Thus, the imperial center might have often chosen to overlook low-level corruption, making it, in turn, endemic to the system.[42]
4. The government might have had political disincentives to fight against abuse by provincial powerholders.

---

[42] According to Kiser and Tong (1992: 306), "Lower level officials are most difficult to monitor because they are the most numerous and the farthest removed from the ruler.... Moreover, salaries tend to be lower for those at the bottom of bureaucratic hierarchies. For these reasons we predict corruption will be the greatest at the lower levels of state fiscal systems."

5. From the perspective of state officials who sought to maximize their interests, it might have made sense to try to accomplish this objective against the interests of the taxpayers rather than those of the ruler.
6. Ottoman imperial documents lack precise prescriptions about how to punish various acts of corruption, compared to the degree of detail available in jurisprudential works, even though the latter focuses narrowly on a handful of judicial functionaries and limited types of misdemeanors. Generally, the lack of consistent punishments for many kinds of non-judicial crimes might have tempted more daring government officials to push the envelope toward excessive extraction when they recognized lucrative opportunities.

If we consider a few factors discussed above in combination with others, additional possibilities emerge. For example, all else being equal, in periods of poor measurement of the tax base, the imperial center could potentially fight corruption by enhancing the monitoring of potential offenders. But if the government remained hesitant to bear the additional cost of monitoring, or if its efforts still failed to keep corruption under a tolerable level, the optimal choice might have been to enhance the frequency of serious sanctions. In contrast, in circumstances where the government's measurement ability was strong but the two control mechanisms (monitoring and sanctions) remained weak, the likelihood of collusion involving state agents and taxpayers at the expense of the ruler's interests might have increased (Kiser and Tong 1992: 306).

We can further complicate the implications of the model, for example by considering the possibility of collusion among multiple state agents or the taxpayers' responses to demands of extraction. In the Ottoman context, connections based on household (*kapı*) affiliations, ethno-regional (*cins*) solidarity (Kunt 1974), and/or long-term association in government service must have made self-interested cooperation among government functionaries viable, if not probable, and attempts to control them more difficult or costlier (Tirole 1986).[43] Then again, the taxpayers' ability to flee persecution, evade extraction by hiding assets, collude with local officials against the state's financial impositions, or rebel against perceived oppression must have also influenced the state agents' and imperial center's actions regarding wealth

---

[43] The policy of awarding short-term tenures to government agents in their posts and rotating them frequently might have been an effective measure against this tendency.

extraction and measures to limit corruption (Kiser and Tong 1992: 307–8).[44] To appreciate the importance of taxpayer strategies to avoid illegitimate extraction, we might reconsider one scenario mentioned above. When the imperial government's ability to measure the tax base was strong but its ability to control the actions of the agents weak, the chances for collusion between the agents and taxpayers might have been high. In circumstances where taxpayers lacked the resources to collude with local officials (against the interests of the imperial center) but were able to cooperate among themselves as a collective, however, they might have rebelled against any act of extraction instead of cooperating with local officials.

Corruption as Represented in the Mühimme, Şikayet, and Kalebend Registers

The previous section helps us think systematically about how the Ottomans controlled corruption in the pre-Tanzimat era and the limitations of these attempts. This section presents a more empirically focused discussion. First, it surveys how acts associated with corruption were represented in one group of documents linked to Ottoman efforts to manage corruption: the petitions to the imperial council as found in select mühimme and şikayet registers. Then it examines the information in kalebend registers regarding punishments imposed on those convicted for crimes of corruption.

As various scholars have detailed (for example, Faroqhi 1993; Emecen 2005), mühimme and şikayet registers contain records of matters discussed and decided in the imperial council and copies of rescripts issued in the name of the ruler, although the documents in the mühimmes seem to include a broader range of concerns, including, for example, diplomatic matters, warfare, and pilgrimage to Mecca.[45] Şikayet registers, which first emerged in the mid-seventeenth century, might be seen as more narrowly focused collections,

---

[44] According to Kiser and Tong (1992: 307–8), a number of factors determine taxpayers' strategies: "Exit strategies will be more frequent among subjects with mobile assets [animals], and among those living close to political borders.... The taxpayers will conceal assets when measurement is difficult or costly.... Colluding with other taxpayers in a revolt... is by far the most costly form of tax avoidance, and thus will only be chosen as a last resort."

[45] Scholars have identified about 260 or so mühimmes in the Ottoman archives that cover, with significant gaps, the years between 1544/45 and 1905 (Faroqhi 1993; Emecen 2005: 108–10). Şikayet registers might have first emerged in 1649 (or perhaps a bit later; see Emecen 2005: 128) and then split into a few more specialized series in the mid-eighteenth century. The collection comprises a couple of hundred registers (Aktaş 1991).

containing documents generally (if not exclusively) about taxation, provincial administration, security, legal disputes and law enforcement, and waqf affairs, and often in response to concerns conveyed to the imperial center by provincial peoples and authorities.[46]

Of interest here in both registers are orders and communications generated by the central bureaucracy in response to petitions regarding allegations of corruption. More specifically, the correspondence I focus on concerns illegal and excessive extraction of resources from common folk; distributive conflicts and improprieties among government functionaries over revenue sources; embezzlement, bribery, and collusion among government authorities; false witnessing, forgery, and the use of fake documents; and, more vaguely, "negligence" in government service.

The following discussion is based on five mühimme and three şikayet registers that selectively cover a period from the mid-sixteenth century to the early eighteenth (Table 4.3). They contain material pertaining mainly to the central lands of the polity in the Balkans and Anatolia but also occasionally to Syria and a few other places. Because mühimme and şikayet registers usually contain hundreds and sometimes thousands of entries, I make the daunting surveying task more manageable by deliberately choosing registers that have been transliterated in Latin script, indexed, and, when possible, made searchable by keyword. I used five mühimme registers published by Turkey's Directorate of State Archives (Devlet Arşivleri Genel Müdürlüğü). To the best of my knowledge, there is no comparable rendering of the complaint registers by archival authorities. For this reason, I used transliterations of three şikayet registers published by graduate students as part of their master's thesis projects. The ones that I chose for my analysis are, to my mind, of high quality.[47] In three registers of significant size (mühimme registers 3 and 7 and şikayet register 4), I surveyed sufficiently large portions of the material in terms of coverage durations or entry numbers, but did not attempt to examine the registers in their entirety.[48] In all registers I surveyed in full or in part, I read every entry to decide whether it contained relevant information and, if so, to properly classify it.

---

[46] But see Emecen 2005: 128–9, for doubts about such attempts to differentiate the two collections based on their substantive coverage. Indeed, in a few late seventeenth-century şikayet registers Tuğluca (2010: 11–14) has observed significant numbers of entries concerning diplomatic and war-related matters.

[47] Reading and analyzing multiple mühimme and şikayet registers "from scratch" is a labor-intensive and time-consuming process. Only a few scholarly studies have pursued this task; the ones that do exist survey only a handful of such registers, and justifiably so. See Taş 2007 and Tuğluca 2010 for good examples of such attempts.

[48] In these registers, I examined all sequentially-dated entries in a particular sub-period, rather than all entries. I have no reason to believe that this selection has an impact on my findings.

Table 4.3 Mühimme and Şikayet Registers Explored

Register	Range of Dates Covered in the Register	Total Number of Entries in the Register	Source
Mühimme #3	Jun. 1559–Dec. 1560	1,665*	*3 Numaralı Mühimme Defteri; 966–968/1558–1560* (1993). Ankara: T. C. Başbakanlık Devlet Arşivleri Genel Müdürlüğü.
Mühimme #7	Aug. 1567–Dec. 1568	1,980*	*7 Numaralı Mühimme Defteri (975–976/1567–1569) [Özet-Transkripsiyon-İndeks]* (1998). Vol. 1. Ankara: T. C. Başbakanlık Devlet Arşivleri Genel Müdürlüğü.
Mühimme #82	Oct. 1617–Nov. 1618	371	*82 Numaralı Mühimme Defteri (1026–1027/1617–1618) [Özet-Transkripsiyon-İndeks ve Tıpkıbasım]* (2000). Ankara: T. C. Başbakanlık Devlet Arşivleri Genel Müdürlüğü.
Mühimme #85	Nov. 1630–Aug. 1631	717	*85 Numaralı Mühimme Defteri (1040–1041 (1042)/1630–1631 (1632)) [Özet-Transkripsiyon-İndeks]* (2002). Ankara: T. C. Başbakanlık Devlet Arşivleri Genel Müdürlüğü.
Mühimme #91	Mar. 1646–Jan. 1647	506	*91 Numaralı Mühimme Defteri (H. 1056/M. 1646–1647) [Özet-Çeviriyazı-Tıpkıbasım]* (2015). Istanbul: T. C. Başbakanlık Devlet Arşivleri Genel Müdürlüğü.
Şikayet #4	May 1665–Jul. 1670	2,065*	Yasemin Tataroğlu (2015). "4 Numaralı Atik Şikâyet Defteri 1665–1670 (H. 1975–1081); Transkripsiyon ve Değerlendirilmesi." Master's thesis, Marmara University, Istanbul.
Şikayet #14	Jul. 1690–Feb. 1691	820	Ümit Baki Erdem (2017). "14 Numaralı Atik Şikâyet Defteri (H. 1101–1102/M. 1690–1691): Transkripsiyon ve Değerlendirilmesi." Master's thesis, Marmara University, Istanbul.
Şikayet #38	Mar.–Aug. 1703	473	Şeyma Çil (2018). "38 Numaralı Atik Şikâyet Defteri (1114–1115/1703) (İnceleme-Metin)." Master's thesis, Marmara University, Istanbul.

* Partially surveyed in the following analysis. See Table 4.4 for details.

A few caveats on these sources and my findings. First, we cannot be sure that bureaucratic conventions remained consistent across different eras in terms of how various types of complaints were received, evaluated, deemed credible (or not), recorded, and acted on. Thus, any comparison across registers should be considered, at best, tentative. Also, specific mühimme or şikayet registers do not necessarily contain all complaints received in a particular period: it is common to find reports from the same era scattered across multiple separate registers. Consequently, comparisons among specific categories or classifications pertaining to crime types or groups involved in them across registers should be based not on absolute numbers or monthly averages, but perhaps on their *relative* representations *within* the same register.

Moreover, despite best efforts to remain consistent when counting and categorizing specific information found in the registers, it is not always possible to guarantee that figures refer to precisely identical phenomena in every single register. In some cases, the categorization of an alleged offender as a military-administrative official is a judgment call: if the document in question does not explicitly specify this point, readers are forced to reconstruct the events and identities mentioned in them in their minds. In others, the distinction between acts of illegal or excessive extraction justified by presumed entitlements and crimes of unjustified usurpation could be vague. Just as importantly, the researcher's ability to make consistent judgments regarding categorization across thousands of documents that change shape over time is not guaranteed.[49] Because of my concerns about how such factors might affect my attempts at categorization, I surveyed my sample of documents two separate times to ensure relatively reliable results.

Finally, the reader should bear in mind that a few of my categorizations may be indirect appraisals, rather than direct measures, of specific types of crimes. For example, a tax yield collected by a local agent on behalf of a government authority but not delivered to the latter on time may or may not be an act of "embezzlement." While in some cases I saw fit to categorize such incidents as tantamount to embezzlement, in others I felt it more appropriate to ignore them based on how I read individual entries. My judgments in some cases might be faulty, so the figures provided in the table for this category (and some others) should be considered *potential* indicators of embezzlement (or bribery, or collusion) rather than actual instances of such acts. At the same time, I take the liberty of considering the prevalence of such suspicions of particular

---

[49] For a comprehensive discussion of how the scribal conventions in responses to petitions vary across time and in mühimme and şikayet registers, see Emecen 2005.

crimes in a specific register as (approximate) indicators of their relative frequency. Despite these caveats I am convinced that the figures presented in the following tables help us appreciate how various acts we might associate with corruption are alluded to in government sources from different periods.

Tables 4.4 to 4.6 provide different categorizations and classifications of complaints pertaining to allegations of corruption, based on various considerations about how to define the term and what specific acts to associate it with (Chapter 3). The first of these, Table 4.4, provides the aggregate numbers of complaints by register.

A comparison of the figures in column 4 of Table 4.4 shows a noticeable difference in the relative frequency of reports about allegations of abuse and misconduct attributed to government officials before and after the turn of the seventeenth century. The most straightforward explanation of this shift might be that abuse by government officials became more common after the turn of the century, which would be consistent with the claims made by many contemporary observers and modern historians. But the change might also be related to how and to what extent allegations of abuse were reported to

Table 4.4 Prevalence of Corruption Related Entries in the Registers

Source	Range of Dates Examined 1	Number of Entries Examined in the Register 2	Number of Related Entries (Average/Month) 3	% 4
Mühimme #3	Jun. 1559–Jun. 1560 (13 months)	1,225	96 (7.4)	8
Mühimme #7	Aug. 1567–Mar. 1568 (7 months)	1,000	80 (11.4)	8
Mühimme #82	Oct. 1617–Nov. 1618 (13 months)	371	107 (8.2)	29
Mühimme #85	Nov. 1630–Aug. 1631 (9 months)	717	146 (16.2)	20
Mühimme #91	Mar. 1646–Jan. 1647 (10 months)	506	146 (14.6)	29
Şikayet #4	May 1665–Apr. 1666 (11 months)	696	235 (21.4)	34
Şikayet #14	Jul. 1690–Feb. 1691 (7 months)	820	277 (39.6)	34
Şikayet #38	Mar.–Aug. 1703 (5 months)	473	115 (23.0)	24

Note: In some long registers, only entries from a specific sub-period are surveyed. Individual entries could contain multiple types of transgressions.

the imperial center based on a variety factors, including possible shifts in scribal-bureaucratic procedures as mentioned earlier, access to means of communication, cost-benefit considerations on the part of the aggrieved parties, and so on.

Table 4.5 categorizes the actors involved in alleged crimes reported to the imperial center.[50] The table divides these actors into three basic groups: alleged perpetrators, those who reported complaints to the imperial center (in person, via representatives, or via written communication), and alleged victims. Each group is subdivided according to official responsibilities and/or tax statuses of actors mentioned in the reports.[51] These comprise military-administrative officials, including tımar- and *zeamet*-holders, members of the local janissary regiments and law-enforcers (sing. *subaşı*), fortress commanders, governors, governors-general, collectors of various taxes, and their deputies, representatives, and sub-contractors (sing. *mütesellim*s, voyvodas, *mültezim*s, and such), plus a few others; religious-judicial authorities, including primarily the qadis and naibs but also, in a few instances, local muftis and court functionaries; waqf administrators and affiliates; and the taxpayers and/or local communities, as collective bodies often represented by multiple individuals (who often included tax-exempt persons).

For reasons I listed earlier, the following discussion is based on the percentile figures given in the second line of every row, not the total numbers of complaints or their monthly averages (given in parentheses). The information provided in columns 1 to 4 in Table 4.5 indicates that complaints about military-administrative officials outnumber those against judicial and religious authorities. Given our lack of knowledge on the proportions of military-administrative and judicial-religious authorities in any region, these observations do not allow us to form any opinion as to whether the two groups are over- or underrepresented among alleged perpetrators. It is noteworthy, however, that the proportion of reports against religious-judicial authorities increases significantly in the later registers (up to 35

---

[50] My categorization is inspired and informed by the choices made by other scholars, such as Taş (2007), Tuğluca (2010), and Yörük (2019), who present comparable classifications. The one presented in Table 4.5 is a modified classification based on the specific concerns of my discussion. The reader should note that total figures reported in Tables 4.4, 4.5, and 4.6 vary because individual entries (reported in Table 4.4) may contain multiple complaints (reported in Tables 4.5 and 4.6).

[51] In Table 4.5, the subtotals reported under "complaints against," "complaints by," and "aggrieved" do not have to match because the numbers of corresponding actors in individual entries vary significantly. In many entries, it is difficult to precisely identify or classify the parties who sent petitions to the imperial center or were aggrieved. Thus, in quite a few cases the relevant data is missing.

Table 4.5 Actors Involved in Corruption

Source (date)	Complaints Against				Complaints By				Aggrieved			
	Mil.-adm.	Rel.-jud.	Waqf aff.	Tax-pay./Comm.	Mil.-adm.	Rel.-jud.	Waqf aff.	Tax-pay./Comm.	Mil.-adm.	Rel.-jud.	Waqf aff.	Tax-pay./Comm.
	1	2	3	4	5	6	7	8	9	10	11	12
M. #3 (1559–60)	83 (6.4) 74%	16 (1.2) 14%	4 (0.3) 4%	9 (0.7) 8%	26 (2.0) 41%	24 (1.8) 38%	3 (0.2) 5%	11 (0.8) 17%	20 (1.5) 29%	0 0%	2 (0.2) 3%	46 (3.5) 68%
M. #7 (1567–8)	56 (8.0) 67%	14 (2.0) 17%	6 (0.9) 7%	7 (1.0) 8%	23 (3.3) 46%	20 (2.9) 40%	4 (0.6) 8%	3 (0.4) 6%	14 (2.0) 25%	0 0%	6 (0.9) 11%	35 (5.0) 64%
M. #82 (1617–18)	76 (5.8) 69%	15 (1.2) 14%	13 (1.0) 12%	6 (0.5) 5%	32 (2.5) 42%	9 (0.7) 12%	18 (1.4) 23%	18 (1.4) 23%	34 (2.6) 33%	1 (0.1) 1%	21 (1.6) 21%	46 (3.5) 45%
M. #85 (1630–1)	102 (11.3) 69%	22 (2.4) 15%	18 (2.0) 12%	6 (0.7) 4%	34 (3.8) 29%	25 (2.8) 21%	20 (2.2) 17%	39 (4.3) 33%	28 (3.1) 20%	2 (0.2) 1%	24 (2.7) 17%	87 (9.7) 62%
M. #91 (1646–7)	88 (8.8) 62%	42 (4.2) 29%	11 (1.1) 8%	2 (0.3) 1%	37 (3.7) 29%	12 (1.2) 10%	15 (1.5) 12%	62 (6.2) 49%	34 (3.4) 25%	0 0%	13 (1.3) 10%	89 (8.9) 65%
Ş. #4 (1665–6)	147 (13.4) 62%	55 (5.0) 23%	29 (2.6) 12%	5 (0.5) 2%	67 (6.1) 30%	24 (2.2) 11%	45 (4.1) 20%	89 (8.1) 40%	58 (5.3) 25%	4 (0.4) 2%	37 (3.4) 16%	132 (12.0) 57%
Ş. #14 (1690–1)	154 (22.0) 57%	57 (8.1) 21%	55 (7.9) 20%	3 (0.4) 1%	54 (7.7) 22%	19 (2.7) 8%	59 (8.4) 24%	118 (16.9) 47%	44 (6.3) 18%	4 (0.6) 2%	58 (8.3) 23%	143 (20.4) 57%
Ş. #38 (1703)	56 (11.2) 53%	37 (7.4) 35%	13 (2.6) 12%	0 0%	25 (5.0) 26%	1 (0.2) 1%	15 (3.0) 16%	55 (11.0) 57%	23 (4.6) 23%	0 0%	16 (3.2) 16%	59 (11.8) 60%

Note: The first figure in the upper line in each category is the total number of cases. The second figure in parenthesis is the number of cases per month. The percentile value in the lower line is the proportion in the sub-group. Mil.-adm.: military-administrative; rel.-jud.: religious-judicial; waqf aff.: waqf affiliates; tax-pay./comm.: tax payers or community. Percentages may not total 100 due to rounding.

Source: see Table 4.3.

percent in the most recent one).⁵² The fact that claims against waqf affiliates increase considerably after the turn of the seventeenth century is interesting and might reflect rising numbers of waqfs around this period. Since the reports in my sample concern primarily the alleged misdemeanors of local officials and those with extractive entitlements (including waqf administrators), it makes sense that we do not observe many taxpayers among alleged perpetrators. The taxpayers we do see here are almost exclusively those who were accused of false witnessing and forging documents and seals.⁵³

Among those who became involved in conveying complaints to the imperial center (columns 5–8), qadis and naibs appear prominently, at least in the earliest registers, which is consistent with the prevalent expectation that the imperial center used provincial judicial authorities to keep an eye on potential oppressors among military-administrative functionaries. In the later registers, however, the qadis' and naibs' tendency to report abuse declines sharply. Given that the representation of the qadis and naibs among alleged perpetrators is significantly higher than their representation among those who reported crimes in the same registers (column 2), this finding indicates that their relative contributions to fighting crime might have diminished considerably from the mid-seventeenth century onward.

Parallel to this trend is the tendency among the taxpayers and local communities to appeal to the imperial center directly, via representatives or by letters composed by their members. While these constitute less than 20 percent of appeals in the first two registers, they range from roughly 40 to 60 percent in the last four. Coupled with the decline in reports of abuse by qadis and naibs, this finding has striking implications. Perhaps it indicates a decline in

---

[52] Many such reports contain complaints about excessive or illegal extractions by the qadis or naibs. For example, in a şikayet entry dated November 1665, the qadi of Gercanis in north-central Anatolia is accused of conducting frequent tours of inspection (*devr*) on nearby villages, illegally imposing on these villages a "court fee" (*mahkeme harcı*) of 2 or 3 guruş and a "permission fee" (*izinname harcı*) of 2.5 guruş; see entry 462 in *4 Numaralı Atik Şikayet Defteri* (Tataroğlu 2015). On "devr," see below. In another entry in the same register dated December 1665, the qadi of Gördüs (perhaps in western Anatolia) is accused of charging an exorbitant fee of 125 guruş for registering documents in the court's archive (*sicil harcı*) and seizing 146 loads of barley; see entry 479 in *4 Numaralı Atik Şikayet Defteri* (Tataroğlu 2015). For more examples, see entries 4 and 41 in *91 Numaralı Mühimme Defteri* (2015); and entries 596 and 657 in *14 Numaralı Atik Şikayet Defteri* (Erdem 2017).

[53] See, for example, entry 915 in *3 Numaralı Mühimme Defteri* (1993), dated March 1559, where a man named Pir Ahmed from Kaş in southern Anatolia is proclaimed guilty of habitual false witnessing based on his own confession. The document demands his apprehension and transfer to the capital for punishment. Another mühimme entry from November 1630 mentions two brothers named Osman and Ömer who forged the seal of the local qadi and used it to prepare fake documents; see entry 320 in *85 Numaralı Mühimme Defteri* (2002).

confidence in the local qadis' and naibs' efforts to keep corruption under control. Alternately, the latter might have become increasingly hesitant to get involved in contentious issues that pitted them against local strongmen and powerholders with titles.[54] Or local communities might have needed their services less urgently or felt increasingly more confident in their ability to personally represent their grievances to the imperial center.

Waqf administrators and affiliates constituted a significant group among those reporting crimes after the sixteenth century. What is not explicit in the table but should be made clear for my purposes is that their allegations often targeted other waqf affiliates and local military-administrative officials and accused these individuals of illegally appropriating and/or embezzling waqf resources.[55] Among the parties aggrieved about crimes associated with corruption (columns 9–12), taxpayers and local communities made up the largest share as expected. Interestingly, religious-judicial officials rarely appear among the alleged victims.

Table 4.6 demonstrates the relative preponderance of corruption crimes as represented in eight mühimme and şikayet registers. In my classification of the crimes, I labeled "excessive extraction" those monetary, in-kind, and service or labor demands based on revenue claims and entitlements that were presumably legitimate but above customary or legally prescribed levels. "Illegal extraction," in contrast, refers to appropriations that pretended to be customary, regular, and legitimate but were not. For example, I include here frequent claims made by both military-administrative and religious-judicial authorities under the names of *kaftan-baha, selamlık akçesi, bi-namaz akçesi,* and so on. Also included in this category are the authorities' so-called tours of inspections in their jurisdictions, for which they were often accompanied by large retinues of aides and militia. Called *devr,* these tours involved crippling demands on local communities: forced to accommodate the authorities and their retinues for extended periods of time, they also suffered the unpaid

---

[54] A mühimme entry dated August 1567 mentions the reticence of the qadis in Vidin, Niğbolu (or Nikopol), and Silistre (or Silistra) in modern-day Bulgaria to support the local taxpayers against the local authorities' acts of oppression; entry 47 in *7 Numaralı Mühimme Defteri* (1998).

[55] See entry 134 in *7 Numaralı Mühimme Defteri* (1998) for a 1567-dated order addressed to the qadis of Selanik (or Thessaloniki) and Siroz (or Serrez) in modern-day Greece concerning a dispute between the administrator (*mütevelli*) of the waqf of Evrenos, a man named Mustafa, and the former scribe of the same waqf, Ahmed. According to the document, Ahmed accused Mustafa of embezzling the waqf's revenues and unfairly dismissing Ahmed from his position because of his inquiries about Mustafa's acts. Mustafa also made untrue claims against Ahmed by using false witnesses and tried to kill him. Finally, Ahmed accused Mustafa of using waqf resources in ways that contradicted the wishes of the waqf's founder. For other examples, see entries 31, 53, and 88 in *4 Numaralı Atik Şikayet Defteri* (Tataroğlu 2015).

appropriation of their supplies when those groups departed.[56] Although such acts bordered on robbery and plunder and were deemed illegal in the registers, the documents also leave the impression that they were common and even regularized, at least until the mid-seventeenth century.[57] I suspect that many local authorities saw them as part of their feudal entitlements. Thus, I tend to differentiate them from blatant robbery or highway banditry, which, whether perpetuated by titleholders or not, made no pretense of legitimacy. Column 1 combines the results for "illegal" and "excessive" extraction.

In addition to alleged extractive improprieties, the registers also contain references to distributive conflicts. The entries that concern such tensions, labeled "conflicts over revenue sources" in Table 4.6, often involve acts of official overreach in pursuit of material resources; in these cases, however, they harmed other officeholders or entities (including waqfs) with extractive entitlements. Such tensions could include, for example, conflicts between tımar- or zeamet-holders over tax privileges associated with specific tax bases that they claimed for themselves, or conflicts between qadis about who could hear and decide disputes and claim the fees associated with this task.[58]

The registers also encompass references to other relevant acts, including embezzlement, which I define as illegal appropriation of wealth or property already collected from their sources at the expense of the ruler or other

---

[56] See, for example, a mühimme entry from October 1630 based on a prior petition by the qadi of Sofya (or Sofia) concerning the alleged transgressions of an unnamed agent (*mütesellim*) of the local sub-governor. According to the petition, the agent descended on a village while accompanied by sixty or seventy men, claimed the villagers' food and supplies without making payments, imposed on them an illegal tax they called "kaftan-baha" (literally, "price of or payment for a caftan") of 5,000 akçes, and apprehended three local men. The order indicates that the agent was dismissed from his position; entry 16 in *85 Numaralı Mühimme Defteri* (2002). Another undated order, probably from 1646, relates that the qadis and their deputies in Bolu (in northwestern Anatolia) frequently performed devrs in the countryside, during which they seized the taxpayers' food and supplies. The order stated that the qadis should stay in their places of residence, not visit rural communities unless invited, and that in cases where they were invited, they should pay for their own supplies based on official prices (*narh*); entry 44 in *91 Numaralı Mühimme Defteri* (2015). For other examples, see entries 83 and 308 in *4 Numaralı Atik Şikayet Defteri* (Tataroğlu 2015), and 98 in *38 Numaralı Atik Şikayet Defteri* (Çil 2018).

[57] See references to cyclical, often thrice-monthly devrs in entries 581 and 593 in *85 Numaralı Mühimme Defteri* (2002). For the statistical representations of devrs in the registers, see the appendix to this chapter.

[58] A mühimme entry of April/May 1646 relates an extended dispute between two individuals, Ali and Ahmed, over certain tımar revenues in the Ayaş subdistrict of Ankara sub-province. According to the report, multiple petitions were sent to the imperial center, and the dispute was heard and decided by the sub-governor of Ankara for Ali. However, the sub-governor's decision did not bring an end to the matter: Ahmed continued to claim the tımar revenues and also raided Ali's home; entry 111 in *91 Numaralı Mühimme Defteri* (2015). Another mühimme entry dated April/May 1618 reports a complaint by the qadi of the Bendereğli district (close to Bolu), Mevlana Ahmed, against the qadi of Samakov (presumably in modern-day Bulgaria), Feyzullah, who held court in Ahmed's jurisdiction and "caused a stir among local people" (ahalisine küllí ihtilal virmeğle). Feyzullah had been warned before not to hold court in a jurisdiction assigned to another judge, but he continued to do so and illegally seized the revenues due to Ahmed; entry 268 in *82 Numaralı Mühimme* (2000).

legitimate claimants of these; bribery; forged or deliberately misleading documents (including forged seals); and false witnessing.[59] Finally, Table 4.6 identifies instances of "collusion" among various government functionaries in their involvement in extractive or distributive improprieties and their "negligence" in fighting crime associated with corruption.[60] The category "other" represents in general other types of misdemeanors or those that are implied in the registers but not explicitly identified.

In Table 4.6, complaints about illegal or excessive extraction constitute the largest category of crime. In fact, in three registers the reports of illegal or excessive extraction make up the majority of all classified acts. This indicates that from the mid-sixteenth century through the early eighteenth, the central government's efforts to control corruption were relatively focused on limiting the exploitation of taxpayers, which aligns well both with the ideological commitments of the polity as articulated in the Circle of Justice and with official imperial pronouncements as found in the kanunnames and adaletnames.[61] Also well represented in the table are conflicts among government officials, embodied in reports pertaining to distributive tensions (column 2) and claims of embezzlement (column 3). Given the presumably limited proportions of government officials and actors with extractive privileges in the entire population, one wonders whether such matters are overrepresented. Particularly interesting here is mühimme register 82, in which reports of distributive conflicts (29 percent) and allegations of embezzlement (14 percent) together account for almost half of all the complaints, outnumbering reports of alleged extractive abuse.[62]

In contrast to jurisprudential discussions of the topic, the specific crimes of bribery, false witnessing, and forged or misleading documentation and seals receive only peripheral attention in the registers. One relevant point here is

---

[59] For an example of embezzlement, see an order sent to the qadis of Köstendil (or Kyustendil) in Bulgaria in March 1631 concerning the crimes of a nameless mütesellim, who collected the revenues of the Köstendil sub-province on behalf of the sub-governor but did not deliver them to him; entry 186 in *85 Numaralı Mühimme Defteri* (2002). For references to bribery, forged documents, and false witnessing in the registers, see below and Note 53.

[60] See entry 332 from 1618 in *82 Numaralı Mühimme Defteri* (2000) for accusations against the former qadi of Molova (or Molyvos on the island of Lesbos), who, in collusion with the agent (*kethüda*) of the local sub-governor, extorted supplies and money from the people of his district. For an order from 1559 that chastises the governor of Aleppo for his negligence to engage with and prevent the oppressive acts of a local strongman named Abu Rish, see entry 622 in *3 Numaralı Mühimme Defteri* (1993).

[61] One would do well to remember that this tendency must be as reflective of the petitioners' expectations from their government as it was indicative of the polity's ideological priorities.

[62] The fact that we observe this result in an era known to be famously difficult in socioeconomic, political, and climatic terms (White 2011) might suggest that in such circumstances, when their extractive efforts failed to generate the much-needed yields, government functionaries tended to turn against one another more intensely.

Table 4.6 Acts of Corruption in Mühimme and Şikayet Registers

Source (date)	Illegal/excessive extraction 1	Conflicts over revenue sources 2	Embezzlement 3	Complaints Bribery 4	False wit. 5	False doc. 6	Collusion 7	Negligence 8	Other 9
M. #3 (1559–60)	43 (3.3) 38%	18 (1.4) 16%	8 (0.6) 7%	1 (0.1) 1%	1 (0.1) 1%	20 (1.5) 18%	3 (0.2) 3%	8 (0.6) 7%	12 (0.9) 11%
M. #7 (1567–8)	29 (4.1) 33%	10 (1.4) 11%	13 (1.9) 15%	4 (0.6) 4%	1 (0.1) 1%	12 (1.7) 13%	4 (0.6) 4%	9 (1.3) 10%	7 (1.0) 8%
M. #82 (1617–18)	48 (3.7) 41%	34 (2.6) 29%	17 (1.3) 14%	2 (0.2) 2%	1 (0.1) 1%	4 (0.3) 3%	4 (0.3) 3%	4 (0.3) 3%	4 (0.3) 3%
M. #85 (1630–1)	79 (8.8) 50%	30 (3.3) 19%	27 (3.0) 17%	1 (0.1) 1%	6 (0.7) 4%	3 (0.3) 2%	4 (0.4) 3%	6 (0.7) 4%	3 (0.3) 2%
M. #91 (1646–7)	95 (9.5) 58%	34 (3.4) 21%	9 (0.9) 6%	2 (0.2) 1%	7 (0.7) 4%	2 (0.2) 1%	9 (0.9) 6%	0 0%	5 (0.5) 3%
Ş. #4 (1665–6)	134 (12.2) 54%	62 (5.6) 25%	28 (2.5) 11%	3 (0.3) 1%	2 (0.2) 1%	4 (0.4) 2%	5 (0.5) 2%	7 (0.6) 3%	5 (0.5) 2%
Ş. #14 (1690–1)	125 (17.9) 43%	64 (9.1) 22%	44 (6.3) 15%	3 (0.4) 1%	13 (1.9) 4%	4 (0.6) 1%	11 (1.6) 4%	0 0%	30 (4.3) 10%
Ş. #38 (1703)	50 (10.0) 37%	20 (4.0) 15%	16 (3.2) 12%	6 (1.2) 4%	18 (3.6) 13%	2 (0.4) 1%	5 (1.0) 4%	0 0%	18 (3.6) 13%

Note: The first figure in the upper line in each category is the total number of cases. The second figure in parenthesis is the number of cases per month. The percentile value in the lower line is the proportion in the entire group. Percentages may not total 100 due to rounding.

Source: see Table 4.3.

that references to such acts can appear as secondary acts—in other words, they can be cited only as means of facilitating unfair extractive or distributive improprieties. For example, in a petition concerning excessive extractions by executive authorities, one can find references to bribes extended to local qadis or naibs to discourage them from interfering with abusers.[63] In other cases, the use of forged or misleading documents is mentioned in disputes involving prebendal authorities or waqf administrators over revenues that these parties claim for themselves.[64] That being said, the relative frequencies of references to forged or misleading documents in the first two registers from the sixteenth century and to false witnesses in the last two registers from the late seventeenth and early eighteenth centuries are noteworthy.

As stated, the registers contain references to government functionaries' "collusion" in illegal extractive schemes and their "negligence" in pursuing crime in their jurisdictions, but infrequently. The latter, in particular, largely disappears in the later periods. Finally, the registers also contain plenty of references to governmental misconduct expressed vaguely and nonspecifically, and I include these in column 9 ("other"). In earlier registers there are cases where the imperial center issued orders to investigate (*teftiş*) the affairs and conduct of certain provincial officials, without explaining the reasons for such actions, or the improprieties that caused them.[65] In the later registers unspecified allusions to the judicial authorities' biases and improper influences in litigations and contractual processes are more common.[66]

Unfortunately, it is almost impossible to provide any systematic answer to the important question of how complaints found in the mühimmes and şikayets were resolved, beyond pointing out how they were initially treated by the imperial bureaucracy. According to Tuğluca (2010: 33), in about 46 percent of the responses to the petitions he examined in five şikayet registers from the late seventeenth century, complaints were forwarded to

---

[63] Entry 202 in *85 Numaralı Mühimme Defteri* (2002), probably from 1631, provides a detailed list of the transgressions and oppressive acts attributed to the sub-governor of Hersek in Bosnia. It also contains a reference to the qadis in the region, who refused to intervene and try to stop the abusive practices of the sub-governor when local people asked for their help because of the bribes that they had allegedly received from the sub-governor. For examples of bribes in judicial processes, see entries 32, 38, and 445 in *38 Numaralı Atik Şikayet Defteri* (Çil 2018).

[64] For examples of references to forged/misleading documents in petitions that primarily concern extractive and distributive conflicts, see entries 611 in *3 Numaralı Mühimme Defteri* (1993); 573 in *7 Numaralı Mühimme Defteri* (1998); and 263 in *14 Numaralı Atik Şikayet Defteri* (Erdem 2017).

[65] See, for example, entries 712, 796, and 870 in *3 Numaralı Mühimme Defteri* (1993).

[66] See, for example, entries 172, 246, 256, and 276 in *38 Numaralı Atik Şikayet Defteri* (Çil 2018). In many of these cases, the allusion to improper relationships between local judicial authorities and individuals of suspicious character or suspected criminals is contained in the vague phrase "hevasına tabii kadıya (or naibe) isnad ile," which can be translated as "with the support of the qadi (or naib) under his (or her) influence."

the original locations for resolution without any further guidance. In 38 percent of the responses, the imperial officials sent specific instructions about how to resolve the complaints in their locations of origin. 6 percent of the responses contain references to inspectors sent from the capital to administer or oversee the resolution processes. In 10 percent of the responses, the center demanded that the alleged perpetrators be brought to Istanbul for interrogation and possible punishment. My own impressions are consistent with Tuğluca's findings. Beyond these initial steps, however, the registers provide no information regarding resolutions for specific complaints, including winners and losers.

More generally, we know little about the overall effectiveness of the imperial center's involvement in corruption allegations brought to its attention. Did the central bureaucracy investigate all reports of abuse? It is likely that some failed to generate any action, but what was their proportion? We also know little about the frequency of investigations leading to any sanctions. Our sources do contain references to dismissals of government officials, and occasionally more serious punishments as well (see below), but how common were they?[67] And when dismissals happened, how likely were they to be permanent or temporary? In cases where dismissals were temporary, how long did they last? More research is required to systematically answer these and many other questions.

To my knowledge, there is no systematic research on punishments actually levied for any sort of crime in the premodern era, let alone those specifically for corruption. Our impressions about punishments, therefore, have been based on a relatively small number of examples casually mentioned in various types of sources, including the chronicles, and largely in passing. In some cases, such incidents were likely recorded because they were exceptional.

Fortunately, this may be changing due to the attention recently given to a particular type of archival source: the kalebend defterleri ("registers of the confined to fortress[es]"), fifty or so registers largely from the eighteenth and early nineteenth centuries that provide clues about a particular subcategory of penalties imposed for a large variety of offences.[68] Specifically, these registers

---

[67] Levent Kuru (2016: 126) has suggested that about 5 percent of the qadis in the Balkan provinces were dismissed from their positions in the first half of the eighteenth century because of allegations of misconduct while in office, often communicated to the imperial center via petitions. I lack comparable information for other eras and types of government service.

[68] Other relevant source types, also underexplored, are *nefy defterleri* ("registers of the exiled") and *kürekçi defterleri* ("registers of those serving in the galleys"). For one survey of the latter records in English, see Zarinebaf 2010. Kalebend registers contain references to a broader variety of punishments that range from simple warning and chastisement to exile, confinement to a fortress, and, more

contain documentation related to the punitive consequences of petitions submitted to the imperial council. By and large, these orders by the central bureaucracy were directed to provincial authorities in particular locales where individuals accused and convicted of a variety of crimes were sent to serve their sentences.[69] In these documents we get useful glimpses of how various acts of corruption were punished at specific points in the premodern period,[70] although it is likely that punishments cited in the kalebend registers constitute a limited selection of possible penalties. For example, the registers contain no examples of fines or capital punishments.[71]

Before turning specifically to how crimes associated with corruption were punished, I will briefly identify some broader patterns in the kalebend registers. First, punishments were not imposed for a predetermined duration (İşbilir 2019). Instead, the release of offenders was often contingent on their rehabilitation (*islah-ı nefs*) or their ability to compensate for the financial damages that their actions caused. In other cases, offenders were released as acts of the ruler's mercy when their relatives, friends, or associates submitted appeals that described their poverty, poor health, or their dependents' destitution. It is not uncommon to observe in the registers gradually more severe punishments for repeat offenders (Sezgin 2022: 233–6).

In many kalebend entries the lengths of the sentences are missing. In cases for which this information is available, punishment durations regardless of the type(s) of crime for specific offenders range from a couple of weeks to a few years. For such entries, most sentences ranged between one to six months. Overall, relatively few people served terms longer than a year. Sentences of confinement in fortresses might have been generally shorter than time spent in exile, which perhaps reflects the more severe anguish associated with these kinds of punishment.[72]

---

occasionally, to hard labor in the galleys. Aksın and Baytimur (2010: 797) insist that the punishments of *confinement* to the boundaries of a fortress should be distinguished from *imprisonment* in a fortress, a more severe punishment type.

[69] The originals of these registers are available in the Presidency of the Republic of Turkey, Department of Ottoman Archives. Keyword-searchable transliterations of select registers have been produced as master's theses since the mid-2010s. My impressions are based on the following theses: Koca 2015; Alakuş 2016; Şahin 2017; Uz 2017; Alemdaroğlu 2018; Çeribaş 2018; Algül 2019; Daş 2019; Erdoğan 2019; Genç 2019; Kara 2019; Toku 2019; Sezgin 2022. According to Aksın and Baytimur (2010: 795), large numbers of other relevant documentation also exist in files containing unbound foils.

[70] The crime-punishment patterns in kalebend registers might not be reflective of those prevalent in earlier times. In fact, confinement to a fortress for an unspecific duration might have become a common punishment only in the eighteenth century (Erim 1984: 80–1; İşbilir 2019).

[71] In a few cases, crimes that "deserve execution" (*katle bedel*) appear to be commuted to confinements in fortresses. See Sezgin 2022: 172–6.

[72] One can also identify a gradation of severity in the variations of exile. Surely, being locked in a distant island (called *cezirebend*) in the Aegean Sea must have generated greater isolation and distress compared to being sent to a large city such as Bursa or to one's native town, which was common. The

Government functionaries often appear among offenders, though this varies across registers. For example, in one register that covers about seven months in 1739, the military and religious titleholders constitute about 15 percent of the 249 offenders (Alakuş 2016: 22). In another register that covers about five years (between 1768 and 1773/74), about 32 percent of the offenders (1,160 or so of them) belong to this group (Koca 2015: 43). The later registers, in particular, contain plenty of references to court officials and military-administrative authorities. For example, in just one portion of a register that covers about sixteen months in 1814 and 1815, at least twenty-three qadis, naibs, and muftis are cited among those who were exiled or confined in a fortress (Erdoğan 2019: 54, 85, and 93). In many registers, military-administrative functionaries are more frequently represented than religious-judicial ones. For the latter, exile might have been the preferred punishment compared to more severe sentences of confinement to a fortress or hard labor in the galleys (Çeribaş 2018: 18; Genç 2019; Sezgin 2022: 273).

Kalebend entries do not reveal how punishments were determined for convicts guilty of multiple crimes, which constitutes a large portion of the entries (see below for examples). Consequently, the easiest way to establish an impression of crime-punishment patterns apropos corruption might be to identify those few records in which particular types of corruption are cited as the exclusive or near-exclusive bases of punishment. The following are specimens of such cases concerning bribery:

- In an order dated November 1789, Feyzullah Efendizade Mehmed Refii Molla, the former qadi of Edirne, was directed to remain in Damascus until the pilgrimage season and then be exiled to Taif, in Arabia, for offering and accepting bribes "in addition to his other offences not befitting of his ulema status" (tarik-i ulemaya na-seza bazı kabayih) until he is remorseful and rehabilitated. A later annotation of June 1790 suggests that he was ordered to reside in his sinecure (arpalık) in Gelibolu in Western Anatolia. The document and annotation indicate a punishment duration of seven months (Uz 2017: [85/3]367–8).
- An order dated April 1813 mandated the exile of Zeynelabidin, a qadi of Rumelia who served as an agent (kapı kethüdası), presumably for a high-ranking official in the judiciary administration,[73] to the island of İstanköy (or Kos) in the Aegean Sea because of his bad deeds (irtikab) and bribery

---

fortresses in which the criminals were confined included those located on the islands of Bozcaada (Tenedos), Limni (Lemnos), Midilli (Mytilene) in the Aegean Sea, and Cyprus, as well as those located in-land in many spots in Anatolia and the Balkans.
[73] On kapı kethüdası, see Nizri 2016.

(*irtişa*), accompanied by his abuse and admonishment of many qadis and naibs, that led to "disorder" (*ihtilal*) in the affairs of many provincial districts. The document is silent as to how exactly Zeynelabidin's acts led to disorder, but they might be tied to decisions of provincial judicial appointments. A subsequent annotation to the entry gives the date of release as June 1813, indicating a sentence of about two months (Çeribaş 2018: [105/3]320–1).

o In an order dated February 1816, Halil, an official in the grand vizier's office presumably responsible for undercover inspections of tradesmen (*tebdil çukadarı*), was sentenced to confinement to the fortress of Magusa (or Famagusta) on the island of Cyprus for accepting bribes from tradesmen. Although the offence was considered serious enough to deserve the death penalty (*katle bedel*), a subsequent annotation indicates that an order was prepared for Halil's release in June 1816, indicating a punishment of four months (Toku 2019: [48/4]286).

The following are examples of punishments for false witnessing:[74]

o In August 1790, Mehmed b. Süleyman, known as "fiqh-master" (*fıkıhçı*), from Istanbul was exiled to Bursa for false witnessing. No annotation exists to indicate his release date (Uz 2017: [152/4]578–9).

o In January 1813, Abbas and Seyyid Mustafa Tahir, a *müezzin* or a mosque official responsible for reciting prayer-calls, were exiled from Istanbul to the district of Tekfurdağı (modern-day Tekirdağ in the Thrace) for false witnessing and acting as proxies in fabricated litigations. Subsequent annotations indicate that a release order for Abbas was prepared in March 1838 and one for Mustafa Tahir in April (Çeribaş 2018: [65/3]228–9). A later entry in the same register indicates that Abbas's earlier release was facilitated by a petition of his wife, who begged the ruler's mercy owing to her destitution ([99/1] 303–4).

o In November 1814, Ahmed, a qadi, was exiled from Istanbul to the island of Limni (or Lemnos) for audaciously providing a false testimony in a litigation that took place in the presence of the grand vizier. A release

---

[74] No references to branding or other types of corporal punishment exist in the documents, though such measures are mentioned in the general kanunnames issued during the reigns of Selim I (d. 1520), Süleyman the Magnificent (d. 1566), Murad III (d. 1595), and Ahmed I (d. 1617). Public shaming (*teşhir*) is another frequent punishment mentioned in the kanunnames for this crime. See Akgündüz 1990–6: 4:303, 8:115, 9:502; and Aydın 2020: 277 and 278.

order was prepared in February 1817, indicating a punishment of about twenty-six months (Erdoğan 2019: [175/1]202).

And here is an example of punishment for forging legal documents:

o In September 1813, Feyzullah Mollazade Mehmed Celaleddîn, a müderris and a court scribe, was exiled to the island of Bozcaada (or Tenedos) for forging copies of court documents. An annotation to the entry specifies that a release order was prepared in December 1813, indicating a sentence of two months (Çeribaş 2018: [93/1]290-1).

The above examples, and others not cited here, suggest that exile and confinement to a fortress were common punishments for many types of offences associated with corruption in the late eighteenth and early nineteenth centuries. Generally, the sentences appear to be short by modern standards,[75] though one should take into account the physical strain and financial costs of traveling to distant locations when considering the overall burden of these punishments.[76] Also consequential for the offenders (and their families) must have been the loss of regular income due to dismissals from their positions (İşbilir 2019),[77] which must have generated serious economic difficulties as indicated in many petitions submitted by relatives for offenders' expedient release.[78]

The entries indicate no strict correlation of crimes and punishment types or durations (cf. Koca 2015: 73; Çeribaş 2018: 18, 50-1; Algül 2019: 37-8, 48-9, 51-2). In addition to the identities of the offenders, considerations such as setting an example for future potential offenders might have contributed to these variations. Qadi Ahmed's impertinence in lying in the grand vizier's

---

[75] According to Koca (2015: 76-7), who examined a register that spanned a period of about five years, the sentences for false witnessing ranged between one and two and a half months, bribery between one and a half and ten and a half months, forgery in legal documents between one and six months, and negligence in government affairs between one and eight and a half months.

[76] It was common for imperial agents to accompany the offenders to their destinations of punishment, possibly at the expense of the latter.

[77] Whether the offenders were eventually allowed to return to their old positions or acquire comparable ones is a question that requires further research. However, I ran into at least one entry that mentions a naib who managed to get reappointed after being dismissed multiple times from the positions of deputy-judgeship in a few districts (Algül 2019: [228/1]150-1).

[78] See, for example, a petition submitted by four orphans of a naib who had been exiled to the island of Limni (or Lemnos) because of his "oppressive actions." The petition mentions that the orphans are minors and that they lack the resources and ability to feed themselves. The petition led to the release of the naib as an "act of mercy towards his children" (Sezgin 2022: [199/5]921).

presence appears to have led to a relatively long sentence. One could also presume that for some groups—those with some combination of know-how, effective networks of support, or financial means—it was easier to arrange for petitions of forgiveness that led to more lenient punishments.

The relative prevalence of entries in which convicts are accused of multiple crimes is consistent with the expectation that minor offenders, whose crimes did not cross a certain threshold of severity, often escaped disciplinary scrutiny. In many such cases, references to illegal or excessive extraction are common. Here are a few examples:

- In an order dated October 1758, Elhac Ibrahim, a janissary and the former governor (voyvoda) and military commander (*serdar*) of the district of Gönen in western Anatolia, is sentenced to confinement in the fortress of Kütahya for being greedy, harassing the inhabitants of the district, threatening to destroy the area because he could not obtain the prebendal revenue resources in the region, extracting illegal taxes, and forcing the people of Gönen to falsely report his good conduct. There is no annotation pertaining to his release date (Algül 2019: [222/1]135).
- In an order dated October 1782, Sarı Molla Ibrahim, a scribe in the court of Leskofça (or Lescovac) in the Balkans, was exiled to Kavala, also in the Balkans, after prior warnings, for being a person of sedition and greed (erbab-ı fitne ve tamaa olmakdan naşi), accepting bribes of 25 to 30 guruş from litigants, denying the lawful rights of people, causing strife and animosity in his community, and provoking the people of his district to resist an order that required them to supply timber to construct the fortress of Niş (or Nish). An order of release was prepared in August 1784, indicating an exile of twenty-two months (Sezgin 2022: [43/3]419–20).
- In an order dated September 1815, Mehmed Emin, the chief scribe of the court of Bolu, is sentenced to exile to Amasra in northern Anatolia for charging fraudulent and excessive scribal fees, preparing forged documents by using the seals of dismissed qadis, using these papers to make and collect false claims of administrative expenses, and evading prosecution among his many crimes. The entry provides no information about his release (Toku 2019: [3/1]151–2).

Despite the difficulty of identifying obvious crime-punishment patterns in such cases, it appears that offenders convicted of multiple transgressions received harsher penalties, regardless of status (cf. Koca 2015: 73). It is noteworthy that in some entries, the convicts' character traits are cited as additional bases of punishment. In many other instances, the reasons are vague, which constitutes another obstacle to discerning precise associations between crime and punishment:

- In May 1784, Ali Efendi, the former mufti of Adana, was exiled to the district of Bursa, following a warning from the şeyhülislam, for colluding with local military-administrative authorities, cooperating with habitual abusers of taxpayers, diverging from the path of justice and fairness, deviating from good behavior, and causing disorder and anguish in his district. An order of release was prepared in August 1784 (Sezgin 2022: [236/4]1059).
- In an order dated June 1783, Kara Hafız Mehmed, a naib from the town of Kuşadası in western Anatolia, was exiled to the island of Limni (or Lemnos) until he was rehabilitated because of "his habit of abusing and harassing the taxpayers" (zulm ü teaddi adet-i müstemirresi olduğuna binaen). An order for his release was issued in response to a petition by his children in December 1783, indicating a sentence of six months (Sezgin 2022: [145/1] 760–1, 921).
- In October 1815, Bostancı Mustafa, the local law-enforcer (subaşı) of the town of Yeniköy on the Bosporus, was exiled to Magusa (or Famagusta) after repeated warnings in the past because of his habit of acting "against the wishes [of the ruler]" (hilaf-ı rıza hareket) and "abusing and coercing the taxpayers" (fukara-yı raiyyeti bila-cürm tecrim ü tazyik). An order of release was prepared three months later, in January 1816 (Toku 2019: [9/4]170–1).
- Ahmed Keşşaf, a scribe in the office of the grand vizier, was exiled to the island of İstanköy (or Kos) for "not minding his business" and "acting against the wishes of the ruler." The order of his exile is dated September 1816. A release order was prepared in December 1816, indicating a punishment duration of three months (Toku 2019: [90/3]414–15).

These examples support the expectation that the consequences of one's actions heavily influenced one's punishment. These consequences include "fomenting sedition and corruption," "abusing and harassing the taxpayers," "causing disorder," and "acting against the wishes of the ruler." Other records, not cited here, also mention the "waste of the public property" (mal-ı mirinin itlafı) and the like (for example, Sezgin 2022: [77/2]531–2). There are some variations in punishments imposed for these types of cases as well.

As to the question of deterrence, the registers offer few answers. Yes, those convicted of corruption were punished, sometimes severely. But we do not know how often formal prosecutions led to punishments. Finally, the registers contain references to former convicts occupying official positions, a possibility, if common, that must have partially mitigated the deterrent effects of their punishments.

The second half of the present chapter offered an empirically driven analysis of corruption crimes reported to and punished by the imperial center. My survey of eight mühimme and şikayet registers from the mid-sixteenth to early eighteenth centuries revealed an increasing frequency of references to crimes that might be associated with corruption. This finding is not easy to interpret: it might reflect actual trends in corruption patterns, but it could also be caused by changes in administrative or record-keeping practices. Or it could indicate that the central government was developing a greater degree of sensitivity to allegations of corruption.

In other respects, the survey generated a clearer picture. For one thing, while complaints against military-administrative authorities were frequent in all registers, those against religious-judicial officials increased noticeably in the second half of the seventeenth century. For another, among those who reported corruption in the seventeenth century, the proportion of religious-judicial authorities declined, while the proportion of taxpayers (as individuals or collective bodies) increased. Finally, illegal or excessive extraction was the predominant form of corruption reported to and addressed by the central government, though distributive conflicts and references to embezzlement are also well represented in the registers. All other forms of corruption, including bribery, false witnessing, and false documentation, appear less frequently in our sources.

According to what we find in the kalebend registers, the exile, confinement, and imprisonment for specific corruption crimes could be short, often limited to a few weeks or months. However, this does not mean that these sentences were light. Also, punishments were influenced by factors unrelated to crime types, including the statuses, reputations, personal histories, and physical conditions of the offenders; societal and political consequences of their actions; and the offenders' abilities to abate their sentences. The latter impression is likely to be valid for those crime-punishment patterns not reflected in the kalebend registers and before the eighteenth century. It is also consistent with the hypotheses presented in the first part of the chapter.

Appendix: Devrs in Mühimme and Şikayet Registers

Table 4.7 gives the frequencies of references to devr and/or unpaid appropriation of communal resources and to imprisonment, violence, or threats of these that accompanied specific instances of illegal/excessive extraction by government functionaries in specific registers.

Table 4.7 Devr, Violence, and Imprisonment in Mühimme and Şikayet Registers

Source (Date)	References to Devr as Illegal Consumption/Appropriation of Supplies	References to Imprisonment, Physical Violence, or Threats of These
M. #3 (1559–60)	8 (0.6) 7%	12 (0.9) 11%
M. #7 (1567–8)	5 (0.7) 6%	6 (0.9) 7%
M. #82 (1617–18)	17 (1.3) 14%	7 (0.5) 6%
M. #85 (1630–1)	21 (2.3) 13%	14 (1.6) 9%
M. #91 (1646–7)	19 (1.9) 12%	13 (1.3) 8%
Ş. #4 (1665–6)	22 (2.0) 9%	9 (0.8) 4%
Ş. #14 (1690–1)	15 (2.1) 5%	14 (2.0) 5%
Ş. #38 (1703)	2 (0.4) 1%	2 (0.4) 1%

Note: The first figure in the upper row in each cell is the total number of cases. The second figure in parenthesis is the number of cases per month. The percentile value in the lower row is the proportion in the entire group of corruption crimes.

Source: See Table 4.3.

5
Corruption in Ottoman Political Literature

Ottoman political literature encompasses commentaries on political ethics, advice literature intended for the ruler and high-level government officials, and reform treatises. I also include in this genre chronicles and more general works of history, based mainly on the thematic concerns of these works. I structure my examination of these texts chronologically: I distinguish writings composed before the sixteenth century from later ones. This temporal threshold corresponds to the major political, bureaucratic, and administrative transformation in the polity, which explains the emergence of novel perspectives on corruption after the sixteenth century. The chapter also identifies major variations within later texts, and divides these into subcategories based on how they highlight specific issues associated with corruption and link the notion to broader political concerns. A caveat before we begin: the hypercritical tone of the perspectives represented in the following pages is an attribute of the discursive field that I explore in this chapter. I do not consider these works as inherently objective depictions of the contemporary social, political, and economic circumstances, although they were certainly influenced by such factors.[1]

Pre-Sixteenth-Century Texts

According to the earliest narrative sources, composed at least a century after the beginnings of the polity, the first Ottoman rulers were great leaders because, among other things, they were generous and charitable: the founders of the dynasty shared with their *ghazi* comrades whatever wealth they accumulated through raids; fed and provided for the poor, widowed, orphaned,

---

[1] See Abou-El-Haj (1991) for the now-standard work attributing critical contemporary opinions about the polity to the personal disillusionments of their bearers.

and the mystics; and established endowments for the needy, as well as soup kitchens, mosques, and madrasas (Neşri 2014: 1:73; Ahmedi 1992: 137-8; Şükrullah 2004: 359; Oruç Beğ 2007: 15-16). In fact, our sources insist, there was a strong relationship between the ruler's benevolence and his success. As the first Ottoman rulers showed compassion toward those who lived in their lands, the support they received from their subjects increased, their realm prospered, and further conquests became easier.

The ideal of a compassionate ruler who provides for his people at the expense of his own material interests perhaps finds its best expression in the example of Osman (d. 1324 or 1326), the eponymous founder of the dynasty, who, according to our sources, left to his heirs no coins or gold, only an outer garment, a single piece of armor, a saltbox, a spoon-box, a few horses and a flock of sheep, aside from the lands he conquered, which in reality "belonged to God" (*vilayet hakkundur*) (Aşıkpaşazade 2013: 51; cf. Oruç Beğ 2007: 16).[2] Consistent with this ideal, in the earliest accounts the first Ottoman rulers are hesitant to regard their subjects as revenue sources. For example, according to Aşıkpaşazade (2013: 30; cf. Neşri 2014: 1:111), Osman was initially not familiar with any form of extraction based on commercial activity in a marketplace. In one incident, someone from Germiyan[3] asked Osman to farm him the tolls (*bac*) generated by a market that Osman had established after a conquest. The request was so alien that the ruler at first failed to understand it, and then became enraged:

> When Osman asked what bac was, the person said, "I [intend to] demand payment from whomever comes to the marketplace." Osman: "what business do you have with anyone in this place that justifies forcing him to pay you?" The person said: "It is custom and tradition (*töre vü adettir*); rulers in all lands collect such tolls (*resm*)." Osman: "Is this based on God's orders or the prophet's example? Or is it something that the rulers established on their own?" The person: "It is customary my Han, based on ancient practice." Osman Gazi, now angry: "Whatever a person earns is their property. How is

---

[2] According to Oruç Beğ (2007: 7), his father, Ertuğrul Gazi, made Osman till the land when he was still a child, presumably to raise him as a humble person. Neşri (2014: 1:287) attributes the following prayer to another early sultan, Murad I (d. 1389): "[O God], I am [nothing but] a humble slave of yours. You know my sincere intentions. It is not my desire to accumulate wealth or property. I did not come [to this world] to gather slaves. What I sincerely desire is to please you."

[3] "Germiyan" refers to the principality in the thirteenth century under the rule of a family with the same name that controlled territories to the south of the Ottoman polity. Its center was what is now Kütahya in western Anatolia (Mélikoff 1965; Varlık 1996).

it acceptable for me to claim a share of their earnings, if I don't contribute to it? You better leave now without saying another word. Otherwise, I will harm you!"[4]

Later, Aşıkpaşazade (2013: 303) relates another interaction, this time between Murad II (d. 1451) and a vizier named Fazlullah, whom the text identifies as from Persia (*acemistan*). According to this report, when Fazlullah suggested collecting obligatory alms (zekat) from "people" (*halk*) to supply the army and replenish the ruler's treasury, Murad II rejected the idea, pointing out that alms were "only for the poor; I cannot force Muslims to pay zekat to me because I do not deserve it."[5] The sultan concluded the conversation by identifying three (and only three) lawful (halal) revenue sources for the ruler: silver mines, poll tax (*haraç*) from non-Muslims living in Ottoman territories, and loot acquired in *ghaza* raids.[6] "Anything else that I might feed to my soldiers would be unlawful (haram)."[7] Noticeable in this remark is the absence of any form of extraction from the Muslim community living in Ottoman lands.

Good government defined as a ruler's financial independence from his subjects is a prominent standard in the earliest narrative sources composed in an era of state-building and bureaucratic-administrative centralization, whose authors either were generally nostalgic for what they imagined to be better times in the past or based their accounts on earlier, now-extinct sources steeped in this nostalgia.

Modern Ottoman historians have identified anti-imperial tendencies in a few of these texts' authors, and/or their own sources, who were bothered by the changes occurring in the first few centuries of Ottoman history.[8] Indeed, the task of state-building—the creation of the janissary core, formulation of novel extraction schemes, and state ownership of agrarian lands—generated winners and losers, and much of the earlier commentary on Ottoman affairs conveys

---

[4] According to Aşıkpaşazade (2013: 30–1; cf. Neşri 2014: 1:111), people around Osman later convinced him that those who protect and serve the market deserve disbursements by those who benefit from the market. Osman subsequently allowed for the extraction of a modest amount, but only from those who managed to sell their goods in the market; he exempted those who did not.

[5] It is not necessarily true that zekat is only for the poor. According to one prominent jurisprudential opinion, it is acceptable to pay zekat to warriors who fight for God, including the ghazis; see Erkal 2013: 205.

[6] Other authors, including Neşri and Ahmedi, identify loot from ghaza as the primary and most cherished revenue source for the early Ottoman polity.

[7] According to the Giese edition of the anonymous *Tevarih-i Al-i Osman* (*Tevarih* 1992: 27), haraç rates were modest in this period and did not burden non-Muslims under Ottoman rule.

[8] There is now an extensive scholarly literature on the political tensions in early Ottoman history. Among other works, Kafadar 1995 and Lowry 2003 have shaped my understanding of the topic.

tensions intrinsic to these processes. Authors of these accounts identify the transition from a dispersed, coequal leadership structure involving the senior ghazi chiefs to a centralized polity under one ruler and his servants, which also entailed the concentration of material resources in the hands of the Ottoman family, as corrupting in the primary meaning of the term: decay and degeneration.

According to the texts identified in Table 5.1, although the first Ottomans were originally wise, fair, benevolent, God-fearing Muslims, they later allowed into their inner circles individuals from older, now-corrupt lands who came to poison the realm with their self-interested and ultimately immoral practices. As noted, the person who proposed that Osman institute the market tax was from Germiyan, and Fazlullah, Murad II's aforementioned vizier, was from Persia. Other examples include the much-despised members of the Çandarlı clan, especially Halil (d. 1387) and his son Ali (d. 1406),[9] with family roots in Karaman, and a Kara or Türk Rüstem, also from Karaman, who is said to have first proposed the idea of taxing prisoners-of-war-turned-slaves whom ghazi warriors had acquired during their raids (Aşıkpaşazade 2013: 75; *Tevarih* 1992: 24–5; Neşri 2014: 1:197–9; Oruç Beğ 2007: 24–5).[10] According to Aşıkpaşazade (2013: 95; cf. *Tevarih* 1992: 31),

> Ottomans is a loyal/faithful (*sadık*) lineage. [Until recently], they committed no illegitimate (*na-meşru*) acts. Whenever the ulema proclaimed a thing forbidden, the Ottomans used to avoid it. There were real qadis during Orhan's time, real ulema during Murad's. They were not mischievous (*müfsid*). [This was] until Çandarlı Halil showed up.[11] When Çandarlı Halil arrived and when Türk Rüstem, also known as Mevlana Rüstem,[12]

---

[9] Oruç Beğ (2007: 32–3) identifies Ali as Halil's (presumably younger) brother.

[10] This practice would later form the basis of the devshirme institution and, consequently, the *kul* system, which the ghazis despised. Incidentally, the principality of Karaman was a longtime rival in central Anatolia (Sümer 2001). The Karamanid rulers are often identified in the sources as impious and immoral leaders, in obvious comparison to their Ottoman counterparts; see, for example, Aşıkpaşazade 2013: 171–3. Interestingly, Oruç Beğ (2007: 33) also accuses Ali Paşa and Türk/Kara Rüstem of debasing the akça by reducing its precious metal content, which the historian attributes to the latter's greed.

[11] Sources indicate that Çandarlı Halil (d. 1387), sometimes referred as "Çandarlı Kara Halil Hayreddin," served as the qadi of Bilecik, Iznik, and Bursa during the reigns of Osman and Orhan and as the kazasker, or chief justice, during the reign of Murad I (d. 1389), which at that time was the highest judicial position in the polity. In addition to his important position in the religious-judicial hierarchy, he also played influential roles in building Ottoman financial and military institutions (Aktepe 1993b). His descendants, members of the extended Çandarlı dynasty, would continue to occupy important offices in the Ottoman government, including the grand vizirate, until at least the mid-fifteenth century.

[12] This title indicates formal training in Islamic jurisprudence and status in the religious-judicial hierarchy. Unfortunately, we do not know much about Türk/Kara Rüstem's personal history.

Table 5.1 Works Reflecting Pre-Sixteenth-Century Perspectives

Title	Author	When the Work Was Composed	Notes about the Author	Notes about the Work
İskendername, or "Alexander's Book"	Ahmedi (d. 1412)	ca. 1410	A native of Anatolia. Studied in Cairo. Served the ruler of Germiyan, Süleyman Şah. Later, served in the Ottoman court.	The work is a world history, the last part of which related the history of the Ottoman dynasty up to Süleyman Çelebi (d. 1411).
Behcetü't Tevarih, or "Beauty of History"	Şükrullah (d. after 1464, perhaps in 1488)	After 1454	Someone with ilmiye credentials who served as the qadi of Bursa. He also served as the Ottoman ambassador to the Karaman and Karakoyunlu courts.	Originally composed in Persian, the work is a history of the world since its beginning to the era of the Ottoman dynasty.
Dürr-i Meknun, or "The Hidden Pearl"	Maybe Yazıcızade Ahmed Bican (d. after 1466)[a]	Mid-fifteenth century	A scholar, Sufi, and translator with interest in astrology. Held scribal posts in government service.	An encyclopedic work that contains information on creation, cosmology, celestial bodies, nature, sciences, religions, societies, and history.
Tevarih-i Al-i Osman, or "History of the House of Osman"	Aşıkpaşazade (d. late fifteenth century)	ca. 1481	A descendant of a mystic from Amasya. A soldier who participated in numerous campaigns in Rumelia.	A history of the Ottoman dynasty based on Yahşi Fakih's (now extinct) early fifteenth-century text, supplemented with later developments.

Tevarih-i Al-i Osman, or "History of the House of Osman"	Multiple unknown authors	Multiple versions; the earliest ones were composed in the late fifteenth century		These are multiple versions of the history of the Ottoman dynasty, produced by anonymous authors, often replicating large sections of parallel narratives. Like Aşıkpaşazade's version, the earliest parts of these may be based on Yahşi Fakih's work. The earliest versions of these texts appeared in the late fifteenth century. Here I relied on the versions edited by Friedrich Giese.
Kitab-ı Cihannüma, also known as *Tarih-i Neşri*, "Book of the Perceptions of the World," or "History of Neşri"	Mehmed Neşri (d. 1520?)	Late fifteenth or very early sixteenth century	Possibly with ilmiye credentials who served in the Ottoman bureaucracy.	A history of the world since the Oghuz to the Ottomans through the late fifteenth century. Heavily reliant on earlier sources, particularly Aşıkpaşazade's work.
Tevarih-i Al-i Osman, or "History of Oruç Beğ"	Oruç Beğ (d. 1502 or 1503)	Multiple versions; the earliest end in 1467–8, the latest in 1502–3.	Possibly a scribe with knowledge of Arabic and Persian who served in the Ottoman bureaucracy.	A history of the Ottoman dynasty that provides extensive information on the reigns of Mehmed II (1451–81) and Beyazıt II (1481–1512). The work also contains information on early Islamic history and Constantinople before its conquest by the Ottomans.

[a] Greiner (2018) disputes that Ahmed Bican was the author of *Dürr-i Meknun*.

Source: The relevant entries in *Türk Diyanet Vakfı İslam Ansiklopedisi* and information provided in the modern editions of the works.

showed up alongside, they brought with them the deception and cheating (*hile*).[13] When [Çandarlı] Halil's son Ali became the vizier, the numbers of religious students/scholars (sing. *danişmend*) increased. Once the Ottomans were a solid (*sulb*) people. Yet when the newcomers arrived, they turned fatwas into means of cheating. They eradicated the fear of God (*takva*).... [At this time,] qadis' mischief became apparent.[14]

Tevarih (1992: 33) is even more explicit about connecting Ottoman rulers' newfound concern with extracting and accumulating wealth from their subjects to the corrupting influences of immoral outsiders who occupied powerful positions in the government. These outsiders used their positions to cheat the broader Muslim community, albeit in ways that might have been technically permissible according to Islamic law:

Whenever Ottoman rulers began to associate with the Persians and people from Karaman, they began committing many sins. Çandarlı Kara Halil and Türk Rüstem of Karaman were [known to be] scholarly and exalted in those times. As they approached the Ottoman rulers, they filled the land with tricks. Ottomans did not know about accounting and calculation before them. After they came to Ottoman lands, they introduced accounting ledgers. It was their practice to accumulate coins and build treasury.

Also:

[In the old days, the Ottoman rulers] knew nothing about massing treasury. Whenever [Çandarlı Halil] Hayreddin Paşa showed up, greedy students/ scholars (danişmends) influenced the rulers. They made them to cast aside fear of God (takva) and they used fatwas [to satisfy their greed]. They said "rulers need treasury." They turned the rulers into themselves. People say "greed and injustice appeared in these times; wherever there is greed there is injustice, and there is a lot of both in our times." The reason that there is

---

[13] The references to "hile," legal scholars/students, and fatwas in the text bring to mind, at least among those familiar with Islamic jurisprudence, *hile-i şeriye* (*hiyal sharia* in Arabic) or legal stratagems to circumvent legal prohibitions, at times against the explicit intent of the law; see Köse 1998. As such, the term could carry a morally ambiguous meaning. For example, various stratagems are known to have been used to sanction charging interest, in the face of well-known regulations against usury in the Ottoman context.

[14] Oruç Beğ (2007: 33) explicitly identifies these developments with Yıldırım Beyazıt's reign (1389–1402).

so much injustice and mischief nowadays is the danişmends. Had they acted according to (religious) knowledge, people would have also acted accordingly. (*Tevarih* 1992: 27)[15]

In this context of moralistic criticism of state-building and centralization by those who "did not belong," we find sporadic references to corruption. Most notable in this regard is a report found in all early narrative sources that recounts Yıldırım Beyazıt's (d. 1402) response to widespread complaints about qadis' actions. The texts are not very explicit or uniformly consistent about the nature of the qadis' offenses. Aşıkpaşazade (2013: 95) calls the ulema of the time müfsid—that is, mischievous, and not possessing takva (fear of God). Şükrullah (2004: 364) suggests that they were tyrannical, acted contrary to the sharia, and accepted bribes. Oruç Beğ (2007: 34) claims that their fesad was apparent and that they "filled the world with bribes" (rişvetle alemi toldurdılar). *Tevarih* (1992: 27) accuses them of committing illicit intercourse with the opposite sex (zina), having same-sex liaisons, practicing usury or charging interest (*riba*), and doing other unlawful (haram) acts. Ahmedi (1992: 143) refers to them as "tyrannical" "bribe-takers," "abusers of God's law," and "confusers of truth." Neşri (2014: 1:337) reports that the qadis were guilty of "many types of" fesad, including, but presumably not limited to, bribery.

For the purposes of our discussion, the texts' vagueness about the specific nature of the qadis' crimes, including bribery, is unfortunate, though one senses in Ahmedi's account of the incident (1992: 143) qadis' willingness to "say 'wrong' to the right, [and] 'right' to the wrong" for the right price.[16] On the other hand, Aşıkpaşazade (2013: 56) and Neşri (2014: 1:155) sometimes refer to bribes extended to the qadis by common people eager to be recruited to the ruler's army, suggesting that such payments did not exclusively take place in litigations.

It might be difficult to identify a fully fleshed-out characterization of corruption in these early sources, yet one can make some general observations. First, the texts associate bribery with greed and all types of immoral

---

[15] By contrast, Oruç Beğ (2007: 33) identifies these developments explicitly with the vizirate of Ali Paşa, whom he identifies as Çandarlı Halil's brother.
[16] Here is what Ahmedi (1992: 143) says in Kemal Sılay's translation: "The Ottoman Sultan [Yıldırım Beyazıt] was the Ömer of justice; he knew that the kadis are tyrannical. / They are the takers of bribes, [and] abusers of the Islamic law; they don't know what 'cause and effect' is. / For [the Sultan] it was not necessary to be interested in this world; [however, the kadis say 'wrong' to the right, [and] 'right' to the wrong! / Gathering them all together, he called them to account; whatever they had taken, he made them return. / He punished them with whatever was necessary."

behavior.[17] The act is symptomatic of poor character—people who commit it are bad Muslims and should not be in positions of authority. Second, because bribery is a consequence of greed, it can be directly associated with a broader group of economic offenses that spring from the same source. It makes sense, for example, to regard it as linked to riba, or usury, another crime attributed to the qadis in one source (*Tevarih* 1992: 27). Generally, however, bribery is akin to any other form of wealth extraction, such as charging fees in the marketplace or taxation, that benefits one party at the expense of the larger Muslim community. Third, the act is specifically associated with no other group but the qadis—and, yet more specifically, the qadis of a particular period (more on this below), who weaponize their knowledge of the sacred law and use it for ill intentions. As is evident elsewhere in the texts, the authors consider themselves good Muslims and are certainly not anti-sharia, but they do seem to be wary of manipulating the law to legitimize any form of exploitation.[18] In fact, the connection proposed between bribery and the instrumental role that the law might play in abetting it is notable in these sources.

The story of Yıldırım Beyazıt's engagement with mischievous qadis also provides clues for an alternative perspective on bribery, though it reaches us only indirectly. According to the accounts, when Beyazıt hears about the complaints he orders that the qadis be imprisoned in a building and makes it known that he intends to burn down the building while they are inside.[19] At this point a counter-hero appears to save the qadis through trickery. This is Ali Paşa (d. 1406), Çandarlı Halil Paşa's son, who, like his father, represents everything our authors despise (cf. Aktepe 1993a, 1993b), especially a disregard for the ghazi ideals. Lacking the courage to personally ask for the ruler's forgiveness, our authors suggest, Ali Paşa uses promises of reward to enlist a

---

[17] The association of bribery with immorality might be most clearly articulated in Yazıcızade Ahmed Bican's mid-fifteenth century *Dürr-i Meknun*, where the author considers bribes accepted by the qadis just one sign of the corrupt state of his time. The other signs include the falling numbers of Muslims who pray and read the Quran; women riding horses and governing the realm; boys acting like princes (*emir*); a rise in same-sex liaisons among men and women; the popularization of zina, sodomy, and alcohol consumption; greed, ignorance, and incompetence among rulers and the ulema; oppression of the poor and the weak; ulema's association with the rulers and their desire to be appointed to important government positions; and so forth (Yazıcıoğlu 1999: 122–3). Yazıcızade was a dervish from Gelibolu and representative of what Sariyannis calls the anti-imperial trend in the earliest phase of the Ottoman polity (Sariyannis 2019: 40–4).

[18] Relevant here are the frequent references in the sources to hile or legal stratagems to circumvent legal prohibitions, mentioned above; see, for example, Aşıkpaşazade 2013: 95; and *Tevarih* 1992: 31.

[19] For readers familiar with medieval European history, the incident is reminiscent of the hanging of forty-four judges by Alfred the Great (d. 899), king of the West Saxons, in a single year for judicial corruption. The incident was reported by Andrew Horn (or Horne; d. 1328) in his *Le mireur a justices*, presumably composed in the early fourteenth century and which remained influential in Europe and presumably elsewhere until much later eras. For the relevant pages, see Horne 1895: 166.

well-liked buffoonish figure in Beyazıt's entourage, one Maskara Arab (or "Arab the fool"), to help save the qadis. Subsequently, Arab approaches the ruler and asks to be sent to Byzantium as Beyazıt's envoy. When the ruler asks why, Arab mentions his plan to request that the Byzantine ruler send the Ottomans a few Christian monks. Beyazıt becomes even more curious and further probes what Arab intends to do with the monks. The latter replies that since all the qadis will be executed, the Ottomans might appoint the monks to their place. When Bayezıt asks why he should appoint the monks rather than his own subjects as qadis, Arab says: "Your subjects [who are not qadis] are not educated (*okumuş*); they are ignorant (*cahil*). These monks are knowledgeable about the Bible. Since by executing the qadis you will make it impossible to enforce the rules of the Quran, the monks could at least enforce the rules of the Bible, which was also revealed from God" (Neşri 2014: 1:337–9; cf. Aşıkpaşazade 2013: 95–6; and Oruç Beğ 2007: 34–5).

Maskara Arab's performance (also see *Tevarih* 1992: 34–6) is supposed to be humorous, yet his words remind the ruler that the qadis' skills and functions are indispensable. The exchange prompts Beyazıt's awareness of the important role the qadis play in his realm, so he summons Ali Paşa to consult with him. Specifically, according to Neşri (2014: 1:339), he asks Ali Paşa why the qadis act as they do if they know God's law. In his response, Ali Paşa justifies the qadis' actions by claiming that they lack sufficient funds to live on,[20] based on which one can deduce that among all other evil acts attributed to qadis, the one that really upsets Beyazıt involves money.[21] When Beyazıt hears Ali Paşa's response, he pardons the qadis and, on Ali Paşa's suggestion, prescribes fees and allowances in return for specific notarial and scribal services, which, according to the sources, became customary at that time.[22]

---

[20] Aşıkpaşazade (2013: 96): "Sultanım! Bunların düşeliği azdır"; *Tevarih* (1992: 36): "İmdi sultanım! Bunlara döşelik gerekdir"; Oruç Beğ (2007: 35): "Sultanım! Bunların düşelikleri azdur, cihetleri yokdur."

[21] Incidentally, the punishment that Beyazıt initially intends to inflict on the qadis is not consistent with the prescriptions in classical works of fiqh for qadis' corruption. Yet it can be justified according to the ruler's siyasa-based discretion (Chapter 4). I am tempted to interpret the lack of explicit protest to this punishment by our authors as evidence of their implicit approval of it. Not unrelated here is the postscript to what happens to Murad II's vizier Fazlullah after he suggests that Murad II extract wealth from his subjects to cover his financial commitments. According to different versions of the text, Murad is so displeased by his vizier's suggestion that he expels him from his position and exiles him. According to at least one version, however, Murad orders that Fazlullah be skinned alive and his skin filled with hay (Aşıkpaşazade 2013: 303n5625).

[22] In a fascinating retelling of Maskara Arab's story much later, Evliya Çelebi (d. 1682) identifies him as Kör Hasan (Hasan "the blind"), whose descendants remained in the entourages of the later sultans as their companions and entertainers. According to Evliya's rendering of the events, Yıldırım becomes enraged at the ulema of his era because of their "acts against law" and their "oppression." He subsequently imprisons about 800 of them, including (anachronistically) şeyhülislams, high-level qadis of Bursa, ranking jurists authorized to issue fatwas, scholars from all legal schools, and authors

Thus, the defense represented in the early narrative sources by Maskara Arab and Ali Paşa is that the ruler needs legal functionaries to serve the needs of the polity; and that it is legitimate, or at least understandable, for legal officials to seek renumeration for their services. Our authors do not necessarily disagree with the first proposition. As they themselves observe, qadis have existed in the Ottoman polity since the earliest times. But the second proposition is clearly problematic for them. Indeed, none of our authors mentions the qadis' financial difficulties during Yıldırım Beyazıt's time. Instead, they repeatedly bring up contemporary qadis' greed and compare them unfavorably to the previous generations. They remind the reader that in the old days, qadiships remained vacant because the ulema of the past were morally scrupulous and feared God. They hesitated to take on the responsibility of interpreting and enforcing sharia, given the risk of making erroneous decisions. Nor did they seek compensation for their services. Later qadis, however, lacked the rectitude to be concerned about offending God and remained fixated on the material benefits associated with the position (*Tevarih* 1992: 33).

While Ali Paşa defends the qadis' actions on the basis of need, he fails to explain how, specifically, they sought compensation. References to bribery might suggest that qadis issued verdicts in litigations according to payments they received from disputants. Yet they might also concern the payments that the qadis received for other types of service.[23] The fact that Beyazıt subsequently allowed the qadis to charge for their notarial and scribal functions—for example, dividing estates, writing letters, and preparing documents (*Tevarih* 1992: 36; Neşri 2014: 1:339; Oruç Beğ 2007: 35)—leads one to think that payments like these (possibly alongside others) were what irked these authors.[24] And this impression is strengthened by their critical reaction

---

of scholarly treatises, with the intention to burn them alive as punishment. He refuses to give in to many pleas of forgiveness for days. Subsequently, Kör Hasan, a companion of Yıldırım, dons the garments of a priest (*metropolid*) and requests the sultan to send him to the Byzantine ruler ("İstanbul tekfuru"). When Yıldırım asks for the purpose of this trip, Hasan declares his intention to ask the Byzantine ruler to lend them forty or fifty priests, who can administer the law in the absence of Muslim jurists capable of issuing fatwas ("'El-cevab: Allah-u alem, olur, olmaz' demeye kadir ulema kalmadıktan sonra"), though their arrival to Bursa, presumably in their dark-colored outfits, might "blacken the Monk Mountain [Keşiş Dağı, or Uludağ, nearby] just like before [its conquest by Muslims]." After this exchange, Yıldırım sees Hasan's point and forgives the ulema. In Evliya's story, Hasan releases the ulema from prison himself, urges the qadis to (re-)convert to Islam ("kadıları Müslüman edeyim"), and warns them against repeating their past crimes. The heads of those who continue with their oppression, he declares, deserve to be pounded in a mortar ("zulm ederlerse kelleleri taş dibekde zedelenir"). Evliya's account does not contain a direct reference to Çandarlı Ali. See Evliya Çelebi 1896: 1:652–3.

[23] Jurisprudential traditions consider the fees charged by the judge for notarial and scribal services legitimate.

[24] Another clue can be found in an interaction that Aşıkpaşazade (2013: 303n5626) reports between Murad I and Çandarlı Halil in which the ruler asks the latter for a loan to finance the funds that he

to Beyazıt's forgiveness: after reporting the ruler's approval of the fees for the qadis' non-adjudicative services, Aşıkpaşazade (2013: 96) suggests that "it was because of Ali Paşa that the Ottomans committed [this] sin." *Tevarih* (1992: 36) too identifies any kind of court fees as "bidat," or innovation against religion. Neşri's (2014: 1:339) assessment of the situation ("the fact that the qadis now charge a toll (resm) of twenty akçes in one thousand [in estate divisions] is Ali Paşa's favor [to them]") can be considered milder only if we disregard the facts that Ali Paşa is a universally despised figure in the early sources and earlier in his text Neşri (2014: 1:187) praises Orhan's decision to make payments (*ulufe*) to the qadis "so that they would not charge anyone [for their services]."[25] For our authors, it very much seems that *any* demand for compensation by the qadis, whether for adjudicative or non-adjudicative functions, was illegitimate. In the case of adjudications, they might have perceived little difference between charging for otherwise fair verdicts and charging for verdicts that favored the paying parties.

These early Ottoman sources have suggested two perspectives on corruption. In the first perspective, which clearly reflects the pro-ghazi, anti-imperial views, bribes are directly associated with the degenerative erosion introduced to the realm by immoral but educated outsiders, especially those with religious-judicial credentials, who used their training and skills in both religious and secular sciences to pursue their state-building and state-centralization project. As such, bribery is associated with the tendency to consider the Muslim community as a source of revenue (that is, a tax base), intrinsic to the political and bureaucratic transformation that the polity experienced in the first couple of centuries in its history. The counter-perspective, indirectly discernible in the voices associated with the new political classes, resists the inclination to associate the term bribery with all forms of extraction, which are not all unjustified, or to view bribery broadly or categorically as a symptom of one's poor, immoral character. Among other things, a bribe might result from the difficult economic circumstances faced by state functionaries and could simply, if not exclusively, indicate confusion

---

intends to send to Mecca, Medina, and Jerusalem. But the ruler insists that the funds should not originate from bribes (*rüşvet florisi*). Given that Halil was a career qadi, the ruler's comments remind the reader of the bribery accusations against the qadis during Beyazıt's reign. Curiously, Halil responds by assuring the ruler that he will lend him funds originating from what he inherited from his father. The fact that he does not vehemently reject any accusation of bribery might lead one to think that the term might have carried a relatively neutral meaning among the likes of Çandarlı.

[25] Other sources of income might have included waqf revenues from Bursa, according to Şükrullah (2004: 359), and the qadis' own personal means.

about which services merit compensation. According to this perspective, the best strategy for preventing such actions is not necessarily to indiscriminately punish those who have sought such payments, but to clearly distinguish legitimate and illegitimate sources of revenue and to enable those who serve the ruler to support themselves in legitimate ways. In fact, it is only by pursuing these policies that the ruler can hope to control the real acts of corruption.

Corruption in Political Commentary between the Sixteenth and Eighteenth Centuries

By the sixteenth century, the Ottoman Empire had become a centralized polity with well-developed judicial, financial, administrative, and military hierarchies. The core provinces of the empire in the Balkans and Anatolia were governed relatively uniformly, directly from the center. The rule of the sultan, built on a coherent system of rules and regulations, strong treasury, sophisticated bureaucracy, and powerful military, ensured an effective control over the empire's lands, taxation of its subjects, enforcement of justice, and protection of the borders. At the time, the polity had fully transformed itself from a conquest state, a ghazi polity, based on a coalition of semi-independent houses, to a strong monarchy run by the sultan's servants according to patrimonial ideals. As Karen Barkey argues (1994: 26), the system featured "a complex compact between state and society" that "incorporated all potentially autonomous elites and organizations into the state." Consequently, earlier tensions between remnants of the ghazi elements and supporters of a dynastic, imperial rule had subsided.[26]

From the second half of the sixteenth century onward, we see a proliferation of political literature based on and combining characteristics from various genres, especially advice literature (Howard 1988; Sariyannis 2019: 7). According to Marinos Sariyannis (2019: 111), while there are exceptions (for example, Kınalızade Ali Efendi's *Ahlak-i Alai*, which appears to be more directly engaged with earlier considerations of political philosophy), many such works that appeared in this period intended to provide direct, practical, and philosophically unencumbered guidance about how to govern the realm.

This literature differs in certain ways from the works examined above. In particular, they take as normative the state's hegemonic presence in

---

[26] For good discussions of the political and bureaucratic transformation in the fifteenth and sixteenth centuries, see Barkey 1994 and 2008.

sociopolitical and economic realms. Relatedly, the stress in the earlier texts on the ruler's austerity and disdain for material, worldly comforts and on the rights of the ghazi establishment appears to have been replaced by an emphasis on the protection of the flock from abuse and the maintenance of a static, hierarchical social order (Sariyannis 2019: 439–40), which Heather Ferguson refers to as (2010: 97) "stability via social hierarchy" under the watchful eyes of a distant and elevated ruler.[27] In what follows, I survey representative texts of the Ottoman political literature, identified in Table 5.2, to detect how various political sources discuss corruption. Specifically, I aim to identify what related offenses are highlighted in these works and the contextual factors that might have shaped the perspectives of their authors, many of whom were former or current government functionaries.[28]

Among the types of acts associated with corruption, our authors universally recognize what they call bribery (in its various forms) as a serious crime that requires policing and punishment. In this sense their judgments are continuous with earlier perspectives surveyed in the previous section. Also prominent in the later works, and consistent with earlier ones, is the link that many authors propose between bribery and moral decrepitude. For example, Lütfi Paşa (1991: 13–15) directly associates bribery, which he identifies as an "infliction without cure" (*maraz-ı bi-ilac*), with greed (*tama*), a riverbed in which evil flows (literally, "greed is a valley of evil"; "tama bir kabih vadidür"). Aşık Çelebi (2018: 85) blames the ill characters ("kişide olmayınca fıtrat-ı pak") of the contemporary qadıs for their evil acts. These statements are consistent with how Mustafa Ali (1982: 2:13) characterizes harmful behavior as a reflection of true character: "One's tyranny is in the self. Weakness hides it; power reveals it" (zulüm nefistedir; acz onu saklar, güç ortaya çıkarır). In fact, for him, avarice also indicates many other failures of personality, including sexual deviancy, drug addiction, and poor lineage, and could even be spotted in one's physiognomy (Mustafa Ali 1982: 2:13, 1:68). The claim that various acts reveal poor character is perhaps best articulated in another sixteenth-century source, Kınalızade's *Ahlak-ı Alai*

---

[27] The texts' frequent references to the Circle of Justice and the need to balance the differential needs of various constituents of the society are related to this significant shift, which resulted in the emergence of a bureaucratic, agrarian empire that valued administrative stability and efficient wealth extraction from productive classes. As I observed in Chapter 3, the Circle played an important role in the polity's official ideology as a basis of its extractive entitlements.

[28] For those familiar with the Ottoman political literature, the sources examined here should not be surprising. They include some of the better-studied texts in the scholarship, composed by those who were considered experienced in and knowledgeable about government affairs and whose opinions have long been deemed by modern researchers to reflect the mood in certain segments of the political class.

Table 5.2 Works Reflecting Perspectives between the Sixteenth and Eighteenth Centuries

Title	Author	When the Work Was Composed	Notes about the Author	Notes about the Work
Asafname, or "Grand Vizier's Book"	Lütfi Pasha (d. 1564)	Early to mid-sixteenth century	Of *devşirme* background from Albania. Served as grand vizier.	Advice to the grand vizier on government, interactions with the ruler, and personal conduct.
Ahlak-ı Alai, or "Sublime Ethics"	Kınalızade Ali Çelebi (d. 1571)	1563–5	Belonged to an ilmiye family. Served as müderris and later as the qadi of Damascus, Cairo, Bursa, and Edirne. Also known for his poems.	A treatise influenced by Persian sources that addresses personal ethics, political philosophy, and household economics.
Miracü'l-Eyale ve Minhacü'l-Adale, or "The Ascent of the Realm and the Path to Justice"	Aşık Çelebi (d. 1572)	Mid-sixteenth century	Served as şeyhülislam Ebussuud's fatwa scribe and as qadi in various courts in Anatolia and the Balkans.	The work is a translation of Ibn Taymiyya's (d. 1328) *al-Siyasa al-Sharia* into Turkish that also contains Aşık Çelebi's critical observations on Ottoman state and government functionaries, especially the qadis.
Usulü'l-Hikem fi Nizami'l-Alem, or "Principles of Wisdom for the Order of the World"	Hasan Kafi Akhisari (d. 1615)	Late sixteenth century	Of ilmiye background. Served as müderris and mid-level qadi.	Advice to those in power about matters related to government, military affairs and organization, and proper social order.
Nushatü's-Selatin, or "Counsel for Sultans"	Mustafa Ali (d. 1600)	Completed in 1581; minor additions in 1586	A madrasa-educated bureaucrat who served various scribal and administrative roles in Istanbul and provincial centers. A prolific writer who produced dozens of titles in many genres.	Advice to those in power about good government and proper conduct of state affairs, including appointments, administration of justice, and wealth extraction.

Tarih-i Selaniki, or "History of Selaniki"	Mustafa Selaniki (d. 1599 or 1600?)	Late sixteenth century	Bureaucrat in the financial service of the palace.	The chronicle covers the events of the late sixteenth century (1563–99/1600).
Kitab-ı Müstetab, or "Book of Remedies"	Unknown	ca. 1620	Presumably of devşirme background and a palace graduate. Someone familiar with fiscal, military, and administrative affairs.	A petition (*layiha*) of reform in government, in particular military/prebendal systems. It also contains observations on financial issues and proposals for reform.
First and second *Risales*, or "Treatises"	Koçi Bey (d. ca. 1650)	First *Risale*: 1630; second *Risale*: 1640	Of devşirme background. He served in the palace in various capacities.	Advice to the ruler and his representatives about good government and proper conduct of state affairs, including the organization of the military and the prebendal system. The second *Risale* might be better characterized as an "administrative manual" about specific functions of various government offices and departments.
Kitab-ı Mesalihi'l-Müslimîn, or "Book on the Proper Courses for Muslims"	Unknown	1637–44	Probably someone who belonged to the ilmiye establishment and served in minor religious-judicial posts.	A compilation of opinions on state, society, and government officials.
Tarih-i Peçevi, or "History of Peçevi"	İbrahim Peçevi (d. 1649?)	1640–9?	Of Bosnian background. Long service in various finance offices in the provincial and military administration. Also served as provincial governor.	The chronicle offers a selective coverage of some important events from the reign of Süleyman until the author's death.

Continued

Table 5.2 Continued

Title	Author	When the Work Was Composed	Notes about the Author	Notes about the Work
Düsturü'l-Amel li Islahi'l-Halel, or "Course of Measures to Redress the Situation"	Katip Çelebi (d. 1657)	1652/3	A prolific scholar with religious and secular credentials who served in important positions in government service.	A philosophically and historically informed reflection on government affairs and how to properly manage them.
Hırzü'l-Mülûk, or "Stronghold of the Kings"	Unknown	Conflicting indications in the text: either late sixteenth or mid-seventeenth century.	Presumably a current government official.	A treatise that provides opinions and information on high-level state officials, including the ruler, viziers, provincial governors, and the religious establishment.
Telhisü'l-Beyan fi Kavanin-i Al-i Osman, or "Memorandum on the Rules of the House of Osman"	Hezarfen Hüseyin Efendi (d. 1678/9)	1675/6	A polymath who served in the financial bureaucracy of the polity.	A treatise that describes the contemporary state of the polity, with particular attention to specific high offices, and one that contains recommendations of reform.
Zeyl-i Fezleke, also known as Tarih-i Silahdar, or "History of Silahdar"	Silahdar Fındıklılı Mehmed Ağa (d. 1726/7)	1695	A man with military roots who served as a palace official and confidant of the ruler.	The chronicle contains a description of the important events between 1654 and 1695.
Tarih-i Naima, or "History of Naima"	Naima (d. 1716)	1697–1704	Originally a son of the janissary commander of Aleppo, he served in the palace. Was the official chronicler from 1697 to 1703 and later served in other administrative offices.	The chronicle contains events from the late sixteenth century to ca. 1660. A treatise on the 1703 Edirne Revolt was added in the end.

Nesayihü'l-Vüzera ve'l-Ümera, or "Advice for Viziers and Statemen"	Defterdar Sarı Mehmed Paşa (d. 1717)	1714–17	Longtime bureaucrat in the financial service of the palace. Served as chief treasurer (*başdefterdar*). Also served in the provincial administration as governor.	The work contains detailed information on the financial affairs of the polity. Also discussed in the work are the provincial administration and military matters. Contains recommendations to fix problems in state affairs.
Nusretname, or "Book of Victory"	Silahdar Fındıklılı Mehmed Ağa (d. 1726/7)	1721	A palace official and confidant of the ruler with military roots.	The chronicle contains a description of the important events between 1695 and 1721 in multiple parts.
Tarih-i Raşid, or "History of Raşid"	Raşid Mehmed Efendi (d. 1735)	1714–23	From an ilmiye background. He served as müderris in various prestigious madrasas, the qadi of Istanbul, and the kazasker of Anatolia. Court chronicler after Naima.	The chronicle contains events from 1660 to 1722.

Source: The relevant entries in *Türk Diyanet Vakfı İslam Ansiklopedisi* and information provided in the modern editions of the works.

(2016: 422–3), where they are associated with a human typology that the author likens to harmful weeds (*nebavit*) in the beautiful garden of the virtuous state (*medine-i fazıla*), which should be eliminated for the good of the polity.[29] Bribery and related crimes as consequences of greed in government appointees can also be observed in Koçi Bey's treatises (1972: 7, 28, 1994: 18, 43), *Kitab-ı Müstetab* (Yücel 1988: 23–5), *Hirzü'l-Mülük* (Yücel 1988: 153–7, 177–9, 195–6), and Defterdar Sarı Mehmed's *Nesayihü'l-Vüzera* (Defterdar 1935: 70, 85, 88, 95, and *passim*), works composed in different eras. References to greed as a source of corruption occur frequently in the chronicles of Selaniki (1999: 1:356–7), Silahdar (—*Tarih* 2012: 785, 797, 986, and *passim*), Naima (2007: 1:29, 2:358, 515), and Raşid (2013: 2:1004).

Yet even among authors who propose a strong connection between bribery and greed, it is possible to find those who acknowledge that otherwise moral people may find themselves offering or accepting bribes in order to survive. For example, while the unnamed author of *Hırzü'l-Mülük* (Yücel 1988: 160, 187) attributes the financial and military troubles of the polity at least partly to the rapacity of high-level administrators, who refused to be satisfied with their legitimate revenue sources and sold prebendal lots to undeserving outsiders, he remains hesitant to blame deserving parties, such as the sons of the deceased tımar-holders, who might consider paying for such allotments because they lacked other means to acquire them. In such cases, it is not *their* greed but that of the higher authorities that is responsible for the corrupt state of affairs.

Moralistic explanations of corruption never completely disappear in the pre-Tanzimat period. Still, a few works, including *Kitab-ı Mesalih*, Hezarfen Hüseyin Efendi's *Telhisü'l-Beyan*, and Naima's *Tarih*, also stress the difficult conditions of their times as explanations for corruption among government officials. As noted, a similar perspective appears in earlier Ottoman accounts

---

[29] According to Kınalızade (ibid.), the "weeds" category, borrowed from Tusi (d. 1274) and Dawwani (d. 1502), is a broad one that contains not only the people he calls the "hypocrites" (*merailer*), "distorters of truth" (*muharrifler*), "rebels to the political authority" (*bagiler*), "apostates" (*marıklar*), and "sophists" (*mugallıtlar*), but also those who "collect property and wealth by false litigations and lies based on animosity" (deavi-i zur ve husumet-i kazibe ile ahz-i emval idenler), "act as false witnesses in litigations," "fine populace excessively," and "accept bribes," along with "qadıs who deliberately misjudge cases" and "müderrises who sell their positions." The English translations here are by Sariyannis (2019: 87). The desirable groups in the virtuous city, which correspond to fruits, flowers, and beneficial plants in the garden, include philosophers, scholars, judges, warriors of faith, those who give advice on good and right things (*zevi'l-elsine*, or "possessors of languages"), those who measure and estimate things (*mukaddırlar*), and people of property (*erbab-ı emval*) who engage in commerce and manufacture goods. In *Ahlak-ı Alai* the acts of rebellion, distortion, apostasy, bribery, and the like correspond to a group identity ("weeds"), which makes it impossible for the individuals associated with them to be included in one of the more desirable constituents of the social order.

attributed to the likes of Çandarlı Ali Paşa. But while Çandarlı is an apologist for disgraced officials, depicted in earlier accounts as someone who overlooks their crimes, references to unfavorable socioeconomic circumstances appear in later texts that are also critical of corrupt acts.

A clearer difference between pre- and post-sixteenth-century political works concerns the broader associations of bribery. For one thing, the earlier inclination to associate bribery with any and all forms of wealth extraction does not appear in later works. Rather, authors explicitly differentiate bribery (and other types of abuse) from legitimate means of raising revenue. Frequent references to the Circle of Justice,[30] which justified the ruler's and his agents' extractive rights over the flock, is revealing in this regard. At the same time, the political literature and chronicles from the era do highlight a particular group of grievances including or frequently linked to bribery. Table 5.3 compiles these offenses based on specific texts.

As Table 5.3 shows, alongside bribery of various sorts the political literature contains recurring references to (mis)appointments of undeserving individuals to important government positions, illegal or excessive extraction of resources from taxpayers (often by force), negligence in government service, and social mixing. But unlike what we observed in mühimme and şikayet registers, they generally exclude concerns about embezzlement.[31] A few (if not all) of the grievances represented in the table are also prominently expressed in jurisprudential and imperial texts, as I observed earlier. What seems distinctive in the political literature, however, is the central concern with acquiring government positions via bribes and, to a lesser extent, favoritism and undue influence—other acts that often required payments to intercessors.[32] Consequently, merit was abandoned as a recruitment criterion, and government offices were assigned to immoral or otherwise unqualified people.[33] Most other grievances the authors raise in these texts—including negligence in government service, mixing of the reaya and the askeri and the consequent social disorder, and the extraction of illegal and/or excessive resources by government appointees (partially to recover the sums they used to purchase

---

[30] See, for example, Lütfi Paşa 1991: 34; Kınalızade 2016: 498; Akhisari 1979–80: 254–5; Koçi Bey 1972: 50, 1994: 65; *Kitab-ı Müstetab* (Yücel 1988): 18, 21–2; Katip Çelebi 1982: 22; Naima 2007: 1:30, 4:1653, and *passim*; and Defterdar 1935: 76, 119–20.

[31] For exceptions, see Aşık Çelebi 2018: 81; Raşid 2013: 1:98.

[32] See, for example, Mustafa Ali 1982: 1:18–19, 66; Peçevi 1968: 11; Silahdar—*Tarih* 2012: 256, 1053–4; Defterdar 1935: 87–90; and Raşid 2013: 2:901, 1166. On favoritism and payments for intercessions, see Koçi Bey 1972: 29, 1994: 43–4; and *Hırzü'l-Mülük* (Yücel 1988): 195–6. For an in-depth discussion of the morality of favoritism in the early modern Ottoman context, see Chapter 8.

[33] See, for example, Aşık Çelebi 2018: 82 and 84–5; Mustafa Ali 1982: 1:18–19, 53, 66, 75; *Kitab-ı Müstetab* (Yücel 1988): 3–5; *Hırzü'l-Mülük* (Yücel 1988): 187; and Silahdar—*Nusretname* 2001: 933–5.

Table 5.3 Harmful Behavior in Government According to Political Texts

Source	Payment-for-appointment schemes/bribes for assignments	Bribery in adjudications	(Mis) Appointments of the immoral and unqualified	Over-extraction; extortion (zulüm)	Favoritism	Social mobility/class mixing	Negligence in gov't and military affairs (including tımar)	Collusion between mil.-admin. and relig.-jud. officials	False witnessing	Sexual deviancy	Drug use
Asafname, by Lütfi Pasha (mid-sixteenth c.)	X				X	X					
Ahlak-ı Alai, by Kınalızade (1563–5)		X	X	X		X	X		X		
Miracü'l-Eyale, by Aşık Çelebi (mid-sixteenth c.)		X	X	X			X				
Usulü'l-Hikem, by Hasan Kafi Akhisari (late sixteenth c.)	X	X	X	X		X	X				
Nushatü's-Selatin, by Mustafa Ali (1581)	X	X	X	X		X	X	X		X	X
Tarih-i Selaniki (late sixteenth c.)	X		X	X		X					
Kitab-ı Müstetab (1620)	X		X	X		X	X				
Risales, by Koçi Bey (1630, 1640)	X	X	X	X	X	X	X				
Kitab-ı Mesalih (1637–44)	X	X	X	X		X					X

Tarih-i Peçevi (1640–9?)	X		X	X				
Düsturü'l-Amel, by Katip Çelebi (1652/3)	X		X	X		X		
Hırzü'l-Mülük (late sixteenth or mid-seventeenth c.)	X	X	X	X	X			
Telhisü'l-Beyan, by Hezarfen Hüseyin Efendi (1675/6)	X		X	X			X	
Tarih-i Silahdar (1695)	X		X	X				X
Tarih-i Naima (1697–1704)	X		X	X	X	X	X	
Nesayihü'l-Vüzera, by Defterdar Sarı Mehmed (1714–17)	X	X	X	X	X	X		
Nusretname, by Silahdar Fındıklılı Mehmed Ağa (1721)	X		X	X	X			
Tarih-i Raşid (1714–23)	X	X	X	X	X		X	X

Notes:

1. The table is an approximate and (at times) inferential representation of the references to various types of relevant behavior in individual sources. While I may have missed references to specific acts cited in individual texts, I feel confident that acts not identified in particular rows are relatively underrepresented.

2. Distributive conflicts, including what moderns call "embezzlement," are rare in the sources and not included in the table.

Source: See the text and accompanying notes.

their posts but also partially to enrich themselves)—are treated as direct consequences of bribery- or influence-induced appointments.[34]

Indeed, the causal relationship among various acts of corruption is explicitly articulated in many works. For example, according to Koçi Bey (1972: 28, 1994: 43),

> it was with the sale of candidacies for judicial positions (*mülazımlıklar*) that many outsiders entered the profession by paying five to ten thousand akçes and subsequently became professors and qadis. [Consequently,] the profession became filled with ignorant people and the differences between good/qualified and bad/unqualified became invisible. These [people who paid for their positions] committed injustices and committed oppression. It is these ignorant individuals and outsiders [who] sully the names of [genuine] scholars.

Katip Çelebi (1982: 24–5, 2010: 89), too, blames the reaya's poverty on the sale of government positions to tyrants and unqualified people for high prices, instead of assigning them based on one's qualifications.[35] Likewise, Selaniki (1999: 1:427) observes that

> government offices were assigned by bribes called pişkeş and gifts ("pişkeş u hedaya namiyle, rüşvetsiz mansıbı u hidmet virilmeyüp"), and thus came to be acquired by unqualified (*na-ehl*) and inappropriate (*na-reva*) people. Those who were concerned with public coffers (beytülmal) were removed [from office] and state resources (*mahsul-ı mülk*) were acquired by incompetent (*na-kardan*) people. Illegal taxes and levies were imposed on the flock continuously and without an end.

In his own formulation of the association among many problems in government, Naima (2007: 3:1111–12) lists the same causal links but adds that the

---

[34] See, for example, Akhisari 1979–80: 250, 269; *Kitab-ı Müstetab* (Yücel 1988): 15; Koçi Bey 1972: 7, 27–8, 1994: 18, 48; Selaniki 1999: 2:479, 482; Mustafa Ali 1982: 1:65, 2:35–6; *Kitab-ı Mesalih* (Yücel 1988): 106–8; Hezarfen 1998: 113, 203; Defterdar 1935: 88; and Silahdar—*Tarih* 2012: 1467–8.

[35] The association of office-selling with bribery might have also been widespread in the Arabic-speaking territories of the empire. Al-Jabarti (d. 1825) claims that payment-for-appointment schemes were considered during the reigns of Süleyman the Magnificent (d. 1566) and Selim II (d. 1574) as a way to raise revenue but were rejected because of their "destructive" potential (al-Jabarti 1994: 1:33–4). The implication of al-Jabarti's discussion is that office-selling became common after the third quarter of the sixteenth century.

frequent replacement of government appointees exasperated the financial difficulties of the masses:

> The officeholders were replaced so frequently... [that] those who had acquired their posts via bribes could often not recuperate the returns of their investments. Many choice sub-provinces and productive provinces were granted to close associates of the ruler or the members of their retinues. Skilled, qualified and experienced provincial administrators could not acquire them and eventually fell into destitution.... Reaya suffered, the public finances were ruined.... The [order of the] world was disrupted.[36]

The (mis)appointments in question were of all kinds and levels. The texts frequently mention such cases with reference to high-status and -income positions in every branch of the administration, including governorships, prominent financial appointments (such as *defterdarlık*s) and inspectorships (*nazırlık*s), army and navy commands, and qadiships.[37] They also describe how the tax-paying common folk managed to obtain janissary or ilmiye affiliation at entry levels (for example, as *acemioğlanları* and *mülazım*s) or acquire prebendal lots by paying or otherwise influencing those in charge.[38] In fact, a perusal of our sources, especially the chronicles, indicates the prevalence of payment-for-appointment schemes and, ironically, how the public despised them—they were so prevalent and so despised that selling government offices to unqualified individuals was an excuse to justify rebellions against the political authority.[39] In one instance, those who sought to bring down the

---

[36] Naima observes in the same place that many offices were assigned by palace women's intercessions (ibid; also, 1:1111). In fact, influence-peddling for money appears to be a clear source of contempt in our sources. The authors mention influential and well-connected brokers, who charged substantial sums for their efforts to sway decision-makers on their clients' behalf. These brokers often included palace functionaries, harem officials, and the ruler's favorites. See, for example, the case of Nasuh "the dwarf" (*cüce*) in Selaniki 1999: 1:136. At times, connections to the Queen Mother were effective. In this regard, consider the tragic story of a Jewish woman named Esperanza Malchi (or "Kira"), a *bohçacı* (peddler of textiles) who acted as an intermediary between Mehmed III's mother, Safiye Sultan (d. 1595), and potential clients from outside who sought Safiye's support in acquiring appointments and revenue sources. According to Naima (2007: 1:162–3), those who regarded Malchi's connections and her knowledge of the arrangements in the palace as threats that eventually brought about her lynching. For a critical and sophisticated take on Malchi's story in various sources, see Kovaleva 2014, who suggested that the character should be seen as a trope based on the conflation of multiple biographies rather than an actual historical personality. Also see Aykan (2021) for a legal discussion of events surrounding Malchi's lynching.

[37] See, for example, Selaniki 1999: 1:328, 332, 409, 427, 2:504, and *passim*; Silahdar—*Tarih* 2012: 1467–8 and *passim*; Naima 2007: 2:414, 703, 3:1097, 1100, 1112, and *passim*; Kitab-ı Müstetab (Yücel 1988): 3–4; Mustafa Ali 1982: 1:66; *Hırzü'l-Mülük* (Yücel 1988): 195–6.

[38] See, for example, Selaniki 1999: 2:471, 479, 518, and *passim*; Naima 2007: 2:637–8, 831–3; *Kitab-ı Müstetab* (Yücel 1988): 3–4; *Hırzü'l-Mülük* (Yücel 1988): 160, 195–6.

[39] See, for example, Naima 2007: 2:487, 704, 3:1152.

ruler obtained a fatwa stating that "a ruler who undermines the order of the state by appointing undeserving people based on bribes instead of the members of the religious and military establishments is deserving of dethronement and eradication" (Naima 2007: 3:1168). Yet Naima (2:704, 3:1184) also makes clear that the parties who complained about such appointments followed the same practices when they had the chance to do so.[40]

Figure 5.1 identifies the distinctive set of wrongdoings associated with corruption as gleaned from many examples from the Ottoman political

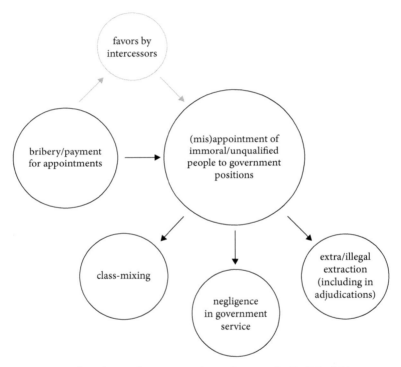

Figure 5.1 Causal Links in Corruption According to the Political Literature (Sixteenth to Eighteenth Centuries)

---

[40] This finding is reminiscent of Olivier de Sardan's (1999) observations on what he calls the "corruption complex" in various modern African communities. According to Olivier de Sardan, practices associated with corruption are "common and routine element[s] of the functioning of the administrative and para-administrative apparatus" in these settings, "from top to bottom." In this sense, "corruption is neither marginal nor sectoralised or repressed, but is generalised and banalised" (28). At the same time, Olivier de Sardan insists, "the stigmatization of corruption, as well as recriminations against it, are a central element of all discourses, public or private, at all levels of society, and have punctuated all the political phases since independence. Corruption is therefore as frequently denounced in words as it is practised in fact. But the verbal stigmatization of corruption rarely leads to legal proceedings or sanctions" (29).

literature composed between the sixteenth and eighteenth centuries. The unique composition of the crimes frequently mentioned in these works, the authors' emphasis on particular types (payment-for-appointment schemes and, especially, (mis)appointment of unqualified people to important positions), and the proposed causal links among particular grievances distinguish the discourses of corruption in these texts from those we observed not only in jurisprudential works and state documents, but also in the political literature composed before the sixteenth century. The lighter shading of "favors by intercessors" connotes the lack of unanimity among our authors on its legitimacy (I'll return to this issue in Chapter 8).

At this point of discussion, a deeper discussion of context might help us appreciate the prevalent concerns in the political literature, especially regarding payments to acquire government posts, a particularly despised practice among many political commentators.[41] In this regard, we can consider a variety of factors that lent credence to claims of impropriety in military, administrative, and judicial appointments, even if intermittently so. In reviewing the relevant literature, one can identify both supply-side and demand-side stimuli for the prevalence of payment-for-appointment arrangements in particular eras.

In terms of supply-side factors there is some consensus among historians that from the last decades of the sixteenth century onward the polity faced significant fiscal problems linked to long wars with powerful European and Middle Eastern adversaries; shifts in military technology, organization, and strategies; and inflationary pressures (Balla and Johnson 2009). The general deterioration of state finances and the increasing need for currency led authorities to seek new revenue sources and find ways to enhance cash flow to the central treasury. The novel forms of direct wealth extraction implemented during this period ranged from multiple types of avarız levies[42] to taxes on tobacco, wine, and coffee production and consumption,[43] along with short- and longer-term tax-farming arrangements.[44]

---

[41] Incidentally, Cemal Kafadar (2018: 291) characterizes the practice as indicative of "the commoditization of public office" and links it to "the inroads made by market forces into the realm of power."

[42] Avarız levies initially referred to a variety of irregular, sometimes in-kind, extractions (including *avarız akçesi, nüzül, sürsat*, and *imdad-ı seferiyye*) intended to finance military expeditions. In the seventeenth century these became regularized in the sense that they were assigned and collected on a habitual basis and turned from partially in-kind (as in the cases of sürsat and nüzül) into completely cash-based revenue sources. According to Tabakoğlu (2016: 364–75, 521) they constituted between 10 and 20 percent of the revenues collected by the central treasury during the seventeenth and eighteenth centuries.

[43] From the end of the seventeenth century on, the government also frequently attempted to restructure the taxes imposed on craftsmen and non-Muslims to enhance their yields and ease their collection (Tabakoğlu 2016: 520–8).

[44] The spread of tax-farming is one response by the Ottoman administration to the post-sixteenth-century financial problems that has been widely recognized and discussed by researchers. In this system, revenue sources were farmed out, sometimes on a lifetime basis, in return for a one-time lump-sum payment at the beginning of the contract, followed by regular subsequent payments. Farmed-out

Despite such attempts at fiscal innovation, Karaman and Pamuk's (2010: 603–11) calculations indicate that the Ottoman Empire's revenues remained low and stagnant compared to those of many European powers, including England, France, Holland, Austria, and Russia. Among other reasons (for example, the empire's size, terrain, agrarian technology, and low levels of urbanization compared to many Western polities), this was because a large portion of the gross tax receipts—perhaps more than half—remained in the hands of state functionaries, local notables, tribal and religious leaders, and others who played critical roles in the assessment, allocation, collection, and delivery of various taxes and revenues due to the government (Karaman and Pamuk 2010: 594–6).

The central government often attempted to remedy this problem by pursuing various policies designed to claim larger proportions of the wealth extracted from taxpayers. In particular, it routinely tapped into the salaries and officially sanctioned revenue sources of tax-exempt groups, including waqf functionaries, tımar-holders, and retired government appointees, at times of need—for instance, during military expeditions or coronations, when new rulers made customary payments to the military and members of the administration.[45] Furthermore, confiscation (*müsadere*) of the property of affluent and high-positioned government officials on their dismissals, or following their executions for real or fictitious crimes they had allegedly committed, became particularly common in the late seventeenth and eighteenth centuries (cf. Arslantaş 2017).

In this context, I interpret payment-for-appointment schemes as another redistributive mechanism. Indeed, our sources contain references to justifications for such arrangements, albeit in ways that undermined their legitimacy: Katip Çelebi (1982: 25, 2010: 89), for example, states that payment-for-appointment schemes were defended on the basis that they benefited the treasury. Naima also indicates that such payments were "excused because of need" (2007: 3:1111) or "justified based on a troubled treasury" (3:1271; see

---

revenue sources often included taxes generated by state-owned agricultural lands and levies associated with manufacturing, customs, mining, and specific services. Individuals who won the right to tax these sources in public auctions paid the state a lump sum and fixed installments for the duration of their contracts. Between the fifteenth and seventeenth centuries, tax-farm contracts did not extend beyond five years. Life-term tax-farming was introduced at the end of the seventeenth century (1695) to enable the government to use "tax-revenues as collateral and borrow on a large term basis" (Pamuk 2004: 17).

[45] At the time of Mahmud I's enthronement in 1730, to give one example, the central government compelled life-term tax-farmers (malikane-holders) to make payments equivalent to 5 percent of the initial lump sum they had paid for their contracts (Tabakoğlu 2016: 542). The malikane-holders were forced to do the same again in the late eighteenth century, but this time at a rate equal to 15 percent of their lump sums, when the Ottomans faced a particularly severe fiscal crisis amid their wars with Russia and Austria (Cezar 1986: 68–74, 137; Tabakoğlu 1986: 295–300).

also 3:1548).⁴⁶ These arrangements, often secured via auctions (ibid.; see also Selaniki 1999: 2:504) but sometimes assigned without the prior consent of appointees (Naima 2007: 4:1676), required immediate payments from appointees and were a significant revenue source. According to Naima, the governorship of Egypt was acquired for 400 purses (around 200,000 guruş) in 1655 (ibid.); the governorship of Aleppo for "more than 50 purses" (25,000 guruş) in 1643 (3:963); the sub-governorship of an unnamed district (sancak) in Anatolia for 30,000 guruş in 1648 (3:1179); and, in 1646, the qadiships of Bursa and Thessaloniki for 10,000 guruş each, and that of Damascus for 19,000 guruş (3:1097, 1112).⁴⁷ These figures probably correspond to advance payments made before or at the time of appointments, followed by subsequent annual contributions by officeholders. The revenue they generated supplemented the ruler's "inner treasury" (or *hazine-i enderun, hazine-i hassa*) and the coffers of high-level state authorities, particularly the grand vizier, governors-general, and military commanders (sing. serdar), which were both frequent auxiliary sources for funds when the government's dedicated sources could not cover its expenses.⁴⁸ The payments made for higher-level appointments had a trickle-down effect: they compelled those who had paid for their positions to seek compensation for the roles they had played in lower-level appointments (Fodor 2018: 77–82). In other words, and as Wilfrid Prest argued in the English context (1991: 78), those who bought had to sell.

---

⁴⁶ Jenny Guardado's (2018) research on office selling in early modern Peru under Spanish control indicates that payment-for-appointment schemes became particularly frequent during military crises, when liquid funds for urgent expenditures were most needed.

⁴⁷ For an articulate depiction of the sales of government posts in the Ottoman context, see the recent work of Pál Fodor (2018: Ch. 2), which benefits from earlier, underappreciated research by Klaus Röhrborn (1973). Outside the Ottoman context in the Islamic world, we find a relatively developed literature on payment-for-appointment schemes in the Mamluk context. Toru Miura (1997) might be the first who noticed the importance of payment-for-appointment schemes as an indispensable revenue source for the late Mamluk state. According to Bernadette Martel-Thoumanian (2005: 55), "Venality of office became so commonplace, indeed, insignificant a practice that it attracted only occasional attention from historians." At some point, Miura observed (1997: 51), wealth became a prerequisite to obtain high offices, and considerations of merit and talent lost importance in appointment considerations. On Ibn Khaldun's views about how Mamluk judges frequently bought their positions, see Morimoto 2002. For more general observations about relevant practices in the Mamluk polity, see van Steenbergen, Wing, and D'hulster 2016a, 2016b.

⁴⁸ Fodor (2018: 80) suggests that the appointment payments not only "enrich[ed] the treasury of the grand vizier or that of the serdars [military commanders]. In fact, most of the money found its way to the ruler's private treasury (*iç hazine*), with the grand vizier receiving far less and apparently having to conceal the amounts from his master." Indeed, contemporary sources indicate a tension among the ruler and his high-level officials on the division of the spoils generated by payment-for-appointment schemes. See Silahdar (—*Nusretname* 2001: 935) for a report in which it is claimed that the grand vizier Nevşehirli İbrahim Paşa (d. 1730) did not share with the ruler (Ahmed III [d. 1730]) the "bribes" he received for appointments. See also Naima 2007: 3:1294.

Unfortunately, our sources, both primary and secondary, fail to provide a systemic description of the appointment processes and their requirements. In fact, it is likely that they varied significantly based on the central government's needs at any given point in time, the qualities and resources of the applicants, and the nature and requirements of specific assignments. This lack of predictability in appointment schemes is a popular source of grievance in the political literature. In particular, authors point out, the central government's inclination to squeeze as much money as possible from its own officials often led to premature and poorly justified dismissals from already-paid-for assignments, which were summarily reassigned to new appointees in return for additional advance or immediate payments.[49] Obviously, this tendency impoverished those in government service and generated major incentives on their part to seek financial resources as fast and as aggressively as they could. Consequently, they led to major acts of abuse directed against taxpayers.[50]

One senses a great deal of anguish and anxiety in the texts over premature dismissals from office; they even go so far as to define this behavior as a measure of morality on its own. According to Peçevi (1968: 20), for example, the grand vizier Rüstem Paşa (d. 1561) was a successful and much-admired statesman, even though he was the person who first instituted the practice of accepting "bribes" to make appointments, because he refused to unjustly dismiss those who made such payments to acquire government posts before the end of their terms.[51] The righteous anger such dismissals must have caused among many officeholders is clearly reflected in Naima's account of Abaza Hasan Paşa's (d. 1658) reaction to his discharge from his post as the voyvoda (overseer) of Yeni İl Turkomans in a letter to the ruler: "I paid the state's treasury (*miri*) 60,000 guruş for this position in addition to making other contributions and facing other expenses. They [the central government; specifically, grand vizier Melek Ahmed Paşa] collected so much from me and yet their greed has still not been satisfied. They want to ruin me.... [The grand vizier] should either allow me to retain my post or return to me what

---

[49] See, for example, Katip Çelebi 1982: 24, 2010: 88; Selaniki 1999: 1:359; *Kitab-ı Müstetab* (Yücel 1988): 4–5; Naima 2007: 2:414, 3:1064, 1111–12, and *passim*; and Hezarfen 1998: 113.

[50] Ali Reza Sheikholeslami (1971: 109–10) describes the consequences of selling offices to highest bidders and the possibility of their arbitrary and premature reassignments based on the inclination to extract funds from officeholders in Qajar Iran as follows: "The result of the sales of offices was mainly the affliction of the peasantry. In the long run, it was the peasantry which footed the bill for the sales. The insecurity of office encouraged the governors to recoup their expenses within the first year. In order to stay for another year, they generally had to pay a new purchase price. Other hopefuls often offered higher prices and thus the governors had to extract even more from the peasantry to remain competitive."

[51] For an impression of the generally favorable views on Rüstem Paşa in Ottoman sources, see Afyoncu 2008.

I contributed to the state's coffers. Or else I remain [in the capital]." When the central government agreed to return to Abaza Hasan only 30 purses (15,000 guruş) and insisted that he leave immediately, he rhetorically asked, "Don't you take pity on what might happen in the provinces if you forced me out of Istanbul in such a state of sorrow and disappointment?" Naima reports that the imperial center did not care "if he put Anatolia to fire as long as he left." And as soon as Abaza Hasan left, in fact, he did begin pillaging the countryside (2007: 3:1309–13).[52] The incident can be read as a striking example of the distributive tensions in the system and their catastrophic consequences in the broader society.

Turning now to the demand side—specifically, demand for government positions—one should consider the natural demographic growth in the households that already belonged to the religious (ilmiye) and military (seyfiye) establishments, as well as outsiders' efforts to attain low-level ilmiye and seyfiye affiliations, which not only provided them with tax-exempt status, but also gave them the opportunity to eventually secure government appointments.

Existing research on Ottoman career patterns indicates a significant propensity toward intergenerational continuity in the ilmiye and seyfiye ranks, which generated much competition for middle- and higher-level government appointments among members of families that already had askeri credentials (Itzkowitz 1962; Abou-El-Haj 1974; Kunt 1983: 57–76; Zilfi 1983, and 1988: Ch. 2; Ergene and Kaygun 2011; Nizri 2014: Chs. 1 and 2). What seems less appreciated in the scholarship is the pressure exerted on the system by those who sought entry from outside. In fact, the withdrawal of rural populations from the agrarian sector, which had stronger effects at some times than others, must have generated a significant appeal for prebendal status and also forced individuals to urban centers, where many tried to attain religious and military affiliation.[53]

According to Sam White (2011), factors that contributed to withdrawals from the agrarian sector in the late sixteenth and early seventeenth centuries included population pressure, limitations to agrarian productivity, and climatic abnormalities (such as droughts). The imperial government also frustrated the rural populations during this period by squeezing them for taxes

---

[52] Evliya Çelebi reports that the amount that Abaza Hasan paid for the position was 70 purses (=35,000 guruş), which was then given to another person for 100 purses (=50,000 guruş); see Evliya Çelebi 1991: 62. For more on Abaza Hasan's rebellion, see Finkel 2005: 257–62. As Naima makes clear in his account, his expulsion from office was the reason for Abaza Hasan's rebellion.

[53] On migration to Istanbul from Anatolia and the Balkans at various times between the sixteenth and eighteenth centuries, see, among others, Aktepe 1958; Özkaya 1981–2; Faroqhi 1998; and, most recently and comprehensively, Başaran 2014.

and by prioritizing the provisioning requirements of urban centers that were experiencing an influx of new immigrants. Finally, insecurity in the countryside, itself a consequence of the agrarian crisis, further disturbed agrarian populations. The scholarship is largely silent on how the rural populations in Anatolia and the Balkans fared in the seventeenth century (cf. Zarinebaf 2010: 37–8). Yet Betül Başaran's research (2014: 27–8) indicates that Istanbul received much migration to urban centers in the eighteenth century, and that movement often intensified at times of trouble, such as "when the cost of internal and external wars intensified economic problems and caused severe shortages, as well as problems associated with natural disasters and epidemics."[54] This might have been a prominent trend in other eras as well.

References to migration from the agrarian sector and enhanced demand for entry-level ilmiye and seyfiye affiliation are frequent in the contemporary political literature.[55] Mustafa Ali writes in his *Nushatü's-Selatin* (1982: 1:78) that peasants of the late sixteenth century often paid the descendants of recently deceased ulema to have their names fraudulently inscribed in the latter's danişmend registers so that they could pretend to be advanced students of the deceased scholars.[56] Through this strategy they could be included in the lists of mülazemet, those waiting to be appointed to judicial and teaching posts.[57] Naima (2007: 2:637–8, 831–3) notes that improper, often bribe-induced admission into the janissary corps was common in his time; the practice could not be eradicated despite the central government's efforts.[58] Our authors seem to regard these developments largely as consequences of enhanced oppression in the provinces by immoral and unqualified authorities motivated to exploit the rural populations, which ended up forcing the latter out of the agrarian economy. While this may not be entirely wrong, the

---

[54] Zarinebaf (2010: 38) also suggests that in the early eighteenth century, "the intensification of rural migration caused congestion in the walled districts of Galata and Istanbul."

[55] See, for example, Lütfi Paşa 1991: 35; Kınalızade 2016: 448–9; Akhisari 1979–80: 254; Mustafa Ali 1982: 1:66, 78; *Kitab-ı Müstetab* (Yücel 1988): 4–5, 8; Koçi Bey 1972: 27–8, 1994: 43; Defterdar 1935: 118.

[56] It was a common practice in the first half of the eighteenth century to auction mülazemet spots to uneducated former peasants (Kuru 2016: 13).

[57] Kazaskers' Ruznamçe Registers indicate that the intense pressure generated by those who wanted to find positions in the judicial administration continued until the eighteenth century, as is evident in shortening terms of appointment for those in office and increasing wait times for those between offices. According to İsmail Gündoğdu (2009: 115), a qadi below the rank of *molla* in Anatolia would have expected to spend on average fifty-one months between appointments in the first half of the eighteenth century. For a consistent picture from the Balkans in the same period, see Kuru 2016: 135–8. Jun Akiba (2005: 45) states for a slightly later period that "there were 5,000 to 6,000 members belonging to the hierarchy of kadıship during the reign of Selim III [r. 1789–1807], despite the number of kadıship posts in the whole Empire being around one thousand at most."

[58] For consistent reports see Selaniki 1999: 2:471, 479; and Raşid 2013: 2:877–8.

authors overlook the possibility that withdrawal from the agrarian sector might have also created a feedback loop, generating incentives to pay for government positions in the face of intensifying competition and thus further exacerbating the inclination to squeeze the rural populations for yet more resources.

Although both supply- and demand-side factors might have contributed to the prevalence of payment-for-appointment schemes, their contributions were not necessarily equal. In fact, the short duration of appointments and the long waits between them indicate that demand for office might have often surpassed the supply. The frequent, almost arbitrary revocation of appointments is another indicator that those who controlled government appointments benefited from a relatively high level of demand.

The association of bribery with greed has direct implications for policing and preventing corruption. For example, Kınalızade (2016: 424) recommended the exile or execution of those guilty of bribery (and other forms of abuse), because he regarded such acts as signals of poor character, which is irredeemable: just as it is impossible to transform weeds into fruits or flowers, people with bad character traits cannot be rehabilitated.[59]

Mustafa Ali, Katip Çelebi, and Defterdar Sarı Mehmed Paşa are some of the authors who called (implicitly and explicitly) for severe punishments for those responsible for corruption, ranging from stern chastisement and dismissal from their positions to execution. A few others, however, including Hazerfen Hüseyin and Naima, recommended restraint in imposing the harshest punishment (execution) on officials guilty of accepting bribes. Table 5.4 summarizes the punitive and other measures proposed by a few prominent voices between the mid-sixteenth and eighteenth centuries to control corruption.

The table provides clues that many authors believed the effort to eliminate corruption merely by the threat of punishments would be ineffective. A few,

---

[59] As Ayşe Sıdıka Oktay (1998: 6–12) suggested in her dissertation, Kınalızade's *Ahlak-i Alai* was closely inspired by Nasr al-Din Tusi's (d. 1274) and Jalal al-Din Dawwani's (d. 1502) works. In fact, both works contain references to "weeds" or nevabit. But while Tusi and Dawwani include in this category five sub-groups—the "hypocrites," "distorters," "rebels," "apostates," and "sophists"—Kınalızade also recognizes corrupt judges who accept bribes and promote injustice, those who litigate false disputes to obtain material benefits, false witnesses, government officials who extort resources from common people, madrasa professors who sub-contract their positions to undeserving people, and usurpers. The emphasis on judicial crimes in Kınalızade's take on the nevabit and his association of these acts with other forms of abuse prominently discussed in Ottoman sources may be related to the fact that he was an Ottoman qadi. In addition, Kınalızade's call for the elimination (by execution or exile) of the nevabit is quite radical compared to what we observe in Tusi and Dawwani's takes, who fall short of recommending these punishments for any sub-groups, except for the "rebels" (Oktay 1998: 365–7; cf. Sariyannis 2019: 87).

Table 5.4 Punishments and Other Measures to Control Corruption as Proposed by Ottoman Commentators

Author/Title (Date of the Work)	Punishments	Other Measures
Lütfi Paşa (mid-sixteenth c.)		Need to appoint individuals who are reliable and without greed; keeping the numbers of state appointees low (1991: 11, 35).
Kınalızade (1563–5)	Exile or execution of offenders (2016: 424).	
Hasan Kafi Akhisari (late sixteenth c.)		Appointing honest, trustworthy, deserving people to government positions (249–50 and *passim*).
Mustafa Ali (1581)	Bribe takers "should not be spared" (1982: 2:11).	Giving positions to those who deserve them; safety of office for qualified, moral people; use of spies to investigate allegations of crime (*passim*).
Kitab-ı Müstetab (1620)		Ruler's direct, personal involvement in appointment decisions and government affairs. Finding the right people for important positions (Yücel 1988: 24–5, 31–2).
Koçi Bey (1631, 1640)	Dismissal and exile; sometimes lifetime ban from appointments; other, unspecified punishments (1972: 30–1, 63, 1994: 46).	Safety of office for deserving appointees; lifetime appointments for moral, deserving individuals; protection of the grand vizier from outside influence when deciding on appointments; strict quotas on mülazamets to restrict the numbers of qadis (1972: 29–30, 63–4, 1994: 44–6, 79–80).
Kitab-ı Mesalih (between 1637 and 1644)		Appointment of excess, "low-quality" qadis to tımars or as slaves of the sultan (kapıkulus) to reduce the pressure on religious-judicial system; sending trustworthy inspectors to provinces (Yücel 1988: 91–2).
Katip Çelebi (1652/3)	"Acts of bribery used to be punished in the past" but not anymore; many offenders used to be exiled and disgraced, and some were executed (1982: 25, 2010: 89).	Appointments should be given to deserving (and presumably moral) people (1982: 33, 2010: 91).

Hırzü'l-Mülük (late sixteenth or mid-seventeenth c.)	Those who hold high positions should be afraid of the ruler. Verdicts of qadis who accept bribes are not valid (Yücel 1988: 159–60, 196).	Finding honest and moral people; sultan should make the appointments of highest positions independent of the grand vizier; sultan should order the kazaskers not to be afraid of anyone when making appointments; kazaskers should make appointments based on merit and experience (Yücel 1988: 195–6). Claims of abuse should be investigated (180).
Hezarfen Hüseyin Efendi (1675/6)	Viziers should frequently be chastised and threatened; state appointees who oppress should be chastised and threatened, may be expelled from office but not executed (perhaps with the exception of provincial governors); kazaskers who sell qadiships should be punished; forgiveness and reappointment should be possible (1998: 73, 203).	Honest state appointees should not be frequently dismissed (113); oppression is due to poverty, so the ruler should keep state appointees (especially ulema) solvent; numbers of mülazemet should be reduced; spies should be used to investigate provincial affairs; unjust qadis should not be allowed to hold positions (203–4).
Naima (1697–1704)	Expulsion from office, exile, confiscation of property might be appropriate, but execution is not (2007: 3:957–8). In punishments, one should be cautious: inappropriate actions of statesmen should be measured against their merits and benefits to the state (3:1220).	Appointing independently wealthy to positions of power and status. See below.
Defterdar Sarı Mehmed (early eighteenth c.)	Warning, admonishment, removal from office. If corruption persists, "severe punishment" (*darb-ı şimşir-i siyaset*) (1935: 87–93, 1969: 42–9).	Position-holders should avoid greed; positions should be given to pious, experienced individuals; lifetime appointments for deserving governors and sub-governors; identical selection procedures for all candidates; appointments by examinations; appointment terms should not be altered; spies should be employed (1935: 76, 87, 89, 92–3).

Note: Empty cells indicate lack of specific recommendations in the associated texts.

including Hezarfen Hüseyin, Defterdar Sarı Mehmed, and the authors of *Kitab-ı Mesalih* and *Hırz'ül-Mülük*, also recommended enhanced monitoring: for example, sending spies to provincial locales to acquire in-depth information about the actions of specific officials.

In addition, the table identifies a large selection of pre-emptive measures, which range from what we might call more moralistic to more systemic. Moralistic measures include appointing honest, non-avaricious, God-fearing individuals to important positions and giving them long tenures. The systemic measures aim to diminish the incentives for predatory actions. They include policies that sought to regulate competition over limited numbers of positions, such as mülazemet quotas; to institute examinations for ulema appointments; and to set appointment terms to reduce the uncertainty that government functionaries faced.

Most authors proposed a combination of these moralistic and systemic measures to fight corruption, which is not surprising: their genre was both cumulative and appropriative, so we can assume that authors were cognizant of their predecessors' and contemporaries' ideas and frequently incorporated them into their own works. Nevertheless, variations do exist among them in terms of their emphasis on either moralistic or systemic measures. For example, while Akhisari and Mustafa Ali appeared to blame the depressing affairs of the state mostly on immoral and undeserving state appointees, Naima and Hezarfen Hüseyin Efendi tended to emphasize pressures on office-seekers to explain why they sought illegitimate ways to enhance their incomes. One source that is worthy of some attention in this regard is *Kitab-ı Mesalih* (Yücel 1988: 120–2), which has a remarkably original interpretation. Possibly composed by a member of the ilmiye order in the first half of the seventeenth century, the work is different not only because it refrained from prescribing *any* punishment for corruption, but also because it assumed that the religious establishment would inevitably contain some morally deficient individuals. Rather than lamenting their existence and consequent incidents of bribery and other forms of abuse, which it presented matter-of-factly, the author proposed a creative solution: turn low-quality qadis and müderrises, many of whom had presumably attained their positions through illegitimate means, to low-level tımar-holders and salaried military personnel (*kapıkulları*). This measure, the author argued, would diminish the numbers of those waiting for appointment, reduce the waiting times in mülazemet status, and thereby lower incentives for payment-for-appointment schemes. It would also increase the numbers of tımar-holders and other military staff who were reasonably knowledgeable about matters of religion.

Alternative Articulations in the Sixteenth to Eighteenth Centuries

Set against these relatively prominent ideas, we might also identify two alternative approaches to public office corruption in the political literature in the same era, perhaps among others undetectable to us for now. The first is what some recent Ottomanists have called the sunna- or sharia-minded voices. The second is what I call the "practical-entrepreneurial" position, a view exemplified by the ideas and observations of the chronicler Naima.

While discussing the theological and sociopolitical differences between the two prominent scholars of the seventeenth century—Abdülmecid Sivasi Efendi (d. 1639), the sheikh of the Halveti order,[60] and Kadızade Mehmed Efendi (d. 1635),[61] the leader of the Kadızadeli movement—Naima lists (2007: 4:1705) sixteen topics on which the two disagreed, including the status of music and dancing as expressions of religious devotion, the legality of the consumption of tobacco and coffee, and the acceptability of visiting saints' tombs. A public debate that pitted the two scholars against one another in 1633 is often cited as an instance in which the pro-Sufi opinions of the well-entrenched establishment figures came under attack by the orthodox, sharia-minded criticisms associated with the Kadızadeli side.[62] Significant for our purposes, also included in the list of disagreements between the two sides, according to Naima, was "the issue of bribery" (*rüşvet bahsi*).

Naima does not describe the nature of this disagreement. And I have not uncovered detailed information about how the two might have diverged on the issue.[63] Nevertheless, the fact that a disagreement about bribery existed

---

[60] Abdülmecid Sivasi Efendi was the sheikh of the Halveti order and a prominent Friday preacher in some of the more important mosques of Istanbul, including those of Şeyhzade, Sultan Selim, Sultan Ahmed, and Hagia Sofia. He is also known to have lectured on hadith- and *tafsir*-related topics. See Zilfi 1988: 133–7; and C. Gündoğdu 2009.

[61] Originally from Balıkesir, Kadızade Mehmed Efendi was the eponymous founder of the Kadızadeli movement in the early seventeenth century. He is said to have been influenced by Birgivi Mehmed Efendi (see below) early in his life. After he arrived in Istanbul, where he completed his training, he served as a Friday preacher in the mosques of Fatih, Sultan Selim, Süleymaniye, and, eventually, Hagia Sofia. See Zilfi 1988: 131–2; and Çavuşoğlu 2001.

[62] For more on this debate that took place in the Sultan Ahmed mosque in the presence of the ruler, see Kātib Chelebi 1957: 132–4; Zilfi 1988: 133–7; and Çavuşoğlu 2001. For more recent takes critical of the older literature, see Terzioğlu 2010; and Shafir 2019.

[63] According to one scholar, whatever the differences were between the two sides, they must have been insignificant: based on a comparative reading of *Tacü'l-Resail ve Minhacü'l-Vesail* that she attributed to Kadızade Mehmed and Abdülmecid Sivasi's *Nesavihü'l-Mülük* and *Letaifü'l-Ezhar ve Lezaizü'l-Esmar*, Semiramis Çavuşoğlu (1990: 230) suggested that "Kadızade and Sivasi essentially agree that bribery is a vice which the people and administrators should refrain from. Probably their views differed only on certain aspects of this practice such as specific acts which constitute bribery, the

suggests that there might have been a distinct sunna-minded perspective on the topic, and perhaps more broadly on corruption, that differed from those in other contemporary works we have examined thus far.[64]

This impression is supported by recent research on Birgivi Mehmed Efendi (d. 1573), who might be one of the best-studied pietistic critics of the Ottoman state and society in the premodern era.[65] According to Katharina Ivanyi (2012, 2020), there are many parallels between Birgivi's political opinions on corruption and the opinions of many of his contemporaries, even those who did not necessarily share his sunna-minded critique of the sociopolitical order. They all regarded bribery and related acts as major problems, and many characterized them as byproducts of the general moral degeneration during their times, associating them specifically with worldly greed. Yet Birgivi's critique was distinctly rooted in the idea that the Muslim community had been in a perpetual state of decline since the Prophet. In this regard, Ivanyi's comparison of Birgivi's ideas to those of his contemporary Mustafa Ali is useful: "Thus, while Birgivī's nostalgia for the past was directed at the age of the Prophet and the ideal community of seventh century Arabia, [Mustafa] ʿĀlī was pining for the 'golden' days of [the Ottoman ruler] Fātiḥ Sultan Meḥmed [d. 1481] and men like the famed Timurid ruler of Herat, Sultan Ḥusayn Bāyqarā (d. 911/1506)" (2020: 108). And

> even though [ʿĀlī] shared with Birgivī a frustration over the nepotism and venality of the official establishment—their respective stances were ultimately very different.... While ʿĀlī would [also] criticize corrupt waqf administrators, tax officials and government agents, he was not interested in reforming the system as a whole, but simply in having more "honest" and

---

classification of bribery into separate categories, etc. These differences did not come out in their writings, but they were expressed presumably in their sermons." This conclusion might now seem problematic, given that Derin Terzioğlu (2007) subsequently cast doubt on the link between Kadızade Mehmed and *Tacü'l-Resail*. In fact, *Tacü'l-Resail* might have been composed not by Kadızade Mehmed, the leader of the Kadızade movement, but by another Halveti sheikh by the same name, Kadızade Mehmed İlmi (d. 1631/32). On the other hand, İbrahim Baz (2019: 172–5) has implicitly agreed with Çavuşoğlu's interpretation in a more recent publication, indicating that the disagreement between the parties might have involved how to differentiate bribery from legitimate compensations for intercessions and assistance in administrative affairs.

[64] I do not mean to suggest that the Kadızadeli ideas should be regarded as the default form of piety-minded positions in premodern Ottoman politics. On this issue, see Terzioğlu 2010; and Sariyannis 2012.

[65] Birgivi has been credited with influencing many later movements, including those who opposed the Kadızadelis, such as the prominent Damascene Sufi and legal scholar Abd al-Ghana al-Nabulusi (d. 1731). He is well known for his uncompromising stance on many acts of popular devotion and his vocal opposition to some Ottoman state practices, such as the cash waqf and contemporary policies of land tenure and taxation. On Birgivi, see Yüksel 1992; and Ivanyi 2012, 2017, and 2020.

"able" men in place. Birgivī, on the other hand, in his call for a dismantling of the institution of the cash waqf,[66] as well as in his demand for a return to the "classical" Ḥanafī doctrine of land ownership and taxation, envisioned a radical overhaul, with unforeseeable consequences for the economic edifice of the Empire as a whole. (109)[67]

Consequently, "Birgivī abhorred the world ʿĀlī was moving in and would probably have seen in him a perfect example of the ambition, or 'vain hope' (*amal*), and 'desire for this world' (*ḥubb al-dunyā*) that pious men should strive to leave behind." According to Ivanyi, Birgivi's critique was not based on "pragmatic considerations of successful statecraft"; instead, it was "rooted in the conviction that societal, as much as individual virtue (and, hence, salvation and closeness to God in the Afterlife) depended on meticulous obedience to God's law, as it had been lived by the Prophet and his community" (111). Thus, he proposed a comprehensive critique of the Ottoman polity: in addition to his unfavorable views about the cash waqf, he also articulated critical opinions about the regime's land system and fiscal practices, including many forms of taxation. He regarded the public treasury (beytülmal) as tainted by illegal sources of revenue and as being used inappropriately to fund the personal expenses of the ruler (104, 222–32).[68]

Since the Ottoman legal, fiscal, and administrative institutions did not comply with sharia, Birgivi insisted, anyone affiliated with them shared the blame for perpetuating the corrupt state of affairs (105). We find here an articulation reminiscent of Theodor Adorno's "wrong lives cannot be lived rightly," one that posited a broader, systemic, and all-encompassing characterization of depravity in every layer of the government. Consequently, Birgivi maintained that God-fearing Muslims should resist any association with a government whose financial and administrative practices lacked religious legitimacy (109–10).

For the members of the religious establishment, the danger of corruption was even higher. Since worldly compensation for religious guidance was

---

[66] According to Birgivi, cash waqfs generated income based on interest payments, which he regarded as against Islamic law. For more on Birgivi's critical opinions on cash waqf, see Mandaville 1979; and Ivanyi 2020: 217–22.

[67] "Unlike that of Birgivī," Ivanyi further suggests (2020: 109), "ʿĀlī's nostalgia was...centered on Persianate court culture, imperial glory and an ideal of worldly erudition and refinement, in which men of learning and literary accomplishment, such as ʿĀlī himself, would be accorded the recognition (and position) they deserved. Instead, however, all ʿĀlī got—as he continuously laments—was to be passed over by the 'unworthy,' 'ignorant,' and 'vile.'"

[68] On the blurred boundaries between the state treasury and the ruler's private purse in pre-Ottoman polities in the Middle East, see van Berkel 2018: 71.

forbidden according to law, men of religion should have vehemently rejected any scheme that rewarded religious service with income or salaries, especially those based on illegitimate sources. Even if an *alim* found himself in the unfortunate position to accept a government post, it was particularly unacceptable for him to provide his services in return for fees, salaries, or other forms of compensation (105). On this point, Birgivi's position is consistent with the jurisprudential traditions I discussed in Chapters 1 and 2.

It has become common in the recent scholarship to identify a "turn toward piety" during the sixteenth and seventeenth centuries, when Sunni Islam became a more central aspect of the official ideology and Muslim subjects' personal lives than ever before.[69] And while researchers interested in the topic have yet to fully trace this turn's effects on contemporary social and political ideals (cf. Shafir 2019: 598), it is also likely that the sunna-minded perspectives on corruption became popular among some segments of the society. In this context, it would be reasonable to expect continuities between Birgivi's opinions and later pietistic articulations.[70]

Indeed, the few publications that explore the writings of piety-minded authors from the seventeenth and eighteenth centuries tend to highlight similar themes,[71] including an emphasis on the moral-religious depravity of the Muslim umma in which the authors lived (Terzioğlu 2010: 267, and *passim*; Kurz 2011: 45–54; Shafir 2019: 614, 617, 619); a condemnation of the laxity of those in power, including the ruler, in enforcing the sharia (Terzioğlu 2010: 291; Shafir 2019: 617); a denunciation of the abuses and moral-religious depravity of government functionaries, especially those at ilmiye ranks (Terzioğlu 2010: 270-1, 295-6; Kurz 2011: 20, 49–50, 59–60, and *passim*; Shafir 2019: 615, 618–19); and the need to reward officials who were honest and devout and punish those who were not (Terzioğlu 2010: 292, 294-5; Shafir 2019: 619). While the particular types of offenses these authors complained about did not necessarily differ from those mentioned by others

---

[69] The most prominent examples of this still-growing literature include Terzioğlu 2010, 2012/13; and Krstić 2011, among others cited in this section.

[70] But there are reasons to expect some variations as well. For example, according to Sariyannis (2012: 284), while Birgivi "had written about 'the corruptness of human transactions that are undertaken for the sake of the vicious thing, coined money'... and taken sides in the debate on cash waqfs... against Ebussuud,... neither the attack upon 'coined money'... nor the cash-waqf controversy, directly touching upon the legitimacy of usury and interest-taking, ever appeared among the issues that the Kadızadelis put forward. Nor did the fundamentalist leaders ever speak against usury (riba), although it was prohibited in the Quran."

[71] These include Derin Terzioğlu 2010, where the author examines a *nasihatname* penned by an obscure sunna-minded Sufi named Hasan in the 1630s; Marlene Kurz (2011), who surveys "a sermon-like book" of a certain preacher named Fazlızade Ali, perhaps composed in the 1740s; and Nir Shafir (2019), who explores poet Nabi's (d. 1712) popular verse-book of advice addressed to his son.

I have already highlighted,[72] the sunna-minded viewed them as direct symptoms of the fallen state of affairs in their times. And just like Birgivi, these figures prioritized the interests of the umma over those of the Ottoman dynasty; de-emphasized (or even rejected) the Circle of Justice as a reference point for a just polity; and stressed the importance of a fully sharia-compliant moral order, rather than, say, the personal benevolence of the ruler, to eliminate all forms of corruption.[73]

I have already reflected on Naima's ideas and observations in my attempts to sketch the broader trends in the discourse on corruption. In fact, it is possible to identify many overlaps between Naima's writings and those of his contemporaries. Like many other commentators who penned their works between the sixteenth and eighteenth centuries, Naima observed the relative prevalence of acts associated with corruption in governmental and administrative processes, recognized the broader societal consequences of such acts, and emphasized the need to reward the efforts of deserving, qualified government functionaries by appointing them to important positions.[74]

Yet it is also possible to detect in Naima's history particular views that separate him somewhat from many of his contemporaries, even given the plurality of the perspectives in the premodern political literature. In fact, his discussion of various examples of bribery, influence-peddling, payment-for-appointment schemes, and such lacks the alarmist and moralistic tone common to most other contemporary accounts and tends to represent them more as practical concerns that needed to be understood in ways commensurate with the circumstances of his time. This interpretation is based on a sophisticated philosophy of history, which Naima credits with shaping the primary attributes, including the shortcomings, of the Ottoman polity during his era (cf. Sariyannis 2019: 311–13). The distinctive remedies that he proposes to control corruption are influenced by the same consideration. And in these reflections we find a somewhat unique take on corruption.

---

[72] Hasan suggests that the judges and provincial officials accepted bribes and robbed common people. "Scribes" were paid to admit unqualified people into official positions (Terzioğlu 2010: 270–1). Fazlızade Ali complained about life-term tax-farming, the purchase and sale of janissary pensions, bribery in litigations and elsewhere, forgery and fraudulent use of legal documents, and the inappropriate use of beytülmal (Kurz 2011: 46–50). Nabi accused the muftis of his time of adulterating fatwas and the judges of accepting bribes (Shafir 2019: 619).
[73] For partial evidence of parallel sensitivities among Arab sources, see al-Jabarti 1994: 1:12–19; and Moreh 2003.
[74] See, for example, Naima 2007: 1:131–2; 2:358–9, 515, 672–3, 695–6, 703, 719–21, 933; 3:1111–14, 1141–3, 1271, 1315–16, and 1366, among other places.

According to Naima, every polity went through five distinct stages: birth (or "victory" over its enemies), growth (or "independence" of the ruler from his followers), maturity ("peace, ease, confidence and security"), gradual decline ("contentment and tranquility"), and dissolution ("prodigality, excessive expenditure, and eventual destruction") (2007: 1:26–30).[75] The Ottoman polity was in the fourth stage during his time, when a sense of passivity had replaced its earlier energy and restlessness. Among other attributes of this stage, Naima identified the pronounced greediness of those in power, intense competition for official appointments, and the prevalence of bribery and nepotism. Naima saw this as a period when the "body" of the state is prone to corruption ("kabul-i fesada mizac-ı devletin istidadı dahi ziyade olur") (1:28–9; cf. Sariyannis 2019: 312).

If pervasive corruption was indeed one symptom of the natural aging of the body politic, as Naima claimed, one could not hope to completely avoid or remedy it. Instead, one should be content to tolerate it as best one could, just as people facing the natural symptoms of aging should aspire to do, by adopting policies that aim to reduce the worst consequences associated with it. Relevant here are various anecdotes that Naima relates in different parts of his history. One such story, mentioned earlier, is that of a Jewish peddler, "Kira" (whose real name was Esperanza Malchi, see Note 36), who was famous for bribing her connections in Mehmed III's harem, possibly even the Queen Mother, Safiye Sultan, to get government positions for her clients. According to Naima, when Malchi's arrangements became particularly notorious and threatened Safiye Sultan's reputation or connections, the Queen Mother's powerful ally Halil Paşa, the *kaymakam* of Istanbul, sent his men to the woman's house to apprehend her, and when they got there they killed Malchi and her sons. They also severed "the hand she used to collect and distribute bribes" and her vagina (*mevzı-ı fercini*), and nailed these on the doors of those who used her services (Naima 2007: 1:162). According to Naima, this punishment was disproportional to Malchi's crimes and did more harm than good: "It is a fact that giving money and gifts [illegitimately] to those in return for providing certain services happens in every age. If it happened within certain limits, it is preferable to deal with such problems [mildly,] with clever tricks that require administrative skills and experience. Shredding the state's honor by such excesses caused by public attacks [and violence] would ensure [greater] damage" (1:163).

---

[75] The translations belong to Sariyannis (2019: 311–12).

Later, Naima (2:637–8) relates another incident that illustrates how *not* to resist temptations of bribery by government officials. The incident, which Naima claims took place in 1628, concerns a janissary scribe's refusal to follow the orders of grand vizier Hüsrev Paşa to unlawfully record the names of numerous new recruits (acemioğlanları) in janissary rosters. Naima describes the scribe as "honest and brave" and Hüsrev Paşa as "arrogant," "tyrannous," "angry," and "a merciless blood-shredder." Yet he also appears to be uncomfortable with the unrelenting, stubborn honesty of the scribe, who resigned from his position under pressure and was subsequently assaulted by those he refused to register:

> Let it be no secret that those who are overzealous about righteousness, stand up against the majority, and resist especially the viziers and influential ulema, cannot get/hold government positions and, thus, remain miserable in all times. In situations like this, it is possible to find solutions with good measures and tricks based on administrative skills and experience. While one could make a name for himself by acting tough, insisting on righteous action, requesting dismissal [when forced to act in such ways], such actions do generate many adverse consequences. (2:638)

Naima does not explain what good measures or tricks might have been appropriate for the scribe.[76] However, he clearly believes that head-on, uncompromising fight against corruption is futile. Indeed, Naima insists, absolute justice in the world existed only during the time of the Prophet, an era that cannot be recreated (and, pace Birgivi, should not be aspired to). In times of disorder and confusion, humans should not expect government affairs to be conducted in ways that are absolutely perfect. It is also inappropriate to dismiss or execute officials every time they do something wrong in these times. Instead of focusing on their shameful affairs, one should compare their good deeds to their bad ones and decide their fate accordingly (3:1220).[77] At another point, Naima (4:1764) proposes another argument against the summary dismissal of unqualified government appointees who attained their

---

[76] Remarkably, Naima relates another very similar incident that seems to have generated results that undermined his suggestion. In 1635, the sultan's agents test a janissary scribe by offering him bribes for unlawfully registering new names in the janissary register. The agents tell him that they could approach the commander of the janissary core to fulfill their objective. The scribe initially refuses their offer, so they pressure him until he accepts. Consequently, he is executed (2:831–3).
[77] In a different point in his discussion, Naima concedes that dismissal, exile, and the confiscation of belongings might be appropriate for various related offenses based on their gravity. Execution, however, is not (3:957).

positions inappropriately: he points out that once they are appointed to those positions, they have the right to hold them. Dismissing them or reducing their incomes would amount to a usurpation of their attained rights.[78]

Clearly, then, while Naima appears to be concerned about acts of corruption, he also warns his readers against policies and measures that might create havoc in administration: "Fixing such issues should be done very cautiously. With patience, very difficult problems could be resolved" (ibid.). Rash and violent acts based on or justified by moral outrage overlook the fact that corruption is systemic in nature given the state of the polity in the fourth stage of its life span. Despite the violence and disruption they often cause, they fail to generate real, enduring change in government affairs. In fact, as I stated earlier, Naima is aware of the irony that while many revolts against state authority have been justified with reference to the corruption of those in power (3:1152, 1168), when such upheavals succeed in bringing down corrupt state officials, corruption is perpetuated by those who replace them (2:703).[79]

The originality of Naima's treatment of the topic is not limited to his pragmatic resistance to moralistic condemnations of contemporary government practices. He also identifies in his account a model administrator whom he deems especially suitable for the circumstances of his times. This is Derviş Mehmed Paşa (d. 1655), who served the polity at the highest levels during the early to mid-seventeenth century (Kunt 1977: 198–200).[80] What made Derviş Mehmed Paşa a successful official was not his excellent moral qualities, including lack of greed, but his ability to accumulate incredible amounts of personal wealth while in office based on his entrepreneurial talents, which

---

[78] Relevant here is an instance when Naima (3:983) relates how he personally addressed the bribery of a scribe named Ahmed Efendi in the service of grand vizier Merzifonlu Kara Mustafa Paşa (d. 1683), whom the latter wanted to have executed because of the bribes he sought from certain officeholders at their appointments. Based on how he tells this story, Naima appears to be an acquaintance of both men. Having observed Kara Mustafa Paşa's anger and Ahmed Efendi's fear of punishment, Naima convinces the grand vizier not to kill Ahmed Efendi, arguing that Ahmed Efendi's blood is beneath the grand vizier. Dismissal is also not an option: Ahmed Efendi knows about the grand vizier's secrets and is a good and efficient scribe who cannot be easily replaced. Naima convinces Mustafa Paşa to keep him in service and merely chastise him ("tenbih ü itab ile iktifa ve hizmette ibka"). On Merzifonlu Kara Mustafa Paşa, see Özcan 2004.

[79] A good example in this regard is the famous uprising of İbşir Mustafa Paşa (d. 1655), who, according to Naima (3:1387–8), cited many acts of corruption by those in power as the main reason for his revolt in 1651. Yet when he himself became the grand vizier in 1654, he committed the very same acts he had complained about before his revolt (4:1562–4; cf. Evliya Çelebi 1991: Ch. 4). For more on İbşir Mustafa Paşa, see Aktepe 2000.

[80] Among other positions he held, Derviş Mehmed Paşa was the governor of Damascus, Diyarbekir, Aleppo, Mosul, Anatolia, Bosnia, and Silistre between 1636 and 1652. In 1653, he was made the grand vizier and remained in that position for about a year and a half (when the average length of tenure at that time was about seven months), until he suffered a stroke and became incapacitated. See Kunt 1977: 197.

allowed him to take advantage of the agricultural, financial, and commercial opportunities available to him in the locations he served. Specifically, Derviş Mehmed built his wealth by lending money at interest; investing in agriculture by, for example, opening up uncultivated lands to large-scale grain production; participating in regional and long-distance trade in grains, live animals, textiles, jewelry, and other luxury materials; and operating retail stores such as bakeries and butcher shops (Kunt 1977: 201–2). These endeavors helped Derviş Mehmed to inexpensively feed and clothe the members of his household, whose number Kunt estimates to be about 10,000, but also to profit immensely from selling leftover foodstuffs and commodities.

Derviş Mehmed's entrepreneurial talent was particularly valuable in his capacity as a high-level government appointee because of the extraordinary financial burden placed on the shoulders of such individuals in the seventeenth century. It was impossible for government appointees during this period to rely solely on officially sanctioned revenue sources to meet their wide-ranging financial obligations, which included sending funds to higher officials, defending their jurisdictions against lawlessness and external enemies, participating in military expeditions, feeding and equipping the members of their households, maintaining the roads, funding charity works, and building mosques and soup kitchens.[81] Such obligations became particularly burdensome at times of shorter and infrequent appointments, elevated monetary inflation, agrarian crisis, and rural depopulation. In this environment, relying exclusively on traditional revenue sources would lead to insolvency if the administrators decided to remain within officially sanctioned levels and forms of revenue extraction, or to administrative abuse, including corruption, if they did not.[82] Derviş Mehmed's efforts to find alternative sources of income helped him to remain solvent in difficult times without burdening the taxpayers by legal or illegal (but otherwise unavoidable) measures.

[81] An account register that belonged to Silahdar (also Koca, Hacı, Öküz) Ömer Paşa while he was the governor of Diyarbekir in the early 1670s provides detailed information regarding the revenues and expenditures of someone who was in an official position comparable to Derviş Mehmed Paşa's at around the same period (Kunt 1981). According to the register, direct and indirect payments to the central government constituted about 45 percent of Ömer Paşa's total expenditures (about 57,000 *esedi guruş*), including those remitted to the palace, to the grand vizier, and for expenses for the representatives of the sultan and the grand vizier while in Diyarbekir. Ömer Paşa's significant expenses also included those made by his steward specifically for food (about 17 percent of the total, roughly 21,500 guruş), other household expenses (about 12 percent, roughly 15,700 guruş), and salary payments (about 13 percent, roughly 16,400 guruş) to those in his military retinue.

[82] Ömer Paşa's account register, which provides information about the governor's revenues and expenses for about one year (November 1670 to November 1671), indicates a deficit of about 5,000 guruş, about 4 percent of the Paşa's total annual earnings—even though the revenue sources listed in the register included certain types of fines and dues that provincial authorities had been forbidden to collect (Kunt 1981: 17, 20).

Overall, Naima's treatment of the topic prizes political stability and demonstrates a commitment to enduring the inherently problematic practices and relationships associated with the polity's level of maturity, albeit in the least painful fashion possible. His insights indicate that public office corruption was systemic and thus might not be eradicated through attempts to punish greed or reward selfless government. It might be rendered tolerable, however, through the promotion of a new type of statesmen, as Metin Kunt suggested decades ago (1977: 203–6). Only men with entrepreneurial skills in commerce and agriculture could meet the considerable financial burdens of the offices they occupied without excessively claiming the resources of others.

* * *

This chapter has examined how corruption was characterized in the premodern Ottoman political literature. Unlike what we have observed in jurisprudential works and state documents, this group of writings contains numerous perspectives. Their authors' positionalities relative to the state before and after the sixteenth century, when the Ottoman polity experienced a radical bureaucratic-administrative transformation, is partly responsible for this variation. Also, uneven influences of particular religious-ideological and historical-pragmatic considerations on the authors contributed to the plurality of opinions.

Among the articulations of corruption surveyed in this chapter, a popular and relatively well-developed one exists in political works composed between the sixteenth and eighteenth centuries by former or then-current government functionaries. In contrast to the pro-ghazi perspectives prevalent in an earlier era, the associated texts recognized the hegemonic presence of the state in the political realm as normative, which is reflected in their authors' anxieties about who should be incorporated into its body and by what means. Regarding corruption, these works highlighted a specific set of grievances—payment-for-appointment schemes, influence-peddling, unqualified appointments, and exploitation of the taxpayer, among others—and often proposed causal links among these practices. Other commentators in the same period identified the roots of corruption in the polity's divorce from true religion. And at least one prominent observer, Naima, excused the prevalence of corruption based on the regime's relative age. These positions called for very different remedies for corruption, ranging from harsh punishments to merit-based appointments, job security and adequate income for government officials, strict observance of fiqh rules, and the promotion of entrepreneurial spirit among state functionaries. Table 5.5 summarizes the differences among the perspectives surveyed in the chapter.

Table 5.5 Perspectives on Corruption in the Ottoman Political Literature

	Pro-ghazi/ antiestablishment	Establishment/bureaucratic-minded	Sharia-minded	Practical-entrepreneurial
Period	Fifteenth century and earlier	Sixteenth to eighteenth centuries	Sixteenth century and afterward	Seventeenth century and presumably afterward
Whose Perspective?	Pro-ghazi/frontier elements	Former and current state functionaries	Pietistic voices, critical of many structural aspects of the polity and its practices	Naima and presumably a few others
Idealized Sociopolitical Order	Egalitarian and undifferentiated Anti-imperial sentiments: the ruler is seen as first among equals Ruler is supposed to be generous and benevolent; should not be parasitic Loot and taxation of non-Muslims as primary revenue sources	Stratified, hierarchical Patrimonial polity in which the ruler shares power with no one and owns everything Centralized bureaucratic government Revenue extraction from the flock as primary revenue source	Umma-centered Strictly sharia-based Disregard of the dynasty's needs, the Circle of Justice; dismissive of the ruler's paternalistic benevolence	Not specifically defined. Naima does not appear to idealize a specific type of sociopolitical order. Implicitly, however, he rejects calcified social divisions of labor among various groups: for example, a vizier should be allowed to engage in trade
Disposition toward Corruption	Moralistic	Largely moralistic, but practical considerations exist	Moralistic and jurisprudentially informed	Pragmatic: corruption is (almost) a technical problem related to the age/phase of the polity; it (or fight against it) should not be allowed to disrupt sociopolitical stability

Continued

Table 5.5 Continued

	Pro-ghazi/ antiestablishment	Establishment/bureaucratic-minded	Sharia-minded	Practical-entrepreneurial
Sources of Corruption	Greed, immorality Decay brought to Ottoman lands by outsiders with religious-judicial credentials	Greed, immorality But corruption may also result from the unfortunate material circumstances of state functionaries	The polity's systemic, structural deficiencies based on its separation from the scriptural and prophetic examples	Lack of financial resources to fund the expenses of government officials
Definition of Corruption	Amorphous: may include most acts that involve extraction of resources from Muslim community	More focused: self-regarding acts that undermine rights and disregard good qualities among government officials; acts that burden taxpayers Not all acts of extraction are illegitimate	Amorphous: any act that lacks jurisprudential justification and harms umma	Amorphous: intolerable amounts of revenue extraction are worse than illegitimate forms of it; the latter, if tolerable, should not be regarded as overly harmful to social order/stability
Specific Acts That May Be Associated with Corruption	Bribery of various types; usury; any form of revenue extraction; sexual deviancy; mixing of gender roles; etc.	Bribery, specifically to obtain government posts; (mis)appointment of unqualified people to official positions; illegal/illegitimate revenue extraction; class mixing; favoritism; negligence in government affairs To a lesser extent, sexual misconduct and deviancy; drug use; etc. (see Table 5.3)	Presumably, specific acts cited in fiqh traditions (including judicial bribery) but also other institutions or practices with dubious legal bases (such as cash-waqf or various forms of taxation common in the polity)	The same acts that Naima's contemporaries have identified (but with less moral outrage)

Remedies against Corruption	Bringing the right people to important positions Severe punishment, including corporal punishment and execution	Appointing the right people to government positions In the worst offenses, severe corporal punishment and execution; also, dismissal from office, exile, and appropriation of property (see Table 5.4) But writers also mention the need for job security and to provide officials with adequate resources	Bringing God-fearing, sharia-minded people to important positions Presumably sanctions elaborated in fiqh traditions	Realize that corruption cannot be fully eradicated; aim instead to manage it Punishments as required but no executions Most important is bringing to positions of power financially independent, entrepreneurial figures who can fund their own needs
Other Observations	Emphasis on the dangers of instrumentalization of the sharia by corrupt legal specialists Prominent anticlerical sentiments Prominent antiestablishment sentiments	Concern with competition for limited number of government positions Emphasis on the negative impact of premature dismissals from office and the negative role they play regarding corruption	May not be a fully fleshed-out perspective on corruption	May not be a fully fleshed-out perspective on corruption

6
Corruption According to Accounts for Foreigners

I have surveyed various types of sources to identify distinctive perspectives on corruption in the early modern Ottoman context. One genre of accounts still left to explore are texts written primarily for Western audiences by authors who were often (though not always) from Europe.[1] These authors include diplomats, travelers, translators, bureaucrats, intellectuals, merchants, and others who were familiar with the Ottoman state, society, history, and institutions.

The use of these sources in researching Ottoman political and administrative practices is contentious. In their critique of Ahmet Mumcu's research on bribery, both Muzaffer Doğan (2002: 38n7) and Yüksel Çelik (2006: 27, 32) took issue with his reliance on such accounts, which they considered uninformed, untrustworthy, or both. Doğan and Çelik only briefly elaborated their criticisms,[2] but there are popular, generic reasons why using foreign sources might provoke criticism. Authors of these works might have been unfamiliar with the culture, language, and institutions of the Ottoman society and thus produced their accounts largely based on subjective and superficial impressions, hearsay, and/or dated sources. Plausibly, Europeans' prevalent feelings of fear, anxiety, and religious antipathy toward the Ottomans before the eighteenth century and possibly those of superiority thereafter unfairly shaped their attitudes.[3] Finally, many European accounts engaged with Ottoman topics

---

[1] In what follows, I sometimes refer to these sources in a shorthand way, as "foreign" or "Western" accounts.

[2] Çelik (2006: 27) suggested that the authors of the accounts lacked "adequate knowledge about Ottoman administrative-fiscal system and in practical processes associated with it." Doğan (2002: 38fn7) claimed that the European accounts conflated the (fully legal, in his opinion) caize payments with bribes due to their "differences in perception."

[3] See Valensi 1993 and Çırakman 2001, 2002 about temporal changes in European perceptions of the Ottoman polity and society before the modern era. According to Engels and Monier (2021: 345), references to corruption in late eighteenth- and early nineteenth-century European accounts represented "a judgement on the behaviour or the culture of [native] office holders—or even whole societies." Also, "the state of corruption within a given society was an indicator of modernity, and vice versa: the more premodern a society, the more it was prone to corruption. The roots of this thinking go back to the time of Enlightenment, bureaucratic reforms and French Revolution, when the Ancien Régime had systematically been associated with corruption" (ibid.).

instrumentally, for example, to support arguments involving intra-European matters, and this might undermine the credibility of their observations (Rouillard 1940: 289–314; Darling 1994: 74; Kaiser 2000).

Reservations toward foreign accounts are consistent with a prevalent trend in the recent scholarship on this literature, which has emphasized how their authors tended to replicate inherited models in their own writings and edited their works to accommodate contemporary expectations and prejudices about their subject (Brentjes 2010: I:449–54).[4] Writing with the "expectation to advance their position or career in their home country," according to this interpretation, the authors composed "standardized narratives" (Varlık 2015: 84) that reproduced a series of tropes, such as the "Fatalistic Turk."[5]

Yet there are also reasons to use these accounts as sources of historical information. For one, we know that many of these authors, though certainly not all, were quite informed about their Ottoman settings, had lived in the Ottoman lands for long periods of time, possessed significant language skills, and had important connections and solid sources of information, including Ottoman sources. A few, such as Demetrius Cantemir, Elias Habesci, and Mouradgea d'Ohsson, cannot even be characterized as foreigners, although they composed their works with foreign audiences in mind.[6] We also cannot assume that these accounts were all *exclusively* shaped by previous narratives or audience expectations with roots in European intellectual trends, or at least to the same degree. In fact, the desire to produce original and factually

---

[4] Referring to works composed in the sixteenth and seventeenth centuries, Brentjes (2010: I:450) argued that "the standardization of travel literature stabilized and extended West European prejudices towards Muslim societies, both negative and positive. The Ottomans were often depicted in more and less negative terms as the destroyers of kingdoms and the world—cruel, lazy, stupid and greedy. If there was something good in the Ottoman culture, Jewish emigrants or Christian renegades were considered its source. This feature applies above all to scholarly and technical knowledge and practices. With regard to social, religious, or legal elements of Ottoman culture, the differences to the traveler's own society more often were positively evaluated and attributed to the Sultan's tolerance with regard to the Empire and their religious creeds or to the efficiency of the Muslim judicial system." For a consistent impression in the late sixteenth- and seventeenth-century Venetian sources, see Valensi 1993: 69–96.

[5] For an example of recent research that indicates the existence of more open-minded characterizations of Middle Eastern subjects in the sixteenth and seventeenth centuries, albeit outside the travel literature, see Bevilacqua 2018.

[6] In this regard, see Carter Findley's careful engagement with the life and work of Mouradgea d'Ohsson, who, Findley (2019: 364) pointed out, "did not write about the Ottoman Empire as an 'Orientalist' or any kind of outside observer. He was more of an 'oriental' than an 'orientalist,' if the terms are to be used at all.... If he had been a generation younger and had studied in a European university as his son did, Mouradgea might have thought of himself as an 'orientalist,' the way Joseph von Hammer thought of himself. However, Orientalism as a scholarly pursuit was hardly more than getting started in Mouradgea's day, his ulema tutors never have heard of it, and the faddish 'Orientalism' of the Romantic and later periods, castigated by Edward Said, was not present either in d'Ohsson's mentality, the work of his artists, or the motivations of his royal patrons in Versailles, Stockholm, or Istanbul. For d'Ohsson, knowing about Islam and the Ottoman Empire was not exotic; it was a matter of practical utility."

accurate depictions of the Orient presumably led many to produce narratives that challenged their readers' prejudices and/or corrected what the authors saw as mistakes and misrepresentations in earlier accounts (Beck 1987; Murphey 1990).[7] In principle, we should regard each account as a unique product of multiple factors, including the author's personal history, interests, and experiences in Ottoman lands, as well as the discursive and genre-specific influences on his or her narrative (Rouillard 1940: 407–20); that is, we should resist the temptation to reduce individual accounts to the tropes they may contain in an a priori manner.[8] What's more, use of these accounts does not amount to an assumption that they are devoid of religious or ideological bias. In fact, and as Ottomanists who specialize in many other narrative and archival sources have pointed out, what we may call "bias" is intrinsic to all historical sources,[9] and this does not undermine their scholarly utility.

It is also possible to make a case for the value of these sources for specific types of research. Foreign accounts could provide significant help on issues that are not well covered in the native sources, including, for example, the lives and institutions of non-Muslim communities and their interactions with Muslim Ottomans and foreign nationals, and commercial affairs and economic relationships between the Ottoman Empire and other polities. Another area where we find some unique and potentially valuable information is the Ottoman administration of justice, including the operations of courts of law in different corners of the empire.[10]

In this chapter, I survey a collection of accounts intended for Western audiences with the objective of characterizing what they considered odd, abusive, or predatory practices in the Ottoman polity.[11] The chapter samples

---

[7] For a good example in this regard, see Ellison's (2002: 66–7) discussion of the disagreements between the accounts of two early seventeenth-century British observers, Richard Knolles and George Sandys.

[8] The existing surveys of this literature illustrate the variability in the accounts, which demonstrates that even if these texts were prone to be filled with errors regarding Ottoman matters and tendencies, they were not uniformly biased. In other words, the accounts cannot be perceived to constitute a homogeneous genre and thus could be utilized in ways that might generate valuable insights on specific issues; on this very issue see Çırakman 2001.

[9] For a general critical survey of various historical sources for Ottoman history-writing, see Faroqhi 2000. For more specialized commentary on two popular types of sources, see Abou-El-Haj 1991 on the accounts of Ottoman political commentators, and Ergene 2003: 125–41 on the archives of the Ottoman Islamic courts of law.

[10] Ottoman-generated (that is, "native") sources provide very limited information on legal practice in or outside the court, since they tended to be prescriptive (like jurisprudential treatises and jurisprudential opinions [fatwa collections]) or too brief and formulaic (like court records). On the other hand, the accounts produced for Western audiences often contain direct insights about actual processes of dispute resolution, insights that are almost ethnographic in nature (Ergene 2003: 115–24, 2004). Regarding the value of foreign sources in corruption-related research, see Herzog 2003: 37.

[11] Although I have tried to read widely (both the primary accounts and the literature on them), I do not presume that my research is comprehensive. I do not read all European languages, so my sources do not include accounts that have not been translated into the languages I can read or are not discussed in

accounts from the late sixteenth century to the early nineteenth to reflect on the insights of authors with different backgrounds and experiences. Table 6.1 lists the accounts *cited* in the following discussion, in chronological order. The choice of accounts is subjective: it partly reflects my interest in the judicial processes of the seventeenth and eighteenth centuries.[12] In what follows, I first identify observations that, in the authors' opinions, concern a few broader and systemic aspects of corruption in the Ottoman context. Then I focus more narrowly on judicial administration and practice.

Systemic Factors Affecting Corruption According to Foreign Accounts

The accounts composed in the premodern period for various Western audiences[13] contain plenty of references to the inherent immorality and venality of the "Turks," a crude way to explain the prevalence of predatory actions by those in power.[14] That said, it is also possible to identify in these sources a characterization of what we might call an ecology of corruption, in which systemic factors, rather than (or in addition to) certain aspects of

---

the secondary literature. Also, my treatment of the accounts is limited in the sense that I focus exclusively on the insights and observations that directly concern corruption or its equivalent(s) in the Ottoman context. Everything else has been left aside based on concerns of time, space, and human energy.

[12] The selection does not include a sub-genre of texts comprising ambassadorial correspondences, consular reports, and documentation generated in consular courts. Although various characterizations of Ottoman corruption in these sources should overlap with those found in the accounts included in my survey, this sub-genre deserves an in-depth analysis. For examples of the growing secondary literature based on these sources, see Valensi 1993; Eldem 1999; van den Boogert 2003, 2005, and 2010; Kadı 2012; Vlami 2015; Talbot 2017; Stefini 2020; and Vanneste 2021. In what follows, I use examples and insights drawn from these works when relevant.

[13] One should be careful in generalizing about the intended readership of these accounts. In fact, it is common in the scholarship to ignore the fact that all these works were composed for specific "Western" audiences and not others. For an informative and interesting take on Russian Orientalism on the Ottoman polity and its differences from the Orientalist literature that emerged elsewhere in Europe, see Taki 2011.

[14] See, among many others, Blount 1650: 174–5, 224; Rycaut 1686: 140; Hill 1709: 16; Cantemir 1734: 189, 433; Porter 1768: 1:84; de Tott 1786: 1(1):viii, 218; and Olivier 1801: 1:175, 182. References to the rapacity and arbitrariness of Ottoman authorities abound in the reports and correspondences composed by English, French, and Dutch commercial and diplomatic officials. Frequent complaints about *avania*, a non-Ottoman term with a connotation of unjust and illegal extraction imposed by the Ottoman authorities on European merchants or their representatives, generate an impression of prevalent lawlessness and predation in the Ottoman polity. For somewhat descriptive references to avania, see Eldem 1999: 231; Kadı 2012: 106–7, 116–20, *passim*; Vlami 2015: 33. A few researchers have suggested that the claims of avania were often mischaracterizations by European entities that had failed to grasp the exact nature of the European entitlements based on the capitulatory regulations, the complexity of the Ottoman legal regime, and/or the Ottoman officials' limits of authority in their jurisdictions. In other instances, Europeans deliberately misrepresented the Ottoman authorities' treatments of them. See Olnon 2000; van den Boogert 2005: 117–57; Vanneste 2021: 232. For references to avania in the texts examined in this chapter, see North 1744: 68, 74–100, *passim*; Report 1913: xxviii, 278, 300, *passim*; Eton 1799: 290, 491, *passim*.

Table 6.1 Information about Foreign Accounts Cited in Chapter 6

Author	Title and Publication Information of the Version Used in the Chapter	Composition and Publication Dates	Notes about the Author/Work
Stephan Gerlach (d. 1612)	Tagebuch der vonzween Glorwurdigsten Romischen Kaysern Maximiliano und Rudolpho... (Franckfurth am Mayn: In Verlegung Johann Savid Zunners, 1674). I used the Turkish translation.	Originally composed in the 1580s. The work was first published in 1674.	The author was a cleric in the entourage of David Ungnad von Sonnegg, the envoy of Maximilian II, the Holy Roman Emperor, to Selim II (1545–74). The work was originally composed in German.
Richard Knolles (d. 1610)	The Generall Historie of the Turkes.... (London: Adam Islip, 1603).	1603	The author was a historian and published the first history of the Ottoman Empire in English (Beck 1987: 40–9).
Salomon Schweigger (d. 1622)	Ein newe Reyssbeschreibung auss Teutschland nach Constantinopel und Jerusalem... (Nuremberg: Lantzenberger, 1608). I used the Turkish translation.	1608	The author was a Protestant theologian and preacher in the entourage of Joachim Freiherr von Sintzendorff (d. 1594), who was sent to Istanbul as the permanent envoy of the Habsburg state. The account is based on his four-year stay in Istanbul.
George Sandys (d. 1644)	A Relation of a Journey Begun An. Dom. 1610... (London: W. Barrett, 1615).	1615	The author was an English poet, traveler, and adventurer who spent two years in the Ottoman lands on his way to Jerusalem for a pilgrimage.
Reinhold Lubenau (d. 1631)	Beschreibung der Reisen des Reinhold Lubenau (Königsberg: F. Beyer [Thomas & Oppermann], 1914). I used the Turkish translation.	Manuscript completed in 1628	The author was a pharmacist in the Habsburg mission to the Ottoman Empire in the late sixteenth century. The work was composed in German.
Henry Blount (d. 1682)	A Voyage into the Levant..., 4th ed. (London: A. Crooke, 1650).	1636	The author was a landowner and traveler who spent eleven months in the Middle East in 1634 and 1635.

Paul Rycaut (d. 1700)	*The History of the Present State of the Ottoman Empire...*, 6th ed. (London: Charles Brome, 1686).	1665	The author served as the secretary of the English ambassador to the Ottoman Empire, the secretary of the Levant Company in Istanbul, and consul for the Levant Company in Smyrna between 1660 and 1678 (Darling 1994: 72; Beck 1987: 75–89).
Not available	*Report on the Manuscripts of Allen Georgie Finch, Esq...* (London: His Majesty's Stationary Office, 1913).	Based on Earl of Winchilsea's correspondence between 1660–68	The *Report* contains the communication of Heneage, Earl of Winchilsea (d. 1689), the British ambassador in the Ottoman Empire during the 1660s, among other miscellaneous collections of papers and documentation.
Roger North (d. 1734)	*The Life of the Honourable Sir Dudley North...* (London: John Whiston, 1744).	Based on Sir Dudley North's observations in the 1660s and 1670s	The work is the biography of Sir Dudley North (d. 1691), a merchant and treasurer of the Levant Company who spent about two decades in Smyrna and Istanbul. The author of the biography, Roger North, Sir Dudley's brother, was a lawyer and historian.
Joseph de Tournefort (d. 1708)	*Relation d'un Voyage du Levant...* (Paris: Imprimerie Royale, 1717). I used the Turkish translation.	Probably completed in 1708	The author was a French botanist who visited the Aegean islands and parts of northern Anatolia between 1700 and 1702.
Aaron Hill (d. 1750)	*A Full and Just Account of the Present State of the Ottoman Empire...* (London: John Mayo, 1709).	1709	The author was a prominent English literary figure who traveled for years in the East, including the Ottoman lands.
Demetrius Cantemir (d. 1723)	*The History of the Growth and Decay of the Othman Empire...* (London: James, John, and Paul Knapton, 1734).	1734	The author was Prince of Moldavia and a historian, composer, and linguist. Between 1687 and 1710 he lived in exile in Istanbul, where he learned Turkish and studied the history of the Ottoman polity (Tuğ 2017: 77n10).

Continued

Table 6.1 Continued

Author	Title and Publication Information of the Version Used in the Chapter	Composition and Publication Dates	Notes about the Author/Work
Alexander Drummond (d. 1764)	*Travels through Different Cities of Germany, Italy, Greece, and Several Parts of Asia...* (London: W. Strahan, 1754).	1754	The author was an English merchant who lived in various parts of the empire for about fifteen years. He served as consul of the Levant Company in Aleppo for about eight years (van den Boogert 2007).
James Porter (d. 1786)	*Observations on the Religion, Law, Government, and the Manners of the Turks*, 2 vols. (London: J. Nourse, 1768).	1768	The author was a British ambassador to the Ottoman Empire between 1747 and 1762.
Christoph Lüdeke (d. 1805)	*Glaubwürdige Nachrichten von dem Türkischen Reiche...* (Leipzig: Junius, 1770). I used the Turkish translation.	1770	The author was a Protestant priest and theologian, originally from Schöneberg. He was the pastor of the Lutheran congregation in Smyrna from 1759 to 1768.
Elias Habesci (d. ?)	*The Present State of the Ottoman Empire* (London: R. Baldwin, 1784).	1784	Of Greek extraction, the author served as secretary in the office of the grand vizier during the reign of Mustafa III (1757–74). The work was translated from its French original.[a]
François Baron de Tott (d. 1793)	*Memoirs of Baron de Tott Containing the State of the Turkish Empire and Crimea during the Late War with Russia...*, 2nd ed, 2 vols. (London: G. G. J. and J. Robinson, 1786).	1785	Originally an aristocrat, the author was a French military adviser to the Ottoman authorities who spent twenty-five years in Ottoman lands. The work originally appeared in French. The second volume contains Claude-Charles de Peyssonnel's (d. 1790) criticism of de Tott's work. De Peyssonnel was the son of Charles de Peyssonnel, French consul at Smyrna in the mid-eighteenth century. Claude-Charles accompanied his father to Smyrna in 1748 and later became the French consul in Crimea and Smyrna. His commentary on de Tott's work appears in both the French and English editions.

Giovanni Mariti (d. 1806)	*Travels through Cyprus, Syria, and Palestine…*, 2 vols. (Dublin: R. Byrne, A. Grueber, J. Moore, W. Jones, and J. Rice, 1792).	1792	Abbe Mariti was an Italian historian, traveler, and diplomat who traveled extensively in the eastern Mediterranean (including Cyprus) after 1760s. The work was originally written in Italian.
William Eton (d.?)	*A Survey of the Turkish Empire…*, 2nd ed. (London: T. Cadell and W. Davies, 1799).	Perhaps 1798 or a few years earlier	The author, a relatively unknown figure, was a long-term resident and self-proclaimed consul in the Ottoman Empire.
Guillaume-Antoine Olivier (d. 1814)	*Travels in the Ottoman Empire, Egypt and Persia…*, 2 vols. (London: T. N. Longman and O. Rees, 1801).	1801	The author was a distinguished French entomologist who spent six years in Ottoman lands (including Egypt) and Persia for research. The work originally appeared in French.
Mouradgea d'Ohsson (d. 1807)	*Tableau général de l'Empire othoman…*, vols. 6–7 (Paris: Firmin Didot, 1824).	D'Ohsson died in 1807. The last two volumes of *Tableau* were published posthumously by his son.	Findley (2019: 1) describes the author as "a half-French Ottoman Armenian Catholic born and educated in Istanbul, professionally serving the Swedish legation in Istanbul, Paris, and Stockholm." In *Tableau* D'Ohsson "gave the Enlightenment its most authoritative, best-illustrated account of Islam and the Ottoman Empire" (ibid.).

[a] There are doubts about the authenticity of this name, which might be an anagram of Sahib-el-Sicia, meaning "friend of the unfortunate." The author used the alias "Alexander Gika" while visiting England; see Mörike 2019.

Note: For the citations of the Turkish translations, see the bibliography.

"Turkish" character, forced government officials toward rent-seeking and exploitation of subject populations.[15]

According to many of the authors, intense political and economic conflict between the dynasty and its ranking officials was a fundamental aspect of the Ottoman polity. Paul Rycaut (1686: 143) wrote in the late seventeenth century that both the property and lives of the "pashas" could be claimed at any time. Elias Habesci (1784: 261–5), a Greek-Ottoman former scribe in the grand vizier's office, insisted a century later that the ruler tried to drain the wealth of those whom he regarded as threats to his power by removing them from their positions, confiscating their properties, and marrying them to his female relatives. The last measure was to appropriate chunks of officials' wealth in the form of payments such as customary gifts and dowries and to ensure that officials' estates were inherited by members of the royal family.[16] Collectively, these policies constituted effective mechanisms of wealth redistribution that benefited the central government (cf. North 1744: 30–1).

Relevant here is the special attention that the accounts devote to various payment-for-appointment schemes as another redistribution mechanism. Such arrangements involved almost all types of government posts, including vizierships, mid- and lower-level offices in the palace and central bureaucracy, governorships and sub-governorships, and appointments in the religious-judicial establishment. For example, Stephan Gerlach (2006: 1:193–4) observed in the late sixteenth century that provincial sub-governors had to offer gifts and bribes to the grand vizier Sokollu Mehmed Paşa (d. 1579) to obtain their appointments. The same was true for prospective college professors and judges, who had to pay not only higher members of the religious establishment, including the kazaskers, but also high-level "pashas" (ibid.), which calls to mind the fatwa by Ibn Kemal discussed in Chapter 2. Richard Knolles (1603: 987), another late sixteenth- and early seventeenth-century observer, suggested that Murad III (d. 1595) granted the governorship of Jerusalem to a Druze Amir in return for 100,000 ducats.

Later accounts indicate the prevalence of the practice and provide ample information about specific arrangements. For example, Rycaut (1686: 140), the well-informed ambassador who served in the latter half of the seventeenth century, observed that no individuals "are advanced in these

---

[15] For an earlier attempt to distinguish bigoted and historically verifiable judgments in one group of foreign accounts, see Valensi 1993.

[16] For a native account of such a predatory marriage arrangement involving the vizier Melek Ahmed Paşa (d. 1662) and Fatma Sultan (d. 1670), daughter of Ahmed I (d. 1617), see Evliya Çelebi 1991: Ch. 10.

times to Office, but pay the Grand Signior vast sums of Money for it, according to the Riches and expectations of profit from the Charge; some pay, as the Pashaws of Grand Cairo and Babylon, 3 to 400000 dollars upon passing the commission; others one, others 200000, some 50000; as their places are more or less considerable." Alexander Drummond (1754: 146–7) wrote in the mid-eighteenth century that the governorship of Cyprus "forms part of the revenue of the prime visier, as first-minister, and is farmed to the governor for three hundred and ten thousand piastres, amounting to about thirty-eight thousand seven hundred and fifty pounds, besides presents of considerable value, which he must give to different people in different ways." And according to Christoph Lüdeke (2013: 157), the qadi of Smyrna paid forty purses (about 20,000 guruş) for a one-year appointment in the mid-eighteenth century, a remarkably specific tidbit given the rarity of information about judicial appointments.

One later account that provides many details about the scale of the practice is Mouradgea d'Ohsson's late eighteenth-century *Tableau général de l'Empire othoman*. Here d'Ohsson (1824: 7:191–201) lists eighty-five annual appointments made by the grand vizier, which the author "divided into three classes, including the high officers in the Sublime Porte (*kapu ricali*, nine in two groups), bureau chiefs (*hacegan*, fifty two scribal officials subdivided into four groups), and 'military' chiefs (*agayan*, ten military commanders and fourteen civilians serving in posts related to the military or the palace, including the directory of the three imperial powder works). Provincial governorships were also annual appointments" (Findley 2019: 290). "This system of selling public offices (*emplois publics*)," d'Ohsson wrote (1824: 7:202; original in French), had been introduced during the reign of Beyazıt II (d. 1512) by our old acquaintance the grand vizier Çandarlı Ali Paşa and was formally established by Rüstem Paşa (d. 1561), a grand vizier of Süleyman I (d. 1566). Given how rarely the notion is used in modern scholarship, it is remarkable that d'Ohsson tended to regard the practice as the "sale of public employments," though he is not alone in this characterization. William Eton (1799: 54) also described the payment-for-appointment schemes as "public sale offices."[17]

The accounts indicate that the sultan and the grand vizier benefited from these arrangements. According to Gerlach (2006: 2:687), when one of the viziers passed away, the grand vizier Sokollu Mehmed Paşa accepted one of the

---

[17] For other references to payment-for-appointment schemes from different periods, see the accounts of Cantemir 1734: 433; North 1744: 30; Habesci 1784: 174; de Tott 1786: 2(3):100–1; Mariti 1792: 1:10; Olivier 1801: 1:199–200; Tournefort 2013: 31. Also, see below.

bids from governors or some other high-level officials who wanted to acquire the vacant position, and these bids could be as high as "fifty to sixty thousand ducats." Later sources provide similar impressions. Habesci (1784: 174) wrote that while the grand viziers received modest stipends from the treasury, the income they received as gifts and annual payments for appointments allowed them to accumulate great wealth. D'Ohsson (1824: 7:183) suggested that the immense income generated by his appointments might have totaled 4 to 5 million guruş per year in the late eighteenth century, and the grand vizier needed every akçe of it, given his own obligations to the ruler and the monetary demands on his personal purses, including what was required for his large household and payments associated with military expeditions.

The sultan and the grand vizier were not alone in profiting from the practice. In fact, there are plenty of references to lower-level military-administrative and religious-judiciary officials who made payments to their higher-ups to secure and keep their positions. Even if ranking officials lacked the authority to make appointments, their support for, or at least acquiescence to, those who occupied the lower positions was habitually monetized. The authors did not distinguish between appointments made in the center and in the provinces.[18]

Obviously, the cost of acquiring and maintaining government posts generated a significant need for financial resources among officeholders, and according to Rycaut (1686: 140), some high-level appointees in the second half of the seventeenth century were forced to borrow from "the covetous Eunuchs of the Seraglio" at "40 or 50 percent [interest] for the year and sometimes at double."[19] The relative infrequency of appointments and inadequate revenues generated by specific posts exacerbated officeholders' financial difficulties. In this regard, authors also note the short durations of the appointments and, more gravely, the tendency to dismiss appointees before the end of their terms in order to collect new payments from their

---

[18] See Gerlach (2006: 1:193–4) for a discussion of how the janissary commanders and kazaskers sold positions under them in the sixteenth century. Tournefort (2013: 201–2) mentions that the judges stationed on the island of Chios sold judicial appointments (presumably *niabet*) on other Aegean islands at the turn of the eighteenth century. D'Ohsson (1824: 7:201–2) suggests that as they themselves were squeezed from the top down, the Grand Admiral, the generals of the militia corps, the department heads, and the provincial governors accepted payments to grant lucrative positions. And Olivier (1801: 1:198) argues that the provincial governors, who, "by dint of money, obtained from the Porte the junction of all the employments of the province," sell them to the highest bidders.

[19] The biographer of Sir Dudley North (North 1744: 61–2) mentions the frequent need on the part of those seeking appointments in the mid-eighteenth century to borrow at interest, ranging from 20 to 30 percent per year.

replacements.[20] Some authors suggested that even frivolous reasons and the smallest complaints could be used to remove officeholders before the end of their terms (Gerlach 2006: 1:193, 251). The selection of officeholders based on their ability to pay high prices for desirable positions demoted merit to a secondary consideration at best: the system, as portrayed in our accounts, often propelled individuals with predatory instincts to official posts, even if they lacked requisite administrative or financial skills.[21]

The intense pressure the central government exerted on officials through various mechanisms of wealth redistribution, especially payment-for-appointment schemes, prompted those officials to extract wealth in illegal or illegitimate ways from those under their jurisdiction. Gerlach (2006: 1:251), who visited the empire in the late sixteenth century, makes this very point when he compares the district governors (*sancakbeyleri*) to sponges ("spongiae") who suck the wealth out of the people under their jurisdictions through every possible means, only to be squeezed themselves by higher-ups, including governors (*beylerbeyleri*) and viziers. According to Rycaut (1686: 140), writing a century later, "Everyone upon his first entrance into Office looks on himself (as indeed he is) greatly indebted and obliged by justice or injustice, right or wrong, speedily to disburthen himself of the debts, and improve his own principal in the world; and this design must not be long in performance, lest the hasty edict overtake him before his work is done, and call him to account for the improvement of his talent." The Earl of Winchilsea, the British ambassador to the Porte in the 1660s, insisted that the "ministers are forced to bee more corrupt by reason that their offices are purchased at high rates and presents, and entertainments exacted daily from them by the Grand Signor, so that Viziers and Bashawes rob and spoyle the people to live themselves and pay their duties"

---

[20] See Hill 1709: 7; Habesci 1784: 264; and Gerlach 2006: 2:573. Rycaut (1686: 145) gives the most dramatic description of the situation: "To make more room for the multitude of officers who crowd the preferments, and to act the cruel edicts of the empire with the least noise; times when a great personage is removed from his place of trust, and sent with a new commission to the charge perhaps of a greater government; and though he depart from the regal seat with all fair demonstrations of favor, before he hath advanced three days in his journey, triumphing in the multitude of his servants, and his late hopes, the fatal command overtakes him; and without any accusation or cause other than the will of the sultan, he is barbarously put to death, and his body is thrown into the dirt of a foreign and unknown country, without solemnity of funeral or monument; that he is no sooner in the grave, than his memory is forgotten."

[21] According to Gerlach (2006: 1:194), it was common for a learned and valuable scholar to be removed from his position in the religious-judiciary administration because he could not continue to pay for his office and be replaced by an incompetent person. Mariti (1792: 1:10) argued that "if interest, and not merit ... [is] the sure path to preferment, it is also the only rule which regulates the actions of the great." According to d'Ohsson (Findley 2019: 290; cf. d'Ohsson 1824: 7:202), "The venality of offices, the uncertainty of those who hold them, excite the whirlwind of intrigues and cabals that constantly agitate the seraglio and the Porte. Personal merit has no price in the eyes of greed, the most important offices are given to avarice and ineptitude" (original in French; translation by Findley).

(*Report* 1913: 319). In the eighteenth century, we find Alexander Drummond (1754: 147) making similar observations:

> The government is annual; so you may well imagine how the wretched people are fleeced. Muhassil ["farmer general" of Cyprus] Mustapha Beg, according to the best information I could obtain, has, this last year, extorted as much as will pay his rent, indemnify him for the presents he made, defray the expence of travelling and living, and put in his pocket five hundred purses, amounting to thirty-one thousand two hundred and fifty pounds, exclusive of innumerable things of value, with which his favour has been courted.
>
> To what purpose has this man oppressed the miserable, and amassed this wealth? Perhaps, in six months after his return to Constantinople, he may not have one asper remaining.

Then he adds (149): "Indeed, nothing can be more absurd than to expect justice in this country, where every office is sold, and the greatest Part of these offices conferred without salary: so that the purchasers have no chance for indemnifying themselves but by rapine and injustice."[22]

What is remarkable about this survey is how closely these overall impressions resemble those in Ottoman political literature. Despite some significant differences between the two genres,[23] both conclude that one major reason for the systemic corruption in the Ottoman Empire is the pressure on

---

[22] Other accounts that tie the institutional setup of the empire to illegitimate extraction include Hill 1709: 9–12; de Tott 1786: 2(3):100–1; Mariti 1792: 1:10; Eton 1799: 51–2; and Tournefort 2013: 31. Based on what we observe in these accounts, however, one could also surmise that the officeholders were not completely helpless against the pressures exerted by the central government. For example, keeping wealth in liquid forms such as cash, valuable metals, or jewelry might have made it easier to keep it from being confiscated. Charitable endowments with generations of family members as their administrators were also established to avoid this very real danger (Porter 1768: 1:87). In addition, ranking provincial authorities tried hard to prevent complaints against them from reaching the capital by pressuring local judges and their own subordinates, and to thwart the impact of those that did reach the capital by finding or buying allies in the palace or the imperial bureaucracy (Porter 1768: 2:50–2; Olivier 1801: 1:198–200). When these efforts failed, it might have been possible to obtain clemency from the sultan or the grand vizier by offering them lavish gifts and/or large sums of money (Gerlach 2006: 1:125). Finally, building large armed retinues (Olivier 1801: 1:198) must have made provincial governors less dispensable during the times of war and offered them a greater degree of security against punitive military expeditions by entities loyal to the center.

[23] The Ottoman commentators had no interest in comparing their polity to its European counterparts. Thus, the European eagerness to debate the merits of labeling the Ottoman government a "tyranny" or "despotism," distinctly Western categorizations that made sense only in the context of contemporary political debates in Europe (Kaiser 2000), must have meant little to them. On the distinction between "tyranny" and "despotism" in early modern European political discourses as applied to the Ottoman polity, see Valensi 1993; Çırakman 2001; Brentjes 2010: I:454–64; and Bevilacqua 2018: Ch. 6.

officeholders to acquire and maintain their posts in an unpredictable institutional setup that made their lives and property generally vulnerable. The overlap in these accounts by two separate groups of observers (though presumably in some communication with one another) is likely no coincidence; it is suggestive of the prevalence of certain historical trends and tendencies.

Corruption in Ottoman Administration of Justice

This section focuses on one realm of government, the administration of justice, for two reasons: First, foreign accounts, especially those composed in later periods, contain abundant observations about judicial actors, institutions, and practices. Second, owing to my previous research, I feel familiar with Ottoman law and legal practices, which makes it easier for me to evaluate the veracity of various assertions made about it in foreign accounts.

There are significant tensions among accounts composed for foreign audiences in how they characterize the Ottoman administration of justice. On the one hand, a prominent inclination among these authors is to condemn all aspects of judicial institutions and practices as crude, senseless, and without merit, implicitly in comparison to their European counterparts. For example, Blount (1650: 163) claimed in the early seventeenth century that "the main points, wherein Turkish injustice differs from that of other Nations, are three: it is more Severe, Speedy, and Arbitrary." Rycaut (1686: 2–5; cf. Beck 1987: 75–89) described Ottoman justice as a reflection of the government's tyrannical nature and, thus, arbitrary and with little virtue: in his opinion the polity had lacked good laws since its foundation, and its government authorities committed the worst crimes against common people. "In no part of the World," Rycaut wrote (141), "can Justice run more out of the current and stream than in Turkey, where [their] Maxims and considerations corrupt both the Judge and Witnesses." Aaron Hill (1709: 16) claimed that "their [viz. Ottoman] Laws are few, but always put in execution with the utmost Severity; and tho' the sentence *Pro* or *Con* depends entirely upon the undisputed will of an Arbitrary Judge, whereby the Subject is depriv'd of that indulgent Liberty that we taste in *Britain*." Hill (6) observed that the purpose of the Ottoman administration of justice was to "make [the subjects] ever ready to obey [the ruler's] most irrational commands with an unexampled willingness; and terrifying their reflections with so deep a sense of his power, as to deter them the smallest inclination to a dangerous disobedience." Baron de Tott (1786: 1[1]:198) argued that "the [Ottoman] Law" let "the Innocent perish" and treated "Monsters...favorably." According to Habesci (1784: 272–3), "The dispensation of the Turkish laws, instead of maintaining justice and equity, tended only to support the three principal objects of the Turkish polity; which are the absolute power of the prince, the oppression of the people, and enriching of the imperial treasury." These are just a few of many examples.

Yet there are also accounts, largely from the latter half of the eighteenth century onward, that aim to provide more nuanced characterizations of the Ottoman government and judicial administration.[24] James Porter (1768: 1:81), for instance, accused earlier authors of "injurious misrepresentation." According to Porter (82–3), his predecessors who were excessively critical of the Ottoman institutions failed to take into consideration the shortcomings and imperfections of their own governments and to acknowledge that

> in every empire which has extended wide, and flourished long, there are some parts of its constitution wise and good: and it is certain, that whatever defects may be in the political system of the Turks, their empire is so solidly founded on the basis of religion, combined with law, and so firmly cemented by general enthusiasm, and the interest, as well as vanity, of the Turkish individual, that it has lasted ages, and bids fair for stability and permanency. (83)

Porter (84) insisted that the judicial system, including its sources and institutions, should be distinguished from legal practice: "It is not their [Ottomans'] laws, but the corrupt administration of them, the flagitious venality of their judges, and the number of false witnesses connived at, and whole testimony is accepted, that is the opprobrium of the Turkish empire."[25] We observe a very similar defense in Claude-Charles de Peyssonnel's critique of de Tott's characterization of the Ottoman jurisprudence (de Tott 1786: 2[4]:206).[26] De Peyssonnel argued that "instead of reciting the [Ottoman] Laws, [he] only

---

[24] The familiarity with the Ottoman judicial system appears to be particularly remarkable in the accounts composed in the late eighteenth century. I discuss below how a few of our later authors portray certain aspects of the court process fairly accurately in my estimation. In addition, Olivier's text (1801: 1:175–81) contains precise descriptions of the jurisprudential hierarchy, how and by whom jurisprudential appointments were made, and nuanced discussions of the court proceedings.

[25] For a contemporary criticism of Porter's characterization of the Ottoman judicial system as non-despotic, see Habesci 1784: 257.

[26] De Peyssonnel (d. 1790) was a long-term resident and French consul in Smyrna. His comments on de Tott's observations are included in the second volume of the second edition (1786) of de Tott's work. A response to de Peyssonnel's critique of de Tott can be found in Eton's account (1799: 33, 56, 86, and elsewhere).

relates how they are abused." While de Peyssonnel agreed that there were frequent abuses in the system, a discussion of the Ottoman administration of justice should allow its reader "some idea of the Law in its purity, and enable him to distinguish it from those violations committed by the Officers charged with its execution, and those abuses by which it is degraded" (213). In fact, if one were to set aside how individuals in charge of the legal system occasionally acted dishonorably, de Peyssonnel suggested (just as Porter had earlier), one could favorably compare the administration of justice in the Ottoman Empire to that in Europe (207). This is consistent with historian Wilfrid Prest's (1991: 68–70) observation that contemporary criticisms of the "corruption and venality" of the English judiciary are similar in tone and prevalence to those directed at the Ottoman legal system.

De Peyssonnel's perspective on the topic is important because the author provides glimpses of his erudition with the sources of Ottoman jurisprudence when he cites the fatwas of (possibly Çatalcalı) "Ali Efendi,"[27] Molla Hüsrev's fifteenth-century commentary *Durar al-Hukkam*, and Ibrahim al-Halabi's popular sixteenth-century manual *Multaqa al-Abhur*.[28] One later account I have examined, that of d'Ohsson,[29] contains comparable references to such sources of Ottoman-Islamic law, which indicates that Porter's and de Peyssonnel's admonition to appreciate the Ottoman judicial system and institutions as a sophisticated realm of learning, and to differentiate them from acts of specific individuals, might have gained popularity by the late eighteenth century.

Hence, we have two representations of the Ottoman administration of justice. The first characterizes it as a simple, cruel, and procedurally unpredictable apparatus that perpetuates the regime's supposed tyranny and enables the powerful to exploit the weak, especially commoners and, above all, Christians. The second depicts it as a realm of sophisticated institutions built on scholarly interpretations and well-established traditions: while the system

---

[27] This is presumably a reference to *Fetava-yı Ali Efendi*, a collection of fatwas by Şeyhülislam Çatalcalı Ali Efendi (d. 1692). The collection was one of the most popular jurisprudential reference works in the eighteenth and nineteenth centuries. The fatwas of Çatalcalı Ali Efendi are known to have influenced the opinions of Ottoman şeyhülislams who came after him; see Uzunçarşılı 1988: 197.

[28] "If [de Tott] had taken the trouble to turn over the *Multeka*, which is the written Code [de Tott ignores in his discussion], and contains all the precepts of religious worship, and the whole of their Jurisprudence, both civil and criminal; if he had consulted the *Durer* and Halebi, its two principal Commentaries; if he had examined the Collections of the *Fetfas*, or sentences of the most celebrated Muftis, and especially those of *Ali Effendi*, the most famous of them all, he would have found a multitude of wise and well digested Laws" (de Tott 1786: 2[4]:206).

[29] In his *Tableau générale*, d'Ohsson (1824: 6:192–222) provides a detailed and fairly accurate characterization of the litigation procedures and rules of evidence, largely based on Halabi's *Multaqa*.

could be (and sometimes was, according to these authors) perverted by ill-intentioned actors, it was not inherently unfair or exploitative.

Broader characterizations of Ottoman justice in these accounts touch on aspects of the judicial system that include observations about corruption. These largely pertain to the qadis: for example, the sources of their incomes, how they litigated disputes, and how they dealt with false witnesses/testimonies. In these focused remarks, more than in our authors' broader generalizations about the Ottoman administration, we find ethnographic insights not found in archival and native narrative sources.

Our accounts agree that the confirmation of judicial appointments in general, and qadiships in particular, required payments.[30] There is also some broad recognition that members of the religious-judicial establishment needed considerable funds to cover the time they spent out of office, though this point comes up less frequently. In any case, and as for many other officeholders, the authors tend to associate these abuses in judicial practice with the appointees' financial needs as well as their venality and lack of integrity.[31]

Qadis' income is a topic of major interest, and the accounts provide a great deal of information on this topic. The Ottoman sources, specifically the kanunnames, provide lists of fees the court officials charged for specific services, including estate divisions and notarial services such as the preparation and registration of marriage and commercial contracts, manumission papers, and letters to higher authorities. As for other income streams for the court personnel, the native sources of information, including court records, are generally silent.[32] As a result, modern scholarship on the Ottoman judicial system and court practice, which relies almost exclusively on official documentation, has failed until very recently to explain how judicial actors were able to cover the significant expenses they incurred during and between their tenures.[33]

---

[30] See, for example, d'Ohsson (1824: 6:187), who observes that "the *Mollas* pay a sum to the *Moupthy* [viz. şeyhülislam?], the *Cadys* to the *Caziaskers*, the *Naïbs* or [deputy judges] to the *Mollas* or *Cadys*. Each month, the *Naïb* also transfers a portion of his earnings to his principal" (original in French). See also North 1744: 50; Drummond 1754: 149; Porter 1768: 1:84; Olivier 1801: 1:175; Gerlach 2006: 1:193–4; Lüdeke 2013: 155; and Tornefort 2013: 31. For consistent French observations from the first half of the seventeenth century, see Rouillard 1940: 308. See Akiba 2023 for a recent, archival examination of how judicial positions were farmed out in the premodern era.

[31] For example, North (1744: 50) writes that the qadis, "paying for their Places, by necessary Consequence are more or less rapacious, and extorting of Money."

[32] The fees that courts were legally entitled to charge for their services do not appear to have changed significantly between the fifteenth and nineteenth centuries, although prices might have increased seven- to eightfold in Ottoman lands over the same period. See Coşgel and Ergene 2016: 81.

[33] One can, for example, consult İnalcık (1986) and Uzunçarşılı (1988: 83–144), perhaps the two most prominent historians of the Ottoman empire and experts on the judicial system, to see how they discuss the incomes of the court personnel.

Most authors of foreign accounts comment on various sources of income for court personnel, but d'Ohsson probably provides the most detailed and systematic information about the provincial qadis in the late eighteenth century. According to d'Ohsson (1824: 6:187–9), who was writing in the late eighteenth century, the qadis had five well-acknowledged revenue sources: fees for litigations, which, according to d'Ohsson, did not have fixed rates and were paid by the winning parties; fees for marriage contracts (12 akçe), notarized documents or *hüccet*s (25 akçes for preparation and 7 akçes for registration), and estate divisions (2 percent of the value of the estate);[34] portions of fines paid by lawbreakers; fees for inspecting charitable endowments; and payments received from mosque imams in their jurisdictions at their appointments.

Not all of these sources of income are visible in Ottoman documents, yet the many accounts composed for foreign audiences corroborate the claim that qadis charged fees for disputes they adjudicated (see Table 6.2). As indicated, d'Ohsson believed there was no fixed rate for this service. Other sources give different opinions: while two seventeenth-century accounts, Knolles and Rycaut, claim that this fee constituted about 2 percent of the sum of money or value of property subject to dispute, later authors, aside from d'Ohsson, cite a figure of 8 to 10 percent (Tournefort) or 10 percent (Lüdeke; Mariti; Drummond; Olivier).[35] Some texts do not clarify who paid these fees; others suggest that in litigations involving money or property, winners paid them—some argue that this guaranteed that the qadi would get his due.[36] I know of only one author, Mariti (1792: 1:14), who suggested that the party who lost the litigation had to pay the litigation fee.[37]

---

[34] The legally prescribed rates were ignored in practice (ibid.). Mariti (1792: 1:14) observes that the qadi in the eighteenth century had "a right also to the tenth part of the effects of every person who dies in his district," which may not be historically accurate or, at least, widely generalizable. But see Dörtok Abacı and Ergene 2022.

[35] According to Olivier (1801: 1:183), per capitulation agreements, "Europeans have...the advantage of paying no more than three per cent. in lieu of ten, which is paid by all the inhabitants of the country; but it may easily be conceived that a judge, ever ready to receive money from one of the parties, cannot bring himself to decide a cause in favour of an European, if he do not promise him beforehand the ten per cent, and even a present calculated on the importance of the trial." In addition to the fees the qadi charged for litigations, d'Ohsson (1824: 6:190–1) also mentions litigation-related fees claimed by other authorities: "In Constantinople, the Chief of Police, *Tchavousch Baschy*, carries the functions of the public prosecutor ("ministère public") in the name and under the authority of the Grand-Vezir. One of his subordinates, a mere *tchavousch*, is responsible for overseeing the accused, bringing him before the magistrate when summoned, and executing the judgment. If the lawsuit is civil, he collects the sum awarded, from which he deducts a tenth as a collection fee, *resm tahsiliyé*, on behalf of *Tchavousch Baschy*. If the action is criminal, he enforces the sentence" (original in French).

[36] According to Olivier (1801: 1:181), "In order that [the qadi] may not lose his fees, it is always the gainer of the cause who pays the costs." According to d'Ohsson (1824: 6:187–8), this situation made the wealthy parties open to harassment through disingenuous litigation, a claim with which Porter agrees (1768: 2:8–9).

[37] "Every person summoned before these tribunals for debt, if he loses his suit, must pay to the cadi the tenth part of the sum in litigation; but, if he gains it, this burthen falls upon the plaintiff" (ibid.).

Table 6.2 Litigation Fees According to Accounts for Foreigners

Source and Approximate Time Period	Litigation Fee	Who Pays For It?
Knolles (1603: 207), late sixteenth/early seventeenth c.	2% in litigations valued over 1,000 "aspers" in Beyazıt I's reign (1389–1402)	Unclear
Rycaut (1686: 142), late seventeenth c.	2% in litigations valued over 1,000 "aspers" in Beyazıt I's reign (1389–1402)	Unclear
Tournefort (2013: 248–9), ca. 1700s	8–10% of the value	Unclear
Drummond (1754: 149), mid-eighteenth c.	10% of the value	"[The qadi] receives as his due, ten per cent. of what is recovered so that he never finds fault with the exorbitancy of the account."
Lüdeke (2013: 155–7), late eighteenth c.	10% of the value	Winner
de Tott (1786: 1[1]:193), late eighteenth c.	10% of the value	"He who gains the Day always pays the Costs."
Mariti (1792: 14), late eighteenth c.	10% of the value subject to litigation	Loser
D'Ohsson (1824: 6:187–9), late eighteenth c.	"fixed [by the qadi] at his will"	"always falling to the charge of the winning party"
Olivier (1801: 1:181, 183), late eighteenth c.	10% of the sum or the value of the items in dispute; 3% for Europeans.	"It is always the gainer of the cause who pays the costs."

To recall, premodern Islamic jurisprudential traditions held that qadis should not receive compensation for adjudicating disputes (see Chapter 2). Ibn Abidin (and likely other jurists) associated such payments with bribery. This is presumably why we do not find any such fees listed in official documents.[38] The

---

[38] Abraham Marcus may be the first modern historian who brought up the possibility of litigation fees in the early modern era. Consistent with many of our accounts, and presumably based on them, he suggested that qadis claimed 10 percent of the sum awarded in litigations in late eighteenth-century Aleppo, payable by the winning parties (1989: 106). Jun Akiba (2021) recently observed references to litigation fees ranging up to 10 percent in court-produced documentation from Vidin (in Bulgaria) from the 1840s. For another recent take on the issue, see Dörtok Abacı and Ergene 2022.

authors of accounts intended for foreign audiences do not appear to be bothered by these payments—there is no evidence that they considered them illegitimate. They were troubled, however, by extractions that accompanied legal or customary procedures, which they saw as arbitrary, excessive, exploitative, or all three. They often refer to tips, gifts, and other such payments that qadis and naibs were said to have demanded for every sort of service. According to Olivier (1801: 1:181–2), in every profession, including legal ones, "the smallest favour, the smallest service are obtained only by presents."

What seems to agitate our authors the most is their impression that payments by litigants influenced the qadis' verdicts. In this regard, we do not find much variation among them. According to Drummond (1754: 149), "In lawsuits, the party who tips the judge highest, will certainly obtain the decree in his favour: but, besides this bribe, he receives as his due, ten per cent. of what is recovered so that he never finds fault with the exorbitancy of the account." Porter (1768: 2:2) alluded to the prevalent tendency of the qadis to accept bribes as follows: "They tell us of some rare examples of uncorrupt judges; I have heard of one, but I have known none." According to William Eton (1799: 33), "The dexterity of the Turkish kadis, or judges, to decide in favour of those who have paid them is often very ingenious." And d'Ohsson (1824: 6:189) observed that qadis without "delicate conscience" had many opportunities besides legitimate revenue sources to build fortunes and that "the abuses of the judicial power [were] frequent, notwithstanding the respect that Mahometans had for their divine laws."[39]

In general, foreign accounts do leave an impression that the Ottoman judicial system and its actors prioritized revenue raising, which often impeded the delivery of justice. It is difficult for a modern historian to sympathize with such a suspiciously monochromatic representation (cf. Olnon 2000; van den Boogert 2005: Ch. 3; Vanneste 2021: 232). But as discussed, other aspects of these accounts make them hard to dismiss, at least entirely. Indeed, a number of them, in explaining how qadis managed to get away with apparently self-serving decisions, offer realistic details about the workings of the court and the procedures that the qadi might have followed based on what we know about the Ottoman administration of justice. Along with the texts by Porter, North, and Olivier, d'Ohsson's description of litigation processes in particular, which is informed by Halabi's detailed characterization of the rules of litigation

---

[39] See Rycaut 1686: 140–1; Hill 1709: 16; Sandys 1615: 62; Gerlach 2006: 2:616; Tournefort 2013: 107; and Lüdeke 2013: 155 for consistent claims. References to gifts, donations, and bribes to the provincial qadis and naibs are frequent in European diplomatic and commercial communications. See, for example, Eldem 1999: 233; Olnon 2000: 171; van den Boogert 2005: 297; Kadı 2012: 116–17, 133.

and evidentiary standards, may offer the most informed and accurate characterization of the qadis' actions in deciding disputes.

According to d'Ohsson (1824: 6:222), qadis had the freedom to construe and interpret the disputes brought to them and decide which parties were allowed to present their evidence in court, a determination that was based on the qadis' consideration of the nature and credibility of the litigants' claims (and counterclaims) as well as the substance of their disputes.[40] In the Ottoman context, the parties who managed to have their evidence (usually witness testimonies) heard in court often won litigations, since according to evidentiary procedures their opponents were not only *not* allowed to present counterevidence, but also could not cross-examine their opponents.[41] A corrupt qadi might have been tempted by the discretion that the rules of evidence allowed to him.

Also, a few of our better-informed authors suggest that qadis could use fatwas to justify legally dubious, even controversial judgments that might have served the interests of actual or potential clients. According to Porter (1768: 2:14), "One principal use to be made of [the fatwas] is that when the judge is well secured by a bribe, though on the unjust side he will then lay a stress on the decision of the *Mufti* as perfectly just and shelter his own justice under that

---

[40] As explained in Chapter 2, premodern jurisprudential conventions did not allow *all* disputants to present evidence in support of their claims or counterclaims. Instead, the "burden of proof" (which in fact generates a potential advantage for litigants skilled in the game of litigation) was placed on a specific party based on the nature of the claims and counterclaims made in court and on the types of disputes. As a rule, the plaintiffs were generally required to prove their claims against their opponents, but it was up to the qadi to decide who played the role of the plaintiff and who the role of defendant, which was not always a straightforward decision. Also, in many cases, and based on the nature of the counter-allegations made in response to initial plaintiff claims, the burden of proof could switch to the defendant if the qadi deemed this appropriate (in which case the plaintiffs were denied the opportunity to present their evidence). Finally, sometimes the qadis assigned proof responsibilities based on the substance of dispute, rather than the specific role the litigants played as plaintiffs or defendants. Premodern jurisprudential manuals contain lengthy and detailed deliberations on how to allocate the proof responsibility among litigants in various combinations of circumstances. See, for example, Halebi n.d.: 275, 289–94; Hüsrev 1980: 158 195–7; and Merginani 1986: 277–9, 308–9.

[41] The following example from North (1744: 51) is not only consistent with d'Ohsson's statement, but also a remarkably accurate description of a typical court process: "The Turkish Law seems to have another Virtue, which lies in the Method of Proof. After the judge hath heard the Demand, and the Witness to the Answer; he considers on which Side the Proof lies. If the Dealing be denied, as by the Defendant's saying, he bought no Goods of the Plaintiff, or the like, the Judge bids the Demander prove it. And if Witnesses are not ready, he gives a few Days to bring them, because he might expect the other Party would have owned the Dealing; but if he said, It's true, I bought the Goods, but I paid him for them; then the Judge bids the Defendant prove. But he will never let Witness come to swear on both Sides to one and the same Fact, for that is to make sure of a Perjury; so, in a Turkish Court, Witnesses never confront, and, upon Oath, contradict one another. But being once taken as Witnesses, the Cause is at an End, the Demand is made and proved, What would you have more?" For other consistent reports, see Porter 1768: 2:4; and de Tott 1786: 1(1):192–4. See Coşgel and Ergene 2016: 213–43, for a discussion of the evidentiary procedures in Ottoman courts and how they might have impacted the consequences of litigations.

sanction; or at the worst, when contradictory *Fetfas* appear, he may favor the unjust by exhorting the contending parties to an accommodation." Because the questions addressed by fatwas were formulated by supplicants, they were shaped by their own characterizations of their concerns, and often neglected much relevant information, so it might have been possible to obtain fatwas that could support both parties in a dispute.[42] It is true that fatwas were technically non-binding in litigations, at least in principle and perhaps with the exception of the şeyhülislams' opinions (Burak 2015b: 41–2). But in practice, reliance on a fatwa composed by a legal expert must have taken some pressure off the qadi.[43]

Finally, d'Ohsson (1824: 6:205, 209) also noted that the "law [tended to admit] no appeals" and that "the law guarantee[d] impunity, protecting the magistrates from all consequences for their judgments" (6:189). Both of these claims are largely accurate. These aspects of the legal system and practice usually shielded qadis from consequences for their actions, even when those actions were controversial. Due to such examples, I am thus inclined to regard the best of the foreign accounts as *plausible* sources of insights about corruption in legal practice. While not all foreign accounts can be taken at face value, they should also not be categorically dismissed.

The topic of witnessing also gets significant attention in these accounts. The status of witness testimony (see Chapters 2 and 4) as the primary evidentiary tool in litigations incentivized false witnessing, often (but not always) in return for compensation, a point that seems to resonate with our authors.[44] Unlike the qadis' bribery, false witnessing was often perpetuated by common folk. Yet in these accounts it is presented as a festering element of the Ottoman administration of justice, at least partly because judicial authorities at best lacked motivation to fight it, and, at worst, sought to actively benefit from it.

There is a general agreement among our authors regarding the prevalence of false witnessing in all periods.[45] Gerlach (2006: 1:96), for example, claimed in

---

[42] Porter (1768: 2:13) agrees: "[The disputant] put the case in his own manner, and instructs the Mufti how he should subscribe it. This is so true, that there frequently appear opposite *Fetfas* in the same cause," presumably, though not certainly, by different muftis. See also de Tott 1786: 1(1):195.

[43] Coşgel and Ergene (2016: 243–5) have demonstrated the high degree of correspondence between winning in litigations and fatwa-use in their statistical exploration of the Kastamonu court records.

[44] See North 1744: 46; Porter 1768: 2:5; de Tott 1786: 1(1):192–4; and d'Ohsson 1824: 6:221–2, for remarks on the importance of witness testimonies in litigations.

[45] This impression might have been broadly shared by the Ottomans themselves, at least in the eighteenth century. According to historian Mehmed Raşid, the grand vizier ordered an official investigation in 1719 because of the pervasiveness of false witnessing in Istanbul due to the "negligence and tolerance" (*tehavün u tesamuh*) of the judges." Consequently, two undercover officers pretending

his sixteenth-century text that "it was possible to pay someone twenty to thirty akçes and demand his testimony on an issue that he knew nothing about." Likewise, Blount (1650: 171), Rycaut (1686: 141), Lüdeke (2013: 155), Porter (1768: 2:8), and Habesci (1784: 272–3), whose collective observations range from the early seventeenth century to the late eighteenth, suggested that false witnessing was widespread and that it could be obtained for trivial sums.[46] And some passages in the accounts might suggest that many engaged in false witnessing as a regular source of income, perhaps even a profession.[47] Admittedly, it is difficult to assess the veracity of these reports, given that various authors read other authors' works and copied them, which tended to duplicate the same tropes across sources. In our case one popular trope is the "bearded witness." For example, Salomon Schweigger (2004: 188), writing in the late sixteenth century, suggested that litigants who wanted to cheat in court often brought in witnesses with long beards. According to Schweigger, "the beard provides credibility to the [false] testimony.... If the judge doubts the testimony of the witness, the latter would stroke his beard and say 'How dare you? I am an honest and respectable person. How can you think that someone with this huge beard could lie?' In this way he could make half a taler or more by using a bit of hair." References to bearded false witnesses can be found not only in other early accounts, such as that of Reinhold Lubenau (2012: 334), who replicates Schweigger's story almost verbatim, but also in later and better-informed ones. They appear, for example, in Dudley North's biography (1744: 47) in a discussion of how the French community, presumably in Istanbul, tried to persuade the local qadi to enlarge their old church. After failing to convince the qadi in a few previous attempts, they accomplished their objective only with the help of "a grave Turk, with long Beard."[48]

---

to sue each other in the Mahmud Paşa court sought and hired multiple false witnesses for money, who were subsequently captured and subjected to public shaming. Some of these offenders were exiled from Istanbul, others were given other (vague) punishments. See Raşid 2013: 2:1149.

[46] European diplomatic and commercial sources also contain frequent references to false witnessing (and fears about false witnessing) in disputes heard in the sharia courts that involved European merchants or their associates; see van den Boogert 2005: 142, 282, 305; Kadı 2012: 118. For an interesting allegation made in 1763 by the Dutch consul in Aleppo of bribes extended to court officials to persuade them to declare known false witnesses reliable, see van den Boogert 2005: 196. Again, one should be cautious about these sources; see Note 14.

[47] According to d'Ohsson (1824: 6:222), for example, "there are men in every town whose only profession is to testify in court for money" (original in French). According to Sir Dudley North, false witnesses were proficient enough to provide credible support to any claim in court and could also endure the qadi's scrutiny (North 1744: 47).

[48] "At length a grave Turk, with a long Beard, came in of his own accord, and, saluting the Judge, asked what the Business was, which being told him, he stroked his Beard, and, by Tide and by Token, made a better Witness than they ever expected to find or procure; which was a greater Surprise, because, by his grave Entry, they, knowing his Character, feared he came to testify against them. Upon

In other instances, however, it is not the duplication across accounts but the very inconsistencies among them that call into question their reliability. For example, how should we regard the report in one sixteenth-century source that false witnesses were branded on the face with a hot iron and publicly shamed (Gerlach 2006: 1:96, 372–3), considering that at least two eighteenth-century sources maintain that false witnessing was rarely punished (Porter 1768: 2:14–15; de Tott 1786: 1[1]:193–4)?[49] The discrepancy may reflect location-based variations or historical changes in how contemporary authorities dealt with the crime, but we cannot be certain.[50]

As a historian I am inclined to attribute credibility to specific accounts based on their degree of nuance in characterizations of multiple incentives, perspectives, and legal strategies. In regard to false witnessing, Porter's text, for example, resists simplistic characterizations. While affirming the prevalence of false witnessing in the Ottoman context, Porter's discussion (1768: 2:5–8) helps the reader to better contextualize a practice that could be associated with multiple motivations:

> There are three species of [false] witnesses; some your neighbours and old acquaintance; others, casual; and lastly, those who make a professed trade of attending courts of judicature, and live by it. On informing them of the merits of the cause, they first declare that they appear in it merely because they see the hardship and injustice intended against you; that, as they know you to be an honest man, on whose veracity they can absolutely depend, they will therefore affirm as truth whatever you shall aver to them as such. This profession, which they make with an affected earnestness is the usual

---

this, the Odgett passed, and the Building went on; and the willing Judge was very well satisfied. But the French had Advice given them to send this old Man his Fee, or else he would have found out a Way to have spoiled all again" (ibid.).

Incidentally, Aşık Çelebi (2018: 86–7), a sixteenth-century Ottoman qadi and commentator, also mentions a long and bushy beard as a basis of credibility among corrupt actors in judicial processes. In his case, it is the qadis who rely on their facial hair to garner respect despite their dishonest actions.

[49] Blount (1650: 171), an early seventeenth-century source, argued that "a false witness endures what the accused should have done, had he been guilty." Early seventeenth-century French sources indicate that false witnesses were "ignominiously branded" (Rouillard 1940: 309).

[50] Relevant to the issue of policing of false witnessing is a document that I cited earlier from Havas-ı Refia (Eyüb) Court Records (vol. 190, 3; dated 1165/1752), one that identifies five individuals as habitual false witnesses. The document gives the names of the accused individuals, the neighborhoods they were from, their distinctive physical characteristics, and occupations. Accordingly, the individuals included a cauldron-maker, a grocer, and a boatman. Consistent with the trope of "bearded witness," four of the five individuals were said to have white beards, and the other one had a black one, though having a beard was common among adult men at the time. One of the individuals was also said to be known as "head of sureties" (kefil başı), indicating that he might have served a semi-formal or informal function in contractual arrangements that required sureties and was thus familiar with legal (including court) processes.

Turkish salvo and seldom fails to appease all their qualms as well as to quiet their scruples.

Or should it not have that effect; if the witnesses insist on better information, they are concealed in a private place, where they can hear all that passes in an adjoining apartment the party with whom you are at variance is decoyed, and there such concessions, by interrogatories, and other artful managements, are drawn from him as may make against himself: these the evidences report on the trial, and declare they have heard. Often indeed, on this occasion, instead of the real party, a friend of your own, who personates him, is introduced into the apartment, where he makes what concessions you please in the hearing of the concealed witnesses, who can neither see nor be seen, and who not chuse to detect the fraud, but report to the judge what they heard, as spoken by the real person. In lawsuits, no practice of this kind can startle a Turk; all he is anxious for, is some pretext, which he thinks may enable him still to pass for an honest man. Thus much of their first species of witness.

The last sort are those who make a professed trade of it, and are always ready at any man's service for a dollar or two. By habit and long practice these need no casuistry, no salvo to their conscience, but swallows their oath, true or false, and will stand or fall by their evidence.

Porter's discussion characterizes venality as only one possible motivation for false witnessing. Another potential factor was social or kin solidarity—commitment to a litigant whom the witness knew and felt obligated to support against a stranger. In this case, the (false) witnessing affirmed the relationship between the parties and signaled trust in the story and the person's character. Here the false testimony was an investment in the parties' enduring relationship.

For Porter, it is clear that many false witnesses who supported one side for reasons seemingly unconnected to profit were aware that their testimony was illegal. Porter differentiates the first two groups according to their attitudes toward this tension. The first type, "neighbours and old acquaintance[s]," were impervious to the technical problems of the arrangement, indicating the strength of their relationship with the litigants. For the second type, "casual" associates of the litigants, a compromise was required to satisfy the letter of the law, though not its spirit. The ruse that Porter describes was not really staged to deceive the potential witness, who was inclined "not to chuse to detect the fraud," but to enable him to deny his culpability if he was exposed. The need for the ruse highlighted the relative weakness of the relationship between the potential witness and the litigant and, at the same time, the parties' willingness to maintain their (fragile) connection nonetheless in the face of a legal obstacle.[51]

Given the minimal enforcement of prescribed punishments against false witnessing according to some of our more informed authors,[52] their impressions regarding the prevalence of false witnessing, if sufficiently accurate, might justify European attempts to level the judicial field in their legal encounters with Ottoman subjects. To be sure, the supposed corruption of the legal system was only one reason that Europeans and their local proxies

---

[51] Lest one regards this ruse Porter describes far fetching, consider the following fatwa by Şeyhülislam Ebussuud Efendi (d. 1574):

> Question: Assume that Zeyd gifted to his daughter Hind a house and a garden that he had purchased from Amr. Afterwards, while Hind was in possession of these properties, Hind's brother Bekir, claiming to be Hind's legal representative (vekil), cancelled the purchase agreement with Amr and issued a [court-generated] document (hüccet) to the latter [Amr] indicating the cancellation. Now, if Amr uses the document to claim the house [and the garden] from Hind, if Hind's [current/actual] representative Bişr objects to court's [previous] decision [to cancel the purchase agreement] by rejecting [Bekr's] claim that Hind had earlier appointed Bekr as her representative, which subsequently leads the judge to question the witnesses listed in the [cancellation] document if they had actually seen Hind designating Bekr [as her representative] and [if the judge] learns from them that they had not but they had "heard a [female] voice behind a wall telling [Bekr] that she was designating him as [her] representative," based on which the judge admits to committing a mistake in the first instance by not questioning the witnesses and then if he rules in Hind's favor, can Amr still claim the house and the garden based on the document in his possession? Answer: He cannot as long as he fails to demonstrate evidence that Hind designated Bekr as her representative in the cancellation agreement.
>
> Mesele: Zeyd, Amr'dan evleri ile iştira etdüği bağçeyi kızı Hind'e hibe ve teslim edüb Hind mutasarrıfe iken karındaşı Bekr, "Hind'in vekiliyim" deyü bey-i mezbûru Amr ile fesh edüb Amr'ın eline hüccet verdikden sonra Amr hüccet-i mezbûreyi ibraz edüb Hind'in elinden mezbûr evi taleb etdikde Hind "Benim vekaletden haberim yokdur" deyü Bişr'i vekil nasb edüb Amr ile hakim'üş-şer'a murafaa oldukda hakim hükmünü istinaf edüb hüccet-i mezbûrun içinde olan şahidlere "Siz Hind'i bi-şahsiha gördünüz mü?" dese şahidler, "Hind'i vechen mine'l-vücüh görmedik ancak dıvar ardından bir avaz işitdik vekilim ol dedi ve yine tevkil etdüğin dahi bilmeziz" deseler, hakim'üş-şer "gaflet olunub şahidlere ol sual etmemişim" deyü tekrar Hind'e hüküm eylese, Hind mutasarrıfe iken Amr hüccet-i mezbûreyi ibraz edüb bağçeyi evleri ile Hind'in elinden almağa kadir olur mu? El-Cevap: Amr bil-fiil Hind sabıkan Bekr'i feshe tevkil etdüğine beyyine ikamet etmeyince kadire olmaz. (Akgündüz 2018: 460).

[52] According to Porter (1768: 2:14–15), "false witnesses should be punished according to the Koran; however, that happens but seldom. Now and then a notorious vagrant and offender, detected in his perjury, if it be in a cause against some great man, is led through the streets on an ass, with his face towards the tail, and an inscription declaring him a Scheat or false witness. But even this is seldom seen, except it be on the accession of a Sultan. A new reign is generally ushered in by some such examples. He declares he will rule according to law, justice and truth: as a proper warning therefore to the people, the Vizir lays hold of half a dozen of these witnesses, and executes that pompous sentence. A punishment so trivial has rather a ridiculous than a serious effect; so that the city of Constantinople swarms with these wretches." See also de Tott 1786: 1(1):193–4. The kalebend registers introduced in Chapter 4 do suggest that false witnesses, in particular the habitual offenders, could be imprisoned or sent to exile as punishment. We do not know, however, how often the crime was prosecuted, or how often prosecutions led to formal punishments.

generally preferred to resolve their disputes with local interests in consular rather than Islamic courts (Vanneste 2021: 274, 291; cf. van den Boogert 2003). After all, the premodern Islamic jurisprudential interpretations contained prescriptions that favored Muslim parties over non-Muslim ones; including, for example, the prohibition on accepting testimonies by non-Muslim witnesses against Muslim litigants. But in litigations that involved them, Europeans appear to be particularly concerned about how their Muslim adversaries with better connections and knowledge might take advantage of a network of false witnesses. It was precisely this concern, Rycaut suggests (1686: 141–2), that

> made an *English* Ambassador upon renewing the Capitulations, to insert an Article of Caution against the testimony of Turks, as never to be admitted nor pleaded in any Court of *Turkish* Justice, against the *English* interest; and nothing to be admitted as evidence in that case, but onely a *Hoget*, which is the nature of a Recognizance made before a Judge, or a Bill or Writing under the hand of him on whom the demand is made; which Article as it was very advisedly and with great Prudence and Wisdom obtained, so it hath proved of admirable consequence and security to the Trafique and Merchants Estates which before being liable the Forgeries and false Pretences of every dissolute *Turk*, have now this point as a defense and fortification, by which false Pretences and Suits for considerable Sums of Money, and matters of great value have been blown away, and decided with great facility and little expense.[53]

---

[53] Here is the relevant clause (clause 9) in *The Capitulations and Articles of Peace between... the King of Great Britain... and the Sultan of the Ottoman Empire* according to the version updated in 1675 (1679: 9): "In all Causes, Businesses and Occasions which shall occur between the said Nation [viz. Great Britain], their Merchants, Interpreters and Brokers, or Servants, and any other whatsoever, that is to say, in selling or buying, in paying or receiving, in giving or taking security, or Pledge, Debt or Credit, and all other such things which appertain to the Ministers of the Law and Justice, they may always (If they please) in such occasions go to the Caddee, who is the Judge of the Law, and there make a Hoget, or publick Authentick Act with Witness, and Register the same, and take a Copy of the same to keep by them, to the end that if in the future any difference or pretence shall arise between the said Parties, they may both have a recourse to the said Hoget and Act. And when the pretence shall be conformable to the tenor of the Hoget Registered, then it shall be accordingly thereunto observed: And if the plaintiff hath not in hands any such Authetick Hoget, but only bringeth partial Witness which makes Cavils or Pretences, our Ministers shall not give ear to them, but observe the written authentick Hoget." See also clause 10 in the same document (9–10), which states that "if anyone within our (viz. Ottoman) Dominions shall accuse any English man to have done him wrong, and shall therefore raise any pretence upon him by violent or partial Witness, our Ministers shall not give ear unto them, nor accept them, but the Cause shall be advised to the Ambassadour or Consul Resident of the English Nation, to the end that the business may be decided with his knowledge and in his presence, that the English may always have recourse to their defence and protection." For the history of the capitulations in the Ottoman empire, see van den Boogert 2005: Ch. 1.

One senses a parallel concern in the peace treaty that the Ottomans and Venetians signed in 1718. According to clause 17 of the treaty, when Venetian subjects in Ottoman lands are involved in any kind of legal affair (presumably with Ottoman subjects), they are expected to have these registered in the court and obtain documents of them ("sebt-i sicil etdirüp hüccet ve ma'mūlün-bih temessükler alalar") so that if disputes emerge later they can be resolved based on these documents (Raşid 2013: 2:1132).[54] Privileging written documentation over witness testimony as evidence in litigations is against Islamic-Ottoman jurisprudential traditions, as our authors themselves recognized,[55] which explains why foreigners often failed to convince local qadis to attribute much evidentiary weight to their documents without witness corroboration, despite guarantees provided to them in the capitulations and other agreements. According to Tommaso Stefini (2020: Ch. 7), judges' disinclination to recognize written documents as adequate proof in the seventeenth century led many European parties either to appeal the decisions of the local courts in the imperial divan or take their disputes with Ottoman subjects directly there.

The two conflicting representations of the Ottoman administration of justice—cruel, senseless, and unpredictable on the one hand; well-founded but poorly run on the other—likewise had conflicting implications for how to fight corruption. According to the first representation there is not much one can do to escape abuse by judicial officials or actors who have the means to manipulate judicial processes. One could try to send petitions to higher authorities against corrupt officials, but with uncertain outcomes. Even if those responsible for predation were replaced, the authors might have insisted, their replacements would behave similarly, since the system was geared toward ensuring wholesale exploitation.

According to the second representation, however, those familiar with the judicial system and legal processes can defend themselves against abuse.

---

[54] In those instances that such documents might not be available, the qadis are instructed to be extra careful to weed out witnesses with ill reputations and to not decide cases based on their testimonies. Incidentally, the same clause also instructs the qadis not to have their decisions influenced by "gifts and bribes" (ibid.).

[55] D'Ohsson (1824: 6:221–2) wrote, "A fact must be established by either the confession of the accused, [oral] testimony, or oath. Any written document, even if presented to a magistrate, is considered only a semi-proof. It acquires validity only by the attestation of two witnesses" (original in French). North (1744: 46) agrees: "The *Turkish* Law rigidly holds every Person to prove all the Facts of his Cafe by two *Turkish* Witnesses, which makes the Dealing, with a View of a Dispute, extremely Difficult; for which Reason the Merchants usually take Writing: But that hath its Infirmity also; for the Witnesses are required to prove, not only the Writing, which with us is enough, but they must prove every Fact contained in it to be true, or else the Evidence is insufficient."

Indeed, such accounts include stories that praise such accomplishments and celebrate the successes of underdogs, commoners, non-Muslims, and Europeans in protecting their rights and interests. Because the system was ultimately based on certain well-established rules and conventions, they could be utilized to protect one's interests against powerful adversaries, based on familiarity with the judicial system and the ability to think strategically about the legal (and sometimes illegal) means available to them. Incidentally, the topic of resisting corruption by such measures is unique to foreign accounts.

We observe a good example of this sort of strategic thinking in de Tott's account (1786 1[1]:193), where he suggests that honest litigants could avoid the threat of hired witnesses by carefully maneuvering in trials to assume the burden of proof, which would make it impossible for the court to hear false testimonies.[56] Porter (1768: 2:5) recommends other ways to manipulate the system when faced with unfair accusations. One method was to continually postpone the verdict, which might frustrate one's adversaries and deplete their financial means: "The means of spinning out a suit, and eluding a decision, are various; a defect in the forms of procedure, absence or death of witnesses, denying the validity of seals, the hand-writing of others, or even their own." One could also appeal the decision of the court by taking the dispute to the imperial council,[57] which would lengthen the process, increase the cost of litigation (albeit for both parties), and potentially put the adversary's false witnesses under a greater level of scrutiny, depending on one's influence over the members of the divan and other ranking officials (Porter 1768: 2:9–13).[58]

---

[56] They could accomplish this by not simply "rejecting" (that is, *inkar*) the wrongful allegations against them supported by false witnesses *in toto* but by "rebutting" (that is, *def*) them—in other words, by strategically agreeing with the accusations in part and proposing a slightly different account. De Tott is correct in suggesting that this maneuver would allow the defendant to assume the proof responsibility and prevent the testimonies of false witnesses from being heard; see Coşgel and Ergene 2016: 218–21. De Tott's general characterization of the Ottoman judicial administration as irrational makes this example surprising. Note that d'Ohsson (1824: 6:222) recognizes the effectiveness of the same strategy in winning litigations when he writes: "It is quite common for a debtor in bad faith to utilize this method: he acknowledges that he owed the sum claimed, but claims that he has paid it, and all he must do is to have his claim confirmed by two [false] witnesses. [In that instance,] documents possessed by the creditor become null and void, since they are inferior to [oral] testimonies" (original in French).

[57] Capitulations granted foreigners the right to appeal a court's decision in the imperial divan under certain conditions—for example, if the sum or value of the property subject to dispute was over a certain amount (4,000 to 5,000 akçes, depending on the period and, presumably, the terms of the specific capitulation agreements), or if the lower court disregarded the evidentiary importance of written documents in their possession; see van den Boogert 2005: 47–72; cf. Olivier 1801: 1:182.

[58] According to Olivier (1801: 1:184), litigants often took their cases to the imperial divan, since "false witnesses dread to come thither, because, being interrogated in his [viz. the grand vizier's] presence, he can send them to prison, order them to be cudgelled, and even cause their hands to be cut off if he perceive that they give a false evidence; while the judges have not the same right, but sometimes find themselves compelled to pronounce their sentence according to the position of the witnesses, notwithstanding the conviction

According to the biographer of Dudley North (North 1744: 44–5), who spent decades in the Ottoman Empire and claimed to be a party to more than 500 litigations "in the Language of the Country" (43), foreigners should "make and cultivate an Interest or Friendship with some grave and reasonable Cadi, or Person learned in the Laws, and keep him in good Humour, by frequent, though small, Presents; much short of what the Feeing of a single Counsel in England would amount to. And, in all his doubtful Matters, he resorted to his learned Friend for Advice, which he faithfully gave him." Seeking advice from legal experts as a personal favor or for a price was both a recognition of the sophisticated nature of the legal system and an acknowledgment that it could be manipulated, within certain bounds, by experienced and well-resourced players.

Incidentally, for those who were thinking about initiating a lawsuit in a court where they might encounter resourceful opponents, there were also tactful ways to test the waters before diving in. What seems remarkable in the following recommendation is a recognition of the judge's professional pride, which requires delicate courting by the potential litigant rather than explicit haggling:

> Before a Trial, to shew the Judge a Respect by making him a small Present, and then to make his Cause known to him, before he brought it on. The Judge ordinarily takes this in better Part, than a great Present, and nothing of the Cause said along with it; for that implied that the Cause was bad, and that he was to be corrupted. If the Suitors, or the Cause, be considerable, and no Present at all is given, the Judge looks upon himself to be slighted, or rather defrauded; for he accounts something is due to him for doing Justice, not much unlike what is here termed Fees, only without State or Rule as the European Way is; and such Omission is not wholesome, even for a good Cause. (45)

But perhaps the best and most common advice for those who wanted to protect themselves against potentially corrupt actors was to utilize the very opportunities available to their opponents. According to Porter (1768: 2:8–9), a good way to protect against false claims and lies of any sort was to "secure the judge" by monetary rewards.[59] Dudley North's biographer wrote that "when

---

which they have of their dishonesty." For references in consular sources pertaining to efforts to change the venue of litigation from provincial courts to the imperial council (and vice versa), see van den Boogert 2005: 192–4, 248.

[59] For a reference in a Dutch source to a "preemptive" bribe extended to a qadi in Aleppo to protect a dragoman against "travesty of justice," see van den Boogert 2005: 297.

he [North] had a righteous Cause, the Adversary was knavish, and would not own the Fact; and he had not regular and true Witnesses to prove it; he made no Scruple, in such Case, to use false ones" (North 1744: 46). This was not "a villainous Subornation, but an Ease under an Oppression, and a lawful Means of coming into a just Right" (ibid.).[60] North

> found by Experience that, in a direct Fact, a false witness was a surer Card than a true one; for, if the Judge has a mind to baffle a Testimony, an harmless honest Witness, that doth not know his Play, cannot so well stand his many captious Questions, as a false Witness, used to the Trade, will do; for he hath been exercised, and is prepared for such handling, and can clear himself, when the other will be confounded; therefore, if there be true Witness, Circumstances may be such as shall make the false ones more eligible. (47)[61]

The discussion above indicates that those who knew how to operate within the judicial system could protect themselves against corruption through legal means or employ strategies that were not completely legitimate to resist legal bullying and extortion. The latter point is important because it implies that strategies and mechanisms that might be considered corrupt could also compensate for inequalities endemic to the system. For example, in an environment where non-Muslims could not testify against Muslims, the existence of (Muslim) witness testimonies for sale must have made it easier for non-Muslim parties to sue their Muslim adversaries or defend against litigations initiated by them.

North's (and presumably a few others') views on the Ottoman administration of justice and how to effectively manage it were colored by a strong sense of pragmatic relativism, which is clear in the following remarks:

> Their [viz. Ottomans'] Law hath so many Turns and Subtilties, that a Judge, if he will use an artful Conduct, may find plausible Colours to sustain or baffle almost any Cause; as may be done even amongst us; for, if a Judge will take a Liberty to presume on the one Side, and hold the other to a strict

---

[60] This brings to mind the well-known Islamic jurisprudential principle that bribing under duress is no crime. See Chapter 2.

[61] Porter (1768: 2:5) gives the same advice to his readers: since "all proof is determined by witnesses and...these are found in abundance who will swear anything for pay, when a cause is desperate, an immediate resource is at hand; for such witnesses may be brought to any point as will puzzle the clearest cause and justify the law's delay" when needed. De Tott (1786: 1[1]:193) also endorses this method.

> Proof, the Cause goes which Way he pleaseth. The Judges in Turky will not ordinarily do flat Injustice for any Present; and if neither Side slights them, how unequal so ever the Presents are, they will determine according to Right. But this argues not that all are such, but many are corrupt Judges, that direct their Decrees to the fairest Chapman; and it were well if there were none such any where else. Here we mean of the Community neither rigidly precise, as some are, nor desperately wicked in their Way, as others may be;... in Opposition to those who think that all Things are arbitrary and corrupt there, as if so mighty an Empire could stand upon those Terms. Allowance ought to be made for the various Sentiments, remote Nations have of the same Methods. Here with us, a Present to a Judge of a Cause depending, tho' silently, made by one of the Parties, is unlawful, and accounted no better than a Bribe; there, it is, not only lawful but, expected as a kind of Duty to the Judge. Here, for a Party to offer at instructing the Judge in private, is intolerable, and the Judge, that endures it, professedly partial. There, it is the best Way for a Suitor to go to the Judge, and make known his Case, by which the Judge esteems himself much better able to judge rightly, when it comes judicially before him. There is no Sight in the Comparison, whether their Methods or ours are best; the Sequel may perhaps shew somewhat tending to a Decision; and, in the mean Time, let it be remembered that there are no Processes, Arrests, Bailiffs, Bails, Spungings, Dilatories, Errors or Appeals... (North 1744: 45–6)

For North, and as with other aspects of Ottoman justice that advantaged some parties and disadvantaged others (for example, unequal rights extended to Muslims and non-Muslims, men and women, bonded and free persons), payments to qadis and false witnessing were part of the system, which he did *not* regard as proof of the deficient, primitive, or irrational nature of Ottoman law. One ought to master their logic and conventions in order to make use of one's potential opportunities to overcome adversaries. Also implicit here is North's distinction between formal rules and processes and a more substantive (rather than procedural) sense of justice, a notion much like what Lawrence Rosen (2000) has proposed in a very different (modern) Islamic context: notions of propriety, fairness, and justice were upheld not because specific guidelines were enforced, proper procedures were followed, or corrupt practices were avoided, but sometimes by ignoring these. Indeed, North (1744: 46–7) told his biographer that in the Ottoman lands, "the Morality of the Action seems to depend on the pure Justice and Right, and not upon the Regularity (in a Christian Sense) of the Means." One wonders how common this sentiment was among Ottomans themselves, including the main actors administering justice.

* * *

Native and foreign observers of the Ottoman polity wrote about corruption from different perspectives, with different objectives, for different audiences. It would be difficult to overstate how their articulations diverged in terms of their broader concerns, worldviews, and religious-ideological inclinations. For example, the question of whether the Ottoman polity was tyrannical or despotic did not concern the Ottomans. Nor were they particularly interested in various regime types or their characteristics in early modern Europe. For their part, foreign observers might have cared the least about the distinctive implications of sharia- and siyasa-discourses on good government and, thus, administrative predation.

Yet there are also clear overlaps in the two genres of writing. For example, the levels of outrage that many native and foreign authors conveyed about corruption appear comparable to modern observers. Also, the two groups seem to agree about the types of corruption and its range of causes. While greed and immorality (among "Turks" in many foreign accounts, and "government officials" according to native ones) were popular explanations for both groups, it is also possible to find both Ottoman and non-Ottoman authors who associated corruption with systemic financial factors. In particular, payment-for-appointment schemes received significant attention in both sets of accounts.

This chapter explored a selection of foreign accounts to identify quasi-ethnographic information about corruption, specifically in the realm of the Ottoman administration of justice. This exercise based on texts of variable quality indicated inconsistent appraisals. Some authors saw the Ottoman judicial system as a crude, irrational realm of government. Others regarded it a sophisticated one. Regarding the particulars of Ottoman justice, I observed an emphasis on the work of the qadi, his sources of income, and how he might have influenced litigation processes based on self interest. I also noted some emphasis on false witnessing, which our sources regarded as common but not always based on greed or immediate material considerations.

Finally, I noted that some foreign accounts engaged with the issue of corruption in order to successfully negotiate with it. According to the authors of these texts, while corruption was an inherent aspect of the Ottoman justice, as it was in many contemporary European settings (at least according to a few of them), it was not senseless or unpredictable. By mastering the knowledge of corruption, one could weaponize it to help those who were systemically disadvantaged by the judicial system.

7
Gifts as Bribes

It might be time to engage with a question that has been lurking in the background since the beginning of the book: How should we think about the relationship between gifts and bribes in the premodern Ottoman society? While the question came up in previous chapters, the topic warrants a more in-depth consideration. In what follows, I review how our sources use the terms and then critically reflect on scholarly deliberations in the Ottoman context on the differences between gifts and bribes. Based on this discussion, I offer in the remainder of the chapter a particular perspective and consider its implications in one case study.

Many premodern jurists tried to distinguish gifts from bribes with reference to the acts' distinctive objectives (see Chapter 2). Al-Tirmidhi, a medieval scholar, stated the difference as follows: "A bribe is what a person gives in order to obtain help, whereas a gift is something to which no condition is attached" (Rosenthal 1964: 136). Later, Ibn Nujaym wrote that gifts were unconditional offerings to express love and friendship (1966: 694). Even in modern texts, gift-giving is differentiated from bribery in much the same way: "A gift is a gift only if it is based on good intentions and love and does not intend to generate favors in exchange. If not, such an offering ceases to become a gift and becomes a bribe, explicitly forbidden by our religion" ("Rüşvet: Alan da Veren de Yanacaktır!" 2013: 196; original in Turkish).[1]

Yet the boundary between gifts and bribes can be imprecise even for legal experts. For example, according to Rosenthal (1964: 139, 139n26), some jurists, such as a certain Jamal al-Din al-Qazwini writing in the twelfth century, argued that gifts could generate legitimate expectations of reciprocity that require satisfaction within certain boundaries. Also, Ottoman jurists struggled to distinguish gifts and bribes in practice (see Chapter 2). Any such attempt remained limited largely to the qadi's work and responsibilities.

Indications of this ambiguity are even more prominent in other discursive fields. It is common, for example, for Ottoman commentators to use the terms

---

[1] It is possible to identify this distinction in non-jurisprudential Ottoman works as well. See, for example, Defterdar 1935: 92; and Kâtib Chelebi 1957: 124.

"gift" and "bribe" interchangeably or identify such tendencies among their contemporaries. For Naima a gift ("caize" or "pişkeş") can be a bribe extended to those in positions of authority to secure admission into government service (2007: 3:1316) and receive protection and intercession (3:1407). He also described a "bribe-giver" (*raşi*) as a person who distributed "gifts" to influential people in the palace (4:1696). Selaniki's history contains multiple references (1999: 1:258, 427; 2:740) to bribes that people called "tributes and gifts." The historian Peçevi (1968: 20) referred to bribes that the grand vizier Rüstem Paşa (d. 1561) received to make appointments as "gifts." The author of *Kitab-ı Müstetab* (Yücel 1988: 23) claimed that bribes were explicitly offered and received among households under the premise of gift exchanges. The literature offers many more examples of this trend.[2]

One notices a parallel tendency in accounts produced for European audiences. According to Stephan Gerlach (2006: 1:193–4), who visited the empire in the late sixteenth century, government officials acquired their posts through "gifts and bribes." George Sandys wrote in the early seventeenth century that "bribery... hath so corrupted their integritie, that those causes (if they beare but a colour of right) do seldome miscarry where gifts are the Advocates" (1615: 62). In litigations, Rycaut (1686: 141) argued "it is the common course for both parties at difference, before they appear together in presence of the judge to apply themselves singly to him, and try whose donative and present hath the most in it of temptation." In a report addressed to the Lord Treasurer of Great Britain, the Earl of Winchilsea, the British ambassador to the Ottoman Empire between 1660 and 1668, wrote that "nothing can be done in this place without 'presents and corruptions'" (*Report* 1913: 127). Aaron Hill suggested in the early eighteenth century that "no subject to the *Grand Signior* dares enter on a place of power, till by the moving rhetoric of some considerable present he has brib'ed the favor of the *Grand Vizier*" (1709: 11). Elias Habesci wrote in the late eighteenth century that in court cases "the best witnesses are generally those whose employers can make the richest presents to the judge" (1784: 273); likewise, in the very early nineteenth century Guillaume-Antoine Olivier wrote that "the smallest favour, the smallest service are obtained only by presents" (1801: 182).

Similar characterizations abound in diplomatic sources as well. For example, Mary Lucille Shay's (1944) study on the internal correspondence of the Venetian *baili* stationed in Istanbul between 1720 and 1734 indicates from the

---

[2] For instances of a parallel conflation of gifts and bribes in the Mamluk context, see Miura 1997; Morimoto 2002; and Martel-Thoumian 2005.

perspective of the giver the unapologetically transactional qualities of "gifts" the Venetian offered to the likes of the grand vizier, *reisülküttab* (head of the sultan's chancery), qadis, and other high officials in the palace and their retinues: "Gifts tempted lips to open, rewarded an informer, coaxed a recalcitrant Turk to reconsider, purchased an official's approval, or in the effective words of the Venetians gifts were used 'to caress' or 'to cultivate'" (46). Such offers were intended to achieve both specific, short-term goals (for example, obtaining a favorable decision in the imperial council pertaining to a trade deal or the release of a compatriot from prison) and open-ended, long-term objectives (for example, recruiting allies among some of the more influential officials in the administration). The gifts were said to be explicitly demanded by the Ottoman officials, intensely negotiated between them and the baili, and at times rejected by the latter.[3]

The vague boundary that separated gifts from bribes in our sources might explain the anxiety in the modern Ottoman scholarship about how to distinguish the two forms of giving. As described, Muzaffer Doğan (2002) and Yüksel Çelik (2006) argue that various types of payment schemes among officials that might look like bribes should be perceived as established and rule-bounded government practices—that they were formally recorded in official ledgers indicates their sanctioned status by the state and legitimacy.[4] Doğan and Çelik do not necessarily deny that bribes were at times extended to and accepted by government authorities under the premise of offering gifts. But they insist that these were aberrations that blurred the difference between legitimate and illegitimate payments as articulated in the state's bureaucratic conventions—thereby implicitly confirming that gifts among officials should be ontologically distinguished from bribes. What is noteworthy in Doğan's and Çelik's attempts to differentiate gifts and bribes is the researchers' implicit affirmation of their shared transactional qualities.[5]

More recent scholarship on gift exchanges in the Ottoman context further elucidates the topic. Fatma Ünyay Açıkgöz (2012, 2018) and Hedda

---

[3] For parallel reports in Venetian sources from the sixteenth and seventeenth centuries, see Valensi 1993: 26, 43. For reports generated by British diplomats, see Talbot 2017: 110. For many consistent references to gifts-cum-bribes in Dutch and French consular and diplomatic sources, see Eldem 1999: 237–40; Kadı 2012: 99, 116–17, 133, 187, *passim*. Between 1732 and 1735, "donations and gratuities" constituted over 35 percent of the general costs incurred by the French nation in the Ottoman Empire (Eldem 1999: 238).

[4] If anything, Doğan (2002) suggested, certain offerings and tributes extended by lower-level officials to their superiors at the times of their appointments, such as pişkeş, caize, and avaid, might be likened to lawful and routine "taxes."

[5] As I argued in the Introduction, the fact that these payments were often arbitrary, negotiable, and could be revoked at a moment's notice casts doubt on Doğan and Çelik's tendency to ascribe a hyper-formal status to them.

Reindl-Kiel (2009, 2012, 2013, and 2017), in particular, have a sophisticated interpretation of the terminology, protocols, and symbolism associated with gift exchanges.[6] According to both researchers, gifts were often memorable, symbolic of the personal connection between the giver and the recipient, which explains the correlations between the identity of the gift-giver and the objects presented as gifts. Gifts to the ruler included highly stylized and personalized items, typically valuable, luxurious objects that aimed to rouse the sovereign, as personal mementos from the presenter. It was common for the ranking members of the ulema, for example, to send the ruler scholarly books. Gifts by members of the military-administrative elite could include jewelry, valuable weapons, horses, slaves, and furs (Reindl-Kiel 2009: 68–72; Açıkgöz 2018: 295; Atik 2019).[7] And official ceremonies involving gift exchanges continued to function as mechanisms to solidify the personal bonds between the ruler and his servants (Açıkgöz 2018: 292, 297).

At the same time, there are clear reasons to resist the assumption that gift exchanges were always selfless, altruistic, non-transactional endeavors.[8] Both Açıkgöz (2012: 235–6; 2018: 293–4) and Reindl-Kiel (2009) have argued that gift exchanges among the political elite were significant ways to articulate relative, mutually acknowledged positions in the political hierarchy. According to Reindl-Kiel (2012: 119), gifts "reflected the degree of honour its addressee ought to obtain, the respective social standing of donor and recipient, the quality of bond connecting them." The type of relationship between the parties was also signified in the terminology used for gifts. For example, pişkeş, a tribute offered to the ruler by his servants, symbolized the giver's

---

[6] See also Turan 2002; Atik 2019; and Sözen 2019.

[7] Anthropologist Chris Gregory (1982: Ch. 1 and *passim*) argued that one criterion that distinguished gifts from other offerings is precisely the personalized nature of the transaction: in market transactions and tax payments, the things exchanged are alienated from their original owners. In gift exchanges, however, the object offered to the recipient carries with it a quality of "inalienability" in the sense that the givers, recipients, and nature of the occasions for the giving are bound to the gifted objects. According to Sancisi-Weerdenburg (1989: 131–2), gifts in the ancient Persian Empire "had undeniable economic value, but more often than that, they also had a surplus value that cannot easily be expressed in economic terms," which she identifies in the "original forms and substance" of gifts that are "capable of bearing and preserving symbolic meanings ... [and] that continue to be recognizable as such long after the moment they were donated."

[8] This claim is consistent with how various scholars described gift exchanges in different settings. Mary Douglas (2002: ix) wrote that "the whole idea of a free gift is based on a misunderstanding." Consistent with the earlier insights of Marcel Mauss (1990), Pierre Bourdieu (2002: 4–6) denied the viability of selfless giving, which he saw as a mere pretension that "veils the objective truth of gift-giving" (cf. Ungureanu 2013: 393). While the act it represents might be instrumental for promoting civic virtues and enhancing group solidarity, Bourdieu recognized its difference from other forms of reciprocity only "subjectively": gifting is a deliberate and strategic "misrecognition" (*meconnaissance*; Bourdieu 2002: 5) and, thus, a misexpression of the true intentions of the parties to the exchange. According to Jacques Derrida (1994: 7), who shared Bourdieu's perspective on the issue, selfless giving is the "very figure of the impossible" (cf. Silber 2009: 180). See also Davis 2000: 3–10, *passim*.

loyalty, gratitude, and personal devotion and thus acknowledged the ruler's claims to sovereignty (Açıkgöz 2018: 297).[9] The ruler's and ranking officials' gifts to their servants and lower-level officials were called *inam* and *ihsan* and indicated the giver's generosity, benevolence, and recognition of the recipient's status as a trusted and dependable ally of lower rank (Açıkgöz 2012: 234–1; Reindl-Kiel 2017: 12–13). Any divergence from the established patterns or standards could be read as an affront to the political and ideological norms of the polity.

The researchers note further the important economic role of gifts as means of revenue extraction. In fact, gift transfers to the ruler constituted a significant economic source provided by those not technically subject to taxation (Reindl-Kiel 2009: 37; Açıkgöz 2018: 292).[10] Relevant to this discussion is Reindl-Kiel's (2017: 11) formulation of a redistributive gift economy that comprised a distinct circuit of wealth appropriation centered on the ruler's personal treasury (*hazine-i birun*), separate from the state treasury (*hazine-i enderun*), which often financed state expenditures when the state's own revenue sources fell short. Açıkgöz's impressions (2012: 292–3) indicate that the imperial center began to consider gifts to the ruler more explicitly as income sources from the second half of the sixteenth century onward, when the polity instituted new occasions for gifting and increased the value thresholds of gifts due to the polity's financial problems.[11] Here, it is important to point out that the occasions, frequency, and composition of gifts to the ruler were not negotiable. These gifts were mandatory, and those whose gifts were late or judged inadequate based on expectations were subject to rebukes and punishments (Açıkgöz 2018: 294).

Given the substantive contributions of their research on the issue, Açıkgöz's and Reindl-Kiel's observations regarding the boundaries between gifts and bribes are significant for the present discussion. Like Doğan and Çelik,

---

[9] For more on pişkeş, see Karaca 2007. In the Iranian context, see Lambton 1994; Floor 2001; and Ashraf 2016. While Ottoman historians who work on official and elite sources tend to translate this term as "tribute" offered to the ruler by his servants as a sign of their loyalty and subservience, it is not entirely clear that this meaning captures the term's full semantic range. Relevant here is Assef Ashraf's (2016: 565) critique of Ann Lambton's definition (1994) of the same term in the late Safavid context. Lambton defines the term in much the same way that Ottoman historians do (as "tribute imposed on individuals and communities and a tax attached to the land and to certain offices" [Lambton 1994: 157]), but according to Ashraf, and based on a broad basis of historical documentation, pişkeş corresponded to a wider range of exchanges. For a preliminary understanding of the word's range of connotations in Ottoman literary texts, see Önal 2008.

[10] Açıkgöz (2018) called the precisely determined and defined gifts that were sent to the ruler according to a predetermined schedule "a type of in-kind tax" collected from highest echelons of the tax-exempt groups.

[11] In fact, cash gifts were also common, and so were the practices of selling valuable gifts and melting silver and gold objects at times of need (Reindl-Kiel 2009: 40, 54; Açıkgöz 2018: 296).

Açıkgöz suggests that gift exchanges among government officials, unlike bribes, were routinized and bounded by rules (2018: 292, 297). In Reindl-Kiel's analysis (2012) of a petition that Cornell Fleischer (1994) had discovered, we find a different attempt to distinguish the two types of giving. The petition belonged to an apprentice in the finance administration during the early sixteenth century who sought promotion.

> The apprentice endeavored to become the successor to his ailing master, a *muhasebeci* [or accountant] who was to recommend him but asked for "a little something" (*bir mikdar nesnecik*) in return. The "little something" was one thousand florin, at that time about 57.000 akçe, a sum for which an unskilled building labourer would have worked more than thirty years. But the deal never worked out, the accountant died, and somebody else got the job. Then the second *ruznameci* promised the young man a position, but when the applicant came along he was brushed off for not bringing a present. (107)

According to Reindl-Kiel, gifting in the Ottoman context habitually involved signals to recipients regarding "the donor's open or secret intentions, and the kind of favour he anticipated from the target of his munificence" (119).[12] And while she acknowledged that in the Ottoman context "the boundaries between gifting and corruption remained fluid and elusive" (ibid.), she remained convinced that "to grace an official with an adequate gift to motivate him to fulfil his duty was evidently not considered to be corruption. Rather, bribery meant paying somebody for an illegal action he would have never done without getting a little something in return" (ibid.).

---

[12] Here is how Cornell Fleischer (1994: 53) interpreted the petition: "One of the most remarkable aspects of [the apprentice's petition]...is the conspicuous absence of that more vigorous language of complaint—complaint about venality of office, complaint about abuse of position, complaint about violation of imperial ideals enshrined in *kanun*, dynastic edict—that would fill the pages of similar petitions penned by a slightly later generation. Here, the tone...is rather one of explanation, apology, and open-ended appeal for personal assistance, assistance that is requested not because the subject has been wronged by greedy and immoral individuals, but because circumstances in an otherwise normal situation have conspired to place him in a difficult position. The matter-of-fact recounting of the events, and the lack of explicit rancor against those who wronged him...suggest that it would be erroneous to read [the scribe's] petition as the sort of protest against corruption of an established, commonly understood system that would be characteristic of a somewhat later era. At this point, relatively early in Süleyman's [d. 1566] reign, the relationship that structured the central administrative apparatus were still understood to be highly personalized ones within which the culture of exchange of 'gifts' was taken as natural, if occasionally problematic. The gift had not yet become a bribe, and [the scribe's] letter has as much the weight and tone of a report as of a complaint." Fleischer's contention that the types of exchanges that might have once been regarded as gifts were perceived as bribes "by a slightly later generation" is thought-provoking, but it is speculative and requires substantiation.

We can detect in Reindl-Kiel's characterization traces of the legalistic articulations explored earlier (cf. Rosenthal 1964: 140; Köse 2008: 138–41). Yet, given the disputed legality of many types of actions and services to others that warranted rewards, the definition fails to clearly distinguish gifts and bribes in numerous instances, a point that is evident in jurisprudential literature (Chapter 2). Moreover, jurists like Ibn Nujaym and Ibn Abidin not only used gifts and bribes interchangeably when discussing identical behavior with dubious legalities; they also employed the term "bribe" to describe a few legally sanctioned transactions for at least some parties. Finally, there is no reason to assume that legalistic considerations solely determined how contemporary Ottomans perceived gifts and bribes in relation to each other.

At this point, I would like to make two (related) interventions regarding how modern Ottoman scholarship has engaged with the topic. First, there are reasons to resist strict functional distinctions between gifts and different transactions. As I observed earlier (Note 8 and elsewhere), scholars of various disciplines, including Ottomanists, have recognized the possibility that gift-giving can be self-serving. But the extensive anthropological literature on the subject goes a step further and reminds us that there may be multiple, even conflicting, ideologies of gifting in any particular setting, to the point that the term "gift" divulges little specificity about its possible meanings and purposes. According to Jonathan Parry (1986: 453, 459, 466), for example, "pure gifts" (or gifts that did not seek reciprocity) emerged only in highly literate, market societies, but even in such contexts they did not eradicate the earlier notions also associated with gifting that required the exchange of goods and services.[13] Research by Yunxiang Yan (2009: 2010) and James Carrier (1990, 1991) shows that different types of gifts (including "conventional/familial," "instrumental," and "personal/pure/perfect"), each with different expectations of reciprocity, are specific to particular types of relationships between transactors. Marshall Sahlins (1972: Chs. 3 and 4; see also Kirk 2007) distinguished between "general," "balanced," and "negative" reciprocity in gifting, associating the first type with generous sharing, the second with strict expectations of equivalence and timely returns, and the last with inequality and exploitation. These insights imply a conceptual and semantic flexibility that is also evident in Ottoman society with the tendency to describe gifts as *both*

---

[13] Because market societies have the least economic dependence on gifts for commodity exchange, Parry argued, they can afford to "idealize" the distinction between gifts and other types of interactions. He suggested (1986: 459) that pure gifts may have first appeared in the late Roman Empire. James Carrier (1990: 23) defined the pure or "perfect gift" as "priceless" because it is a "material expression of the immaterial." Also, it is "free, unconstrained and unconstraining."

unreciprocated tokens of love *and* explicitly transactional offers in various discursive fields.

Second, the concerted effort to distinguish gifts from bribes tends to divert our attention from their shared functions and what they imply about the broader context in which these interactions took place. In the case mentioned above, for example, while calling the apprentice's payment a gift or a bribe might betray a modern preoccupation or sensitivity on the part of the historian, the ambiguity itself points to the acts' common features, which tend to get overlooked in the effort to distinguish them. In fact, the difference might have been immaterial for the apprentice. His payment to his master represented an offer that required reciprocity based on mutual agreement that remained unfulfilled. As such, it was central to his grievance.

Here I propose that gifts and bribes might be viewed primarily as interactions that both conform to the "macro patterns of economic organization" in the premodern Ottoman society (Kirk 2007: 187). Indeed, one could imagine various forms of gift exchanges, tributes, bribes, payments for appointments, and the like, all as various modalities of reciprocity that served important social, political, and economic purposes. In this regard, Karl Polanyi's (2001) insights are crucial: in characterizing how premodern societies functioned, he emphasized the critical importance of reciprocal ties, either alone or in combination with other forms of "economic organization."[14] In these settings, the acts of giving, receiving, and countering, in whatever form they took, helped establish personal connections that individuals relied on to belong, to protect themselves from external threats, and to thrive.[15] From this perspective,

---

[14] In Polanyi's work (2001: 45–58), "reciprocity" is one of the three primary forms of economic organization, along with "redistribution" and "market exchange," that describe how economic interactions are structured. It refers to exchanging goods and services among kin and non-kin that involve reciprocated offers and counteroffers. Polanyi did not assume these forms to be mutually exclusive; instead, one could identify combined aspects of multiple forms in a given society. On Polanyi's economic categorizations, see also Dalton 1968: Chs. 1 and 7.

[15] What Willem Floor (2001: 615) has stated for Qajar Iran might also be relevant for the Ottomans, although Floor needlessly limits various forms of reciprocity to gift exchanges without acknowledging the variability of the term's meaning: "The act of giving has not been an incidental, but rather a structural, institutionalized element of Persian society and polity.... Because the socio-political hierarchy was based on reciprocity and personal transactions, the judicious distribution of gifts was a natural instrument within this value system to serve as a reward for services rendered or gifts received, as well as an expression of the continued appreciation and the sustained confirmation of the system. Therefore, this habit of gift giving was part of the fabric of Persian life and held for all classes and ranks or social and ethnic groups." More recently, Assef Ashraf (2016: 555) recognized the relevance of Polanyi's modeling (though, again, in a fashion that is unnecessarily restricted to gift exchanges) for Qajar Iran as follows: "The exchange of gifts to and from the Qajar state reflected a culture of exchange that existed within broader nineteenth-century Iranian society, and enmeshed the elite in social and economic relations that helped sustain their rule. The depictions of Qajar rulers as 'autocratic' and 'arbitrary,' which often features in the historiography of Iran, obscures the fact that political practices

there is little difference among many types of gifts exchanged between kin, tributes offered to the ruler, favors granted to the sultan's servants, payments made for appointments, and bribes paid to government officials, despite variations in their enactment, symbolism, or temporality: they were all means to create the mutual ties and obligations on which individuals and groups relied. The centrality of reciprocal relationships and the parallel functions that gifts and bribes served in premodern Ottoman society require greater emphasis in our analyses, at least as the starting point for the ensuing discussions.[16]

We can identify both of these tendencies—the often uncertain, complex meanings of gift and the centrality of reciprocity in premodern Ottoman society—in the sixteenth-century account of Hans Ulrich Krafft (1997).[17] Krafft was a German merchant who was first jailed in Tripoli (in Syria) in 1574 because of his company's debts to local Jewish creditors and then, after the appointment of a new qadi a few years later, got involved in a lengthy litigation with creditors who sought compensation from him for his company's debts. Krafft's account is useful because it demonstrates how litigants often struggled to influence judges to achieve their desired outcomes (115–31). Aided in this endeavor by the local French consul, a few Venetian merchants, and a friendly fortress commander, Krafft first tried to gain the qadi's favor by repairing his golden watch, which compelled his opponents to send the qadi presents to level the playing field. Krafft was subsequently advised to appeal to the qadi's wife and arranged to send her two silk dresses along with a request that she intercede with her husband on his behalf.[18] Based on the reports of the person or persons who presented Krafft's gifts to the wife (who remain nameless in the account), she listened to Krafft's story, sympathized with his

---

like gift giving were an extension of the cultural norms of giving that existed in broader society.... Gift exchange in Qajar Iran reminds us that, as Karl Polanyi and others have pointed out, premodern political and economic systems, were 'as a rule, embedded in social relations.'" Incidentally, acknowledging the importance of the broader conception of reciprocity, instead of a particular modality associated with it, allows us to perceive particular forms of giving-and-countering as individual aspects of a bigger whole without regarding any one form as paradigmatic.

[16] To be clear, it is not my purpose to question the merits of research that seeks to distinguish gifts from bribes. After all, that is in part what I attempt to accomplish in this chapter. My point is that such efforts should be based on a broader conceptual framework, such as the one sketched above.

[17] My interest in Krafft's account is not new. In fact, I have been fascinated with the story since I first encountered it during my dissertation research because of the text's ethnographic import. See Ergene 2003: 115–23, and 2004 for the evolution of my thinking about Krafft's experiences and how they might reflect various aspects of legal practice and dispute resolution processes in the Ottoman context. The interpretation presented in this chapter has not appeared before.

[18] As I mentioned earlier, references to gifts extended to local qadis and naibs to curry favor with them are common in European sources. See, for example, Olnon 2000: 171; van den Boogert 2005: 297; Kadı 2012: 116–17, 133, *passim*.

situation, admired and accepted the dresses, promised to approach the qadi on his behalf, and pledged to return the gifts if the qadi decided against the German. She may also have subsequently disregarded the countergifts from Krafft's adversaries (126) because of her commitment to the merchant's cause. Krafft later heard from his sources that the wife did in fact ask her husband to be lenient toward him and advocated for him. More specifically, when the qadi suggested that Krafft's company's debts were so large that the creditors would not be able to agree on a settlement low enough for Krafft to pay to secure his release, she suggested that he threaten to send all parties to Istanbul, presumably to settle their problems in the imperial council. The wife claimed that the creditors would be unwilling to take this risk, since Krafft could easily secure the support of European ambassadors in Istanbul.[19] When the qadi asked his wife how he could profit from Krafft's release, she showed him the clothes Krafft had sent and assured him that the merchant would be willing to reward the qadi generously if he showed him favor. Indeed, the qadi ultimately strongarmed the creditors to accept a settlement of 1,000 gold pieces—significantly less than the debt owed by Krafft's company—and Krafft paid the qadi about one hundred gold pieces, or 10 percent of the settlement award. On his release from prison, Krafft returned to Europe (115–31).

The fact that Krafft remained in prison for more than two years (from August 1574 to October 1576) before the arrival of the new qadi[20] illustrates the dire consequences of not having support based on personal connections in an environment that lacked effective and adequate guardrails against arbitrary behavior by judicial and administrative authorities.[21] As I explained in Chapter 2, there is little doubt that the litigants' offers to the qadi or his close relatives were unsanctioned according to jurisprudential standards.[22] It is also obvious that the wife's involvement in Krafft's case was self-interested, as evident in her appreciation of the expensive dresses and her (and her husband's)

---

[19] For other references in European sources to changing the litigation venue as a legal strategy, see van den Boogert 2005: 192–4, 248.

[20] Presumably because the previous naib, himself a local person, was more inclined to accommodate the local creditors' desires to keep the German in prison, forcing him to agree to a more substantial settlement.

[21] Krafft would finally be released in August 1577. According to Peters (2005: 34–5), "The most common function of imprisonment lies outside the domain of penal law. It is the ultimate means of coercion in private law to force debtors to fulfil their obligations. They can be imprisoned by the *qāḍī* until they pay their debts or carry out their obligations or prove that that they are indigent or incapable of fulfilling their obligations.... The length of imprisonment is left to the discretion of the authority imposing it." Nevertheless, a three-year imprisonment is extraordinarily long.

[22] On the other hand, Krafft's offerings, whether called gifts or bribes, might have been legal for him according to some jurisprudential interpretations, since they constituted measures to eliminate unfair threats to himself or his property. See Chapter 2.

interest in possible material rewards for facilitating a settlement. At the same time, the wife's concern with the material aspects of the relationship was complemented by behavior that signals her virtues, demonstrated in her commitment to make Krafft's case to her husband in a compelling manner, and her promise to return the gifts to Krafft if her support proved useless. Her display of integrity thus complicates her relationship with Krafft, forcing us to view the arrangement as something that should not be reduced to a simple, impersonal quid pro quo.

The ethnographic insights on *guanxi* relations in the context of modern China are relevant to this discussion. Guanxi refers to informal associations often (though not always) involving kin, friends, classmates, neighbors, fellow village or town residents, and so on. These relationships are solidified and reproduced by reciprocal favors, including material and informational exchanges for those involved in them, based on a shared sense of belonging, communal responsibility, and companionship (Xin and Pearce 1996). As in the Ottoman case, such connections often guarantee a degree of assurance in a highly insecure world: "In a situation where there is pervasive distrust of the system and great gaps exist in the legal and societal infrastructure necessary for capitalism, the consolidation of social relationships built on gift exchange provides a substitute form of trust that can improve the profitability of investment and reduce the risk of arbitrary bureaucratic interference that is not in the interests of the investors" (Smart 1993: 398). Guanxi could help someone gain access to strategic information, share rare resources, and obtain support from powerful or influential parties in potentially lucrative or advantageous ventures. This last aspect of guanxi relations has led many to associate them with corruption (Torsello and Venard 2016). Yet, while researchers acknowledge the possibility that guanxi might be utilized to achieve legally dubious objectives, they also insist that reducing guanxi to a sheer means-to-ends transactionality neglects the complexity of the connections it envelops and the functions it serves.

Scholarship on guanxi helps us understand how the exchanges between Krafft and the qadi's wife conveyed a sense of legitimacy without reducing them to mutually exclusive formulations of gifts and bribes. It might be that what qualified a particular type of giving as justifiable was (perhaps among other things) how it was carried out: "Clearly, guanxi can be used for instrumental purposes, and this usage is recognized by members of the society. However, it is referred to as the art of guanxi, because the style of exchange and the appropriateness of the performance are critical to its effectiveness. The style and manner of gift exchange is not optional; rather, it is fundamental to its operation" (Smart 1993: 399; cf. Smart and Hsu 2007). A failure to follow the correct forms in the exchange might devalue the offer: "The blatant intention to obligate may fail precisely because of its open motivation" (Smart 1993: 395). The appropriate forms of giving should also be sensitive to the givers' and receivers' tastes and status, the reasons and occasions for the exchange, and the form and time frame for reciprocation. They should promote strong, forward-looking, relationships between the parties involved (ibid.; see also Silin 1972: 342–3). From this perspective, one can regard the wife's expressions of compassion toward a poor stranger in an alien land, her assurances to Krafft after she accepted his offers, and her loyalty to him even when she was presumably tempted by the creditors' counteroffers as evidence of her performative mastery of the role she played.

I believe that such a performance was not only common but often expected in the Ottoman context. Let us reconsider the following quotation from the biography of Sir Dudley North (d. 1691), originally discussed in Chapter 6, presumably based on the author's familiarity with local practice:

> Another of [Dudley North's] Schemes (not a little the Practice of most Franks residing in Turky) was, before a Trial, to shew the Judge a Respect by making him a small Present, and then to make his Cause known to him, before he brought it on. The Judge ordinarily takes this in better Part, than a great Present, and nothing of the Cause said along with it; for that implied that the Cause was bad, and that he was to be corrupted. If the Suitors, or the Cause, be considerable, and no Present at all is given, the Judge looks upon himself to be slighted, or rather defrauded; for he accounts something is due to him for doing Justice, not much unlike what is here termed Fees, only without State or Rule as the European Way is; and such Omission is not wholesome, even for a good Cause. (North 1744: 45)

The performance described in the quotation is instrumental in building trust and generating a sense of intimacy between the judge and the supplicant. Moreover, the text implicitly recognizes a line between corrupting and non-corrupting payments that should not be crossed. Yet it also resists categorical distinctions between "gifts" and "bribes" *based on reciprocity* by discounting the possibility of offering the judge a present that is too small in value—that is, purely symbolic. Just like offering the judge "no Present," such an offer would be insulting. The present must have some economic worth, "not much unlike what is here [viz. England?] termed Fees," in order to generate a return. Coupled with the supplicant's demonstration of respect for the judge's sense of virtue, an apt determination of the proper value of the present, neither too low nor too high, becomes part of the performance.[23]

It is not surprising that the performance of giving-and-countering would be a basis of legitimacy when the material boundaries that separate gifts from bribes are indiscernible. Thus, I am inclined to see various types of gifts, bribes, and everything in between not as discrete categories, but as overlapping notions on a conceptual spectrum (cf. Appadurai 1986; Carrier 1991: 132). In the eyes of many premodern commentators, Ottoman and foreign, the critical importance attached to the shared functions that gifts and bribes served in facilitating or reproducing reciprocity seems to have eased their interchangeable use. In this context, calling an exchange "gifting" or "bribery" in a mutually exclusive way might have reflected judgments regarding the act's performative aspects or stemmed from the subjective positions of the people who did the labeling.

* * *

I close this chapter with a note of caution about the broader implications of the above discussion. One might be tempted to regard the often-untraceable functional distinctions between gifts and bribes in a premodern environment as a reason to question the relatability of corruption in premodern and modern settings. According to Peter Bratsis (2003a: 10–11), for example,

> The apparent lack of a word for bribery in Ancient Greek presents a problem for those who assume an unbroken line in the concept of corruption. Mark Philp (1997) notes that there are many words in Ancient Greek that make no distinction between a gift and a bribe (*doron, lemma, chresmasi peithein*) since, for the Greeks, to persuade through gift giving was acceptable and no perversion of judgment could be assumed. Philp makes the point that if the Greeks have no conception of bribery, then the whole idea of a public body in Ancient Greece is put into question: "If these were the only terms for bribery in the Ancient Greek world we would have to take the view that there is a

---

[23] Natalie Zemon Davis (2000: 88) seems to agree with the above analysis, at least in sixteenth-century France: "In a world of gifts that created 'friendships' and grateful obligations, where did bribery begin? There was not even a special word for bribery in Old Regime France.... In France 'bribe' meant and still means a little morsel of bread. The phrase 'pot-e-vin,' which came by the nineteenth century to refer to something illicit (but still not as clear-cut as the English 'bribe'), was in the sixteenth century an amount of wine that one might buy at supper or an inn, or that might be used for the friendly drink between traders clinching sale agreements, also called 'le vin de marché.' Thus in France, one just used the word 'dons' or 'présents' and had to decide by context and performance whether the gift was a good one or a bad one."

basic untranslatability of the terms between us and them—that they not only failed to distinguish gifts and bribes, but that they also had no real concept of public office or trust." On this point, Philp is absolutely right.

I remain unconvinced. Aside from misrepresenting Mark Philp's argument,[24] Bratsis's claim lacks validity in our context since the potential indistinguishability of gifts and bribes as modalities of reciprocity does not entirely erase the different moral connotations of the terms in Ottoman Turkish. The Ottomans routinely used the terms "gift" and "bribe" interchangeably, but this generally happened when the former was tainted by the appearance of the latter. The tendency did not shield the associated acts from criticism and thus indicates no lack of awareness of the conceivably objectionable uses of the terminological substitution, which is expected given the diversity (and sophistication) of viewpoints on corruption in the Ottoman context. Surely Krafft's adversaries did not regard his service to the qadi and gifts to his wife as mere tokens of affection. Indeed, we find a good example of such conflicting perspectives on the legitimacy of gifts in Olivier de Sardan's (1999) work on modern Africa. According to the researcher, gift-giving and reciprocity are essential aspects of the "moral economy" in many African communities and instrumental in ordinary people's daily interactions with state authorities. However, while it is common in these settings to use notions and terminology associated with gifting to justify certain technically illegal practices in official business, this tendency is also widely condemned based on prevailing legal-bureaucratic norms. One's positionality concerning such interactions often shapes his or her perspective on a case-by-case basis (34–40).

---

[24] Philp (1997: 442) actually disputes the claim that "the (ancient) Greeks did not have a word for bribes because all gifts are bribes" by referring to John Noonan's (1984) work. Also, here is how Philp immediately qualifies the section that Bratsis quotes: "In fact, although there were a number of terms for bribery which were essentially neutral, there were also powerfully negative terms, such as *diaphtheirein*, which implied the destruction of a person's independent judgment and action. There is also ample evidence that the Greeks could recognize both the concept of a public trust, and the use of gifts to subvert the ends of that trust. There was a general law in Athens concerning bribery which laid down penalties for giving or taking bribes to the detriment of the interests of the people, and 'cata-political bribery' was accorded the most powerful condemnatory adjective in Greek, namely *aischron*, or shameful."

8

On the Morality of Patronage

The Case of Ilmiye

This chapter explores the morality of patronage and associated practices in the Ottoman context. Like the previous chapter, this one elaborates on a topic that came up in my discussion of specific discursive realms on corruption. Building on my earlier impressions, I reflect here on an under-studied topic in Ottoman history-writing. The specific focus on patronage is partly due to its unique status among other acts linked to corruption as both a well-institutionalized mechanism of recruitment to government service *and* a potential source of abuse by government officials in the Ottoman polity. Also, this is one issue where one might expect significant variations in premodern and modern societies. While it is common to associate various kinds of patronage with corruption in modern contexts, the academic literature based on European settings confirms the need for restraint about such assumptions in premodern ones.

The chapter begins with a comparative consideration of the relationship between patrimonial state and patronage networks in the Ottoman context. My discussion centers on the ilmiye—that is, the Ottoman religious-judicial establishment—not only because of my general familiarity with this part of Ottoman government and society, but also because of the relatively well-developed literature on this group. The ensuing survey builds on insights and information found in jurisprudential works, political literature, and state-generated documents. The chapter excludes foreign accounts because they contain limited and hardly unique evaluative perspectives on patronage practices in the ilmiye.

A few terms I use in this chapter require some elaboration. By "patronage," I mean the material support and advantages provided by patrons with political, administrative, professional, and economic clout to clients with whom they may or may not have prior personal connections. For clients, patronage-based support might generate economic benefits, career advancement, or both. The support provided by patrons could be based on their existing links to their clients (or their desire to establish such connections) or might indicate their appreciation of the clients' talents and other qualities. Patronage might generate feelings of charitable fulfillment for patrons. It could also be a means to build or bolster networks of influence that could translate into political capital, support against actual or potential rivals, or economic benefits (Buchan and Hill 2014: 108–11). "Favoritism" is a related term, but one with more negative connotations that presumes a patron-client interaction based primarily, if not exclusively, on unsanctioned considerations of self-interest by the involved parties that often undermine the interests of third parties. In the context of this discussion, it could be defined as privileging a person in considerations of career advancement based on his (rarely her) personal associations and less on merit. Terms such as "cronyism" and "nepotism" refer to narrower subtypes of this relationship, the former involving friends and associates and the latter family and kin.[1]

Patrimonialism and Patronage in the Ilmiye

There is a relatively well-developed academic literature on the connection between patrimonial state and patronage relations in early modern Europe. In patrimonial settings, according to Julia Adams, government positions and sources of revenue tended to be distributed by those in power based on a "wide discretion" (2005a: 16, 17) and not necessarily in line with the requirements of "rational-legal procedure" (34; see also Peck 1993: 4). Such grants often generated reciprocal obligations by their beneficiaries in the form of future payments, political support, and service commitments (Adams 1994: 506; Peck 1993: 15). The grants could also extend the ruler's patrimonial privileges to those on whom they were bestowed. In other words, recipients' claims to the offices and economic sources could mimic the ruler's entitlements, as in the case of hereditary offices in the Netherlands, France, England, and elsewhere (Adams 2005a: 17, 76).

A reader of recent European historiography on the subject may feel that appropriation of social, economic, and political privileges via favoritism tends to be no transgression in settings where patrimonial claims to office and

---

[1] These definitions are inspired by the elaborations found in the following site in addition to the sources cited in the text: "Favoritism, Cronyism, and Nepotism," Markkula Center for Applied Ethics at Santa Clara University, https://www.scu.edu/government-ethics/resources/what-is-government-ethics/favoritism-cronyism-and-nepotism/, accessed March 6, 2022.

authority are standard for the rulers and ruling elite.[2] In fact, the scholarly literature emphasizes the normalcy of family- and client-based favoritism in Europe since the earliest times. According to Bruce Buchan and Lisa Hill (2014: 30), "Patronage and nepotism were the norm rather than the exception in Athenian and Roman public life." Though her research focuses on the institution of the papacy in the medieval era, Birgit Emich (2020: 72) argued more generally that "the premodern age considered nepotism legitimate, even morally imperative as well as functional." In the Netherlands, the "blatant nepotism" of fathers appointing their sons to non-venal offices "was deemed perfectly acceptable" between the late-sixteenth and eighteenth centuries (Adams 1994: 508, 2005a: 82). In early modern France, patronage was an accepted method "for appointment to public offices and ecclesiastical benefices, and for the award of titles, honors, certain privileges, fiscal exemptions, money gifts, lands, and pensions. The alternative... [to] patronage was not a modern system of recruitment and reward decided by examinations, level of training, and other objective standards of expertise. The alternative that came to mind was venality" (Harding 1981: 50). In early Stuart England, "patronage structured the society" (Peck 1993: 5). William Gibson (1993: 180) argued that nepotism "was accorded moral legitimacy by contemporaries" in appointments in the Church of England during the eighteenth century. Adams (2005a: 83) summarized the general attitudes toward nepotism in most Western societies as follows: "Until Enlightenment ideas of merit became popular in the eighteenth century... nepotism remained an expectation shared by both the givers and receivers of privilege, and one that contemporaries acknowledged and approved."[3]

---

[2] A different tendency seems to have existed in Imperial China, where the patrimonial privileges of the ruling dynasty were not shared with the imperial bureaucracy. According to Man-Cheong (1997), the administrative system in Qing China was geared toward eliminating possible competition to the throne by office-holding families and minimizing family-based factionalism. Consequently, admission to the imperial civil service was done by examinations administered by censors whose relatives were disqualified from these exams and who evaluated the examinees' work without knowing their identities. In subsequent career advancements of later-stage officials as well, "the rule of seniority and other norms operated in such a way as to equalize the chances for advancement of officials from family backgrounds as disparate in privilege as official families and commoner families" (Marsh 1960: 132). Under these circumstances, "any office-holding family found it difficult to maintain status for more than three generations" (Man-Cheong 1997: 53). The system treated nepotism as a crime that could be punished by execution (64).

[3] While the normalcy of patronage in premodern Europe might be rooted in the prevalence of patrimonial claims to authority, modern historians have also identified other factors that might have further contributed to its popularity. Gibson (1993: 188), for example, suggested that patronage, and specifically nepotism, was the prevalent method to staff the Church of England prior to the nineteenth century due to the absence of modern methods of professional training and recruitment. However, one could argue that other methods of staffing might have remained undeveloped in this setting precisely

It has been suggested that in settings where the distribution of privileges, sources, and appointments via patronage is common, criticism of unqualified people in positions of power tends to focus less on the *system* of patronage and more on the patrons' *individual* disregard for or misjudgment of their clients' abilities (Engels 2018: 171). Indeed, the direct, personal nature of patron-client relationships and kin networks was supposed to help patrons to observe their clients' qualities and reward those deemed worthy. For many European commentators, patronage was a more justifiable method of recruitment in the hands of virtuous patrons than, for example, simply selling appointments to those who paid the highest sums (Hurstfield 1967: 28; Harding 1981: 52, 57; Gibson 1993: 186; Emich 2020: 71). My discussion in this chapter is driven by such considerations.

In the Ottoman context, Halil İnalcık (2018: 14) described the connection between the patrimonial character of the polity and the prevalence of patron-client relationships as follows:

> Cultivation, servitude, and affiliation (*terbiyet, kulluk, intisab*, respectively), constituted the bases of social relationships in the Ottoman patrimonial society.... [They represented] an essential social link by the patron and his servants/dependents (sing. kul). Connections (or dependency; *bağlılık*) was necessary to promote the prominence and wealth of the patron and to survive and advance for the servants. This patrimonial principle, articulated in the patron-servant relationship, is evident in the Ottoman state's fundamentals and nature.... In the Ottoman patrimonial society, affiliation (intisab) and patronage constituted the basic principle of social relations and hierarchy in every segment of the elite [and] in status groups, bureaucracy, military, even in the religious establishment.[4]

---

because of the pervasiveness of patronage. The same author also highlighted how favoritism toward kin and clients functioned at times as charity extended toward the needy (182, 188; see also Buchan and Hill 2014: 110–11).

[4] For an earlier articulation of the same sentiment by the same author in direct conversation with Max Weber's own formulations, see İnalcık 1992. In this publication, while İnalcık acknowledged the patrimonial character of the Ottoman polity based on Weber's articulations, he also challenged the Weberian position that the polity stagnated because of its patrimonial character. For him, the polity's dynamism was evident in its ability to develop progressively complex administrative apparatuses in the service of the ruler, but these apparatuses also increasingly routinized and rationalized government. For a more recent and comprehensive articulation of the "bureaucratization of the patrimonial authority" in the Ottoman context, see Barkey 2016. This interpretation is in line with Julia Adams's (2005a: 18) take on the possibility of institutional change in patrimonial settings based on Shmuel Eisenstadt's earlier insights: "Patrimonial rule is a fixed form that paradoxically allows for institutional innovation.... In his pioneering analysis of what he calls 'historical bureaucratic empires,' Shmuel N. Eisenstadt... stresses the capacity of patrimonial rulers and their dependents to capture

In the specific case of the Ottoman religious-judicial establishment, the patrimonial character of the group is evident in its (almost) exclusive entitlement to particular offices, claimed through various types of patron-client relationships or kinship ties. Systematic inquiries into patronage connections within the ilmiye hierarchy go back to the early 1980s, and those inquiries have become increasingly sophisticated (Zilfi 1983, 1988; Tezcan 2009; Atçıl 2009, 2017; Beyazıt 2014a; and others cited in the following discussion).[5] This literature leaves the strong impression that the highest-ranking members of the ilmiye establishment found ways to monopolize the top positions for themselves, their children, and their clients. Abdurrahman Atçıl (2017: 134) wrote that "the vision of a self-reproducing hierarchy that would admit only those who were affiliated with the [ilmiye] dignitaries...was almost completely realized" by the sixteenth century. Baki Tezcan (2009: 396) suggested that the ilmiye dignitaries merit the label "lords of the law" because they had "both the ability to pass their sons and the power to create clienteles that showed them and connected them with financial resources." According to Madeline Zilfi, "blind-favoritism" (1983: 339) and patronage, particularly "patronage of a relative" (2006: 220), shaped the judicial-religious hierarchy so as to "reflect the interests of eminent ulema families and the workings of patrimonial prerogative" (1983: 318) and formed the basis of the "ulema aristocracy" by the eighteenth century (343, 353, 358).[6]

Atçıl's (2017: 181–6) categorical differentiation among different patronage networks in the ilmiye shows us how different types of favoritism were institutionalized. One prevalent type was premised on the privileges extended

---

uncommitted, 'free-floating resources' and redirect them to substantially new enterprises, which may run the gamut from mere spendthrift waste to a more productive expansion of sovereignty into new substantive areas to new moves toward rational-legal bureaucratic centralization, strengthening the lineaments of state formation." For two sophisticated treatments of Ottoman patrimonialism, see Findley 1980a and Kobas 2019. For the relationship between patrimonial government and patronage practices in the Mamluk context, see van Steenbergen 2006: 57–62.

[5] For patronage relations involving the non-ilmiye elite, see, among others, Abou-El-Haj 1974 and 1991; Kunt 1974, 1983; and Findley 1980a and 2006. Most recently, Günhan Börekçi's research (2021) also explored patronage networks in the Ottoman palace and political-military administration.

[6] According to Adams (1994: 506), European patrimonialism "is typified by a segmentation of sovereignty between rulers and corporate elites," where "sovereignty is institutionalized in a set of interdependent relationships among rulers and the corporate bodies...that undergird their rule. It is dual, not unitary, with pronounced tendencies toward further segmentation and fragmentation." Zilfi (2006: 224) describes the interlocking patrimonialisms of the Ottoman dynasty and the ilmiye establishment in the eighteenth century as follows: "A balance was struck between palace interventionism and *ulema* aristocracy [in affairs of the ilmiye]. Their complementary patrimonialisms mutually guaranteed each other's right of access, and together set the conditions for others' entry. The partnership was fueled in the first instance, however, not by the amicable division of *ilmiye* resources, but by shared interests in social conservatism and in the continuing paramount status of Islamic law in Ottoman governance."

to high-level ilmiye dignitaries—including şeyhülislams, kazaskers, ranking qadis, and madrasa professors—that allowed them to bring their students and disciples into the hierarchy as mülazıms (or novices), a status that made them eligible for future appointments as qadis or madrasa instructors.[7] In addition, the ranking ulema could support their former pupils in subsequent appointments to teaching and judiciary positions (Atçıl 2009: 494, 2017: 182).

A second type of patronage was based on family connections (Atçıl 2017: 183–5; see also Uzunçarşılı 1988: 48–50). The sons of high ilmiye families, in particular, could collect stipends at a very young age, receive mülazım status almost automatically, and often obtain appointments with little to no wait compared to many other mülazıms. At those times when other novices had to demonstrate their competency for appointments by passing examinations,[8] the sons of the established ulema families, the *mollazade*s or *ulemazade*s, could be exempted from them (İpşirli 2021: 178–9; Yurdakul 2022: 53–81).[9] And after their appointments to specific teaching or judiciary posts, they rose fast in the hierarchy. "The privileged hierarchical status of the sons of the dignitaries became established in law and practice and gave them a tremendous advantage in the competition for advancement in the hierarchy" (Atçıl 2017: 184).[10]

There are obvious justifications for both types of patronage. One could argue that the most accomplished minds in the ilmiye establishment

---

[7] Mülazım labels were habitually granted every seven years and on special occasions such as the ruler's enthronement, his first military expedition, and the births of princes. Specific quotas were assigned to individual dignitaries according to their ranks. In the mid-sixteenth century, former and current şeyhülislams could name ten, the kazasker of Rumelia seven, the kazasker of Anatolia five, the qadi of Istanbul three, the qadi of Edirne two, and the highest-ranking müderrises three mülazıms. These quotas increased in later periods and extended to other dignitaries, including, for example, the tutors of the rulers, until the early eighteenth century. High-level ilmiye dignitaries could also name mülazıms when they received promotions or participated in military expeditions. When they passed away, their students could be allowed to adopt the mülazım status. For more details on the label and how its bestowal changed over time, see Uzunçarşılı 1988: 45–53; Beyazıt 2009; Aykanat 2018; İpşirli 2021: 365–9; and Yurdakul 2022: 54–61.

[8] Administering examinations to test competency for specific teaching appointments goes back to the early sixteenth century (Uzunçarşılı 1988: 63–6; Atçıl 2017: 170–1). While such examinations were the basis for assignments of madrasa positions in later periods (Beyazıt 2009: 432, 437; Furat 2017: 250), Uzunçarşılı (1988: 105) argued that appointments to judgeships were rarely decided by this method "from the seventeenth century onward." Aykanat (2018: 173) argued that references to examinations for mülazemet status first appear in the late sixteenth century. As we will see shortly, calls for frequent examinations that exempted few candidates became a common aspect of the proposals to reform the ilmiye establishment in the late eighteenth century.

[9] Akiba (2023) demonstrates how mollazades and ulemazades claimed particular qadiships in the eighteenth century.

[10] See Kılıç 2019 for a distribution of müderris appointments among people of different backgrounds in the early nineteenth century, which revealed that the children of senior ulema families made up about 40 percent of the ilmiye appointments at all levels. At the highest levels in the ilmiye hierarchy, their share reached to 80 percent. Zilfi (1983: 327) observed that "of the 188 and Kadıaskers and Şeyhülislams for whom such information is known, 112 were the sons of Great Molla fathers" in the eighteenth and early nineteenth centuries.

constituted the best judges of scholarly merit and potential. Also, sons of the prominent ilmiye families had access to the best training in religious sciences from birth, often from their own relatives (cf. İpşirli 2021: 179).[11] They could reasonably expect to benefit from the latter's guidance during their lifetimes. Thus, their easy access to and fast rise in the ilmiye hierarchy could be attributed to the erudition they had already acquired at a young age and their expected future excellence. These considerations would even justify the appointments granted to mollazades and ulemazades while they were still children.[12]

As a third type, patronage could also encompass relationships of support beyond teacher-student and family connections. Favors shown to friends, associates, or potential clients appear to have been common in the ilmiye (Uzunçarşılı 1988: 102, 105, 242, *passim*), as observed by many contemporary sources. Such support could be received from powerful individuals outside the judicial-religious establishment, including the sultan, members of the ruling dynasty, viziers, provincial governors, and other ranking members of the administration (Uzunçarşılı 1988: 61, 68, *passim*; Beyazıt 2009: 432; Atçıl 2017: 185–6; İpşirli 2021: 267). These might have lacked the institutionalized framework associated with other forms of patronage and may thus be less visible to the historian beyond anecdotal evidence, but they were likely no less effective.

The literature on the ilmiye establishment in general and its recruitment patterns in particular is extensive, but modern scholarship has paid much less attention to contemporary opinions on the legitimacy of kin- and client-based favoritism. One exception that proves the rule might be Madeline Zilfi's (1983: 341n48) casual statement in passing that "nepotism was not of itself an abuse in the Ottoman view," a judgment that one can perhaps extend to other kinds of favoritism given the prominence of extended households in Ottoman bureaucratic and political structures.[13] Zilfi did not attempt to justify this

---

[11] For example, we learn from Şeyhülislam Feyzullah Efendi's (d. 1703) autobiography that he received his initial training in religious sciences, languages, and poetry from his father, maternal uncle, and other relatives, all of whom happened to be prominent scholars. See Türek and Derin 1969: 206.

[12] Zilfi (1983: 343) suggests that "the younger age of some Great Mollas may have stemmed from precocious exposure to learning and more preparation for the qualifying examinations than the less pedigreed. Indeed, patrimonial privileges derived from precisely that rationale and those who would create an ulema aristocracy were quite willing to proclaim the inherent virtues of the ulema-born."

[13] Michael Nizri (2014: 56) shares this opinion, it seems, without any qualification: "As early as the 16th century, the Ottoman ruling class regarded nepotism as a legitimate practice and took it for granted, as was the case in Europe at that time. Consequently, the Ottoman system enabled the sons and relatives of officeholders to enter its ranks. At the beginning of the 17th century, it had become accepted practice for sons to follow in their fathers' footsteps." Abou-el-Haj (1991: 55) argued more generally that the Ottoman elites "took nepotism and personal influence (intisap) for granted." A recent dissertation (Çerçinli 2022) related to this discussion came to my attention too late while the book was in production at the press.

claim. Yet it is reminiscent of scholarly opinions on European settings, which is unsurprising given her point that patronage in the Ottoman polity was systemic. On the other hand, some scholars have also noted, albeit too briefly for the present discussion, criticism of favoritism among a few contemporary observers (İpşirli 1988, 2014; Uzunçarşılı 1988: 241–60; Beyazıt 2009; Erdoğan 2018; see also Zilfi 1988, 58).

Jurisprudential Considerations of Favoritism

It may be that justification of favoritism (based on patrimonial considerations or not) is limited in jurisprudential treatments of the topic, given the distinctive, umma-focused ideological tendencies of classical Islamic jurisprudence.[14] In fact, constraints on favoritism are clear in expectations pertaining to the qadis that the Ottomans adopted from earlier jurisprudential traditions. Qadis were required to recuse themselves from hearing disputes involving their relatives (Chapter 2). They were also supposed to reject invitations to private gatherings and celebrations if these might generate the appearance of favoritism toward particular individuals who might subsequently appear in court as parties to litigations.

I also noted a reticence toward favoritism in the qadis' appointments, though the consequences for such appointments might not have been as severe as those for bribery. According to fatwas by sixteenth-century şeyhülislams Ibn Kemal and Ebussuud, appointments to qadiship secured by uncompensated intercessions of influential parties might have been considered undesirable but not necessarily illegal.[15] There seems to be some disagreement among jurists about this issue, however. For example, while Ibn Abidin (1982–94:

---

[14] Here I refer the reader to the material in the Quran and hadith literature, mentioned in Chapter 1, that can be interpreted against nepotism and, more generally, favoritism.

[15] To remind the reader, here are my translations of Ibn Kemal's and Ebussuud's fatwas, respectively: "Question: If a [prospective] qadi bribed a kazasker or [specific] paşas to have their names to be submitted to the ruler [hüdavendigar] and if the ruler remains unaware of the bribes and does not receive these bribes [himself], would the appointments and subsequent judgments of this qadi be valid? Answer: If his appointment is based on bribery, that qadi's judgments are void. [However,] if the appointment is based on intercession and the bribe is received by the intercessor, [his judgments] would be valid. His appointment cannot be considered to be attained by bribes" (İnanır 2011: 119). "Question: If a qadi named Zeyd acquires his qadiship by the intercession of someone other than the ruler whom he had paid or as a result of someone's favor, would his judgments be legally valid? Answer: [If he acquires the position] through bribery, his judgments would not be valid. This is the accepted opinion [among jurists]. His qadiship would be void [literally: "fully dismissed"]. And even though attainment of the position by favor is also impermissible, the judgments [of those who had acquired their positions in this way] that are consistent with the law cannot be reversed" (Düzdağ 1972: 133).

12:123, 128) agreed with Ibn Kemal and Ebussuud's interpretations, he also acknowledged opinions that categorized appointments based on favor as unlawful.

In appointments other than qadiship, however, the jurisprudential expectations appear to be more protective of the interests of the ilmiye families. For example, Ibn Abidin (8:511–12) considered the sons' guaranteed appropriation of their deceased fathers' positions other than qadiship (such as the post of imamate in mosques, teaching posts in madrasas, and preacherships) and the associated stipends from the public treasury as appropriate if the sons, like their fathers, strived to serve religion. He also observed that according to some jurists, this rule should even apply to infants, effectively sanctioning the statuses of underaged mollazades and ulemazades who held non-judiciary ilmiye positions. The practice, which he claimed was common in Hijaz, Egypt, and Anatolia, promoted the study of religion and shielded the families of the servants of Islam from financial ruin.

Ibn Abidin's agreement that certain positions of privilege and income should be concentrated in the hands of specific families across generations does not necessarily betray disregard of merit as a desirable qualification. Indeed, Ibn Abidin (8:512) insisted that only capable sons should be allowed to inherit their fathers' appointments and incomes. Yet the jurist did not elaborate what constituted merit or how it should be assessed in cases of multiple candidates for a single position. He did observe, however, that it was common in the nineteenth century for religious posts to be inherited by those who were ignorant, uninterested in serving religion, or determined to subcontract their entitlements to those who paid the most for them, to the detriment of many mosques, charitable endowments, and madrasas. The jurist warned that "if the ruler appoints an undeserving person to a teaching position, that appointment is void" (ibid.). Ibn Abidin also insisted that if the ruler granted a position to an inept person, he committed a misdeed by allowing that person to hurt the Muslim community and by denying a deserving person his due. According to Islamic law, the jurist continued, the ruler was obligated to take positions from incompetent people and give them to competent ones (ibid.).

This summarizes the full extent of discussions on favoritism that I have been able to locate in Ottoman jurisprudential sources. Noticeable in this material is a certain anxiety about appointments to qadiship and qadis' judicial operations, both of which underscore the special importance attributed to this office for the legitimacy of the legal system and practice. And while many premodern jurists did not believe that favoritism was as intolerable as bribery in appointments to qadiship, the fact that they compared the two at all indicates the former's potential stigma. Concerns about favoritism appear less prominently with regard to other offices and interactions. Yet, in these discussions merit and competency also were important, although perhaps under-substantiated, considerations.

Patronage in Ottoman Political Literature

A survey of premodern views on the morality of patronage as found in the political literature reveals relatively infrequent critical takes on various forms of patronage and favoritism among many other types of abuse (see Table 5.3), a finding that is partially consistent with Zilfi's position on the issue.[16] Yet even though an antipatronage sentiment might not have been prevalent in premodern political works, it is still possible to identify conflicting opinions among contemporary commentators. A prominent example is Mustafa Ali: in his *Nushatü's-Selatin*, the writer complained about Sokollu Mehmed Paşa (d. 1579), the grand vizier to Selim II, whose patronage "became the privilege of his own men. His lavish favors became the unquestionable monopoly of his relatives and dependents" and left out others who deserved support (1982: 2:72).[17] Regarding the ilmiye establishment, Mustafa Ali observed that whenever "judiciary and scholastic positions... become vacant, qualification and priorities are disregarded and the offices are not given to the right person, for, one says: 'This one is one of such and such person's men,' 'This one recommends himself as being the *khōja* of such and such pasha...'" (1:75). Because of the rampant practice of rewarding connections, Mustafa Ali contended, the ulema of his era felt compelled to make "frequent visits" to the viziers' houses and demonstrated "zeal in wandering from reception to reception in order to prevent the ignorants from overtaking them and becoming their superiors through the intercession of the great," which interfered with their studies and "prevent[ed] them from rising up through 'the composition of' books and [other] works" (ibid.). While Mustafa Ali held that "bribery," by which he meant payment-for-appointment schemes, was

---

[16] Included in this group are *Kitab-ı Müstetab*; *Tarih-i Selaniki*; *Tarih-i Silahdar*; *Usulü'l-Hikem fi Nizami'l-Alem*, by Akhisari; *Düstürü'l-Amel li Islahi'l-Halel*, by Katip Çelebi; and *Telhisü'l-Beyan bi Kavanin-i Al-i Osman*, by Hezarfen Hüseyin Efendi.

[17] For more on Mustafa Ali's complaints about Sokollu Mehmed Paşa, see Fleischer 1986: 56, 86, 202, 305. According to Fleischer (1986: 305), while Ali criticized Sokollu Mehmed Paşa "because he practiced nepotism on a scale that purportedly surpassed anything that had occurred in Suleyman's time," he also "tempered his criticisms with the observation that at least most of Sokollu's proteges were in fact able and worthy people."

primarily responsible for the deteriorating quality of the state officials in every sector of the government, favoritism toward undeserving men also played a role (1982: 1:75–7; 2003a: 68–73).[18]

In his later *Künhü'l-Ahbar* (2003b: 79), completed around 1600, Mustafa Ali had more specific criticisms, including complaints about the privileges extended to the children of prominent ilmiye officials (*mevalizadeler*). He claimed that these children regularly obtained mülazım status and were appointed to important positions at very young ages and, implicitly, without the required qualifications. Conversely, those who were qualified found it difficult, if not impossible, to rise in the hierarchy without family connections (79–80). In fact, the element of nepotism in the ilmiye hierarchy even discouraged those who could not hope to rely on patronage from seeking education in religious sciences. And since merit while in office went unrewarded, many chose not to pursue further training after they reached a certain point in their careers, instead devoting their energies to seeking patronage from high-level government officials. Consequently, both the madrasas and the court system failed to fulfill the needs of the religion, polity, and society (cf. İpşirli 2014: 170–1).

Mustafa Ali's disillusionment with the system was no doubt related to his personal frustrations (Fleischer 1986: 38–40, 90, 134, Ch. 5).[19] Although he was fortunate enough to hold the status of mülazım (25–33), which made him eligible for an ilmiye position, his efforts to gain the sultan's favors by dedicating a poetic work to him that he had composed with the intention of obtaining a teaching position or a judgeship went nowhere and later forced him to vacate his mülazemet (Mustafa Ali 1982: 2:71).[20] Subsequently, his attempts to earn the support of Sokollu Mehmed Paşa by submitting to him an original work of military history also failed (1982: 2:72–3).[21] For Mustafa Ali, the patron-client networks and consequent favors extended in recruitment to government positions could have generated favorable results if the patrons were able to recognize merit and talent. Given the type of people in power during Mustafa

---

[18] For a more general assessment of Mustafa Ali's critique of the ilmiye establishment, see İpşirli 1988, 2014; Beyazıt 2009; and Erdoğan 2018.

[19] And despite his above-mentioned criticisms, he himself made frequent efforts to influence appointment decisions for himself and his friends (Fleischer 1986: 116, 125–6).

[20] In the early eighteenth century, mülazıms who lacked backing had to wait eighteen years or more before they were admitted to examinations for madrasa positions. See Raşid 2013: 2:718; Uzunçarşılı 1988: 65n3; and Furat 2017: 250n18.

[21] This must be *Heft Meclis*, or *The Seven Scenes*, which Fleischer (1986: 58) describes as a work that "treats the 1566 Sigetvar campaign, the death of Sultan Süleyman, and the accession of Selim; it praises Sokollu Mehmed Paşa lavishly and exhibits a greater concern with style and panegyric than with history." Apparently Sokollu misunderstood the nature of this manuscript, mistaking it as a copy of someone else's work in Mustafa Ali's calligraphy (Mustafa Ali 1982: 2:74).

Ali's era,[22] however, their patronage only harmed the society. Thus he recommended—at least in the cases of "great mollahs" (*mevali-i izam*), presumably a reference to the highest-ranking judges—that appointments should be linked to their performance on examinations (1982: 1:77, 177).

It is difficult to find another critique of favoritism as comprehensive as Mustafa Ali's, but a few other commentators did express similar sentiments. Koçi Bey (1972: 27–9, 1994: 43–4), who composed his two *Risales* in the 1630s and 1640s, described as harmful the inclination to please third parties (*hatır*) and intercede with favors (şefaat) in appointment decisions, especially the ilmiye ones. While he did not specifically comment on different types of favoritism as Mustafa Ali did, Koçi Bey did argue that judgeships should "absolutely not" be granted based on bribes or as acts of favor (1972: 129). Instead, when there was excessive demand for a limited number of judgeships, as happened in his era, appointments should be based on examination results (ibid.).[23]

The anonymous author of *Hırzü'l-Mülük*, composed in the late sixteenth or mid-seventeenth century, also regretted that the kazaskers of his time often made appointments to judgeships as favors to viziers and other high-ranking military-administrative authorities (*ümera*) or because they were afraid of them (Yücel 1988: 195–7). Like Koçi Bey, the author pointedly questioned the legitimacy of appointments to judgeships based on bribes and favors, which he claimed was a prevalent practice, and mentioned the existence of (unidentified) fatwas against this practice. Unlike Koçi Bey, but like Mustafa Ali, he specifically recognized both kin- and client-based favoritism as two reasons, among others, for the declining quality of education in the madrasas. And unlike both, the author proposed no examinations to advance merit in the ilmiye hierarchy. Instead, he insisted that candidates' scholarly credentials—including the names of their teachers and of those from whom they received their novitiate status, the books they studied, and such—should be properly recorded and the appointment decisions should be made based solely on this information.[24]

---

[22] See also Mustafa Ali's recounting of grand vizier Lütfi Paşa's (d. 1564) uninformed dismissal of Mevlana Ali Çelebi's *Hümayunname*, a work that Mustafa Ali regards as exemplary in its penmanship and indicative of its author's praiseworthy skills (1982: 2:74–5).

[23] Without going into much detail, Defterdar Sarı Mehmed Paşa (1935: 92; cf. 1969: 49) also recommends that judges be subjected to examinations to ascertain that they deserve their positions.

[24] Other works that contain critical commentary on various forms of favoritism include *Tevarih-i Al-i Osman*, by an anonymous author (*Tevarih* 1992: 34); Silahdar's *Nusretname* (2001: 933–5); and Defterdar Sarı Mehmed Paşa's *Nesayihü'l-Vüzera ve'l-Ümera* (Defterdar 1935: 87, 95, 113, and *passim*), but these are often brief and not focused on the ilmiye.

A few points about these commentaries warrant reflection. For one, there are reasons to suspect that they were not complete aberrations despite their small numbers: while the systemic—and thus normalized—patrimonial qualities of the ilmiye establishment might have somewhat curbed the intensity of opposition to sanctioned practices of favoritism, other factors might have also provoked irritation. In particular, the gradual but progressive bureaucratization of the Ottoman patrimonial authority in the early modern era (Barkey 2016; see also Findley 1980b, 1989) might have popularized merit-based claims to office long before the nineteenth century.[25] Specifically for the ilmiye, the idealized (and likely enduring) regard for scholarly knowledge as one legitimate basis of status in the religious hierarchy must also have influenced contemporary perspectives about the results of any type of favoritism. Finally, despite the prevalence of patronage relationships, the ilmiye establishment did continue to admit individuals from outside groups, including those from modest backgrounds. As long as individuals without patronage connections found their ways in, only to get stuck at positions they deemed beneath them, critical assessments of the system must have remained.

One interesting aspect of the critical commentaries is their tendency to freely associate bribery with favors and intercessions in appointment decisions, which is also apparent in later remarks. Obviously, it is possible to distinguish bribes from patronage and acts of favor as methods of recruitment: while the first was an unambiguous mechanism of transactional rent-seeking by those in power, the latter did not have to be, at least in principle, since patronage could be a way to reward recipients' talents and skills. And unlike bribery, which often appears in Ottoman commentaries as evidence of greed and poor character, failures of patronage-based recruitment could be attributed to unintended errors in evaluating clients' qualifications. Yet our authors, and others who expressed similar opinions in non-ilmiye contexts,[26] associated the two. The likelihood that most acts of favor generated reciprocal tokens of appreciation from the clients, whether immediate or

---

[25] According to Tolga Kobas (2019: 20), while most studies on patrimonialism consider a government office an extension of the person who controls it in any manner that he considers appropriate, they ignore the possibility of an opposite relationship between the two in complex administrative-bureaucratic settings: "The relations between the person and the office (P/O) have been considered in a one-sided manner, i.e., P→O, personalism undermines office. Patrimonialism studies have focused solely on the impact of 'the personalization of the office.' Yet, there is also the flipside of the coin, i.e., O→P, officialization of the person, the incumbent being subjected to such elements that when he receives an official position, he is already transformed, there are internalized limits and barriers to his exercises of personal discretion. As part of a culture of office, raised within a particular habitus the flesh and bones individual and his conduct are made to comply with sets of criteria e.g., a degree of merit, technical knowledge and expertise, performance, manners, knowledge of protocol and etiquette, etc."

[26] See, for example, Defterdar 1935: 87.

delayed, might have made the differences between bribery and patronage immaterial.

Finally, the three authors express a particular concern about judgeship appointments based on favoritism, which is reminiscent of a sensitivity I observed in the jurisprudential works, particularly those that Ibn Abidin described as more stringent (Chapter 2).[27] And these authors, like Ibn Abidin, hesitated to question the legitimacy of patrimonial privilege in other ilmiye positions. Here, it is significant that both Mustafa Ali and Koçi Bey proposed examinations as the exclusive means to measure and reward merit for judgeship appointments, a position that implies a wholesale condemnation of favoritism as an unredeemable method of staffing in at least one sector of the ilmiye. While scholars have not observed similar tendencies in contemporary Europe, the tension between patronage and examinations as competing methods of recruitment and advancement is clear in the context of premodern China.[28] As we will see, the idea of implementing examinations more comprehensively as a way to prevent further degeneration of the judiciary would continue, and perhaps grow stronger, in later eras.

The above discussion indicates that the criticism of patronage and favoritism might have been familiar, though perhaps not hegemonic, in the premodern Ottoman political discourses. In addition, there were other perspectives that cannot be reduced to a simple acceptance or condemnation of the relevant practices. One such nuanced take belongs to Naima, who produced his *Tarih* at the turn of the eighteenth century. References to kin- and client-based favoritism where Naima makes his opinions about the matter known appear in multiple places in this work. In one instance, Naima mentions Şeyhülislam Balizade Mustafa Efendi's (d. 1662) tendency to appoint many of his friends and acquaintances to ilmiye posts during his tenure (Naima 2007: 4:1735).[29] According to Naima, Balizade was proud of showing such favors "regardless of what other people might say," which exemplifies one unapologetic stance on

---

[27] There are reasons to believe that this stringent interpretation was not the dominant opinion. Chronicler Raşid (2013: 2:1166) mentions accusations directed at Kevakibizade Veliyüddin Efendi (d. 1727), the kazasker of Anatolia, that a number of qadiship appointments he made as favors to those who pled for these positions ("bi-hasebi'l-iktiza şefaat-i şüfe'a ile verdiği bir kaç mansıb içün") were actually based on bribes. The accusers, who were qadis themselves, made no issue of favor-based appointments but questioned the legality of those based on bribes. The way Raşid himself relates this incident makes the reader think that he agreed with this distinction. The complaint ultimately led to Kevakibizade's exile to the island of Lesbos (Midilli) in 1719.

[28] See Note 2.

[29] According to Naima, Balizade was dismissed from his position because he was too casual or lax (*laubali*) and he disregarded the formal ceremonial expectations of his post ("*riayet-i merasim-i tarik kaydından azade*"). He was also accused of receiving payments for appointments of unqualified individuals (ibid.). For more on Balizade Mustafa Efendi, see İpşirli and Kaya 2020.

the propriety of what we moderns might call cronyism.[30] Interestingly, Naima does not reject Balizade's position in a wholesale manner. In fact, he praises Balizade's inclination to show favors to those close to him as an indication of his benevolence (*himmet*), while also suggesting that Balizade's good intentions should have been tempered, in appointment decisions, by some attention to competency (*liyakat*) and aptitude (*istidad*) (ibid.). In other words, Naima appears to assume that acts of favoritism as expressions of benevolence or considerations of merit are not necessarily mutually exclusive if decision-makers find ways to balance them. Consequently, those in positions of authority should not always feel compelled to find the *best* individuals for vacant positions. Merely *adequate* people might in fact be appropriate choices if they also happen to be among those the decision-makers are obliged to—an interpretation that resonates with patrimonial entitlements to office, within limits.

In Naima's extensive commentary on the execution of Şeyhülislam Feyzullah Efendi (d. 1703), who was notorious for placing his many children, relatives, and clients in important ilmiye positions (Nizri 2014: Chs. 2 and 3), we find additional insights on the morality of favoritism (Naima 2007: 4:1858–61). According to Naima, Feyzullah's tendency to favor his kin and clients played a role in his eventual fall, but not because such behavior was inherently illegitimate or unacceptable. In fact, in response to a hypothetical "objection" (*itiraz*) that he considered for rhetorical purposes—one that highlighted the prerogatives of the ruler and, presumably, other people in positions of authority to "push forward" whomever they desired—he explicitly recognized the legitimacy of such privileges as long as those promoted were qualified and the rights of other members of the corporate body to which the favored appointees belonged remained untrampled. In Feyzullah's case, however, his zeal to exercise unrestrained favoritism not only cast doubt on the qualities of those he supported, but also barred many other deserving members of the ilmiye from attaining desirable positions and much-needed livelihoods. In his discussion, Naima used the counterexample of Şeyhülislam Hoca Sadedin Efendi (d. 1599), who also had established an ilmiye dynasty but only gradually and only by favoring relatives of recognized merit. By contrast, Feyzullah's untampered desire to quickly elevate his offspring and other dependents generated much ill will among his colleagues because his behavior

---

[30] Relevant here are Gibson's attempts to link patronage as acts of benevolence and charity toward relatives and dependents in eighteenth-century England (1993: 182, 188).

threatened their collective interests, which led the ilmiye establishment to turn against him, and this played a major role in his execution.[31]

Madeline Zilfi (2006: 223) observed that "class-based patrimonialism" became even more structurally embedded in high-level ilmiye careers during the eighteenth century.[32] Thus, there are reasons to suspect that criticisms directed at patronage intensified in this era.[33] Indeed, complaints about appointments based on "intercession," "pleas" (*rica*), and regard for others (hatır or *gönül*)—often cited in an undifferentiated manner along with bribery—appear in multiple reform proposals (*layiha*s) submitted to Selim III (d. 1808) in 1792 (Çağman 2010).[34] Regarding the ilmiye more specifically, chronicler Enveri Efendi's (d. 1794; Aktepe 1995) layiha criticized the practice of granting teaching and judicial posts "based on pleas and intercessions" to undeserving individuals in the past "one hundred and fifty years." Because these people rose in the hierarchy and perpetuated the same habits while in office, undeserving officeholders now outnumbered deserving ones. According to Enveri, if the government ensured granting ilmiye posts based on merit "just like in the past," the situation would improve "slowly but surely," within the next fifteen to twenty years (Çağman 2010: 3–4).

---

[31] In a later treatment of the topic, chronicler Raşid (2013: 2:649–51) blames Feyzullah for appointing his kin and clients to important offices in unprecedented and unsanctioned manners. One such example was his attempt to grant his son Fethullah the honorary rank of şeyhülislam and reserve the actual office for him to assume after his own passing. But like Naima, Raşid also emphasized that Feyzullah Efendi's tendency to monopolize high-level offices kept many members of the ilmiye out of office and devoid of income. For the details of Fethullah's rise in the ilmiye hierarchy, see Nizri 2014: 91–2. According to Madeline Zilfi (2006: 222), "Nepotism was common throughout the elites, but Feyzullah's eight years as şeyhülislam seemed to be staking a permanent claim to the hierarchy.... For the ulema, Feyzullah's manipulations were deeply offensive not so much because he elevated relatives out of turn, but because he appropriated virtually all positions worth having." After Feyzullah's execution, "nepotistic advantage was condemned in so far as it promoted individualized, exclusivist extremes. It was upheld, however, as a class entitlement" (223).

[32] Based on her impressions of the information found in one late eighteenth-century mülazım "day register" (*ruznamçe*), Yasemin Beyazıt (2009: 435–41) calculated the proportion of novices who owed their designation and the accompanying entitlements to family-based patronage and other forms of favoritism as about 45 percent. This proportion might have been under 5 percent in the late sixteenth century. On sixteenth-century admission patterns to mülazamet status, see Beyazıt 2012–13: 206–9. Also see Note 10.

[33] If true, this tendency might also be related to the further bureaucratization of the ilmiye establishment (see Note 25) and/or increasing demand for ilmiye positions in the seventeenth and eighteenth centuries; there is some evidence for both possibilities. Regarding the first, see the literature on the developments of the şeyhülislam's office and the Ottoman judicial bureaucracy, including Heyd 1969; Uzunçarşılı 1988: 195–9; Koca 1995; Ayar 2011–12, 2012, and 2014; Kuru 2020; and Kuru and Önal 2018. Regarding the second, consider Jun Akiba's (2005: 45) claim that "there were 5,000 to 6,000 members belonging to the hierarchy of kadıship during the reign of Selim III [r. 1789–1807], despite the number of kadıship posts in the whole Empire being around one thousand at most."

[34] See, in particular, the layihas by Muhasebe-i Evvel El-Hac Ibrahim Efendi, Tevkii El-Hac Mehmed Hakkı Bey Efendi, Sadrazam Koca Yusuf Paşa, Reisü'l-küttab Vekili Firdevsi Emin Efendi, and Beylikçi Suni Efendi transcribed in Çağman 2010.

In the group of layihas submitted to Selim III, the one that contained the most comprehensive treatment of the problems in the ilmiye belonged to Tatarcık Abdullah Efendi, a former kazasker of Anatolia and Rumelia.[35] As with many earlier critiques, Abdullah linked the degeneration of madrasa education and the administration of justice to the prevalence of bribery and favoritism in the appropriation of novitiate status and appointment decisions of all sorts (Tatarcık Abdullah Efendi 1916/7: 270–8). More prominently than the authors described earlier, Abdullah stressed the need for properly administered examinations to ensure merit at every level in the ilmiye career, including the mülazemet status and the teaching and judicial appointments. To recall, Mustafa Ali's and Koçi Bey's recommendations to implement examinations had been limited to the judgeship appointments.

By proposing examinations as the primary basis of ilmiye appointments, Abdullah implored authorities, if only implicitly, to quash favoritism of many types, including favoritism that (a) involved non-ilmiye patrons and ilmiye clients and (b) was based on non-kin patrons and clients. Yet he did not go so far as to call for a complete and principled rejection of high-level ilmiye dignitaries' family-based entitlements. In appointments to entry-level madrasa positions, his layiha held, the deserving sons of ilmiye dignitaries should be allowed to be exempted from examinations, albeit with the approval of the imperial authority.[36] And while the undeserving sons of high ilmiye families should be kept away from madrasa positions, he argued, the state should still provide them with income equal to entry-level teaching stipends so that they could support themselves.[37]

This survey indicates that in the early modern Ottoman polity acts of favoritism were not universally regarded as transgressions on par with many other abuses that we moderns associate with corruption. Yet it also seems that some, perhaps many, Ottomans disapproved of it as a basis for government appointments—more so for certain offices than for others—and freely associated it with payment-for-appointment schemes. It also appears that

---

[35] Tatarcık Abdullah Efendi's layiha proposed reforms on many aspects of the government, not just the functioning of the ilmiye establishment. For more on Tatarcık Abdullah and his layiha, see Furat 2017; Özkul 2018; and İpşirli 2021: 272–3.

[36] İlhami Yurdakul (2021; 2022: 81–126) has observed that the sons of ilmiye dignitaries remained exempt from examinations for various teaching positions, including those in the madrasas, until the early twentieth century.

[37] The influence and popularity of Tatarcık Abdullah's layiha can be observed in the nineteenth-century chronicle of Ahmed Cevdet Paşa (1891: 43–52), who provides an extensive summary of and commentary on the text. On Ahmed Cevdet Paşa's opinions on the madrasa system in the nineteenth century, including many criticisms that resemble those of Tatarcık Abdullah, see Çadırcı 1997.

while a few Ottomans proposed remedies (some more far-reaching than others) to ameliorate the ill consequences of favoritism, these did not generally include calls for a complete eradication of patron-client relationships in government affairs.

Favoritism in Official Documents

In her research on the development of ilmiye institutions during the sixteenth century, Yasemin Beyazıt (2014b) identified five state-issued documents, including three law codes (kanunnames), one imperial order (*hüküm*), and an imperial edict (*hatt-ı hümayun*).[38] The four earliest documents contain primarily curricular and organizational prescriptions in madrasa education that aimed to ensure high standards among madrasa students. Although these works do refer to the need to curb students' inclinations to skip their training, rise too fast in the ilmiye ranks, and, in the case of the 1577 edict, prohibit the appointment of undeserving individuals based on (presumably illegitimate forms of otherwise undefined) favoritism (*iltimas*; Uzunçarşılı 1988: 242), they do not offer detailed insights on the legitimacy of different types of patronage.

The edict dated 1598 is different because it expresses the need to control entry into the ilmiye establishment and limit the numbers who could claim mülazım status, given the increasing demand for ilmiye positions in the late-sixteenth century (244–5; Akgündüz 1990–6: 8:633–8; see also Beyazıt 2012–13). Specifically, the edict restricted the privilege of granting mülazemets to ilmiye dignitaries, based on either teacher-student relationships or family connections. The groups specifically mentioned in the document as those that should be barred from the mülazemet status, either completely or in part, included the personnel of non-ilmiye branches of the government, such as janissaries, artillerymen, and members of the provincial cavalry; religious instructors (*hoca*s) serving in various departments of the palace; graduates of provincial madrasas; and nominees of non-mevali qadis, unless these individuals also received formal madrasa training in sanctioned institutions and

---

[38] These are "Kanûnnâme-i Talebe-i İlm," an undated document presumably from the early sixteenth century, transliterated copies of which are available in Uzunçarşılı 1988: 13, and Akgündüz 1990–6: 4:662–4, among other places; "Mevâlî-i İzâm ve Müderrisîn-i Kirâmın Tedrise Muvazebetleri İçün Nişân-ı Humâyun" from 1538, available in Uzunçarşılı 1988: 15–16, and Akgündüz 1990–6: 4:667–9, among other publications; an order dated 1576, available in Uzunçarşılı 1988: 13–14, among others; an imperial edict dated 1577, available in Uzunçarşılı 1988: 241–2; and a law code dated 1598, available in Uzunçarşılı 1988: 243–5, and Akgündüz 1990–6: 8:633–8.

served as assistants to madrasa teachers. Even in such cases, the edict required, these individuals should receive appointments only after they took and passed the required examinations. These requirements might be seen as the polity's attempts to ensure merit and, as such, might align with the objectives of earlier state-generated documentation concerning the ilmiye establishment. Yet they also institutionalized ilmiye dignitaries' control over access to ilmiye careers (cf. Beyazıt 2012–13).

We have considerably less information about comparable documentation in the seventeenth century. In one study, Mehmet İpşirli (1988: 282–4) mentions an imperial order from 1636 that highlighted the need to ensure high-quality madrasa training, the madrasa teachers' power to grant mülazemets to their most deserving students, the requirement that candidates who lacked such support must pass examinations to acquire mülazım status, and the expectation that the children of senior ilmiye families be properly trained and credentialed by recognized teachers before they were granted mülazemet status. These conditions are consistent with those articulated in the official documentation issued in the sixteenth century. And while the last requirement aimed to ensure merit among ulema children, the fact that this group was mentioned separately indirectly underscores their unique status. An edict dated 1653 makes a brief reference to the expectation that judgeships be granted based on examinations and that authorities pay particular attention to mülazemet grants (Naima 2007: 3:1503; cf. Beyazıt 2009: 432). Another edict dated 1689 also required examinations for appointments to teaching positions, but only for those in upper-level madrasas (that is, those with stipends of forty akçes per day) and with the formal approval of the şeyhülislam (Beyazıt 2009: 433).

The imperial government might have issued more documents related to the ilmiye appointments in the eighteenth century, possibly indicating the growing tensions I highlighted earlier. An edict dated 1715 again addresses the mülazemet system's degeneration and the need to ensure merit among the novices.[39] To this end, the document ordered authorities to note candidates' names, ages, reputations, and what they studied during their madrasa trainings and under whose supervision. For the children of the ulema families, however, it was not necessary to confirm their ages or their training credentials. Instead, the edict instructed authorities to merely record their fathers'

---

[39] A particular concern during this period according to Raşid (2013: 2:901) was the practice of selling and buying mülazemet status, which allowed unqualified individuals to enter the system and greatly increased the numbers of those waiting for teaching and judicial posts.

names, which implies relaxed expectations for this group (Raşid 2013: 2:901; Furat 2017: 254). Chronicler Raşid (2013: 2:902–3) notes another decree in the same year that reduced the quotas allowed to high-level ilmiye authorities to nominate novices—another attempt to relieve the pressure on the mülazemet system by clamping down on non-kin-based patronage. Professors in the madrasas of Edirne and Bursa were especially affected by this decree, which completely stripped their power to select novices (ibid.).[40]

Regarding judicial appointments, an edict issued in 1729 mentioned that some qadis waiting for appointments were seeking favors from and pleading with the authorities to reduce the tenure of those already in office so that their own appointments could be expedited. Such intercessions caused harm to qadis in office and forced them to oppress those in their jurisdictions by subjecting them to excessive and illegal impositions to compensate for their losses. The edict also required that the appointment order of the out-of-office qadis should be based on wait times: those who had been out of office the longest should receive the first vacant positions. Among the qadis with equal wait times, examinations should be conducted, and appointments should be made accordingly (Raşid 2013: 3:1618–19).

References to unjustified favoritism continued in official documents in the latter half of the eighteenth century. For example, an edict dated 1750 specifically mentioned "excessive intercessions" (*kesret-i şufaa*) based on considerations of benevolence and "compassion" (*terahhüm*) by those in office as one of the reasons that unqualified individuals were granted mülazemet status and teaching positions in madrasas (Uzunçarşılı 1988: 254, 254n2). The same concerns were also articulated in a later order (dated 1793), one that decried the decrepit state of the judicial administration and blamed it on the presence of many unqualified individuals who had found their ways into the judiciary through favors and pleas (şefaat ve rica). The order insisted that neither mülazemet status nor judgeships should be granted without examinations (Uzunçarşılı 1988: 257–8; Feyzioğlu and Kılıç 2005: 38–9).

An undated communication that Selim III (d. 1807) sent to his şeyhülislam conveys a slightly different impression of how the polity attempted to ensure merit in decisions pertaining to teaching positions: by restricting these appointments to those who excelled in periodic examinations *and* to the adult (*mültehi*) and capable (*müstaid*) children of the dignitary families (mevalizadeler) and only with imperial approval. It seems that the polity continued to recognize the

---

[40] Thus, while "individual ulema officials at Istanbul...lost some of their novitiate patronage...they emerged as the only men empowered to grant ulema novitiates" (Zilfi 1988: 59).

patrimonial claims of ilmiye dignitaries as applied to kin at least in the madrasa posts, which is consistent with what we observed in Tatarcık's layiha around the same time. That the system continued to link the special status of the ulema children to their presumed merits is evident in how the document highlights the need to eliminate the role of third-party influence in appointment decisions ("bade'l-yevm rica ve şefaat ile asla rüus verülmeye") immediately after it recognizes mevalizade privileges as legitimate (Uzunçarşılı 1988: 260; Feyzioğlu and Kılıç 2005: 41).[41]

Overall, official documents indicate a concern with the harmful consequences of favoritism in training for and staffing ilmiye positions. This concern led those in power, time and again, to take administrative measures that involved a few bureaucratic strategies tailored to fit the patrimonial character of the polity. One such strategy was to differentiate various types of patronage and recognize some as more legitimate than others. Thus, official documents appear to elevate intra-ilmiye links over connections of support involving those who belonged to different parts of the government. Within the ilmiye, the patronage of those closer to the top of the hierarchy and the center of the polity was more favorably regarded than that of others. When the government tried to further restrict access to the ilmiye ranks in later eras, it did not focus on circumscribing the kin-based privileges of the ilmiye dignitaries. Instead, its primary strategy was to reduce the influence of favoritism in certain types of appointments, specifically judgeships, which indicates the government's increasing sensitivity to criticisms about unqualified and/or oppressive qadis, a tendency that also resonated with the jurisprudential opinions and quite a few contemporary observers.

All these attempts indicate that the Ottoman polity was geared toward regulating patronage and checking its potential harms without completely eliminating it, which should not surprise us given the influence of ranking members of the ilmiye hierarchy over government decisions. It is plausible that many members of this group were invested both in curbing some of the worst possible consequences of favoritism and, simultaneously, perpetuating their own patrimonial privileges. Incidentally, this consideration would explain the significant overlaps between the reform proposal of Tatarcık Abdullah, a high-level ilmiye dignitary, and official documents issued at the very end of the eighteenth century.

* * *

---

[41] I should note that variations exist in Uzunçarşılı's and Feyzioğlu and Kılıç's readings of the document.

This chapter has demonstrated in various discursive fields multiple perspectives on the legitimacy of favoritism pertaining to ilmiye appointments. While the patrimonial aspects of the polity, shared by its corporate ilmiye elites, must have influenced how many Ottomans thought about this issue, so did jurisprudential doubts about qadi appointments based on favors, and the system's failure to bring deserving people to the appropriate positions, possibly influenced by bureaucratic developments and the growing demand for ilmiye positions. The fact that many otherwise vocal observers of the polity remained silent about favoritism suggests a general acquiescence, but this sentiment was not necessarily an enthusiastic one, nor was it universal.

Thus it is reasonable to distinguish favoritism in the premodern Ottoman context from other acts that we moderns associate with corruption. Some Ottomans saw the boundaries between favors and bribes as disconcertingly vague, yet many would agree that not every favor extended to family, friends, and clients was unacceptable. And although other techniques to assess and reward merit, such as examinations, were also promoted, patronage-based recruitment and staffing never seems to have completely lost its legitimacy in the ilmiye hierarchy. That said, this was not necessarily a static environment: the chapter has also raised the possibility that the Ottomans became increasingly critical of favoritism during the eighteenth century and beyond.

Conclusion

Possible Rationalizations of Corruption and Other Afterthoughts

An imperial order (entry 64 in *91 Numaralı Mühimme Defteri* [2015]) from 1645 that was addressed to the governor of Anatolia and the qadi of unstated judgeship lists a variety of accusations directed at the qadi of Bozöyük in northwestern Anatolia as follows:

> The inhabitants of the judgeship of Bozöyük petitioned [to the imperial council] that although conducting tour of inspections (devr) is outlawed, Ahmed, the qadi of Bozöyük, [habitually] visits many villages, stays in the dwellings of the poor people and their families thereby forcing them to host him, and seizes their supplies without any compensation. He [illegally] fines them great sums in the inspections of those who neglect the daily prayers (bi-namaz teftişi),[1] charges them seventy-seven guruş per oarsman for their share of oarsmen levy (kürekçi bedeli),[2] and claims for himself [from this amount] more than what is allowed in the imperial orders. After he decides a dispute and prepares documentation to this effect, he habitually readjudicates the same quarrel, and rules for the other [previously defeated] party after accepting bribes based on greed from the latter. While it is forbidden to adjudicate disputes that had not been heard for ten years with no legal excuse, he adjudicates them. He prepares [and charges for the copies of] documentation in the court records and forwards these to local military-administrative authorities even when the plaintiff does not request these. He charges excessive fees for registrations in the court records, issuing documentation [to private parties], dispensing any approval that requires his signature, recording marriages, and estate assessments and divisions. The people of Bozöyük reported many such endless acts of oppression of his,

---

[1] On bi-namaz teftişi see Tosun 2017: 63–4.
[2] The oarsmen levy (kürekçi bedeli) was a cash substitute for the oarsmen that the local people were supposed to send to the navy; see Bostan 2002.

requested that the sums that he had collected be returned to them. Tours of inspection are forbidden. If the accusations are true, the proceedings from such acts should be returned to their owners.

When you receive this order, you should bring Ahmed, the qadi, and his adversaries to the court and investigate the matter according to fairness and justice. If the accusations against Ahmed are proven accurate, you should rule in favor of the latter, and collect and return the sums to their owners in full. You should also forcefully chastise (*muhkem tenbîh*) him so that he would not charge excessive fees for scribal and notarial services [in the future].

Many of the accusations against Ahmed are common in the mühimme and şikayet registers from different periods, although their representations vary over time (Chapter 4). Assuming that these were partially or completely accurate in Ahmed's case, how could he justify his actions to people under his jurisdiction, to higher authorities, or to himself?

To conclude this book, I initially reflect on these questions and attempt to represent the perspectives of government officials guilty of predatory misconduct. Given the relative silence of these actors in historical sources, the challenge of formulating systematic claims in this regard urged me to explore how researchers from other disciplines (sociology, psychology, anthropology, and organizational ethics, among others) might have represented Ahmed's thought processes. It is true that the efforts of non-historians cannot entirely make up for the gaps in historical information. And their findings should be properly contextualized for our purposes. Yet insights generated in other disciplines make it possible to contemplate, if provisionally, various justifications of corruption in sophisticated ways. I intend the following discussion as a forward-looking reflection on an understudied topic; it is supposed to inspire future research as much as enlighten current readers, a task appropriate for a conclusion. The discussion, supported by the empirical information presented in the previous chapters, should also help the reader to recall and reconsider this material in a different light. In the last section of this conclusion, I recapitulate and connect the book's main arguments.

Existing research on corruption and its perpetrators, albeit mostly in modern contexts, indicates that corrupt agents often regard themselves as honest people who claim to care about justice and fairness (Sykes and Matza 1957; Conklin 1977; Benson 1985; Allison, Messick, and Goethals 1989; and Rabl and Kühlmann 2009, among many others). Much scholarship has tried to explain this paradox, and researchers have identified many rationalizations for transgressions. A common task in corruption research has been to organize these rationalizations, often based on earlier publications with a narrower focus, into a comprehensive taxonomy (see, for example, Sykes and Matza 1957; Bandura, Underwood, and Fromson 1975; Robinson and Kraatz 1998; Fritsche 2002, 2005; Ashforth and Anand 2003; Murphy and Dacin 2011; Shigihara 2013; Kaptein and van Helvoort 2019). Though the justifications presented in these studies vary somewhat, there are also major overlaps among them, since the scholarship that informs the endeavor is based on a close dialogue among works that constitute it. For this reason, instead of producing my own synthesis of the existing attempts, I adopt a specific list of rationalizations and consider their relevance to the premodern Ottoman context. This list is based on Blake Ashforth and Vikas Anand's "The Normalization of Corruption in Organizations" (2003), a popular and frequently cited study that has received widespread support in other publications.[3]

The first rationalization is "**legality**," which means excusing practices that may be seen as corrupt because they are not technically illegal, or because the applicable laws are dated, unenforced, or unenforceable (ibid.: 18). Claiming ignorance of the law and noting gray areas between obviously legal and obviously illegal practices are other possible ways to rationalize actions with questionable legitimacy (cf. De Klerk 2017: 257). In the Ottoman context, the vague boundaries between bribes and gifts in administrative practices and jurisprudential traditions (Chapters 2, 7) must have made the legal conflation of the two common. Also, the piecemeal development of the Ottoman legal and administrative system kept many local customs and traditions in place, which in turn allowed for the persistence of significant ambiguities and inconsistencies that might have supported legalistic rationalizations for redundant and excessive extractions (İnalcık 1965: 52–3).[4] Finally, the habitual

---

[3] A Google Scholar search identifies more than 2,000 citations of this study as of December 2023.
[4] "Thus is one of the sources of illegal and unfair practices [in the Ottoman polity]: in recently conquered locales, the Ottomans used to leave intact old laws of taxation for a time. This is because the subjects were used to old taxes. [However,] the amalgamation of old and new forms of taxation could generate many problems. Even after the promulgation and enforcement of the Ottoman Dynastic Law-code (*kanun-i Osmani*)... state functionaries continued to demand older taxes by claiming that 'they have been collected since ancient times.' The Ottoman Empire's general attachment to and respect for 'ancient laws' (*kanun-i kadim*) aided this situation" (İnalcık 1965: 52). Also, "it was an inclination of the subgovernors, tımar-holders, and other officials to continue the older taxes as established customs even after the promulgation of the *kanun-i Osmani*. In this way the older taxes were perpetuated as corrupt innovation (*bidat*) and new ones were added to them.... We should not forget that the *salguns* [that is, excruciating demands for money and supplies from the populace] imposed by the members of the military establishment in the seventeenth century and constituted a disaster for the empire were

non-punishment of minor inferences and inconstant punishment of more egregious ones based on the identity of the offender or contextual circumstances, a tendency we observed earlier (Chapter 4), could be construed by actors accused of corruption as evidence of the relative legality of their transgressions. In other words, unpunished crimes might have been considered minor misdemeanors, or even no crimes at all.

The second rationalization, "**denial of responsibility,**" refers to the inclination to blame corruption on external factors, actors, or circumstances beyond one's control that make it impossible to avoid objectionable practices. The tendency also includes behavior perceived to be common, generally accepted, or based on precedent (Ashforth and Anand 2003: 18).[5] In the Ottoman context, economic pressures on state functionaries might be the most obvious basis for this type of rationalization, as we have seen in Chapter 5.[6] Moreover, the ruler's patrimonial claims to the reaya's wealth and his servants' privileges as extensions of the ruler's authority might have justified excessive extractions in the eyes of state functionaries. In other words, what legitimized avarız and nüzül akçesi and imdad-ı seferiye as subsequently regularized but originally extraordinary forms of taxation might also have legitimized other forms of extraction that fulfilled the needs of the sultan's agents and allowed them to serve the ruler (Chapter 3).[7] This possibility might have amplified rationalizations that could be perceived both as "legalistic," because they could proclaim consistency with the imperial ideology, and as "denials of responsibility," because the associated acts were common and based on precedent.

The third rationalization, "**denial of injury,**" involves claims that transgressions caused little to no damage, little to no protest by victims, or insignificant harm compared to other transgressions (Ashforth and Anand 2003: 18–19; cf.

---

based on old taxes" (ibid.: 67). Indeed, the kanunname of Wallachia (Eflak), dated 1516, warns local authorities not to demand food or supplies from taxpayers claiming that this was a long-established, customary practice; see Akgündüz 1990–6: 3:458.

[5] In a slightly different articulation, De Klerk (2017: 257) identifies three variations of the same justification: "*Denial of personal responsibility*—Blaming it on circumstances beyond your control... *Displacing responsibility*—Shifting responsibility to another person or thing... *Diffusing responsibility*—Manifold excuses such as, 'Everybody does it.'"

[6] Bursa's sixteenth-century market inspection regulations (Akgündüz 1990–6: 2:194) indicate that one frequent excuse among those market officials accused of excessive extraction was that "the amount required to acquire the positions that they served cannot be otherwise raised" (ya beğlik akçeyi ne yerden versem gerekdir). The author of *Hırzü'l-Mülūk* (1994: 187) attributes the following words to a hypothetical governor accused of illegal extractions from actual or potential tımar-holders: "What can I do? I am obligated to send the grand-vizier thousands of florins every six months. Our prebendal assignments generate revenues barely adequate for our own expenditures. If not for these 'bribes,' from whom can I extract (*tahdil*) this many florins [due to the grand vizier]?"

[7] "Also, just like the imposition of 'avarız-ı divaniyye' on the reaya at times of the state's extraordinary needs, the provincial authorities were allowed to generate revenue via extractions such as *salma* at times of severe need" (İnalcık 1965: 52).

Rabl and Kühlmann 2009: 273; and De Klerk 2017: 257). In the operations of the Ottoman courts, minor transgressions such as fee extractions only slightly higher than officially prescribed levels might have been rationalized in this fashion (Chapter 4).[8]

The fourth rationalization, "**denial of victim**," involves denying that victimization has occurred: for example, by construing transgressions as acts of retaliation or revenge, by alleging that victims voluntarily participated in interactions (and thus should not be construed as victims), or by rejecting "the victim's individuality through depersonalization" (Ashforth and Anand 2003: 19–20).[9] In the Ottoman context, it is conceivable that some government officials saw certain groups, such as religious, ethnic, or linguistic minorities, as inferior or contemptible and used this view to justify their abuse of them. I should point out that although allegations of discrimination against non-Muslims are common in foreign accounts, I have encountered no justification of discrimination beyond what the legal and administrative system required.

"**Social weighting**," the fifth rationalization, means discrediting the moral authority of those who judge the behaviors of corrupt actors ("condemnation of the condemner") or questioning the laws or criteria on which such judgments can be made. Ashforth and Anand also include in this category what they call "selective social comparisons," which refers to sentiments that can be articulated thus: "There are others who cause more harm than us" (ibid.: 20–1). In the Ottoman context, the last version of this rationalization brings to mind historian Peçevi's defense of the grand vizier Rüstem Paşa (d. 1561). According to Peçevi (1968: 20), although Rüstem Paşa initiated the practice of receiving bribes for appointments, he never succumbed to prematurely dismissing officeholders from whom he had received payments (Chapter 5).

"**Appeal to higher loyalties**," the sixth rationalization, refers to the sacrifice of ethical and/or professional principles for causes said to be of greater importance to the transgressing actors, especially family or group loyalty (Ashforth and Anand 2003: 21). Implicit here is the possibility of a

---

[8] Relevant here is Bradly Reed's (1995: 366, *passim*) argument in the context of late imperial China that while many fees that the court clerks and runners charged for their services were illicit by legal standards, they were not considered corrupt or immoral by the court officials or clients and thus required little justification, as long as they remained below certain levels.

[9] This is how Ashforth and Anand (ibid.: 20) explain the last possibility: "The third variant is a denial of the victim's individuality through depersonalization (the victim is an interchangeable member of a social category) or of the victim's very humanity through dehumanization (the victim is an object or of a lesser species).... This psychological distancing is often abetted by physical and social distance and makes it easier to deny the impact of corruption on the victims—to practice 'moral exclusion.' ... Depersonalization is evident in accounts of Wall Street traders who viewed clients not as unique individuals but as suckers asking to be conned."

"normative plurality," which enables actors to prioritize conflicting objectives depending on circumstances and thus justify actions based on their "situated moralities."[10] In the Ottoman context, a striking example of this type of rationalization can be found in Naima's discussion of Şeyhülislam Balizade Mustafa Efendi's (d. 1662) favoritism in appointment decisions (Chapter 8). According to Naima (2007: 4:1735), the şeyhülislam excused his actions by proudly suggesting that during his tenure "I made a deliberate effort to favor my friends and acquaintances. I do not care what other people might say." Generally, the importance of reciprocity and the widespread acceptance of patronage networks and kin-based favoritism might have made it easier to represent various transgressions as acts that served important social functions.

The seventh rationalization, the "**metaphor of the ledger**," refers to the sense of entitlement to commit transgressions or the tendency to excuse them based on one's past or planned (future) good deeds, or "credits" (Ashforth and Anand 2003: 21).[11] In the Ottoman context, an official might have perceived his previous acts of value or moral fortitude as counterbalancing his transgressions. As we have seen, Naima advised excusing the crimes of officeholders based on their good deeds if the latter outweighed the former (Chapter 5).

The final rationalization, "**refocusing attention**," includes attempts to shift the focus away from individuals' transgressions and toward their more commendable actions (ibid.: 21–2). This could be done by "willfully deemphasiz[ing], compartmentaliz[ing], or suppress[ing] knowledge of their [corrupt] acts in favor of more normatively redeeming features of [one's] work" (ibid.: 22). In the Ottoman context, I have encountered no examples of this type of justification.

---

[10] The role of normative plurality in justifying corruption is well explored in anthropological research on various African contexts; see, for example, Chauveau, Le Pape, and Olivier de Sardan 2001; and Blundo and Olivier de Sardan 2006: 97. For discussions of normative plurality as a factor in corruption research, see Grüne and Tölle 2013; and Kerkhoff 2013. Situated morality is associated with the actors' tendency to internalize different moral expectations without exclusively identifying with any one of them. Based on the circumstances and whom the actor is interacting with, differing priorities might influence his or her actions. According to Chibnall and Saunders (1977: 144), individuals often face the prospect of making multiple choices in their lives, some of which might contradict officially prescribed norms (Chapter 7). On this point, see also Olivier de Sardan 1999: 34: "The practices that come under the complex of corruption, while being legally culpable and widely reproved, are none the less considered by their perpetrators as being legitimate, and often as not being corruption at all. In other words, the real borderline between what is corruption and what is not fluctuates, and depends on the context and on the position of the actors involved."

[11] Other research even indicates that individuals could excuse their transgressions by expressing their original intentions to act morally, by pointing out that they had not committed any transgressions in the near past, or by arguing that they would have acted morally under different circumstances. See, for example, Effron 2016.

There might be additional types of rationalizations in the Ottoman setting that could be difficult to place in any of these categories.[12] Nevertheless, this list of rationalizations is comprehensive enough to encompass most of the potential defenses used by transgressing agents.

With these insights in hand, let us return to the very specific case of Ahmed, the voiceless qadi of Bozöyük. How might he have justified his actions based on the model presented above, assuming that he committed the crimes he was accused of and that he still considered himself a just and moral person? Ahmed might have argued that conducting inspection tours (devrs) was necessary to maintain peace and reduce criminal activity in the countryside,[13] which was part of his job as the highest judicial authority in his jurisdiction, whether or not the imperial administration sanctioned these tours in every situation. This would have been a legalistic argument. Or he might have insisted that the services and supplies he had acquired from the taxpayers during these tours were customary and, therefore, legal entitlements, at least within limits. The mühimme entry also lists inappropriate extractions for a variety of fiscal, notarial, and legal services. Though these services might have been fraudulently rendered, the fact that they were technically associated with qadis' functions might have allowed Ahmed to try to justify them on a legalistic basis. At the very least, he might have argued, the payments he received from court clients were gifts, signifying their appreciation of his learning or gratitude for his services, permissible according to fiqh traditions.[14]

I find it significant as well that the mühimme entry cites no punishment for Ahmed's proven crimes other than a chastisement. We know that the qadis were occasionally dismissed from their positions for similar types of crimes.[15] But the possibility that this was not always the case must have made his

---

[12] For example, claims of ignorance by authorities regarding the crimes of other actors whom they were expected to police might be perceived as another way to proclaim their moral rectitude amid failures of proper conduct. For example, we find a warning in Bursa's "Market-Inspection Kanunname" to local market inspectors (muhtesibs) that they cannot plead ignorance if they neglect to discipline local shop owners' misconduct (Akgündüz 1990–6: 2:194).

[13] İnalcık (1965: 77) suggested that the imperial government periodically sanctioned tours of inspection to apprehend outlaws in the countryside, which might have constituted a legal ground for local authorities to justify their illegitimate forays on rural communities.

[14] As I argued in Chapter 2, gifts in recognition of a qadi's status could be legitimate under certain circumstances. Also, according to Akiba (2021), qadis and other court personnel could accept unsolicited "gifts" for their scribal functions, such as preparing legal deeds.

[15] See, for example, entry 63 in *14 Numaralı Şikayet Defteri* (Erdem 2017), which indicates that the naib of Malkara in Rumelia was dismissed from his position in 1690 for accepting bribes in adjudications. According to Kuru (2016: 126), about 5 percent of the qadis in the Balkan provinces were dismissed in the early eighteenth century because of allegations of misconduct while in office.

transgressions not only less consequential in terms of their career consequences, but also more excusable in his eyes.

Not every transgression attributed to Ahmed can be rationalized based on legalistic considerations. But Ahmed might have denied responsibility for them based on the claim that these transgressions were necessary for him to meet his financial needs, not only during his tenure in Bozöyük, but also during the years-long gap he must have anticipated before his next appointment. The system's inability to provide adequate compensation to court officials must have promoted this type of rationalization. In an environment of increasingly shorter tenures and longer wait times,[16] prevalent venality, and official court fees that had remained fixed over centuries,[17] judicial authorities must have been tempted to justify alternative—including illegitimate—forms of revenue extraction. In fact, given the financial pressures the judicial personnel faced at the time, Ahmed might have regarded the expectation that he should derive revenue only from sanctioned sources, by sanctioned means, at sanctioned levels, as akin to what premodern Chinese historians call a "structural hypocrisy."[18]

Overall, we should expect legalistic and need-based rationalizations to be relatively popular for qadis like Ahmed. But there might have been at least one other type of rationalization for which we find clues in the mühimme entry. The emphasis on tours in the entry might indicate that Ahmed's extractive impositions were particularly harsh in his interactions with remote, isolated communities. And the claim that he imposed fines on these communities for neglecting their daily prayers might suggest that their piety did not impress

---

[16] By the end of the sixteenth century, the average term of tenure for the appointments of the judges was about three years. Over the centuries, because of the increasing number of candidates for a relatively stagnant number of judicial positions, the durations of appointments declined, and the waiting times increased significantly. The length of tenure ranged from twelve to twenty months in the late seventeenth century, depending on the status of the judgeship. A regular judge in the province of Anatolia would have expected to spend, on average, fifty-one months between appointments in the first half of the eighteenth century. In the Balkans, most judges spent twenty-five to sixty months between appointments. See İ. Gündoğdu 2009b: 115; and Kuru 2016: 135–6. According to Kuru (ibid.), only in thirty-six of the 3,048 appointments in the Balkans did the qadis have waiting times less than twelve months.

[17] According to the information found in the kanunnames and other official documentation, the prescribed fees for court services did not change much between the fifteenth and eighteenth centuries, although prices in Istanbul increased substantially during that period. See Dörtok Abacı and Ergene 2022.

[18] Here Madeleine Zelin's (1984) description of Qing provincial courts is of particular interest. According to Zelin, the reason provincial officials were compelled to use technically illegal but in reality common and tolerated strategies for raising enough revenue to cover their expenses was that the Chinese government prescribed impractically low fees and taxes for political reasons and was resistant to changing them even when circumstances demanded it. See also Park 1997. The phrase "structural hypocrisy" is from Will 2004: 39, *passim*.

him. Thus, one could hypothesize that these communities displayed certain qualities he disapproved of, leading him to deny their victimhood.

It is likely that the popularity of particular rationalizations varied according to the realm of government in which an official served and the specific functions he performed. Thus, we should expect that officials in, say, the palace, the provincial administration, or the finance department would rely on different justifications than Ahmed might have. We need more research to better understand how these individuals (including Ahmed) perceived their crimes and explained the reasons for them.

* * *

Let me conclude by briefly reviewing my main arguments in the previous chapters. This book has probed the tension between modern and premodern Ottoman definitions of public office corruption. The prevailing tendency in the field has been to ignore this conceptual-cum-historical problem, evident in the often-indiscriminate use of the word "corruption" as if it were a timeless concept. At the same time, the few historians who have challenged the decontextualized treatment of corruption appear to have rejected a priori *any* possible connection between potentially corresponding notions across history. The book proposed an alternative position capable of identifying both the affinities and differences between modern and premodern characterizations by examining how the Ottomans (and non-Ottomans) portrayed self-interested abuse of power by government officials before the nineteenth century.

Among the genres of sources that I examined, the jurisprudential ones (Chapters 1 and 2) tend to concentrate on certain transgressions and judicial actors, especially bribes by the qadis and, to a lesser extent, by the court witnesses and muftis. I have argued that this choice might stem from the tradition's self-referentiality, which reproduced in the Ottoman context the genre's original focus—the judicial realm and its practices—and its ideological commitments to preserving the collective interests of the Muslim community. Chapters 3 and 4 explored state-generated documents, which highlighted transgressions that threatened the taxpayers' wellbeing and, therefore, the hierarchical patrimonial order under the ruler's authority. These documents paid the most attention to crimes associated with excessive and illegal extraction by military-administrative authorities and non-adjudicative transgressions by judicial actors.

Authors of Ottoman political literature (Chapter 5) characterized corruption in ways that varied widely. In general, their perspectives were shaped by their positionalities in relation to the polity and its policies. Until the sixteenth century, the bureaucratic-administrative transformation of the

Ottoman state and the broader socioeconomic implications of this process influenced the relevant discussions: here one observes a tendency to link corruption to the state's extractive practices, which benefited the dynasty at the expense of the polity's other constituents. Afterward, the focus shifted to the inappropriate acquisition of government offices by unqualified individuals, often via venality, and the adverse consequences of this practice both for state officials and taxpayers. Finally, I noted the existence of more pietistic and pragmatic articulations related to corruption.

We saw in Chapter 6 that accounts intended for foreign audiences bring a different perspective on the issue. Often motivated by concerns different from those of native authors—including, for example, intra-European debates on just government—and shaped by genre- and audience-specific expectations, these works reveal multiple opinions on the sources and state of corruption in the Ottoman context, ranging from a sense of appalled indignation (especially in earlier accounts) to fascination with and normalization of the associated acts, coupled with the desire in later texts to master these. The operations of the sharia court and aspects of Ottoman high politics received close attention in accounts written for foreigners. At the same time, I also identified significant thematic and substantive parallels between these sources and those intended for native audiences regarding the types of problems they recognized in the polity.

The discourses examined in this book, including the potential rationalizations by corrupt actors that I considered in the conclusion, illustrate multiple perspectives on public office corruption. Yet they may not be comprehensive. There might have been intra-genre variations that I was unable to detect in specific discursive fields. Also, a few discourses may be entirely missing. In the latter regard, the absence of provincial, non-Muslim, and non-elite voices is conspicuous. It is possible that many features of the discourses that I have discussed resonated with these viewpoints, including the association of corruption with the state's extractive measures (which is prominent in early political texts) or the expectation of a paternalistic and protective relationship between the ruler and his subjects (which is evident in state-generated documents). However, we should also anticipate perspectives unique to the omitted groups. I leave the important task of exploring their worldviews to future research, which should benefit from the ongoing explorations of Ottoman moral economies—a promising endeavor in our field.[19]

---

[19] Two panels on moral economy in the most recent Early Modern Ottoman Studies Conference held in Ankara (July 12-15, 2023) brought together largely exploratory papers by Cemal Kafadar, Mehmet Kuru, Eda Özel, İklil Selçuk, and Onur Usta.

The multi-genre survey presented in this book has indicated that many modern connotations of corruption would mesh with premodern Ottomans, though there may be no single overarching notion that encapsulates all the specific transgressions we associate with the concept today (even if zulüm comes close). Instead, what might have distinguished premodern perceptions was the significant variation across different genres of sources and, in a few cases, within them. In addition to these multiple meanings, I have also noted the often tentative, potentially unstable boundaries that separated legitimate and illegitimate justifications of extraction (Chapter 3); the cost-sensitive and negotiable consequences of predatory behavior for those who engaged in it (Chapter 4); and the context-dependent and frequently disputed moralities of gifts-as-bribes and patronage (Chapters 7 and 8).

More effort is needed to determine how various discourses of corruption shifted in later eras. The available literature in the Ottoman context indicates that the modern state attempted to reduce the gray areas in the official depictions of corruption in the nineteenth century by more concretely differentiating gifts from bribes; instituting a comprehensive salary system for state functionaries that excluded gifts as means for compensation; better defining the bases of extortion by government officials; limiting the influence of patronage in government service; and imposing more precise and inflexible punitive regulations for offenses deemed illegitimate in new criminal codes (Mumcu 2005: 274–89; Çelik 2006; Kırlı 2006 and 2015; cf. Saraçoğlu 2021). One also senses in these works that the state sought to make its perspective hegemonic by challenging the conflicting perceptions and practices in other realms of Ottoman society, although Çelik (2006) notes that such attempts encountered some resistance, at least in provincial settings.

Long-term continuities certainly emerge in how Ottomans in premodern and modern times perceived certain acts associated with government abuse and predation and judged them on their morality. In the context of these continuities, the transition to modernity vis-à-vis public office corruption might be located, at least provisionally, in the state's efforts to define corruption from its vantagepoint and how such attempts accentuated particular characterizations and de-emphasized others. If one result was a relative loss of plurality and ambiguity in the meanings of corruption, this would be consistent with select European experiences (Hirschman 1977; Kerkhoff 2013; Engels 2018). Because of the book's premodern temporal focus, I have not tested this hypothesis here, but it is worth probing in future research.

References

Primary Sources

Hadith Collections

Abu Dawud, Sulaiman ibn Ash'ath. 2008. *English Translation of Sunan Abu Davud.* 5 vols. Edited by Hafiz Abu Tahir Zubair Ali Za'i, Huda Khattab, and Abu Khaliyl. Translated by Nasiruddin al-Khattab. Riyadh: Darussalam.

al-Bukhari, Muhammad ibn Isma'il. 1997. *The Translation of the Meanings of Sahih al-Bukhari: Arabic-English.* 9 vols. Edited by Muhammad Muhsin Khan. Riyadh: Darussalam.

Ibn Majah, Muhammad ibn Yazid. 2007. *English Translation of Sunan Ibn Majah.* 5 vols. Edited by Hafiz Abu Tahir Zubair 'Ali Za'i, Huda Khattab, and Abu Khaliyl. Translated by Nasiruddin Khattab. Riyadh: Darussalam.

Muslim, Ibn al Hajjaj. 2007. *English Translation of Sahih Muslim.* 7 vols. Edited by Hafiz Abu Tahir Zubair 'Ali Za'i, Huda Khattab, and Abu Khaliyl. Translated by Nasiruddin al-Khattab. Riyadh: Darussalam.

an-Nasa'i, Ahmad ibn Shu'ayb. 2007. *English Translation of Sunan an-Nasa'i.* 6 vols. Edited by Hafiz Abu Tahir Zubair 'Ali Za'i, Huda Khattab, and Abu Khaliyl. Translated by Nasiruddin al-Khattab. Riyadh: Darussalam.

at-Tirmidhi, Abu 'Eisa Mohammad ibn 'Eisa. 2007. *English Translation of Jami'at-Tirmidhi.* 6 vols. Edited by Hafiz Abu Tahir Zubair 'Ali Za'i. Translated by Abu Khaliyl. Riyadh: Darussalam.

Kalebend Registers in Theses

Alakuş, Murat. 2016. "BOA 6 (H.1151–1152/M.1739) ve 31 (H.1221–1222/M.1806–1807) Numaralı Kalebend Defterleri (İnceleme ve Metin)." Master's thesis, Mimar Sinan University, Istanbul.

Alemdaroğlu, Şahin. 2018. "20 Numaralı Kalebend Defteri (1780–1782) Değerlendirme ve Metin." Master's thesis, Mimar Sinan University, Istanbul.

Algül, Faruk. 2019. "11 Numaralı Kalebend Defteri'ne (H.1167–1169/M. 1754–1756) Göre Suç ve Suçlu Profili." Master's thesis, Mimar Sinan University, Istanbul.

Çeribaş, Volkan. 2018. "33 Numaralı Kalebend Defteri (s. 1–133/H. 1227–1229/ M. 1812–1814) (Metin ve İnceleme)." Master's thesis, Mimar Sinan University, Istanbul.

Daş, Esra. 2019. "37 Numaralı Kalebend Defterine Göre (s. 1–147) H. 1238–1239/ M. 1823–1824 Yılları Arasında Osmanlı Devleti'nde Suç, Suçlu ve Cezalar (Değerlendirme-Metin)." Master's thesis, Mimar Sinan University, Istanbul.

Erdoğan, Mustafa Cengiz. 2019. "33 Numaralı Kalebend Defteri (s. 134–264) (Evâhir-i Rabiü'l-âhir 1229– Şevval 1230) (Muharrem. 1814–1815) (Metin ve İnceleme)." Master's thesis, Mimar Sinan University, Istanbul.

Genç, Hakan. 2019. "35 Numaralı Kalebend Defterine Göre (1818–1819) Osmanlı Devleti'nde Suç ve Suçlu Profili." Master's thesis, Mimar Sinan University, Istanbul.

Kara, Melahat. 2019. "18 Numaralı Kalebend Defterine Göre (s. 147-290) H. 1190-1191/ M. 1776-1777 Yılları Arasında Osmanlı Devleti'nde Suç, Suçlu ve Cezalar (Değerlendirme-Metin)." Master's thesis, Mimar Sinan University, Istanbul.

Koca, Uğur. 2015. "17 Numaralı Kalebend Defterine Göre Hicri 1182-1188 (M. 1768-1774) Yılları Arasında Osmanlı Devleti'nde Suç, Suçlu, Hapishaneler ve Cezalar." Master's thesis, Mimar Sinan University, Istanbul.

Sezgin, Hale. 2022. "21 Numaralı Kalebend Defterine Göre H. 1196-1199/M. 1782-1784 Yılları Arasında Osmanlı Devleti'nde Suç, Suçlu ve Cezalar (Değerlendirme ve Metin)." Mimar Sinan University, Istanbul.

Şahin, Fatma. 2017. "11 Numaralı Kalebend Defterine Göre (s. 1-196) H. 1166-1167/ M. 1753-1754 Yılları Arasında Osmanlı Devleti'nde Suç, Suçlu ve Cezalar (Değerlendirme-Metin)." Master's thesis, Mimar Sinan University, Istanbul.

Toku, Zeynep. 2019. "34 Numaralı Kalebend Defterine Göre (s. 1-106) H. 1230-1231/ M. 1815-1816 Yılları Arasında Osmanlı Devleti'nde Suç, Suçlu ve Cezalar (Değerlendirme-Metin)." Master's thesis, Mimar Sinan University, Istanbul.

Uz, Ramazan. 2017. "24 Numaralı Kalebend Defterine (H. 1203-1205/M. 1788-1790) Göre Osmanlı Devleti'nde Suçlar, Suçlular ve Cezalar (Değerlendirme ve Metin)." Mimar Sinan University, Istanbul.

Mühimme and Şikayet Registers in Print and Theses

3 Numaralı Mühimme Defteri; 966-968/1558-1560. 1993. Ankara: T. C. Başbakanlık Devlet Arşivleri Genel Müdürlüğü.

4 Numaralı Atik Şikâyet Defteri 1665-1670 (H. 1075-1081): see Tataroğlu 2015.

7 Numaralı Mühimme Defteri (975-976/1567-1569) [Özet-Transkripsiyon-İndeks]. 1998. Vol. 1. Ankara: T. C. Başbakanlık Devlet Arşivleri Genel Müdürlüğü.

14 Numaralı Atik Şikâyet Defteri (H. 1101-1102/M. 1690-1691): see Erdem 2017.

38 Numaralı Atik Şikâyet Defteri (1114-1115/1703) (İnceleme-Metin): see Çil 2018.

82 Numaralı Mühimme Defteri (1026-1027/1617-1618) [Özet-Transkripsiyon-İndeks ve Tıpkıbasım]. 2000. Ankara: T. C. Başbakanlık Devlet Arşivleri Genel Müdürlüğü.

85 Numaralı Mühimme Defteri (1040-1041 (1042)/1630-1631 (1632)) [Özet-Transkripsiyon-İndeks]. 2002. Ankara: T. C. Başbakanlık Devlet Arşivleri Genel Müdürlüğü.

91 Numaralı Mühimme Defteri (H. 1056/M. 1646-1647) [Özet-Çeviriyazı-Tıpkıbasım]. 2015. Istanbul: T. C. Başbakanlık Devlet Arşivleri Genel Müdürlüğü.

Çil, Şeyma. 2018. "38 Numaralı Atik Şikâyet Defteri (1114-1115/1703) (İnceleme-Metin)." Master's thesis, Marmara University, Istanbul.

Erdem, Ümit Baki. 2017. "14 Numaralı Atik Şikâyet Defteri (H. 1101-1102/M. 1690-1691); Transkripsiyon ve Değerlendirilmesi." Master's thesis, Marmara University, Istanbul.

Tataroğlu, Yasemin. 2015. "4 Numaralı Atik Şikâyet Defteri 1665-1670 (H. 1075-1081) Transkripsiyon ve Değerlendirilmesi." Master's thesis, Marmara University, Istanbul.

Yörük, Gül. 2019. "Osmanlı'da Devlet-Toplum İlişkilerine Bir Örnek: 112 Numaralı Atik Şikayet Defteri (1727)." Master's thesis, Ankara Üniversitesi, Ankara.

Premodern Chronicles, Kanunnames, Jurisprudential Works, Political Literature

Ahmed Cevdet Paşa. 1891. *Târîh-i Cevdet* (tertib-i cedid). Volume 6. Dersaadet: Matbaa-i Osmaniye.

Ahmed Efendi, es-Seyyid, and es-Seyyid Hafız Mehmed ibn Ahmed el-Gedusi, eds. 2014. *Netîcetü'l Fetâvâ: Şeyhülislam Fetvaları*. Prepared for publication by Süleyman Kaya, Betül Algın, Ayşe Nagehan Çelikçi, and Emine Kaval. Istanbul: Klasik Yayınları.

REFERENCES 275

Ahmedi 1992: Sılay, Kemal. 1992. "Aḥmedī's History of the Ottoman Dynasty." *Journal of Turkish Studies/Türklük Bilgisi Araştırmaları* 16: 129–200.
Akgündüz, Ahmed, ed. 1990–6. *Osmanlı Kanunnameleri ve Hukuki Tahlilleri*. 9 vols. Istanbul: Fey Vakfı Yayınları.
Akgündüz, Ahmed, ed. 2018. *Şeyhü'l-İslam Ebüssu'ud Efendi Fetvaları*. Istanbul: Osmanlı Araştırmaları Vakfı Yayınları.
Akhisari 1979–80: İpşirli, Mehmet. 1979–80. "Hasan Kâfî el-Akhisârî ve Devlet Düzenine Ait Eseri." *Tarih Enstitüsü Dergisi* 10–11: 239–78.
Aşık Çelebi. 2018. *Mi'racü'l-Eyâle: Âşık Çelebi'nin Siyâsetnâmesi*. Edited by Muhammed Usame Onuş, Abdurrahman Bulut, Ahmet Çelik, Özgür Kavak, and Hızır Murat Köse. Istanbul: Türkiye Yazma Eserler Kurumu Başkanlığı.
Aşıkpaşazade 2013: Aşıkpaşazade Derviş Ahmed. 2013. *Âşıpaşazâde Tarihi [Osmanlı Tarihi (1285–1502)]*. Edited by Necdet Öztürk. Istanbul: Bilge Kültür Sanat.
Aziz Efendi. 1985. *Kanūn-Nāme-i Sultani li 'Aziz Efendi. 'Aziz Efendi's Book of Sultanic Laws and Regulations: An Agenda for Reform by a Seventeenth-Century Ottoman Statesman*. Prepared by Rhoads Murphy. Cambridge, MA: Harvard University Press.
Defterdar 1935: Defterdar Sarı Meḥmed Pasha. 1935. *Ottoman Statecraft: The Book of Counsel for Vezirs and Governors*. Translated by Walter Livingston Wright Jr. Princeton Oriental Texts 2. Princeton, NJ: Princeton University Press.
Defterdar 1969: Defterdar Sarı Mehmed Paşa. 1969. *Devlet Adamlarına Öğütler/Nesayıh'ul-Vüzera v'el-Ümerâ*. Translated by Hüseyin Ragıp Uğural. Ankara: Türk Tarih Kurumu Basımevi.
Demirtaş, H. Necâti, ed. 2011–2. *Açıklamalı Osmanlı Fetvaları*, 2 vols. (Istanbul: Kubbealtı Neşriyat).
Demirtaş, H. Necâti, ed. 2014. *Açıklamalı Osmanlı Fetvâları: Fetâvâ-yı Ali Efendi; Şeyhülislâm Çatalcalı Ali Efendi (1674–1686)*. 2 vols. Istanbul: Kubbealtı Yayınları.
Evliya Çelebi. 1896. *Evliya Çelebi Seyahatnamesi*. Vol. 1. Der Saadet: İkdam Matbaası.
Evliya Çelebi. 1991. *The Intimate Life of an Ottoman Statesman: Melek Ahmed Pasha (1588–1662): As Portrayed in Evliya Çelebi's Book of Travels (Seyahat-name)*. Translation and Commentary by Robert Dankoff. Albany, NY: SUNY Press.
Halebi, İbrahim. n.d. *İzahlı Mülteka el-Ebhur Tercümesi*. Vol. 3. Translated by Mustafa Uysal. Istanbul: Çelik Yayınları.
Hezarfen 1998: İlgürel, Sevim, ed. 1998. *Hezârfen Hüseyin Efendi: Telhîsü'l Beyân fî Kavânin-i Âl-i Osmân*. Ankara: Türk Tarih Kurumu Yayınları.
Hırzü'l Mülük. 1994. In *Osmanlı Kanunnameleri ve Hukuki Tahlilleri*, edited by Ahmed Akgündüz, 4: 29–96. Istanbul: Fey Yayınları.
Hüsrev, Molla. 1980. *Gurer ve Dürer Tercümesi (Islam Fıkhı ve Hukuku)*. Vol. 4. Translated by Arif Erkan. Istanbul: Eser Neşriyat.
İbn Abidin 1982–94: İbn-i Âbidin, Muhammed Emīn. 1982–94. *Reddü'l Muhtar Ale'd Dürri'l Muhtar*. Translated by Ahmet Davutoğlu et al. 17 vols. Istanbul: Şamil Yayınları.
İbn Nujaym 1966: Sahillioğlu, Halil. 1966. "İbn-i Nüceym'in Rüşvet Hakkındaki Risalesi." *Ankara Üniversitesi Hukuk Fakültesi Dergisi* 22 (1): 691–7.
İbn Nujaym 2004: Pekcan, Ali. 2004. "Son Dönem Hanefî Fakihlerinden İbn Nüceym'in (970/1563) Fıkhî Risâlelerinin Tanıtımı ve 'Rüşvet' Risâlesi'nin Çevirisi." *İslam Hukuku Araştırmaları Dergisi* 3: 253–63.
İdris Bitlisi. 1991. "Kanun-ı Şehinşahi." In *Osmanlı Kanunnameleri ve Hukuki Tahlilleri*, edited by Ahmet Akgündüz, 3:11–85. Istanbul: Fey Vakfı.
al-Jabarti 1994: Philipp, Thomas, and Moshe Perlmann, eds. 1994. *'Abd al-Raḥmān al-Jabartī's History of Egypt: 'Ajā'ib al-Āthār fī'l-Tarājim wa'l-Akhbār*. 3 vols. Stuttgart: Franz Steiner Verlag.

Kâtib Chelebi. 1957. *The Balance of Truth*. Translated by G. L. Lewis. Ethical and Religious Classics of East and West 19. London: George Allen and Unwin.

Katip Çelebi. 1982. *Bozuklukluların Düzeltilmesinde Tutulacak Yollar (Düsturu'l-amel li-ıslahi'l-halel)*. Edited by Ali Can. Ankara: Başbakanlık Yayınevi.

Katip Çelebi 2010: Gündoğdu, Hüseyin. 2010. "An Ottoman Scribe and Intellectual: Katib Çelebi and the Analysis of His Work 'Düsturu'l-'Amel li-Islahi'l-Halel'." *ODÜ Sosyal Bilimler Enstitüsü Sosyal Bilimler Araştırmaları Dergisi* 1 (1): 81–92.

Kâtip Çelebi. 2016. *Mîzânü'l-Hakk fî İhtiyâri'l-Ehakk*. Edited by Süleyman Uludağ. Istanbul: Dergâh.

Kaya, Süleyman, ed. 2009. *Fetâvâ-yı Feyziyye: Şeyhülislam Feyzullah Efendi*. Istanbul: Klasik Yayınları.

Kaya, Süleyman, Betül Algın, Zeynep Trabzonlu, and Asuman Erkan, eds. 2011. *Behcetü'l Fetâvâ: Şeyhülislam Yenişehirli Abdullah Efendi*. Istanbul: Klasik Yayınları.

Kınalızade 2016: Kınalızade Ali Çelebi. 2016. *Ahlâk-ı Alâî (Günümüz Türkçesiyle)*. Edited by Mehmet Demirkol. Ankara: Fecr Yayınları.

Koçi Bey. 1972. *Koçi Bey Risalesi*. Edited by Zuhuri Danışman. Ankara: Milli Eğitim Bakanlığı Yayınları.

Koçi Bey. 1994. *Koçi Bey Risalesi (Eski ve Yeni Harflerle)*. Edited by Yılmaz Kurt. Ankara: Ecdad Yayınları.

Lütfi Paşa 1991: Kütükoğlu, Mübahat S., ed. 1991. *Lütfi Paşa Âsafnâmesi (Yeni Bir Metin Tesisi Denemesi)*. Istanbul: İstanbul Üniversitesi Edebiyat Fakültesi Basımevi.

Lütfi Paşa. 2001. *Lütfi Paşa ve Tevârih-i Âl-i Osman*. Edited by Kayhan Atik. Ankara: T. C. Kültür Bakanlığı.

al-Marghinani, Burhan al-Din. 1870. *The Hedaya or Guide: A Commentary on the Mussulman Laws*. Translated by Charles Hamilton. Vol. 2. London: T. Bensley.

al-Māwardī, Abu'l-Hasan 'Ali ibn Muhammad ibn Habib al-Basri al-Baghdadi. n.d. *al-Ahkam as-Sultaniyyah: The Ordinances of Government*. Translated by Asadullah Yate. London: Ta Ha.

Merginani, B. E. l. H. A. b. E. B. 1986. *İslam Fıkhında Tahkikli ve Tahriçli el-Hidaye Tercemesi*. Vol. 3. Translated by Ahmet Meylani. Istanbul: Kahraman Yayınları.

Mustafa Ali. 1982. *Mustafa Ali's Counsel for Sultans of 1581*. Edited by Andreas Tietze. 2 vols. Vienna: Austrian Academy of Sciences Press.

Mustafa Ali. 2003a. *XVI. Yüzyıl Osmanlı Efendisi Muṣṭafā 'Alī: Mevā'idü'n-Nefāis fī Kavā'idi'l-Mecālis*. Translated by Douglas Scott Brookes. Cambridge, MA: Harvard University Press.

Mustafa Ali. 2003b. *Künhü'l-Aḫbār C. II: Fātiḥ Sulṭān Meḥmed Devri, 1451–1481*. Edited by Hüdai Şentürk. Ankara: Türk Tarih Kurumu Basımevi.

Naima 2007: Naîmâ Mustafa Efendi. 2007. *Târih-i Na'îmâ (Ravzatü'l-Hüseyn fî Hulâsati Ahbâri'l-Hâfıkayn)*. 4 vols. Edited by Mehmet İpşirli. Ankara: Türk Tarih Kurumu Yayınları.

Neşri 2014: Mehmed Neşri. 2014. *Kitab-ı Cihan-nümâ (Neşri Tarihi)*. 2 vols. Edited by Faik Reşit Unat and Mehmed A. Köymen. Ankara: Türk Tarih Kurumu Yayınları.

Oruç Beğ 2007: Öztürk, Necdet, ed. 2007. *Oruç Beğ Tarihi (Giriş, Metin, Kronoloji, Dizin, Tıpkıbasım)*. Istanbul: Çamlıca Basım Yayın.

Peçevi 1968: İbrahim Peçevi. 1968. *Peçevî Tarihi*. Translated by Murat Uraz. Istanbul: Neşriyat Yurdu.

Raşid 2013: Râşid Mehmed Efendi ve Çelebizâde İsmaîl Âsım Efendi. 2013. *Târîh-i Râşid ve Zeyli*. 3 vols. Istanbul: Klasik Yayınları.

Selaniki 1999. Selâniki Mustafa Efendi. 1999. *Tarih-i Selâniki*. 2 vols. Edited by Mehmet İpşirli. Ankara: Türk Tarih Kurumu Basımevi.

Silahdar—*Nusretname* 2001: Topal, Mehmet. 2001. "Silâhdar Fındıklılı Mehmed Ağa: Nusretnâme." PhD diss., Marmara University, Istanbul.

Silahdar—*Tarih* 2012: Türkal, Nazire Karaçay. 2012. "Silahdar Fındıklılı Mehmed Ağa: Zeyl-i Fezleke (1065–22 Ca.1106/1654–7 Şubat 1695)." PhD diss., Marmara University, Istanbul.

Şükrullah 2004: Almaz, Hasan. 2004. "Şükrullah, B. Şihâbeddin Ahmed B. Zeyneddîn Zekî; Behcetü't-Tevârîh (İnceleme-Metin-Tercüme)." PhD diss., Ankara University.

Tatarcık Abdullah Efendi. 1916/7. "Nizâm-ı Devlet Hakkında Mutâla'ât." *Târih-i Osmâni Encümeni* 41: 257–84.

Tevarih 1992: *Anonim Tevârîh-i Âl-i Osman*. 1992. Edited by Friedrich Giese and Nihat Azamat. Istanbul: Marmara Universitesi Yayınları.

Ural, İbrahim, and Mehmed Ali Sarı, eds. 1996. *El-Muhtarat Minel Fetava*. Istanbul: Fey Vakfı.

Yazıcıoğlu 1999: Sakaoğlu, Necdet, ed. 1999. *Dürr-i Meknun: Saklı İnciler*. Istanbul: Tarih Vakfı Yurt Yayınları.

Yücel, Yaşar, ed. 1988. *Osmanlı Devlet Teşkilatına Dair Kaynaklar: Kitab-ı Müstetab, Kitâbu Mesâlihi'l Müslimîn, Hırzü'l Mülük*. Ankara: Türk Tarih Kurumu Basımevi.

Accounts by Foreign Authors or for Foreign Audiences

[Blount, Sir Henry]. 1650. *A Voyage into the Levant: A Brief Relation of a Journey Lately Performed by Mr. Henry Blunt Gentleman, from England by the way of Venice, into Dalmatia, Sclavonia, Bosna, Hungary, Macedonia, Thessaly, Thrace, Rhodes and Egypt, unto Gran Cairo: With particular Observations Concerning the Moderne Condition of the Turks, and Other People Under that Empire*. 4th ed. London: A. Crooke.

Busbequius, A. G. 1744. *Travels into Turkey: Containing the Most Accurate Account of the Turks, and Neighbouring Nations, Their Manners, Customs, Religion, Superstition, Policy, Riches, Coins, &c. The Whole Being a Series of Remarkable Observations and Events, Interspers'd with Great Variety of Entertaining Incidents, Never before Printed*. London: J. Robinson.

Cantemir, Demetrius. 1734. *The History of the Growth and Decay of the Othman Empire, Part I; Containing the Growth of the Othman Empire, from the Reign of Othman the Founder, to the Reign of Mahomet IV. That Is, From the Year 1300, to the Siege of Vienna, in 1683*. Translated by N. Tindal. London: James, John, and Paul Knapton.

The Capitulations and Articles of Peace between The Majesty of the King of Great Britain, France, and Ireland, &c. and The Sultan of the Ottoman Empire..., as They Have Been Augmented and Altered in the Times of Several Ambassadors: And Particularly as They Have Been Renewed, Augmented, and Amplified at the City of Adrianople in the Month of January 166½.by Heneage Earl of Winchelsea, Ambassador Extraordinary from His Majesty: And also as They Have Been since Renewed in the Month of September 1675. with Divers Additional Articles and Priviledges, by Sir John Finch, Knight, Ambassador in Ordinary from His Majesty to Sultan Mahomet Han, the Most Puissant Prince and Emperor of the Turks. 1679. London: J. S. MDCLXXIX. https://ota.bodleian.ox.ac.uk/repository/xmlui/bitstream/handle/20.500.12024/A32196/A32196.html?sequence=5.

Chesneau, Jean. 2012. *D'Aramon Seyahatnamesi: Kanuni Devrinde İstanbul-Anadolu-Mezopotamya*. Istanbul: Dergah Yayınları.

Drummond, Alexander. 1754. *Travels through Different Cities of Germany, Italy, Greece, and Several Parts of Asia, as Far as the Banks of the Euphrates: In a Series of Letters. Containing, an Account of What Is Most Remarkable in the Present State, as Well as in Their Monuments of Antiquity*. London: W. Strahan.

Eton, W. 1799. *A Survey of the Turkish Empire. In Which Are Considered, I. Its Government, Finances, Military and Naval Force, Religion, History, Arts, Sciences, Manners, Commerce, and Population. II. The State of the Provinces, Including the Ancient Government of the Crim Tatars, The Subjection of the Greeks, Their Efforts toward Emancipation, and the Interest of Other Nations, Particularly of Great Britain, in Their Success. III. The Causes of the Decline of Turkey, and Those Which Tend to the Prolongation of Its Existence, with a Development of the Political System of the Late Empress of Russia. IV. The British Commerce with Turkey, The Necessity of Abolishing the Levant Company, and the Danger of Our Quarantine Regulations with Many Other Important Particulars.* 2nd ed. London: T. Cadell and W. Davies.

Gerlach, Stephan. 2006. *Türkiye Günlüğü*. Edited by Kemal Beydilli; translated by Türkis Noyan. 2 vols. Istanbul: Kitap Yayınevi.

Habesci, Elias. 1784. *The Present State of the Ottoman Empire Containing a More Accurate and Interesting Account of the Religion, Government, Military Establishment, Manners, Customs, and Amusements of the Turks than Any Yet Extant. Including a Particular Description of the Court and Seraglio of the Grand Signor. And Interspersed with Many Singular and Entertaining Anecdotes*. Translated from French. London: R. Baldwin.

Hill, Aaron. 1709. *A Full and Just Account of the Present State of the Ottoman Empire in All Its Branches: With the Government, and Policy, Religion, Customs, and Way of Living of the Turks, in General. Faithfully Related from a Serious Observation, Taken in Many Years Travels thro' Those Countries*. London: John Mayo.

Knolles, Richard. 1603. *The Generall Historie of the Turkes from the First Beginning of the Nation to the Rising of the Othoman Familie with All the Notable Expeditions of the Christian Princes against Them. Together with the Lives and Conquests of the Othoman Kings and Emperors; Faithfullie Collected out of the Best Histories, Both Ancient and Moderne, and Digested into One Continuat Historie Untill This Present Yeare 1603.* London: Adam Islip.

Knolles, Richard, and Paul Rycaut. 1701. *The Turkish History, Comprehending the Origin of That Nation, and the Growth of the Othoman Empire, with the Lives and Conquests of Their Several Kings and Emperors*. Vol. 2, edited by John Savage. London: Isaac Cleave.

Krafft, Hans Ulrich. 1997. *Türklerin Elinde Bir Alman Tacir*. Translated by Turgut Akpınar. Istanbul: İletişim.

Lubenau, Reinhold. 2012. *Osmanlı Ülkesinde*. Translated by Türkis Noyan. 2 vols. Istanbul: Kitap Yayınevi.

Lüdeke, Christoph Wilhelm. 2013. *Türklerde Din ve Devlet Yönetimi: İzmir-İstanbul 1759-1768*. Translated by Türkis Noyan. Istanbul: Kitap Yayınevi.

Mariti, [Giovanni]. 1792. *Travels through Cyprus, Syria, and Palestine: With a General History of the Levant*. Vol. 1. Dublin: R. Byrne, A. Grueber, J. Moore, W. Jones, and J. Rice.

Mignot. 1787. *The History of the Turkish, or Ottoman Empire, from Its Foundation in 1300, to the Peace of Belgrade in 1740. To Which Is Prefixed an Historical Discourse on Mahomet and His Successors*. Translated by A. Hawkins. Vol. 2. Exeter, UK: R. Thorn.

North, Roger. 1744. *The Life of the Honourable Sir Dudley North, Knt. Commissioner of the Customs, and Afterwards of the Treasury to His Majesty King Charles the Second. And of the Honourable and Reverend Dr. John North, Master of Trinity College in Cambridge, and Greek Professor, Prebend of Westminster, and Sometime Clerk of the Closet to the Same King Charles the Second*. London: John Whiston.

d'Ohsson, [Abraham Constantine Mouradgea]. 1824. *Tableau général de l'empire Othoman, divisé en deux parties, dont l'une comprend la législation mahométane, l'autre l'histoire de l'Empire othoman*. Vols. 6 and 7. Paris: Firmin Didot.

Olivier, Guillaume-Antoine. 1801. *Travels in the Ottoman Empire, Egypt, and Persia, Undertaken by Order of the Government of France, during the First Six Years of the Republic*. 2 vols. London: T. N. Longman and O. Rees.

Pococke, Richard. 1745. *A Description of the East, and Some Other Countries*. Vol. 2. London: W. Bowyer.

Porter, James. 1768. *Observations on the Religion, Law, Government, and Manners, of the Turks*. Vol. 1. London: J. Nourse.

Report on the Manuscripts of Allen Georgie Finch, Esq, of Burley-on-the-Hill, Rutland. Vol. 1. 1913. Historical Manuscripts Commission. London: His Majesty's Stationery Office.

Rycaut, Paul. 1652. *The Present State of the Ottoman Empire. Containing the Maxims of the Turkish Politie, the Most Material Points of the Mahometan Religion, Their Sects and Heresies, Their Convents and Religious Votaries. Their Military Discipline, With an Exact Computation of Their Forces Both by Land and Sea. Illustrated with Divers Pieces of Sculpture, Representing the Variety of Habits amongst the Turks*. 3rd ed. London: John Starkey and Henry Erome.

Rycaut, Paul. 1686. *The History of the Present State of the Ottoman Empire. Containing the Maxims of the Turkish Polity, the Most Material Points of the Mahometan Religion, Their Sects and Heresies, Their Convents and Religious Votaries. Their Military Discipline, with an Exact Computation of Their Forces Both by Sea and Land. Illustrated with Divers Pieces of Sculture, Representing the Variety of Habits amongst the Turks*. 6th ed. London: Charles Brome.

Sandys, George. 1615. *A Relation of a Journey Begun An. Dom. 1610. Foure Books. Containing a Description of the Turkish Empire, of Ægypt, of the Holy Land, of the Remote Parts of Italy, and Islands Adioyning*. London: W. Barrett.

Schweigger, Salomon. 2004. *Sultanlar Kentine Yolculuk, 1578–1581*. Edited by Heidi Stein. Translated by S. Türkis Noyan. Istanbul: Kitap Yayınevi.

Shay, Mary Lucille. 1944. *The Ottoman Empire from 1720 to 1734, as Revealed in Despatches of the Venetian Baili*. Urbana: University of Illinois Press.

Sonnini, C. S. 1801. *Travels in Greece and Turkey, Undertaken by Order of Louis XVI. And with the Authority of the Ottoman Court*. 2 vols. London: T. N. Longman and O. Rees.

de Tott, [François] Baron. 1786. *Memoirs of Baron de Tott: Containing the State of the Turkish Empire and the Crimea, during the Late War with Russia. With Numerous Anecdotes, Facts, and Observations, on the Manners and Customs of the Turks and Tartars*. 2nd ed. 2 vols. London: G. G. J. and J. Robinson.

Tournefort, Joseph de. 2013. *Tournefort Seyahatnamesi*. Edited by Stefanos Yerasimos, translated by Ali Berktay and Teoman Tunçdoğan, 4th ed. Istanbul: Kitap Yayınevi.

Secondary Sources

Abou El Fadl, Khaled. 2002. "The Place of Tolerance in Islam." In *The Place of Tolerance in Islam*, edited by Khaled Abou El Fadl, Joshua Cohen, and Ian Lague, 3–26. Boston: Beacon.

Abou El Fadl, Khaled. 2003. "The Human Rights Commitment in Modern Islam." In *Human Rights and Responsibilities in the World Religions*, edited by J. Runzo, N. Martin, and A. Sharma, 301–64. Oxford: Oneworld Publications.

Abou-El-Haj, Rifaʻat. 1974. "The Ottoman Vezir and Pasha Households 1683–1703: A Preliminary Report." *Journal of American Oriental Society* 94 (4): 438–47.

Abou-El-Haj, Rifaʻat. 1984. *The 1703 Rebellion and the Structure of Ottoman Politics*. Istanbul: Nederlands Historisch-Archaeologisch Instituut te Istanbul.

Abou-El-Haj, Rifaʻat. 1991. *Formation of the Modern State: The Ottoman Empire, Sixteenth to Eighteenth Centuries*. Albany, NY: SUNY Press.

Abu-el-Haj, R. A. 1986. "Review Article: Metin Kunt, The Sultan's Servants: Transformation of Ottoman Provincial Government 1550–1650." *Osmanlı Araştırmaları/The Journal of Ottoman Studies* 6: 221–46.

Acer, Zabit. 2009. "Corruption of the Ottoman Inheritance System and Reform Studies Carried Out in the 17th Century." *Zeitschrift für die Welt der Türken* 1 (2): 119–30.

Açıkgöz, Fatma Ünyay. 2012. "XVII. Yüzyılda Osmanlı Devleti'nde Hediye ve Hediyeleşme (Padişahlara Sunulan ve Padişahların Verdiği Hediyeler Üzerine Bir Araştırma)." PhD diss., Gazi University, Ankara.

Açıkgöz, Fatma Ünyay. 2018. "Osmanlı Devleti'nde Pîşkeş (XXII. Yüzyıl)." *Turkish Studies* 13 (24): 287–300.

Acun, Fatma, and Ramazan Acun. 2007. "Demand for Justice and Response of the Sultan: Decision Making in the Ottoman Empire in the Early 16th Century." *Études balkaniques* 2: 125–48.

Adams, Julia. 1994. "The Familial State: Elite Family Practices and State-Making in the Early Modern Netherlands." *Theory and Society* 23 (4): 505–39.

Adams, Julia. 1996. "Principals and Agents, Colonialists and Company Men: The Decay of Colonial Control in the Dutch East Indies." *American Sociological Review* 61 (1): 12–28.

Adams, Julia. 2005a. *The Familial State: Ruling Families and Merchant Capitalism in Early Modern Europe*. Ithaca, NY: Cornell University Press.

Adams, Julia. 2005b. "The Rule of the Father: Patriarchy and Patrimonialism in Early Modern Europe." In *Max Weber's "Economy and Society": A Critical Companion*, edited by Charles Camic, Philip S. Gorski, and David M. Trubek, 237–66. Stanford, CA: Stanford University Press.

Adıyaman, Ceyda. 2015. "Eski Türkçede Orunç/Urunç: Rüşvet Sözcüğü Üzerinde Bir Araştırma." *Turkish Studies* 10 (16): 1–16.

Afyoncu, Erhan. 2008. "Rüstem Paşa." In *TDV İslâm Ansiklopedisi*, 35: 288–90. Istanbul: Türk Diyanet Vakfı.

Agmon, Iris. 2017. "State, Family, and Anticorruption Practices in the Late Ottoman Empire." In *Anti-Corruption in History: From Antiquity to the Modern Era*, edited by Ronald Kroeze, André Vitória, and Guy Geltner, 251–63. Oxford: Oxford University Press.

Ahmad, Atif Ahmad. 2009. *Islam, Modernity, Violence, and Everyday Life*. New York: Palgrave Macmillan.

Akçetin, Elif. 2021. "Corruption, Security, and Law in Early Qing China." Paper presented at the "Ottoman Corruption" online workshop. November 19, 2021.

Akçetin, Elif. 2023. "Ottoman Corruption: The View from Qing China." Unpublished paper.

Akgündüz, Ahmed. 1987. "1274/1858 Tarihli Osmanlı Ceza Kanunnamesinin Hukuki Kaynakları, Tatbik Şekli ve Men'-i İrtikâb Kanunnamesi." *Belleten* 51 (199): 153–92.

Akiba, Jun. 2005. "From *Kadı* to *Naib*: Reorganization of the Ottoman Sharia Judiciary in the Tanzimat Period." In *Frontiers of Ottoman Studies*, edited by Colin Imber and Keiko Kiyotaki, 43–60. London: I. B. Tauris.

Akiba, Jun. 2021. "Between Law, Custom, and Corruption: Ottoman Judges' Collection of Fees during the Late Eighteenth and Early Nineteenth Centuries." Paper presented at the "Ottoman Corruption" online workshop. November 12, 2021.

Akiba, Jun. 2023. "Farming Out Judicial Offices in the Ottoman Empire, c. 1750–1839." *Bulleting of the School of Oriental and African Studies.* Online access only. doi:10.1017/S0041977X23000940. Last accessed December 19, 2023.

Aksın, Ahmet, and Süha Oğuz Baytimur. 2010. "25 Numaralı Kalbend Defterinin Tanıtımı ve Kalebend Defterlerinin Osmanlı Sosyal Tarihi Bakımından Önemi." In *XV. Türk Tarih Kurumu Kongresi: Kongreye Sunulan Bildiriler. IV. Cilt—I. Kısım*, 793–812. Ankara: Türk Tarih Kurumu Basımevi.

Aktan, Hamza. 2002. "Kazf." In *TDV İslâm Ansiklopedisi*, 25: 148–9. Istanbul: Türk Diyanet Vakfı.

Aktaş, Necati. 1991. "Atik Şikâyet Defteri." In *TDV İslâm Ansiklopedisi*, 4: 68. Istanbul: Türk Diyanet Vakfı.

Aktepe, Münir. 1958. "İstanbul'un Nüfus Meselesine Dair Bazı Vesikalar." *Tarih Dergisi* 9 (13): 1–30.

Aktepe, Münir. 1993a. "Çandarlı Ali Paşa." In *TDV İslâm Ansiklopedisi*, 8: 211–12. Istanbul: Türk Diyanet Vakfı.

Aktepe, Münir. 1993b. "Çandarlı Kara Halil Hayreddin Paşa." In *TDV İslâm Ansiklopedisi*, 8: 214–15. Istanbul: Türk Diyanet Vakfı.

Aktepe, Münir. 1995. "Enverî, Sâdullah." In *TDV İslâm Ansiklopedisi*, 11: 268–70. Istanbul: Türk Diyanet Vakfı.

Aktepe, Münir. 2000. "İpşir Mustafa Paşa." In *TDV İslâm Ansiklopedisi*, 22: 375–6. Istanbul: Türk Diyanet Vakfı.

Alan, Ercan. 2013. "Kadıasker Ruznamçe Defterlerine Göre XVII. Yüzyılda Rumeli'de Kaza Teşkilatı ve Kadılar." *Güney-Doğu Avrupa Araştırmaları Dergisi* 1 (23): 53–97.

Alexander, John. 1999. "Counting the Grains: Conceptual and Methodological Issues in Reading the Ottoman Mufassal Tahrir Defters." *Arab Historical Review for Ottoman Studies* 19–20: 55–70.

Allison, Scott T., David M. Messick, and George R. Goethals. 1989. "On Being Better but Not Smarter Than Others: The Muhammad Ali Effect." *Social Cognition* 7: 275–95.

Altay, Ahmet. 2011. "Klâsik Dönem Osmanlı Siyasetnâme Geleneğine Genel Bir Bakış." *Turkish Studies* 6 (3): 1795–1809.

Anastasopoulos, Antonios. 2013. "Non-Muslims and Ottoman Justice(s?)." In *Law and Empire: Ideas, Practices, Actors*, edited by Jeroen Duindam, Jill Harries, Caroline Humfress, and Nimrod Hurvitz, 275–92. Leiden: Brill.

Appadurai, Arjun. 1986. "Commodities and the Politics of Value." In *The Social Life of Things: Commodities in Cultural Perspective*, edited by Arjun Appadurai, 3–63. Cambridge: Cambridge University Press.

Arafa, Mohamed A. 2012. "Corruption and Bribery in Islamic Law: Are Islamic Ideals Being Met in Practice?" *Annual Survey of International and Comparative Law* 18 (1): 171–242.

Arı, Ferit. 2021. "İlmiye Mesleğinde Ulemâzâde Yükselişine Bir Örnek: Dürrîzâde es-Seyyid Mehmed Tahir ve es-Seyyid Mehmed Arif Efendilerin Kariyer Basamakları." *Uluslararası Tarih Araştırmaları Dergisi* 13 (6): 1713–27.

Arjomand, Said. 1984. *The Shadow of God and the Hidden Imam: Religion, Political Order, and Societal Change in Shi'ite Iran from the Beginning to 1890.* Chicago: University of Chicago Press.

Arjomand, Saïd Amir. 2003. "Medieval Persianate Political Ethic." *Studies on Persianate Societies* 1: 3–28.

Arslantaş, Yasin. 2017. "Confiscation by the Ruler: A Study of the Ottoman Practice of Müsadere, 1700s–1839." PhD diss., London School of Economics and Political Science.

Arslantaş, Yasin, 2021. "The Sale of Public Offices in the Ottoman Empire: An Economic Analysis." Paper presented at the "Ottoman Corruption" online workshop. November 12, 2021.

Ashforth, Blake E., and Vikas Anand. 2003. "The Normalization of Corruption in Organizations." *Research in Organizational Behavior* 25: 1–52.

Ashraf, Assef. 2016. "The Politics of Gift Exchange in Early Qajar Iran, 1785–1834." *Comparative Studies in Society and History* 58 (2): 550–76.

Atar, Fahrettin. 2001. "Kadı." In *TDV İslâm Ansiklopedisi*, 24: 66–9. Istanbul: Türk Diyanet Vakfı.

Atçıl, Abdurrahman. 2009. "The Route to the Top in the Ottoman Ilmiye Hierarchy of the Sixteenth Century." *Bulletin of the School of Oriental and African Studies* 72 (3): 489–512.

Atçıl, Abdurrahman. 2017. *Scholars and Sultans in the Early Modern Ottoman Empire*. Cambridge: Cambridge University Press.

Atik, Kayhan. 2019. "Osmanlı Bürokratlarının Padişaha Sunduğu Hediyeler." *Uluslararası Sosyal Araştırmalar Dergisi* 12 (65): 166–76.

Atik, Sefa. 2021. "Hanefî Fakih İbn Nüceym'in Risâleleri Üzerine." *Diyanet İlmî Dergi* 57: 205–40.

Ayar, Talip. 2011–12. "Osmanlı Dönemi Fetva Hizmetlerinde Etkin Bir Birim: Fetva Eminliği." *bilimname* 21: 159–77.

Ayar, Talip. 2012. "Osmanlı Devlet Teşkilatında Fetvâ Eminlerinin Görevleri." *Atatürk Üniversitesi İlahiyat Fakültesi Dergisi* 38: 403–21.

Ayar, Talip. 2014. *Osmanlı Devleti'nde Fetvâ Eminliği (1826–1922)*. Ankara: Diyanet İşleri Başkanlığı Yayınları, 2014.

Aydın, Melikşah. 2020. "Osmanlı Yargılama Hukukunda Tanıklık." PhD diss., Selçuk University, Konya.

Aykan, Yavuz. 2016. *Rendre la justice à Amid: Procédures, acteurs et doctrines dans le contexte ottoman du XVIIIème siècle*. Leiden: Brill.

Aykan, Yavuz. 2021. "On Bribery and Confiscation: Revisiting the Case of Kira, the Jew (April 1, 1600)." Unpublished paper.

Aykanat, Mehmet. 2018. "Klasik Dönemde Osmanlı Devletinde Hâkim Adaylığı: Mülâzemet." *Türkiye Adalet Akademisi Dergisi* 9 (34): 165–88.

Aylmer, Gerald E. 1973. *The State's Servants: The Civil Service of the English Republic 1649–1660*. London and Boston: Routledge & Kegan Paul.

Ayoub, Samy. 2016. "'The Sulṭān Says': State Authority in the Late Ḥanafī Tradition." *Islamic Law and Society* 23: 239–78.

Ayoub, Samy. 2020. *Law, Empire, and the Sultan: Ottoman Imperial Authority and Late Hanafi Jurisprudence*. Oxford Islamic Legal Studies.

Bacqué-Grammont, Jean-Louis (1979) "Notes et documents sur Dîvâne Hüsrev Paşa." *Rocznik Orientalistyczny* 41 (1): 21–55.

Badawi, Elsaid M., and Muhammad Abdel Haleem, eds. 2008. *Arabic-English Dictionary of Qur'anic Usage*. Leiden: Brill.

Bălan, Sergiu. 2012. "Substantivism, Culturalism and Formalism in Economic Anthropology." *Cogito: Multicultural Research Journal* 2: 27–36. http://cogito.ucdc.ro/2012/vol4n2/en/4_substantivism-culturalism-and-formalism-in-economic-anthropology.pdf.

Balla, Eliana, and Noel D. Johnson. 2009. "Fiscal Crisis and Institutional Change in the Ottoman Empire and France." *Journal of Economic History* 69 (3): 809–45.

Bandura, Albert, Bill Underwood, and Michael E. Fromson. 1975. "Disinhibition of Aggression through Diffusion of Responsibility and Dehumanization of Victims." *Journal of Research in Personality* 9: 253–69.

Banerjee, Abhijit, Rema Hanna, and Sendhil Mullainathan. 2013. "Corruption." In *The Handbook of Organizational Economics*, edited by Robert Gibbons and John Robert, 1109–47. Princeton: Princeton University Press.
Barcham, Manuhuia, Barry Hindess, and Peter Larmour, eds. 2012. *Corruption: Expanding the Focus*. Canberra: ANU E Press.
Bardakoğlu, Ali. 2016. "Hediye." In *TDV İslâm Ansiklopedisi*, 1: 151–5. Istanbul: Türk Diyanet Vakfı.
Bardhan, Pranab. 1997. "Corruption and Development: A Review of Issues." *Journal of Economic Literature* 35 (3): 1320–46.
Barkan, Ömer Lütfi. 1943. *XV ve XVIıncı Asırlarda Osmanlı İmparatorluğunda Zirai Ekonominin Hukuki ve Mali esasları: Kanunlar*. Istanbul: Burhaneddin Matbaası.
Barkan, Ömer Lütfi. 1952. "Kanunnameler." In *İslam Ansiklopedisi*, 6: 185–95. Ankara: Milli Eğitim Bakanlığı Yayınevi.
Barkey, Karen. 1994. *Bandits and Bureaucrats: The Ottoman Route to State Centralization*. Ithaca, NY: Cornell University Press.
Barkey, Karen. 2008. *Empire of Difference: The Ottomans in Comparative Perspective*. Cambridge: Cambridge University Press.
Barkey, Karen. 2014. "Political Legitimacy and Islam in the Ottoman Empire: Lessons Learned." *Philosophy and Social Criticism* 40 (4–5): 469–77.
Barkey, Karen. 2016. "The Ottoman Empire (1299–1923): The Bureaucratization of Patrimonial Authority." In *Empires and Bureaucracy in World History: From Late Antiquity to the Twentieth Century*, edited by Peter Crooks and Timothy H. Parsons, 102–26. Cambridge: Cambridge University Press.
Başaran, Betül. 2014. *Between Crisis and Order: Selim III, Social Control and Policing in Istanbul at the End of the 18th Century: Between Crisis and Order*. Leiden: Brill.
Başoğlu, Tuncay. 2011. "Ta'zir." In *TDV İslâm Ansiklopedisi*, 40: 198–202. Istanbul: Türk Diyanet Vakfı.
Bayder, Osman. 2022. "İbn Nüceym'in el-Eşbâh ve'n-Nezâir'ine Hamevî Tarafından Yöneltilen Eleştiriler." *bilimname* 48: 535–65.
Baz, İbrahim. 2019. *Kadızadeliler Sivasiler Tartışması*. Ankara: Otto.
Beck, Adrian, and Ruth Lee. 2002. "Attitudes to Corruption amongst Russian Police Officers and Trainees." *Crime, Law and Social Change* 38: 357–72.
Beck, Brandon. 1987. *From the Rising of the Sun: English Images of the Ottoman Empire to 1715*. New York: Peter Lang.
Becker, Gary S. 1978. *The Economic Approach to Human Behavior*. Chicago: University of Chicago Press.
Benson, Michael. 1985. "Denying the Guilty Mind: Accounting for Involvement in a White-Collar Crime." *Criminology* 23: 583–607.
Berkes, Niyazi. 1964. *The Development of Secularism in Turkey*. Montreal: McGill University Press.
Berki, Ali Himmet, ed. 1986. *Açıklamalı Mecelle (Mecelle-i Ahkâm-ı Adliyye)*. Istanbul: Hikmet Yayınları.
Berktay, Halil. 1987. "The Feudalism Debate: The Turkish End—Is 'Tax-vs.-Rent' Necessarily the Product and Sign of a Modal Difference?" *Journal of Peasant Studies* 14 (3): 291–333.
Bevilacqua, Alexander. 2018. *The Republic of Arabic Letters: Islam and European Enlightenment*. Cambridge, MA: Belknap Press of Harvard University Press.
Beyazıt, Yasemin. 2009. "Osmanlı İlmiyye Bürokrasisinde Şeyhülislamlığın Değişen Rolü ve Mülâzemet Sistemi (XVI.–XVIII. Yüzyıllar)." *Belleten* 73: 423–41.

Beyazıt, Yasemin. 2012-13. "Efforts to Reform Entry into the Ottoman Ilmiyye Career towards the End of the 16th Century: The 1598 Ottoman Ilmiyye Kanunnamesi." *Turcica* 44: 201-18.
Beyazıt, Yasemin. 2014a. *Osmanlı İlmiyye Mesleğinde İstihdam (XVI. Yüzyıl)*. Ankara: Türk Tarih Kurumu.
Beyazıt, Yasemin. 2014b. "XVI. Yüzyıl Osmanlı İlmiyye Kanûnnâmeleri ve Medrese Eğitimi." *Belleten* 78 (283): 955-81.
Beydilli, Kemal. 1999. "Küçük Kaynarca'dan Tanzimât'a Islâhât Düşünceleri." *İlmî Araştırmalar*, 8: 25-64.
Bilge, Sadık Müfit. 2015. *Sultanlar, Sipahiler, Köylüler, İktisatçılar: Osmanlı Klasik Çağı'nda (1300-1600) Tarım, Tarımın Vergilendirilmesi ve Vergileme İlkeleri Bakımından İncelenmesi*. Istanbul: Kitabevi.
Blundo, Giorgio. 2007. "Hidden Acts, Open Talks: How Anthropology Can 'Observe' and Describe Corruption." In *Corruption and the Secret of Law: A Legal Anthropological Perspective*, edited by Monique Nuijten and Gerhard Anders, 27-52. Aldershot, UK: Ashgate.
Blundo, Giorgio, and Jean-Pierre Olivier de Sardan. 2006. *Everyday Corruption and the State Citizens and Public Officials in Africa*. London: Zed Books.
Bolat, Kasım. 2012. "Naima'ya Göre Devlet Adamları Arasında Muhalefet." *Tarih Okulu* 13: 89-114.
Börekçi, Günhan. 2021. "On the Power, Political Career and Patronage Networks of the Ottoman Royal Favourites (Late Sixteenth and Early Seventeenth Centuries)." In *Social Networking in South-Eastern Europe, 15th-19th Century*, edited by Maria Baramova, Grigor Boykov, and Ivan Parvev, 17-61. Zurich: LIT Verlag.
Bostan, İdris. 2002. "Osmanlı Donanmasında Kürekçi Temini ve 958 (1551) Tarihli Kürekçi Defterleri." *Tarih Dergisi* 37: 59-76.
Bourdieu, Pierre. 1990. *The Logic of Practice*. Translated by Richard Nice. Stanford, CA: Stanford University Press.
Bourdieu, Pierre. 2002. *The Outline of a Theory of Practice*. Translated by Richard Nice. 16th ed. Cambridge: Cambridge University Press.
Bozkurt, Nebi. 2016. "İltimas." In *Türkiye Diyanet Vakfı İslâm Ansiklopedisi*, 1: 154. Istanbul: Türk Diyanet Vakfı.
Bratsis, Peter. 2003a. "Corrupt Compared to What? Greece, Capitalist Interests, and the Specular Purity of the State." Discussion Paper 8. London: Hellenic Observatory, London School of Economics.
Bratsis, Peter. 2003b. "The Construction of Corruption, or Rules of Separation and Illusions of Purity in Bourgeois Societies." *Social Text* 21 (4): 9-33.
Brentjes, Sonja. 2010. *Travellers from Europe in the Ottoman and Safavid Empires, 16th-17th Centuries: Seeking, Transforming, Discarding Knowledge*. Burlington, VT: Ashgate.
Brockopp, Jonathan. 2003. "Justice and Injustice." In *Encyclopaedia of the Qur'ān*, 3: 69-74. Leiden: Brill.
Buchan, Bruce. 2012. "Changing Contours of Corruption in Western Political Thought, c. 1200-1700." In *Corruption: Expanding the Focus*, edited by Manuhuia Barcham, Barry Hindess, and Peter Larmour, 73-95. Canberra: ANU E Press.
Buchan, Bruce, and Lisa Hill. 2014. *An Intellectual History of Political Corruption*. Political Corruption and Governance. Basingstoke, UK: Palgrave Macmillan.
Burak, Guy. 2015a. "Between the Ḳānūn of Qāytbāy and Ottoman Yasaq: A Note on the Ottomans' Dynastic Law." *Journal of Islamic Studies* 26 (1): 1-23.

Burak, Guy. 2015b. *The Second Formation of Islamic Law: The Hanafi School in the Early Modern Ottoman Empire*. Cambridge: Cambridge University Press.
Çadırcı, Musa. 1997. "Cevdet Paşa'nın Medreselerle İlgili Görüşleri." In *Ahmet Cevdet Paşa (1823–1895): Vefatının 100. Yılına Aramağan*, 79–84. Istanbul: Türk Diyanet Vakfı Yayınları.
Çağman, Ergin, ed. 2010. *III. Selim'e Sunulan Islahat Lâyihaları*. Osmanlı Tarih Kaynakları 11. Istanbul: Kitabevi.
Çakmakçıoğlu, Seda. 2007. *Koçi Bey Risaleleri*. Istanbul: Kabalcı Yayınevi.
Calhoun, Craig ed. 1996. *Habermas and the Public Sphere*. Cambridge, MA: The MIT Press.
Carrier, James G. 1990. "Gifts in a World of Commodities: The Ideology of the Perfect Gift in American Society." *Social Analysis* 29: 19–37.
Carrier, James G. 1991. "Gifts, Commodities, and Social Relations: A Maussian View of Exchange." *Sociological Forum* 6 (1): 119–136.
Carrier, James G. 2018. "Moral Economy: What's in a Name." *Anthropological Theory* 18 (1): 18–35.
Çavuşoğlu, Semiramis. 1990. "The Ḳāḍīzādelı Movement: An Attempt of Şerī'at-Minded Reform in the Ottoman Empire." PhD diss., Princeton University.
Çavuşoğlu, Semiramis. 2001. "Kadızâdelilier." In *TDV İslâm Ansiklopedisi*, 24: 100–2. Istanbul: Türk Diyanet Vakfı.
Çerçinli, Meliha Nur. 2022. "Tanzimat Döneminde Osmanlı Devletinde Sadakat ve Liyakat Kavramlarının Toplumsal Tezahürü (1839–1876)." PhD diss., Yeditepe University, Istanbul.
Çelik, Yüksel. 2006. "Tanzimat Devrinde Rüşvet-Hediye İkilemi ve Bu Alandaki Yolsuzlukları Önleme Çabaları." *Türk Kültürü İncelemeleri Dergisi* 15: 25–64.
Cezar, Yavuz. 1986. *Osmanlı Maliyesinde Bunalım ve Değişim Dönemi: XVIII. yy. dan Tanzimat'a Mali Tarih*. Istanbul: Alan Yayıncılık.
Charrad, Mounira M., and Julia Adams. 2011. "Patrimonialism, Past and Present." *Annals of the American Academy of Political and Social Science* 636: 6–15.
Chauveau, Jean-Pierre, Marc Le Pape, and Jean-Pierre Olivier de Sardan. 2001. "La pluralité des normes et leurs dynamiques en Afrique." In *Inégalités et politiques publiques en Afrique: Pluralité des normes et jeux d'acteurs*, edited by Gerard Winter, 145–62. Paris: IRD, Karthala.
Chibnall, Steven, and Peter Saunders. 1977. "Worlds Apart: Notes on the Social Reality of Corruption." *British Journal of Sociology* 28 (2): 138–54.
Cin, Halil. 1986. *Miri Arazi ve Bu Arazinin Özel Mülkiyete Dönüşümü*. Konya: Selçuk Üniversitesi Yayınları.
Çırakman, Aslı. 2001. "From Tyranny to Despotism: The Enlightenment's Unenlightened Image of the Turks." *International Journal of Middle East Studies* 33 (1): 49–68.
Çırakman, Aslı. 2002. *From the "Terror of the World" to the "Sick Man of Europe": European Images of Ottoman Empire and Society from the Sixteenth Century to the Nineteenth*. New York: Peter Lang.
Çizakça, Murat. 1995. "Cash *Waqfs* of Bursa, 1555–1823." *Journal of the Economic and Social History of the Orient* 38 (3): 313–54.
Collins, Stephanie, and Holly Lawford-Smith. 2021. "We the People: Is the Polity the State?" *Journal of the American Philosophical Association* 7(1): 78–97.
Conklin, John E. 1977. *"Illegal but Not Criminal": Business Crime in America*. Englewood Cliffs, NJ: Prentice-Hall.
Cook, M. A. 1972. *Population Pressure in Rural Anatolia, 1450–1600*. London: Oxford University Press.
Cook, Michael. 2000. *Commanding Right and Forbidding Wrong in Islamic Thought*. Cambridge: Cambridge University Press.

Coşgel, Metin M. 2004. "Ottoman Tax Registers (*Tahrir Defterleri*)." *Historical Methods: Journal of Quantitative and Interdisciplinary History* 37 (2): 87–100.
Coşgel, Metin M. 2005. "Efficiency and Continuity in Public Finance: The Ottoman System of Taxation." *International Journal of Middle East Studies* 37: 567–85.
Coşgel, Metin M. 2013. "The Fiscal Regime of an Expanding State: Political Economy of Ottoman Taxation." Working Paper 2013-28. Department of Economics Working Paper Series. Storrs: University of Connecticut.
Coşgel, Metin M. 2015. "The Ottoman Empire." In *Fiscal Regimes and the Political Economy of Premodern States*, edited by Andrew Monson and Walter Scheidel, 404–28. Cambridge: Cambridge University Press.
Coşgel, Metin M., and Boğaç Ergene. 2014. "'Law and Economics' Literature and Ottoman Legal Studies." *Islamic Law and Society* 21: 114–44.
Coşgel, Metin M., and Boğaç Ergene. 2016. *The Economics of Ottoman Justice: Settlement and Trial in the Sharia Courts*. Cambridge: Cambridge University Press.
Coşgel, Metin M., Boğaç Ergene, Haggay Etkes, and Thomas J. Miceli. 2013. "Crime and Punishment in Ottoman Times: Corruption and Fines." *Journal of Interdisciplinary History* 53 (3): 353–76.
Coşgel, Metin M., Haggay Etkes, and Thomas J. Miceli. 2011. "Private Law Enforcement, Fine Sharing, and Tax Collection: Theory and Historical Evidence." *Journal of Economic Behavior and Organization* 80 (3): 546–52.
Crone, Patricia. 2004. *God's Rule—Government and Islam: Six Centuries of Medieval Islamic Political Thought*. New York: Columbia University Press.
Curta, Florin. 2006. "Merovingian and Carolingian Gift Giving." *Speculum* 81 (3): 671–99.
Dalton, George, ed. 1968. *Polanyi, Primitive, Archaic and Modern Economies: Essays of Karl Polanyi*. Boston: Beacon.
Davis, Natalie Z. 2000. *The Gift in Sixteenth-Century France*. Madison, WI: The University of Wisconsin Press.
Darling, Linda T. 1993. "Formation of the Modern State: The Ottoman Empire Sixteenth to Eighteenth Centuries by Rifaʿat Ali Abou-El-Haj." *International Journal of Middle East Studies* 25 (1): 118–20.
Darling, Linda T. 1994. "Ottoman Politics through British Eyes: Paul Rycaut's 'The Present State of the Ottoman Empire.'" *Journal of World History* 5 (1): 71–97.
Darling, Linda T. 1996. *Revenue-Raising and Legitimacy: Tax Collection and Financial Administration in the Ottoman Empire 1560–1660*. Leiden: Brill.
Darling, Linda T. 2013. *A History of Social Justice and Political Power in the Middle East: The Circle of Justice from Mesopotamia to Globalization*. New York: Routledge.
Darling, Linda T. 2014. "Political Literature and the Development of an Ottoman Imperial Culture in the Fifteenth Century." *Journal of the Ottoman and Turkish Studies Association* 1 (1–2): 57–69.
de Klerk, Jeremias J. 2017. "'The Devil Made Me Do It!': An Inquiry into the Unconscious 'Devils Within' of Rationalized Corruption." *Journal of Management Inquiry* 26 (3): 254–69.
Denny, Frederick. 2001. "Community and Society in the Qur'ān." In *Encyclopaedia of the Qur'ān*, 1: 367–86. Leiden: Brill.
Derrida, Jacques. 1994. *Given Time: I. Counterfeit Money*. Translated by Peggy Camuf. Chicago: University of Chicago Press.
Dikici, Ayşe Ezgi. 2006. "Imperfect Bodies, Perfect Companions? Dwarfs and Mutes at the Ottoman Court in the Sixteenth and Seventeenth Centuries." Master's thesis, Sabancı University, Istanbul.

Dion, Michel. 2010. "Corruption and Ethical Relativism: What Is at Stake?" *Journal of Financial Crime* 17 (2): 240–50.
Doğan, Cem. 2013. "16. ve 17. Yüzyıl Osmanlı Siyasetnâme ve Ahlâknâmelerinde İbn Haldûnizm: Kinalızâde Ali Efendi, Kâtip Çelebi ve Na'îmâ Örnekleri." *Uluslararası Sosyal Araştırmalar Dergisi* 6 (27): 197–214.
Doğan, Hasan. 2017. "İslam Muhakeme Hukunda Ta'dîl ve Tezkiye." *İslam Hukuku Araştırmaları Dergisi* 29: 9–20.
Doğan, Muzaffer. 2002. "Osmanlı İmparatorluğunda Makam Vergisi: Caize." *Türk Kültürü İncelemeleri Dergisi* 7: 35–74.
Doğan, Muzaffer. 2009. "Osmanlı Merkez Bürokrasisinde Genel Maaş Sistemine Geçiş Çalışmaları." *Türk Kültürü İncelemeleri Dergisi* (20): 33–68.
Dörtok Abacı, Zeynep, and Boğaç Ergene. 2022. "The Price of Justice: Revenues Generated by Ottoman Courts of Law in the Late Seventeenth and Early Eighteenth Centuries." *Journal of Near Eastern Studies* 81 (1): 25–52.
Dörtok Abacı, Zeynep, Jun Akiba, Metin Coşgel, and Boğaç Ergene. 2023. "Judiciary and Wealth in the Ottoman Empire, 1689–1843." *Journal of the Economic and Social History of the Orient* 66 (1–2): 43–84.
Douglas, Mary. 2002. "Foreword: No Free Gifts." In Marcel Mauss, *The Gift*, ix–xxiii. London: Routledge.
Drechsler, Wolfgang. 2013. "Three Paradigms of Governance and Administration: Chinese, Western and Islamic." *Society and Economy* 35 (3): 319–42.
Düzbakar, Ömer. 2008. "İslâm-Osmanlı Ceza Hukukunda Rüşvet ve Bursa Şer'iyye Sicillerine Yansıyan Örnekler." *e-Journal of New World Sciences Academy* 3 (3): 532–50.
Düzbakar, Ömer. 2009. "Bribery in Islam-Ottoman Penal Codes and Examples from the Bursa Shari'a Court Records of 18th Century." *Bilig* 51: 55–84.
Düzdağ, M. Ertuğrul. 1972. *Şeyhülislâm Ebussuud Efendi Fetvaları Işığında 16. Asır Türk Hayatı*. Istanbul: Enderun Kitabevi.
Effron, Daniel A. 2016. "Beyond 'Being Good Frees Us to Be Bad': Moral Self-Licensing and the Fabrication of Moral Credentials." In *Cheating, Corruption, and Concealment: The Roots of Dishonesty*, edited by Jan W. van Prooijen and Paul A. M. van Lange, 33–54. Cambridge: Cambridge University Press.
Egmond, Florike. 2001. "*Crooked Justice*: Corruption, Inequality and Civic Rights in the Early Modern Netherlands." *Memoria y Civilización* 4: 43–91.
Eickelman, Dale, and Armando Salvatore. 2004. "Muslim Publics." In *Public Islam and the Common Good*, edited by Armando Salvatore and Dale Eickelman, 3–37. Leiden: Brill.
Eisenstadt, Shmuel. 2002. "Concluding Remarks: Public Sphere, Civil Society, and Political Dynamics in Islamic Societies." In *The Public Sphere in Muslim Societies*, edited by Miriam Hoexter, Shmuel N. Eisenstadt, and Nehemia Levtzion, 139–61. Albany, NY: SUNY Press.
Eisenstadt, Shmuel N. 2006a. "Civil Society and Public Spheres in a Comparative Perspective." *Polish Sociological Review* 2 (154): 143–66.
Eisenstadt, Shmuel N. 2006b. "Public Spheres and Civil Society in Selected Premodern Societies: Some Comparative Observations." *Comparative Sociology* 5 (1): 1–31.
Ekinci, Ekrem Buğra. 2002. "Osmanlı Hukunda Mahkeme Kararlarının Kontrolü (Klasik Devir)." *Belleten* 65 (244): 959–1005.
Elardo, Justin A., and Al Campbell. 2006. "Revisiting the Substantivist/Formalist Debate: A Formal Presentation of Three Substantivist Criticisms." *Research in Economic Anthropology* 25: 267–84.
Eldem, Edhem. 1999. *French Trade in Istanbul in the Eighteenth Century*. Leiden: Brill.

Ellison, James. 2002. *George Sandys: Travel, Colonialism, and Tolerance in the Seventeenth Century*. Cambridge, UK: D. S. Brewer.
Emecen, Feridun. 2005. "Osmanlı Divanının Ana Defter Serileri: *Ahkâm-ı Mîrî, Ahkâm-ı Kuyûd-ı Mühimme* ve *Ahkâm-ı Şikâyet*." *Türkiye Araştırmaları Literatür Dergisi* 3 (5): 107–39.
Emich, Birgit. 2020. "The Cardinal Nephew." In *A Companion to the Early Modern Cardinal*, edited by Mary Hollingsworth, Miles Pattenden, and Arnold Witte, 71–87. Leiden: Brill.
Engels, Jens Ivo. 2018. "Corruption and Anticorruption in the Era of Modernity and Beyond." In *Anti-corruption in History: From Antiquity to the Modern Era*, edited by Ronald Kroeze, André Vitória, and Guy Geltner, 167–80. Oxford: Oxford University Press.
Engels, Jens Ivo, and Frédéric Monier. 2021. "Colonial and Corruption History: Conclusions and Future Research Perspectives." In *Corruption, Empire and Colonialism in the Modern Era: A Global Perspective*, edited by Ronald Kroeze, Pol Dalmau, and Frédéric Monier, 339–56. Singapore: Palgrave Macmillan.
Erdoğan, Mert Can. 2018. "XVI. ve XVII. Yüzyıl Osmanlı Nasihathanemelerinde Ulema-Ümera İlişkisine Yönelik Eleştiri ve Öneriler." In *Osmanlı Medreseleri: Eğitim, Yönetim ve Finans*, edited by Fuat Aydın, Mahmut Zengin, Kübra Cevherli, and Yunus Kaymaz, 689–705. Istanbul: Mahya Yayıncılık.
Ergene, Boğaç. 2001. "On Ottoman Justice: Interpretations in Conflict (16th–18th Century)." *Islamic Law and Society* 8 (1): 52–87.
Ergene, Boğaç. 2003. *Local Court, Provincial Society and Justice in the Ottoman Empire: Legal Practice and Dispute Resolution in Çankırı and Kastamonu (1652–1744)*. Boston: Brill.
Ergene, Boğaç. 2004. "Pursuing Justice in an Islamic Context: Dispute Resolution in Ottoman Courts of Law." *Political and Legal Anthropology Review* 27 (1): 51–71.
Ergene, Boğaç. 2014. "Qanun and Sharia." In *The Ashgate Research Companion to Islamic Law*, edited by Ruud Peters and Peri Bearman, 109–22. Burlington, VT: Ashgate.
Ergene, Boğaç. 2020. "On Ottoman Early Modernity." *Journal of the Ottoman and Turkish Studies Association* 7 (1): 24–6.
Ergene, Boğaç, and Atabey Kaygun. 2011. "Intergenerational Mobility in the Ottoman Empire: Observations from Eighteenth-Century Kastamonu." *History of the Family* 16 (1): 30–46.
Erim, Neşe 1984. "Osmanlı İmparatorluğunda Kalebendlik Cezası ve Suçluların Sınıflandırılması Üzerine Bir Deneme." *Osmanlı Araştırmaları* 4: 79–88.
Erkal, Mehmet. 2013. "Zekat." In *TDV İslâm Ansiklopedisi*, 44: 197–207. Istanbul: Türk Diyanet Vakfı.
Ermiş, Fatih. 2014. *A History of Ottoman Economic Thought: Developments before the Nineteenth Century*. Abingdon, UK: Routledge.
Faroqhi, Suraiya. 1986. "Political Initiatives 'From the Bottom Up' in the Sixteenth- and Seventeenth-Century Ottoman Empire: Some Evidence for Their Existence." In *Osmanistische Studien zur Wirtschafts- und Sozialgeschichte: In Memoriam Vančo Boškov*, edited by Hans Georg Majer, 24–33. Wiesbaden: Harrassowitz Verlag.
Faroqhi, Suraiya. 1992. "Political Activity among Ottoman Taxpayers and the Problem of Sultanic Legitimation (1570–1650)." *Journal of the Economic and Social History of the Orient* 35 (1): 1–39.

Faroqhi, Suraiya. 1993. "Mühimme Defterleri." In *Encyclopedia of Islam*, 2nd ed., 7: 470–2. Leiden: Brill.
Faroqhi, Suraiya. 1998. "Migration into Eighteenth-Century 'Greater Istanbul' as Reflected in the Kadı Registers of Eyüp." *Turcica* 30: 163–83.
Faroqhi, Suraiya. 2000. *Approaching Ottoman History: An Introduction to the Sources*. Cambridge: Cambridge University Press.
Ferguson, Heather L. 2010. "Genres of Power: Constructing a Discourse of Decline in Ottoman *Nasihatname*." *Archivum Ottomanicum* 35: 81–116.
Ferguson, Heather L. 2018. *The Proper Order of Things: Language, Power and Law in Ottoman Administrative Discourses*. Stanford: Stanford University Press.
Feyzioğlu, Hamiyet Sezer, and Selda Kılıç. 2005. "Tanzimat Arifesinde Kadılık-Naiplik Kurumu." *Tarih Araştırmaları Dergisi* 24 (38): 31–53.
Findley, Carter V. 1980a. *Bureaucratic Reform in the Ottoman Empire*. Princeton, NJ: Princeton University Press.
Findley, Carter V. 1980b. "Patrimonial Household Organization and Factional Activity in the Ottoman Ruling Class." In *Türkiye'nin Sosyal ve Ekonomic Tarihi (1071–1920)*, edited by Osman Okyar and Halil İnalcık, 227–35. Ankara: Meteksan.
Findley, Carter V. 1989. *Ottoman Civil Officialdom*. Princeton, NJ: Princeton University Press.
Findley, Carter V. 2006. "Political Culture and the Great Households." In *The Cambridge History of Turkey*, edited by Suraiya Faroqhi, 3: 65–80. Cambridge: Cambridge University Press.
Findley, Carter. 2019. *Enlightening Europe on Islam and the Ottomans: Mouradgea d'Ohsson and His Masterpiece*. Leiden: Brill.
Finkel, Caroline. 2005. *Osman's Dream: The History of the Ottoman Empire 1300–1923*. New York: Basic Books.
Fleischer, Cornell H. 1986. *Bureaucrat and Intellectual in the Ottoman Empire: The Historian Mustafa Âli (1541–1600)*. Princeton, NJ: Princeton University Press.
Fleischer, Cornell H. 1994. "Between the Lines: Realities of Scribal Life in the Sixteenth Century." In *Studies in Ottoman History in Honour of Professor V. L. Ménage*, edited by Colin Heywood and Colin Imber, 45–62. Istanbul: Isis Press.
Floor, Willem. 2001. "Gift Giving v. in the Qajar Period." In *Encyclopædia Iranica*, 10: 615–17. New York: Encyclopædia Iranica Foundation. http://www.iranicaonline.org/articles/gift-giving-v. Last accessed 30 July 2020.
Fodor, Pál. 1995. "How to Forge Documents? (A Case of Corruption within the Ottoman Bureaucracy around 1590)." *Acta Orientalia Academiae Scientiarum Hungaricae* 48 (3): 383–9.
Fodor, Pál. 2018. *The Business of State: Ottoman Finance Administration and the Ruling Elites in Transition (1580s–1615)*. Berlin: Klaus Schwarz Verlag.
Foucault, Michel. 1981. "The Order of Discourse." In *Untying the Text: A Post-structuralist Reader*, edited by Robert Young, 48–78. London: Routledge & Kegan Paul.
Foucault, Michel. 2002. *The Archeology of Knowledge*. New York: Routledge.
Frierson, Elizabeth. 2004. "Gender, Consumption, and Patriotism: The Emergence of an Ottoman Public Sphere." In *Public Islam and the Common Good*, edited by Armando Salvatore and Dale Eickelman, 99–125. Leiden: Brill.
Fritsche, Immo. 2002. "Account Strategies for the Violation of Social Norms: Integration and Extension of Sociological and Social Psychological Typologies." *Journal for the Theory of Social Behaviour* 32 (4): 371–94.

Fritsche, Immo. 2005. "Predicting Deviant Behavior by Neutralization: Myths and Findings." *Deviant Behavior* 26 (5): 483–510.

Fuess, Albrecht. 2009. "Ẓulm by Maẓālim? The Political Implications of the Use of *Maẓālim* Jurisdiction by the Mamluk Sultans." *Mamlūk Studies Review* 13 (1): 121–47.

Furat, Ayşe Zişan. 2017. "XVIII. Yüzyıl Osmanlı Eğitiminde Dönüşüm: Islah mı? Yenilenme mi?" In *Sahn-ı Semân'dan Dârülfünûn'a Osmanlı'da İlim ve Fikir Dünyası (Âlimler, Müesseseler ve Fikrî Eserler)—XVIII. Yüzyıl*, edited by Ahmet Hamdi Furat, Nilüfer Kalkan Yorulmaz, and Osman Sacid Ar, 243-72. Istanbul: Zeytinburnu Belediyesi Yayınları.

Garoupa, Nuno, and Daniel Klerman. 2002. "Optimal Law Enforcement with a Rent-Seeking Government." *American Law and Economics Review* 4 (1): 116–40.

Garoupa, Nuno, and Daniel Klerman. 2004. "Corruption and the Optimal Use of Nonmonetary Sanctions." *International Review of Law and Economics* 24 (2): 219–25.

Garoupa, Nuno, and Daniel Klerman. 2009. "Corruption and Private Law Enforcement: Theory and History." Research Paper LE09-016, Illinois Law and Economics Research Papers Series, University of Illinois College of Law.

Geltner, G., and Maaike van Berkel. 2013. "Fighting Corruption in Premodernity, East and West: A Literature Review." Work Package WP 2. Anti-Corruption Policies Revisited. European Commission. http://anticorrp.org/wp-content/uploads/2013/08/Literature-Review-for-History-of-Medieval-Corruption.pdf.

Genç, Mehmet. 2007. "Osmanlılar: İktisadî ve Ticarî Yapı." In *TDV İslâm Ansiklopedisi*, 33: 525–32. Istanbul: Türk Diyanet Vakfı.

Genç, Mehmet. 2009. "Economy and Economic Policy [in the Ottoman Empire]." In *Encyclopedia of the Ottoman Empire*, edited by Gábor Ágoston and Bruce Masters. New York: Facts on File.

Gerber, Haim. 1994. *State, Society and Law in Islam: Ottoman Law in Comparative Perspective*. Albany, NY: SUNY Press.

Gerber, Haim. 1999. *Islamic Law and Culture, 1600–1840*. Leiden: Brill.

Gerber, Haim. 2018. *Oppression and Salvation: Annotated Legal Documents from the Ottoman Book of Complaints of 1675*. Berlin: Klaus Schwarz.

Gibb, Hamilton A. R. 1962. "Luṭfī Paşa on the Ottoman Caliphate." *Oriens* 15: 287–95.

Gibson, William. 1993. "Nepotism, Family, and Merit: The Church of England." *Journal of Family History* 18 (2): 179–90.

Giladi, Avner. 2002. "Family." In *Encyclopaedia of the Qur'ān*, 2: 173–6. Leiden: Brill.

Graaf, Gjalt de. 2007. "Causes of Corruption: Towards a Contextual Theory of Corruption." *Public Administration Quarterly* 31 (1): 39–86.

Gregory, Chris. 1982. *Gifts and Commodities*. London: Academic Press.

Greiner, Carlos. 2018. "Reassessing the Authorship of the *Dürr-i Meknun*." *Archivum Ottomanicum* 35: 193–212.

Grüne, Niels, and Tom Tölle. 2013. "Corruption in the Ancien Régime: Systems-Theoretical Considerations on Normative Plurality." *Journal of Modern European History* 11 (1): 31–51.

Guardado, Jenny. 2018. "Office-Selling, Corruption, and Long-Term Development in Peru." *American Political Science Review* 112 (4): 971–95.

Gündoğdu, Cengiz. 2009. "Sivâsî, Abdülmecid." In *TDV İslâm Ansiklopedisi*, 37: 286–7. Istanbul: Türk Diyanet Vakfı.

Gündoğdu, İsmail. 2009a. "Osmanlı Tarihi Kaynaklarından Kazaskerlik Rûznâmçe Defterleri ve Önemi." *Uluslararası İnsan Bilimleri Dergisi* 6 (2): 698–722.

Gündoğdu, İsmail. 2009b. "The Ottoman *Ulema* Group and State of Practicing '*Kaza*' Authority during the 18th Century." PhD diss., Middle East Technical University, Ankara.

Gündoğdu, İsmail. 2009c. "Some Observations on the Ottoman Judicial System and *Ilmiye* Group in the 18th Century." *International Journal of Human Sciences* 6 (2): 793–805.

Guo, Li. 2002. "Gift-Giving." In *Encyclopaedia of the Qur'ān*, 2: 313–14. Leiden: Brill.

Gupta, Akhil. 1995. "Blurred Boundaries: The Discourse of Corruption, the Culture of Politics, and the Imagined State." *American Ethnologist* 22 (2): 375–402.

Gupta, Akhil. 2005. "Narratives of Corruption: Anthropological and Fictional Accounts of the Indian State." *Ethnography* 6 (1): 5–34.

Gürbüzel, Aslıhan. 2023. *Taming the Messiah: The Formation of an Ottoman Political Public Sphere, 1600–1700*. Oakland: California University Press.

Habermas, Jürgen. 1991. *The Structural Transformation of the Public Sphere: An Inquiry into a Category of Bourgeois Society*. Translated by Thomas Burger. Cambridge, MA: MIT Press.

Hagen, Gottfried. 2005. "Legitimacy and World Order." In *Legitimizing the Order: The Ottoman Rhetoric of State Power*, edited by Hakan T. Karateke and Maurus Reinkowski, 55–83. Leiden: Brill.

Haldon, John. 1993. *The State and the Tributary Mode of Production*. London: Verso.

Hallaq, Wael B. 2002. "A Prelude to Ottoman Reform: Ibn 'Ābidīn on Custom and Legal Change." In *Histories of the Modern Middle East: New Directions*, edited by Israel Gershoni, Hakan Erdem, and Ursula Woköck, 37–61. Boulder, CO: Lynne Rienner.

Hallaq, Wael B. 2009. *Sharī'a: Theory, Practice, Transformations*. Cambridge: Cambridge University Press.

Hamilton, Gary G. 1990. "Patriarchy, Patrimonialism, and Filial Piety: A Comparison of China and Western Europe." *British Journal of Sociology* 41 (1): 77–104.

Hann, Chris. 2006. "The Gift and Reciprocity: Perspectives from Economic Anthropology." In *Handbook of the Economics of Giving, Altruism and Reciprocity*, edited by Serge-Christophe Kolm and Jean Mercier Ythier, 1: 207–23. Amsterdam: Elsevier.

Harding, Robert. 1981. "Corruption and the Moral Boundaries of Patronage in the Renaissance." In *Patronage in the Renaissance*, edited by Guy Fitch Lytle and Stephen Orgel, 47–64. Princeton, NJ: Princeton University Press.

Hathaway, Jane. 1996. "Problems of Periodization in Ottoman History: The Fifteenth Through the Eighteenth Centuries." *The Turkish Studies Association Bulletin* 20: 25–31.

Heidenheimer, Arnold I., and Michael Johnston. 2002. *Political Corruption: Concepts and Contexts*. New York: Routledge.

Herzog, Christoph. "Corruption and Limits of the State in the Ottoman Province of Baghdad during the Tanzimat." *MIT Electronic Journal of Middle East Studies* 3 (2003): 35–43.

Heyd, Uriel. 1967. "Ḳānūn and Sharī'a in Old Ottoman Criminal Justice." *Proceedings of the Israel Academy of Sciences and Humanities* 3 (1): 1–18.

Heyd, Uriel. 1969. "Some Aspects of the Ottoman Fetvā." *Bulletin of the School of Oriental and African Studies* 32 (1): 35–56.

Heyd, Uriel. 1973. *Studies in Old Ottoman Criminal Law*. Edited by V. L. Ménage. Oxford: Oxford University Press.

Hindess, Barry. 2012. "Introduction: How Should We Think about Corruption?" In *Corruption: Expanding the Focus*, edited by Manuhuia Barcham, Barry Hindess, and Peter Larmour, 1–24. Canberra: ANU E Press.

Hirschman, Albert. 1977. *The Passions and the Interests: Political Arguments for Capitalism Before Its Triumph.* Princeton, NJ: Princeton University Press.
Holmes, Leslie. 2015. *Corruption: A Very Short Introduction.* Oxford: Oxford University Press.
Horne, Andrew. 1895. *The Mirror of Justices.* Edited by William Joseph Whittaker. London: Bernard Quaritch. https://books.google.gr/books?id=h0oKr_7OV28C&dq=Andrew%20horne%20the%20mirror%20for%20justices&pg=PP11#v=onepage&q&f=false.
Howard, Douglas. 1988. "Ottoman Historiography and the Literature of 'Decline' of the Sixteenth and Seventeenth Centuries." *Journal of Asian History* 22 (1): 52–77.
Howard, Douglas. 1995/6. "Historical Scholarship and the Classical Ottoman Ḳānūnnāmes." *Archivum Ottomanicum* 14: 79–107.
Huntington, Samuel. 1968. *Political Order in Changing Societies.* Clinton, MA: The Colonial Press.
Hurstfield, Joel. 1967. "Political Corruption in Modern England: The Historian's Problem." *History* 52 (174): 16–34.
Hurvitz, Nimrod. 2007. *Competing Texts: The Relationship between al-Mawardi's and Abu Ya'la's "al-Ahkam al-Sultaniyya."* Cambridge, MA: Islamic Legal Studies Program, Harvard Law School.
Hurvitz, Nimrod. 2013. "The Contribution of Early Islamic Ruler to Adjudication and Legislation: The Case of the *Mazalim* Tribunals." In *Law and Empire: Ideas, Practices, Actors*, edited by Jeroen Frans Jozef Duindam, Jill Harries, Caroline Humfress, and Nimrod Hurvitz, 135–56. Rulers & Elites 3. Leiden: Brill.
Imber, Colin. 1997a. *Ebu's-Suʿud: The Islamic Legal Tradition.* Stanford, CA: Stanford University Press.
Imber, Colin. 1997b. "Women, Marriage, and Property: Mahr in the Behçetü'l Fetawa of Yenişehirli Abdullah." In *Women in the Ottoman Empire: Middle Eastern Women in the Early Modern Era*, edited by Madeline Zilfi, 81–104. Leiden: Brill.
İnalcık, Halil. 1965. "Adaletnameler." *Belgeler* 2 (3–4): 49–142.
İnalcık, Halil. 1978a. "Ḳānūn." In *Encyclopedia of Islam*, 2nd ed., 4: 558–62. Leiden: Brill.
İnalcık, Halil. 1978b. "Ḳānūnnāme." In *Encyclopadia of Islam*, 2nd ed., 4: 562–6. Leiden: Brill.
İnalcık, Halil. 1980. "Osmanlı Bürokrasisinde Aklâm ve Muâmelât." *Osmanlı Araştırmaları* 1: 1–14.
İnalcık, Halil. 1986. "Maḥkama." In *Encyclopedia of Islam*, 2nd ed., 6: 3–11. Leiden: Brill.
İnalcık, Halil. 1988a. "Adâletnâme." In *TDV İslâm Ansiklopedisi*, 1: 346–7. Istanbul: Türk Diyanet Vakfı.
İnalcık, Halil. 1988b. "Şikâyet Hakkı: ʿArż-i Ḥâl ve ʿArz-i Maḥżar'lar." Edited by İsmail E. Erünsal, Christopher Ferrard, and Christine Woodhead. *Osmanlı Araştırmaları* 7–8: 33–54.
İnalcık, Halil. 1991. "Tax Collection, Embezzlement and Bribery in Ottoman Finances." *Turkish Studies Association Bulletin* 15 (2): 327–46.
İnalcık, Halil. 1992. "Comments on 'Sultanism': Max Weber's Typification of the Ottoman Polity." *Princeton Papers in Near Eastern Studies* (1): 49–72.
İnalcık, Halil. 1993. "State and Ideology Under Suleyman I." In *The Middle East and the Balkans under the Ottoman Empire: Essays on Economy and Society*, 70–93. Bloomington: Indiana University Press.
İnalcık, Halil. 1995. "Resm." In *Encyclopedia of Islam*, 2nd ed., 8: 486–7. Leiden: Brill.
İnalcık, Halil. 2001. "Kanunnâme." In *TDV İslâm Ansiklopedisi*, 24: 333–7. Istanbul: Türk Diyanet Vakfı.

İnalcık, Halil. 2018. *Şâir ve Patron: Patrimonyal Devlet ve Sanat Üzerinde [sic] Sosyolojik Bir İnceleme*. Istanbul: Doğu Batı Yayınları.
İnanır, Ahmet. 2011. *Şeyhülislâm İbn Kemal'in Fetvaları Işığında Kanûnî Devrinde Osmanlı'da Hukukî Hayat*. Istanbul: Osmanlı Araştırmaları Vakfı.
İpşirli, Mehmet. 1988. "Osmanlı İlmiye Mesleği Hakkında Gözlemler, XVI–XVII. Asırlar." *Osmanlı Araştırmaları* 7: 273–85.
İpşirli, Mehmet. 1997. "Nahîfî'nin Nasîhatü'l-vüzera'sı." *Tarih Enstitüsü Dergisi* 15: 15–27.
İpşirli, Mehmet. 2006. "Mülâzemet." In *TDV İslâm Ansiklopedisi*, 31: 537–9. Istanbul: Türk Diyanet Vakfı.
İpşirli, Mehmet. 2010. "Şeyhülislâm." In *TDV İslâm Ansiklopedisi*, 39: 91–6. Istanbul: Türk Diyanet Vakfı.
İpşirli, Mehmet. 2014. "Âlî ve Selanikî: Çağdaş İki Tarihçinin Tenkit Tarzı, Üslubu ve Anlayışı Üzerine Gözlemler." In *Gelibolulu Mustafa Âlî Çalıştayı Bildirileri*, edited by İ. Hakkı Aksoyak, 167–74. Ankara: Türk Tarih Kurumu Yayınları.
İpşirli, Mehmet. 2015. "Mısır Eyaletinin Teşkili Döneminde İki Beylerbeyi Soruşturması." *Marmara Üniversitesi Hukuk Fakültesi Hukuk Araştırmaları Dergisi* 21 (2): 3–19.
İpşirli, Mehmet. 2021. *Osmanlı İlmiyesi*. Istanbul: Kronik.
İpşirli, Mehmet, and Eyyüp Said Kaya. 2020. "Mustafa Efendi, Bâlîzâde." In *Türk Diyanet Vakfı İslâm Ansiklopedisi*, 31: 294–5. Istanbul: Türk Diyanet Vakfı.
Iqbal, Zafar, and Mervyn K. Lewis. 2014. "The Islamic Position on Corruption." In *Handbook on Islam and Economic Life*, edited by M. Kabir Hassan and Mervyn K. Lewis, 283–308. Cheltenham, UK: Edward Elgar.
İşbilir, Ömer. 2019. "Kalebend: Osmanlı Devleti'nde Bir Ceza Türü." In *TDV İslâm Ansiklopedisi*, supplement 2: 5–7. Istanbul: Türk Diyanet Vakfı.
İslamoğlu, Huri, and Çağlar Keyder. 1977. "Agenda for Ottoman History." *Review (Fernand Braudel Center)* 1 (1): 31–55.
İslamoğlu-İnan, Huri. 1994. *State and Peasant in the Ottoman Empire: Agrarian Power Relations and Regional Development in Ottoman Anatolia During the Sixteenth Century*. Leiden: Brill.
Itzkowitz, Norman. 1962. "Eighteenth-Century Ottoman Realities." *Studia Islamica* 16: 73–94.
Ivanyi, Katharina. 2012. "Virtue, Piety and the Law: A Study of Birgivī Meḥmed Efendi's *al-Ṭarīqa al-Muḥammadiyya*." PhD diss., Princeton University.
Ivanyi, Katharina. 2017. "Birgivī Meḥmed." In *Encyclopaedia of Islam*, 3rd ed. Leiden: Brill. http://dx.doi.org/10.1163/1573-3912_ei3_COM_25347. Last accessed December 24, 2023.
Ivanyi, Katharina. 2020. *Virtue, Piety and the Law: A Study of Birgivī Meḥmed Efendi's "al-Ṭarīqa al-muḥammadiyya."* Leiden: Brill.
Izutsu, Toshihiko. 1964. *God and Man in the Qur'an: Semantics of the Koranic Weltanschaaung*. Tokyo: Keio Institute of Cultural and Linguistic Studies.
Jacoby, Tim. 2010. "Turkey and Europe: Culture, Capital and Corruption." *Review of International Studies* 36 (3): 663–84.
Johansen, Baber. 1988. *The Islamic Law on Land Tax and Rent: The Peasants' Loss of Property Rights as Interpreted in the Hanafite Legal Literature of the Mamluk and Ottoman Periods*. London: Croom Helm.
Johansen, Baber. 2002. "La corruption: Un délit contre l'ordre social. Les qāḍī-s de Bukhārā." *Annales: Histoire, Sciences Sociales* 57 (6): 1561–89.
Johnson, Melissa N. P., and Ethan McLean. 2020. "Discourse Analysis." In *International Encyclopedia of Human Geography*, edited by Audrey Kobayashi, 377–8. Amsterdam, Oxford, Cambridge: Elsevier.

Johnston, Michael. 1996. "The Search for Definitions: The Vitality of Politics and the Issue of Corruption." *International Social Science Journal* 48: 321–35.

Kadı, İsmail Hakkı. 2012. *Ottoman and Dutch Merchants in the Eighteenth Century: Competition and Cooperation in Ankara, Izmir, and Amsterdam*. Leiden: Brill.

Kadivar, Mohsen. 2003. "An Introduction to the Public and Private Debate in Islam." *Social Research* 70 (3): 659–80.

Kafadar, Cemal. 1991. "On the Purity and Corruption of the Janissaries." *Turkish Studies Association Bulletin* 15 (2): 273–80.

Kafadar, Cemal. 1993. "The Myth of the Golden Age: Ottoman Historical Consciousness in the Post-Süleymânic Era." In *Süleymân the Second and His Time*, edited by Halil İnalcık and Cemal Kafadar, 45–57. Istanbul: Isis Press.

Kafadar, Cemal. 1995. *Between Two Worlds: The Construction of the Ottoman State*. Berkeley: University of California Press.

Kafadar, Cemal. 1997. "The Question of Ottoman Decline." *Harvard Middle Eastern and Islamic Review* 4 (1–2): 30–75.

Kafadar, Cemal. 2018. "Prelude to Ottoman Decline Consciousness: Monetary Turbulence at the End of the Sixteenth Century and the Intellectual Response." *Osmanlı Araştırmaları* 51: 265–95.

Kaiser, Thomas. 2000. "The Evil Empire? The Debate on Turkish Despotism in Eighteenth-Century French Political Culture." *Journal of Modern History* 72 (1): 6–34.

Kamali, Mohammad Hashim. 2013. "Islam Prohibits All Forms of Corruption." *New Strait Times*, 19 January, Saturday ed., sec. Comment.

Kaptein, Muel, and Martien van Helvoort. 2019. "A Model of Neutralization Techniques." *Deviant Behavior* 40 (10): 1260–85.

Karaca, Filiz. 2007. "Pişkeş." In *TDV İslâm Ansiklopedisi*, 34: 294–6. Istanbul: Türk Diyanet Vakfı.

Karaman, K. Kıvanç, and Şevket Pamuk. 2010. "Ottoman State Finances in European Perspective, 1500–1914." *Journal of Economic History* 70 (3): 593–629.

Kaya, Alp Yücel. 2022. "Üretim Tarzı, Sınıf, Devlet: Solun Türkiye Tarihiyle Sınavı." *Devrimci Marksizm* 50: 159–206.

Kenanoğlu, Macit M. 2013. "Vergi." In *TDV İslâm Ansiklopedisi*, 43: 52–8. Istanbul: Türk Diyanet Vakfı.

Kendall, Gavin, and Gary Wickham. 1999. *Using Foucault's Methods*. London: Sage.

Kerkhoff, Toon. 2012. "Hidden Morals, Explicit Scandals: Public Values and Political Corruption in the Netherlands (1748–1813)." PhD diss., University of Leiden.

Kerkhoff, Toon. 2013. "Corruption in the Netherlands: Changing Perceptions from Early Modern Pluralism to Modern Coherence." *Journal of Modern European History* 11 (1): 88–108.

Kettering, Sharon. 1986. *Patrons, Brokers, and Clients in Seventeenth-Century France*. New York: Oxford University Press.

Khadduri, Majid. 2002. *The Islamic Conception of Justice*. Baltimore: Johns Hopkins University Press.

Kılıç, Cihan. 2019. "Osmanlı İlmiye Teşkilatında Müderrislerin Merâtibi (1245/1829 Tarihli Tarîk Defterine Göre)." *Türkiyat Araştırmaları Enstitüsü Dergisi* 65: 265–87.

Kirk, Alan. 2007. "Karl Polanyi, Marshall Sahlins, and the Study of Ancient Social Relations." *Journal of Biblical Literature* 126 (1): 182–91.

Kırlı, Cengiz. 2006. "Yolsuzluğun İcadı: 1840 Ceza Kanunu, İktidar ve Bürokrasi." *Tarih ve Toplum Yeni Yaklaşımlar* 4: 45–119.

Kırlı, Cengiz. 2015. *Yolsuzluğun İcadı: 1840 Ceza Kanunu, İktidar ve Bürokrasi*. Istanbul: Verita.

Kiser, Edgar, and Xiaoxi Tong. 1992. "Determinants of the Amount and Type of Corruption in State Fiscal Bureaucracies: An Analysis of Late Imperial China." *Comparative Political Studies* 25 (3): 300–31.
Klerman, Daniel. 2007. "Jurisdictional Competition and the Evolution of the Common Law." *University of Chicago Law Review* 74 (4): 1179–226.
Kobas, Tolga. 2019. "Understanding Patrimonial Resilience: Lessons from the Ottoman Empire." PhD diss., Columbia University.
Koç, Mehmet. 2017. "Osmanlı Hukukunda Ta'zir Suç ve Cezaları." PhD diss., Necmettin Erbakan Üniversitesi, Konya.
Koca, Ferhat. 1995. "Fetvahâne." In *TDV İslâm Ansiklopedisi*, 12: 496–500. Istanbul: Türk Diyanet Vakfı.
Köksal, Cüneyd. 2016. *Fıkıh ve Siyaset: Osmanlı'larda Siyaset-i Şer'iyye*. Istanbul: Klasik Yayınları.
Kolbaşı, Ahmet. 2008. "Koçi Bey Risalesi'ne Göre XVII. Yüzyılda Osmanlı İmparatorluğu'nda Devlet-Halk Münasebetlerini Etkileyen Faktörler." *Sosyal Bilimler Araştırma Dergisi* 12 (September): 119–29.
Kolovos, Elias. 2007. "Beyond 'Classical' Ottoman *Defter*ology: A Preliminary Assessment of the *Tahrir* Registers of 1670/71 concerning Crete and the Aegean Islands." In *The Ottoman Empire, the Balkans, the Greek Lands: Toward a Social and Economic History. Studies in Honor of John C. Alexander*, edited by Elias Kolovos, Phokion Kotzageorgis, Sophia Laiou, and Marinos Sariyannis, 201–35. Istanbul: The Isis Press.
Kovaleva, Daria. 2014. "The Trope of Kyra as a Jewish Female Intermediary in the Sixteenth-Century Ottoman Imperial Harem: Theory and Practice, Fiction and History." Master's thesis, Central European University, Budapest.
Köse, Saffet. 1998. "Hiyal." In *TDV İslâm Ansiklopedisi*, 18: 170–8. Istanbul: Türk Diyanet Vakfı.
Köse, Saffet. 2008. "İslam Hukukuna Göre Rüşvet Suçu ve Cezası." *İslam Hukuku Araştırmaları Dergisi* 11: 139–66.
Kroeze, Ronald, Pol Dalmau, and Frédéric Monier. 2021. "Introduction: Corruption, Empire and Colonialism in the Modern Era: Towards a Global Perspective." In *Corruption, Empire and Colonialism in the Modern Era: A Global Perspective*, edited by Ronald Kroeze, Pol Dalmau, and Frédéric Monier, 1–19. Singapore: Palgrave Macmillan.
Kroeze, Ronald, André Vitoria, and Guy Geltner. 2018. "Introduction: Debating Corruption and Anticorruption in History." In *Anticorruption in History: From Antiquity to the Modern Era*, edited by Ronald Kroeze, André Vitoria, and Guy Geltner, 1–17. Oxford: Oxford University Press.
Krstić, Tjiana. 2011. *Contested Conversions to Islam: Narratives of Religious Change in the Early Modern Ottoman Empire*. Stanford, CA: Stanford University Press.
Kunt, Metin. 1974. "Ethnic-Regional (*Cins*) Solidarity in the Seventeenth-Century Ottoman Establishment." *International Journal of Middle East Studies* 5 (3): 233–9.
Kunt, Metin. 1977. "Derviş Mehmed Paşa, Vezir and Entrepreneur: A Study in Ottoman Political Economic Theory and Practice." *Turcica* 9: 197–214.
Kunt, Metin. 1978. *Sancaktan Eyalete: 1550–1650 Arasında Osmanlı Ümerası ve İl İdaresi*. Istanbul: Boğaziçi Üniversitesi Matbaası.
Kunt, Metin. 1981. *Bir Osmanlı Valisinin Yıllık Gelir-Gideri: Diyarbekir, 1670–1*. Istanbul: Boğaziçi Üniversitesi Yayınları.
Kunt, Metin. 1983. *The Sultan's Servants: The Transformation of the Ottoman Provincial Government, 1550–1650*. New York: Columbia University Press.

Kuran, Timur. 2001. "The Provision of Public Goods under Islamic Law: Origins, Impact, and Limitations of the Waqf System." *Law and Society Review* 35 (4): 841–98.
Kuran, Timur. 2004. "Why the Middle East Is Economically Underdeveloped: Historical Mechanisms of Institutional Stagnation." *Journal of Economic Perspectives* 18 (3): 71–90.
Kuran, Timur. 2011. *The Long Divergence: How Islamic Law Held Back the Middle East*. Princeton, NJ: Princeton University Press.
Kuru, Levent. 2016. "Kazasker Ruznamçelerine Göre 18. Yüzyılın İlk Yarısında Rumeli'de Kadılık Müessesesi." PhD diss., Marmara University, Istanbul.
Kuru, Levent. 2020. *Osmanlı İlmiye Tevcihâtı (1693–1725)*. Çanakkale: Paradigma Akademi.
Kuru, Levent, and Kuru Ahmet Önal. 2018. *Osmanlı Kaza Teşkilatı (1078/1667–1668 Düzenlemesine Göre)*. Istanbul: Yeditepe Yayınları.
Kuru, Selim. 2008. "[Review of] Dror ZE'EVI. Producing Desire: Changing Social Discourse in the Middle East, 1500–1900." *Journal of the Economic and Social History of the Orient* 51: 675–96.
Kurz, Marlene. 2011. *Ways to Heaven, Gates to Hell: Fażlīzāde 'Alī's Struggle with the Diversity of Ottoman Islam*. Berlin: EB-Verlag.
Lambton, Ann K. S. 1980. *Theory and Practice in Medieval Persian Government*. London: Variorum.
Lambton, Ann K. S. 1994. "'Pīshkash': Present or Tribute?" *Bulletin of the School of Oriental and African Studies* 57 (1): 145–58.
Lambton, Ann K. S. 2013. *State and Government in Medieval Islam: An Introduction to the Study of Islamic Political Theory: The Jurists*. London: RoutledgeCurzon.
Ledeneva, Alena V. 2013. "A Critique of the Global Corruption 'Paradigm'." In *Postcommunism from Within: Social Justice, Mobilization, and Hegemony*, edited by Jan Kubik and Amy Linch, 297–333. New York: New York University Press.
Ledeneva, Alena, Roxana Bratu, and Philipp Köker. 2017. "Corruption Studies for the Twenty-First Century: Paradigm Shifts and Innovative Approaches." *Slavonic and East European Review* 95 (1): 1–20.
Lewis, Bernard. 1958. "Ottoman Observers of Ottoman Decline." *Studia Islamica* IX: 111–27.
Lewis, Bernard. 1961. *The Emergence of Modern Turkey*. London: Oxford University Press.
Liebersohn, Harry. 2011. *The Return of the Gift: European History of a Global Idea*. Cambridge: Cambridge University Press.
Lindeman, Mary. 2012. "Dirty Politics or 'Harmonie'? Defining Corruption in Early Modern Amsterdam and Hamburg." *Journal of Social History* 45 (3): 582–604.
Lockman, Zachary. 2004. *Contending Visions of the Middle East: The History and Politics of Orientalism*. Cambridge: Cambridge University Press.
Lowry, Heath. 1992. *Studies in Defterology*. Istanbul: Isis Press.
Lowry, Heath. 2003. *The Nature of the Early Ottoman State*. Albany, NY: SUNY Press.
Lowry, Joseph E. 2003. "Lawful and Unlawful." In *Encyclopaedia of the Qur'ān*, edited by Jane Dammen McAuliffe, 3: 172–6. Leiden: Brill.
Lucchini, Ricardo. 1995. "Universalisme et relativisme dans l'approche de la corruption: Réflexions sociologiques." In *La corruption: L'envers des droits de l'homme*, edited by Marco Borghi and Patrice Meyer-Bisch, 47–65. Fribourg: Editions Universitaires Fribourg Suisse.
Mah, Harold. 2000. "Phantasies of the Public Sphere: Rethinking the Habermas of Historians." *Journal of Modern History* 72: 153–82.
Man-Cheong, Iona D. 1997. "Fair Fraud and Fraudulent Fairness: The 1761 Examination Case." *Late Imperial China* 18 (2): 51–85.

Mandaville, Jon E. 1979. "Usurious Piety: The Cash Waqf Controversy in the Ottoman Empire." *International Journal of Middle East Studies* 10 (3): 289-308.
Marcus, Abraham. 1989. *The Middle East on the Eve of Modernity: Aleppo in the Eighteenth Century*. New York: Columbia University Press.
Mardin, Şerif. 1969. "Power, Civil Society and Culture in the Ottoman Empire." *Comparative Studies in Society and History* 2: 258-81.
Markiewicz, Christopher. 2018. "Europeanist Trends and Islamicate Trajectories in Early Modern Ottoman History." *Past and Present* 239 (January): 265-81.
Marlow, Louise. 1997. *Hierarchy and Egalitarianism in Islamic Thought*. Cambridge: Cambridge University Press.
Marsh, Robert. 1960. "Bureaucratic Constraints on Nepotism in the Ch`ing Period." *Journal of Asian Studies* 19 (2): 117-33.
Martel-Thoumian, Bernadette. 2005. "The Sale of Office and Its Economic Consequences during the Rule of the Last Circassians (872-922/1468-1516)." *Mamlūk Studies Review* 9 (2): 49-83.
Martin, Vanessa. 1996. "An Evaluation of Reform and Development of the State in the Early Qājār Period." *Die Welt des Islams*, n.s., 36 (1): 1-24.
Matuz, Josef. 1982. "The Nature and Stages of Ottoman Feudalism." *Journal of Asian and African Studies* 16: 281-92.
Mauss, Marcel. 1990. *The Gift: The Form and Reason for Exchange in Archaic Societies*. Translated by W. D. Halls. New York: W. W. Norton.
Meeker, Michael M. 2001. *A Nation of Empire: The Ottoman Legacy of Turkish Modernity*. Berkeley: University of California Press.
Mélikoff, Irène. 1965. "Germiyān-Oghullari." In *Encyclopaedia of Islam*, 2nd ed., 2: 989-90. Leiden: Brill.
Meloy, John L. 2004. "The Privatization of Protection: Extortion and the State in the Circassian Mamluk Period." *Journal of the Economic and Social History of the Orient* 47 (2): 195-212.
Menchinger, Ethan Lewis. 2014. "An Ottoman Historian in an Age of Reform: Ahmed Vâsıf Efendi (ca. 1730-1806)." PhD diss., University of Michigan.
Meredith, Colin. 1971. "Early Qajar Administration: An Analysis of Its Development and Functions." *Iranian Studies* 4 (2-3): 59-84.
Messick, Brinkley. 2003. "Property and the Private in a Sharia System." *Social Research* 70 (3): 711-34.
Midilli, Muharrem. 2019. *Klasik Osmanlı Ceza Hukukunda Şeriat-Kanun Ayrımı*. Istanbul: Klasik.
Miura, Toru. 1997. "Administrative Networks in the Mamlūk Period: Taxation, Legal Execution, and Bribery." In *Islamic Urbanism in Human History: Political Power and Social Networks*, edited by Sato Tsugitaka, 39-76. London: Kegan Paul International.
Miura, Toru. 2021. "Reconsidering Administrative Networks of Taxation, Legal Execution and Bribery from the Mamluk to the Ottoman Period." Paper presented at the "Ottoman Corruption" online workshop, November 19, 2021.
Moreh, Shmuel. 2003. "Napoleon and the French Impact on Egyptian Society in the Eyes of al-Jabarti." In *Napoleon in Egypt*, edited by Irene A. Bierman, 77-98. Reading, UK: Ithaca Press.
Mörike, Tobias. 2019. "Elias Habesci." In *Christian-Muslim Relations 1500 - 1900*, edited by David Thomas. Leiden: Brill. http://dx.doi.org/10.1163/2451-9537_cmrii_COM_30562. Last accessed December 22, 2013.
Morimoto, Kosei. 2002. "What Ibn Khaldūn Saw: The Judiciary of Mamluk Egypt." *Mamlūk Studies Review* 6: 109-31.

Moseley, K. P., and Immanuel Wallerstein. 1978. "Precapitalist Social Structures." *Annual Review of Sociology* 4: 259–90.
Mottahedeh, Roy. 1980. *Loyalty and Leadership in Early Islamic Society*. Princeton, NJ: Princeton University Press.
Moutafchieva, Vera. 1988. *Agrarian Relations in the Ottoman Empire*. Boulder, CO: Eastern European Monographs.
Muir, Sarah, and Akhil Gupta. 2018. "Rethinking the Anthropology of Corruption: An Introduction to Supplement 18." *Current Anthropology* 59 (18): S4–S15.
Mumcu, Ahmet. 1985. *Osmanlı Hukukunda Zulüm Kavramı (Deneme)*. 2nd ed.. Ankara: Birey ve Toplum.
Mumcu, Ahmet. 2005. *Tarih İçinde Genel Gelişimiyle Birlikte Osmanlı Devleti'nde Rüşvet—Özellikle Adli Rüşvet*. Istanbul: İnkilap Yayınevi.
Mumcu, Ahmet. 2007. *Osmanlı Devleti'nde Siyaseten Katl*. Ankara: Phoenix Yayınevi.
Mundy, Martha, and Richard S. Smith. 2007. *Governing Property, Making the Modern State: Law, Administration and Production in Ottoman Syria*. London: I. B. Tauris.
Mungiu-Pippidi, Alina and Till Hartmann. 2019. "Corruption and Development: A Reappraisal." In *Oxford Research Encyclopedia of Economics and Finance*. Oxford: Oxford University Press. https://doi.org/10.1093/acrefore/9780190625979.013.237.
Murphey, Rhoads. 1990. "Bigots or Informed Observers? A Periodization of Pre-Colonial English and European Writing on the Middle East." *Journal of the American Oriental Society* 110 (2): 291–303.
Murphy, Pamela R., and M. Tina Dacin. 2011. "Psychological Pathways to Fraud: Understanding and Preventing Fraud in Organizations." *Journal of Business Ethics* 101 (4): 601–18.
Mustak, Aykut. 2007. "A Study on the Gift Log, MAD 1279: Making Sense of Gift-Giving in the Eighteenth Century Ottoman Society." Master's thesis, Boğaziçi University, Istanbul.
Nasr, Seyyed Hossein, Caner Dağlı, Maria M. Dakake, Joseph E. B. Lumbard, and Mohammed Rustom, eds. 2015. *The Study Quran: A New Translation and Edition*. New York: HarperCollins.
Ni, Shawn, and Pham Hoang Van. 2006. "High Corruption Income in Ming and Qing China." *Journal of Development Economics* 81 (2): 316–36.
Nielsen, Jørgen S. 1985. *Secular Justice in an Islamic State: Maẓālim under Baḥrī Mamlūks 662/1264–789/1387*. Istanbul: Nederlands Historisch-Archeologisch Instituut.
Nielsen, Jørgen S. 1990. "Maẓālim." In *Encyclopaedia of Islam*, 2nd ed., 6: 933–5. Leiden: Brill.
Niyazioğlu, Aslı. 2007. "On Altıncı Yüzyıl Sonunda Osmanlı'da Kadılık Kabusu ve Nihânî'nin Rüyası." "In Memoriam; Şinasi Tekin II," edited by Yücel Dağlı, Yorgos Dedes, and Selim S. Kuru. Special issue, *Journal of Turkish Studies* 31 (2): 133–43.
Nizri, Michael. 2014. *Ottoman High Politics and the Ulema Household*. Basingstoke, UK: Palgrave Macmillan.
Nizri, Michael. 2016. "Rethinking Center-Periphery Communication in the Ottoman Empire: The Kapı-Kethüdası." *Journal of the Economic and Social History of the Orient* 59 (3): 473–98.
Noonan, John T. 1984. *Bribes: The Intellectual History of a Moral Idea*. Berkeley: University of California Press.
Nye, Joseph. 1967. "Corruption and Political Development: A Cost-Benefit Analysis." *American Political Science Review* 61 (2): 417–27.
Ocak, Ahmet Yaşar. 2002. "Klasik Dönem Osmanlı Düşünce Hayatı." In *Türkler Ansiklopedisi*, edited by Hasan Celal Güzel, Kemal Çiçek, and Salim Koca, 11: 10–29. Ankara: Yeni Türkiye Yayınları.

Oğuz, Gülser. 2014. "Tereke Kayıtlarının Güvenilirliği ve Kadıların Mirastan Mal Kaçırma Yöntemleri." *Turkish Studies* 9 (1): 409-26.
Oktay, Ayşe Sıdıka. 1998. "Kınalızâde Ali Efendi ve Ahlâk-ı Alâî." PhD diss., Marmara University, Istanbul.
Okumuş, Ejder. 1999. "İbn Haldun ve Osmanlı'da çöküş tartışmaları." *Dîvân* 4 (6): 183-209.
Okur Gümrükçüoğlu, Saliha. 2012. "Şikâyet Defterlerine Göre Osmanlı Teb'asının Şikâyetleri." *Ankara Üniversitesi Hukuk Fakültesi Dergisi* 61 (1): 175-206.
Olivier de Sardan, Jean-Pierre. 1996. "L'economie morale de la corruption en Afrique." *Politique Africaine* 63: 99-116.
Olivier de Sardan, Jean-Pierre. 1999. "A Moral Economy of Corruption in Africa?" *Journal of Modern African Studies* 37 (1): 25-52.
Olnon, Merlijn. 2000. "Towards Classifying *Avania*s: A Study of Two Cases involving the English and Dutch Nations in Seventeenth-Century Izmir." In *Friends and Rivals in the East: Studies in Anglo-Dutch Relations in the Levant from the Seventeenth to the Early Nineteenth Century*, edited by Alastair Hamilton, Alexander de Groot, and Maurits van den Boogert, 157-86. Leiden: Brill.
Olson, Carl. 2002. "Excess, Time, and the Pure Gift: Postmodern Transformations of Marcel Mauss' Theory." *Method and Theory in the Study of Religion* 14 (3-4): 350-74.
Önal, Sevda. 2008. "Edebi Metinlere Yansıyan Yönüyle Osmanlı Toplumunda Hediyeleşme." *Atatürk Üniversitesi, Sosyal Bilimler Enstitüsü Dergisi* 11 (1): 103-13.
Osrecki, Fran. 2017. "A Short History of the Sociology of Corruption: The Demise of Counter-Intuitivity and the Rise of Numerical Comparisons." *The American Sociologist* 48 (1): 103-25.
Öz, Mehmet. 1999. "Klasik Dönem Osmanlı Siyasi Düşüncesi: Tarihi Temeller ve Ana İlkeler." *İslami Araştırmalar Dergisi* 12 (1): 27-33.
Öz, Mehmet. 2010. "Tahrir." In *TDV İslâm Ansiklopedisi*, 39: 425-9. Istanbul: Türk Diyanet Vakfı.
Özcan, Abdülkadir. 1989. "Küçük Ahmed Paşa." In *TDV İslâm Ansiklopedisi*, 2: 113-14. Istanbul: Türk Diyanet Vakfı.
Özcan, Abdülkadir. 2004. "Merzifonlu Kara Mustafa Paşa." In *TDV İslâm Ansiklopedisi*, 29: 246-9. Istanbul: Türk Diyanet Vakfı.
Özcan, Almıla Gökçe. 2008. "Kâtip Çelebi'nin Düsturü'l-Amel li-Islâhi'l-Halel ve Defterdar Sarı Mehmed Paşa'nın 'Nesâyihü'l-Vüzerâ ve'l-Ümerâ' Adlı Eserlerine Göre Osmanlı Yönetim Anlayışı ve Toplum Düzeni." Master's thesis, Gazi Üniversitesi, Ankara.
Özdeğer, Mehtap. 2007. "Kıbrıs'ta Malî Kaynaklı Bir İsyan Girişim: Muhassıl Çil Osman Ağa Vak'ası ve Tahkikatı (1764-1765)." *Türk Dünyası Araştırmaları* 171: 47-68.
Özel, Ahmet. 1999. "İbn Nüceym, Zeynüddin." In *TDV İslâm Ansiklopedisi*, 20: 236-7. Istanbul: Türk Diyanet Vakfı.
Özel, Oktay. 2016. *The Collapse of Rural Order in Ottoman Anatolia: Amasya 1576-1643*. The Ottoman Empire and Its Heritage: Politics, Society and Economy 61. Leiden: Brill.
Özen, Şükrü. 2008. "Sadrüşşeria." In *TDV İslâm Ansiklopedisi*, 35: 427-41. Istanbul: Türk Diyanet Vakfı
Özkaya, Yücel. 1981-2. "Osmanlı İmparatorluğu'nda XVIII. Yüzyılda Göç Sorunu." *Dil ve Tarih Coğrafya Fakültesi Tarih Araştırmaları Dergisi*, 171-208.
Özkul, Osman. 2018. "Osmanlı İlmiye Sistemine İçerden Bir Eleştiri: Kazasker Tatarcık Abdullah Molla'nın Layihasının Analizi." *Tarih Okulu Dergisi* 11 (34): 233-46.
Özmucur, Süleyman, and Şevket Pamuk. 2002. "Real Wages and Standards of Living in the Ottoman Empire 1489-1941." *Journal of Economic History* 62: 293-321.

Pamuk, Şevket. 2000. *A Monetary History of the Ottoman Empire*. Cambridge: Cambridge University Press.
Pamuk, Şevket. 2004. "Institutional Change and the Longevity of the Ottoman Empire, 1500–1800." *Journal of Interdisciplinary History* 35 (2): 225–47.
Panoff, Michel. 1970. "Marcel Mauss's *The Gift* Revisited." *Man*, n.s., 5 (1): 60–70.
Pardo, Italo. 2013. "Who Is Corrupt? Anthropological Reflections on the Moral, the Criminal and the Borderline." *Human Affairs* 23 (2): 124–47.
Park, Nancy E. 1997. "Corruption in Eighteenth-Century China." *Journal of Asian Studies* 56 (4): 967–1005.
Parry, Jonathan. 1986. "*The Gift*, the Indian Gift and the 'Indian Gift.'" *Man*, n.s., 21 (3): 453–73.
Peck, Linda L. 1993. *Court Patronage and Corruption in Early Stuart England*. London: Routledge.
Peirce, Leslie. 2003. *Morality Tales: Law and Gender in the Ottoman Court of Aintab*. Berkeley and Los Angeles: University of California Press.
Peters, Rudolph. 1997. "Shahid." In *Encyclopedia of Islam*, 2nd ed., 9: 297–8. Leiden: Brill.
Peters, Rudolph. 2005. *Crime and Punishment in Islamic Law: Theory and Practice from the Sixteenth to the Twenty-First Century*. Cambridge: Cambridge University Press.
Philp, Mark. 1997. "Defining Political Corruption." *Political Studies* 45: 436–62.
Pierce, Steven. 2016. *Moral Economies of Corruption: State Formation and Political Culture in China*. Durham and London: Duke University Press.
Polanyi, Karl. 2001. *The Great Transformation: The Political and Economic Origins of Our Time*. 2nd ed. Boston: Beacon.
Powers, David S. 1992. "On Judicial Review in Islamic Law." *Law and Society Review* 26 (2): 315–42.
Powers, David S. 2007. "Appeal." In *Encyclopedia of Islam*, 3rd ed. Leiden: Brill. http://dx.doi.org/10.1163/1573-3912_ei3_COM_0158.
Prest, Wilfrid. 1991. "Judicial Corruption in Early Modern England." *Past and Present* 133 (November): 67–95.
Quataert, Donald. 2003. "Ottoman History Writing and Changing Attitudes Towards the Notion of 'Decline'." *History Compass* 1: 1–10.
Rabl, Tanja, and Torsten Kühlmann. 2009. "Why or Why Not? Rationalizing Corruption in Organizations." *Cross Cultural Management: An International Journal* 16: 268–86.
Rebstock, Ulrich. 1999. "A Qāḍī's Errors." *Islamic Law and Society* 6 (1): 1–37.
Reed, Bradly W. 1995. "Money and Justice: Clerks, Runners, and the Magistrate's Court in Late Imperial Sichuan." *Modern China* 21 (3): 345–82.
Reed, Bradly. 2000. *Talons and Teeth: County Clerks and Runners in the Qing Dynasty*. Stanford: Stanford University Press.
Reindl-Kiel, Hedda. 2009. "Power and Submission: Gifting at Royal Circumcision Festivals in the Ottoman Empire (16th–18th Centuries)." *Turcica* 41: 37–88.
Reindl-Kiel, Hedda. 2012. "Luxury, Power Strategies, and the Question of Corruption: Gifting in the Ottoman Elite (16th–18th Centuries)." In *Şehrâyîn. Illuminating the Ottoman World: Perceptions, Encounters and Boundaries*, edited by Yavuz Köse, 107–20. Wiesbaden: Harrassowitz Verlag.
Reindl-Kiel, Hedda. 2013. "Osmanlı Yöneticileri, Lüks Tüketimi ve Hediyeleşme." In *İSAM Konuşmaları*, edited by Seyfi Kenan, 137–51. Istanbul: İSAM Yayınları.
Reindl-Kiel, Hedda. 2017. "Kullara Tayın, Efendiye Gümüş Takım: Osmanlı İmparatorluğu'nda Dağıtım ve Bölüştürme Düzeni (16.–18. yüzyıl)." *Yemek ve Kültür* 47: 10–15.

Reinhart, A. Kevin. 2002. "Ethics and the Qur'ān." In *Encyclopaedia of the Qur'ān*, 2: 55–79. Leiden: Brill.
Robinson, Sandra L., and Matthew S. Kraatz. 1998. "Constructing the Reality of Normative Behavior: The Use of Neutralization Strategies by Organizational Deviants." In *Dysfunctional Behavior in Organizations*, edited by R. W. Griffin, A. O'Leary-Kelly, and J. M. Collins, 1: 203–20. Stamford, CT: JAI Press.
Robson, J. 1960. "Bid'a." In *Encyclopedia of Islam*, 2nd ed. 1: 1199. Leiden: Brill.
Rodinson, Maxime. 1973. *Islam and Capitalism*. Translated by Brian Pearce. New York: Pantheon.
Röhrborn, Klaus. 1973. *Untersuchungen zur osmanischen Verwaltungsgeschichte*. Berlin: Walter de Gruyter.
Rose, Jonathan. 2018. "The Meaning of Corruption: Testing the Coherence and Adequacy of Corruption Definitions." *Public Integrity* 20: 220–33.
Rose-Ackerman, Susan. 2010. "Corruption: Greed, Culture, and the State." *The Yale Law Journal Online* 120: 125–40.
Rosen, Lawrence. 2000. *The Justice of Islam*. Oxford: Oxford University Press.
Rosenthal, Franz. 1964. "Gifts and Bribes: The Muslim View." *Proceedings of the American Philosophical Society* 108 (2): 135–44.
Rosenthal, Franz. 1995. "Rashwa." In *Encyclopaedia of Islam*, 2nd ed., 8: 466–7. Leiden: Brill.
Rouillard, Clarence Dana. 1940. *The Turk in French History, Thought, and Literature (1520–1660)*. Paris: Boivin & Cie.
Rubin, Avi. 2011. *Ottoman Nizamiye Courts: Law and Modernity*. New York: Palgrave Macmillan.
Rubin, Avi. 2018. *Ottoman Rule of Law and the Modern Political Trial: The Yıldız Case*. Syracuse: Syracuse University Press.
Rubin, Avi. 2021. "The Positivization of Ottoman Law and the Question of Continuity." In *State Law and Legal Positivism: The Global Rise of a New Paradigm*, edited by Badouin Dupret and Jean-Louis Halpérin, 150–77. Leiden: Brill.
Rubin, Avi, and Iris Agmon. 2021. "Writing History Backwards and Forwards: Thoughts on the Notion of 'Ottoman Corruption.'" Paper presented at the "Ottoman Corruption" online workshop. November 19, 2021.
Rubinstein, W. D. 1983. "The End of 'Old Corruption' in Britain 1780–1860." *Past and Present* 101: 55–86.
"Rüşvet: Alan da Veren de Yanacaktır!" 2013. In *Hadislerle Islam*, edited by Mehmet Emin Özafsar et al., 5: 191–200. Ankara: Diyanet İşleri Yayınları. http://hadislerleislam.diyanet.gov.tr/?p=kitap&i=5.0.196. Last accessed 12 January 2020.
Ryad, Umar. 2015. "Ledine." In *Christian-Muslim Relations 1500–1900*, edited by David Thomas. Leiden: Brill. http://dx.doi.org/10.1163/2451-9537_cmrii_COM_26188. Last accessed December 19, 2023.
Sahlins, Marshall. 1972. *Stone Age Economics*. New York: Aldine.
Salvatore, Armando, and Dale Eickelman. 2004. "Preface." In *Public Islam and the Common Good*, edited by Armando Salvatore and Dale Eickelman, xi–xxv. Leiden: Brill.
Salzmann, Ariel. 1993. "An *Ancien Régime* Revisited: 'Privatization' and Political Economy in the Eighteenth-Century Ottoman Empire." *Politics and Society* 21 (4): 393–423.
Salzmann, Ariel. 2003. *Tocqueville in the Ottoman Empire: Rival Paths to the Modern State*. Leiden: Brill.
Sancisi-Weerdenburg, Heleen. 1989. "Gifts in the Persian Empire." In *Le Tribut dans l'Empire Perse: Actes de la Table Ronde de Paris, 12–13 Décembre 1986*, edited by Pierre Briant and Clarisse Herrenschmidt, 129–46. Paris: Peeters.

Saraçoğlu, Safa. 2021. "Approaching Corruption Indirectly: Impressions Based on 19th Century Codification Processes." Paper presented at the "Ottoman Corruption" online workshop. November 26, 2021.

Sariyannis, Marinos. 2008. "Ottoman Critics of Society and State, Fifteenth to Early Eighteenth Centuries: Toward a Corpus for the Study of Ottoman Political Thought." *Archivum Ottomanicum* 25: 127–50.

Sariyannis, Marinos. 2011. "The Princely Virtues as Presented in Ottoman Political and Moral Literature." *Turcica* 43: 121–44.

Sariyannis, Marinos. 2012. "The Kadızadeli Movement as a Social and Political Phenomenon: The Rise of the 'Mercantile Ethic'?" In *Political Initiatives: "From the Bottom Up" in the Ottoman Empire*, edited by Antonis Anastasopoulos, 263–89. Heraklion, Greece: Crete University Press.

Sariyannis, Marinos. 2013. "Ruler and State, State and Society in Ottoman Political Thought." *Turkish Historical Review* 4 (1): 83–117.

Sariyannis, Marinos. 2015. *Ottoman Political Thought up to the Tanzimat: A Concise History*. Rethymno, Greece: Foundation for Research and Technology-Hellas, Institute for Mediterranean Studies.

Sariyannis, Marinos. 2016. "Ottoman Ideas on Monarchy before the Tanzimat Reforms: Toward a Conceptual History of Ottoman Political Notions." *Turcica* 47: 33–72.

Sariyannis, Marinos. 2019. *A History of Ottoman Political Thought up to the Early Nineteenth Century*. Leiden: Brill.

Savcı Güçlü, Nuray. 1998. "Nâima'ya Göre XVII: Yüzyıl Osmanlı İktisadi Yapısı ve Toplumsal Sonuçları." Master's thesis, Marmara University, Istanbul.

Sawyer, Jeffrey K. 1988. "Judicial Corruption and Legal Reform in Early Seventeenth-Century France." *Law and History Review* 6 (1): 95–117.

Schull, Kent. 2014. *Prisons in the Late Ottoman Empire: Microcosms of Modernity*. Edinburgh: Edinburgh University Press.

Selçuk, İklil. 2021. "Ottoman Market Regulation and Inspection in the Early Modern Period." *ADALYA* 24: 355–74.

Serrano Ruano, Delfina. 2007. "'Amal (Judicial Practice)." In *Encyclopaedia of Islam*, 3rd ed. Leiden: Brill. https://referenceworks.brillonline.com/entries/encyclopaedia-of-islam-3/*-COM_0156. Last accessed January 18, 2020.

Shafir, Nir. 2019. "Moral Revolutions: The Politics of Piety in the Ottoman Empire Reimagined." *Comparative Studies in Society and History* 61 (3): 595–623.

Shaw, Stanford. 1976. *History of the Ottoman Empire and Modern Turkey. Volume I: The Rise and Decline of The Ottoman Empire 1280–1808*. Cambridge: Cambridge University Press.

Shaw, Stanford, and Ezel Kural Shaw. 1977. *History of the Ottoman Empire and Modern Turkey. Volume II: The Rise of Modern Turkey 1808–1975*. Cambridge: Cambridge University Press.

Sheikholeslami, Ali Reza. 1971. "The Sale of Offices in Qajar Iran, 1858–1896." *Iranian Studies* 4 (2/3): 104–18.

Sherry, John F., Jr. 1983. "Gift Giving in Anthropological Perspective." *Journal of Consumer Research* 10 (2): 157–68.

Shigihara, Amanda. 2013. "It's Only Stealing a Little a Lot: Techniques of Neutralization for Theft among Restaurant Workers." *Deviant Behavior* 34 (6): 494–512.

Silber, Ilana F. 2009. "Bourdieu's Gift to Gift Theory: An Unacknowledged Trajectory." *Sociological Theory* 27 (2): 173–90.

Silin, Robert. 1972. "Marketing and Credit in a Hong Kong Wholesale Market." In *Economic Organization in Chinese Society*, edited by William Willmot, 327-52. Stanford, CA: Stanford University Press.
Smart, Alan. 1993. "Gifts, Bribes, and *Guanxi*: A Reconsideration of Bourdieu's Social Capital." *Cultural Anthropology* 8 (3): 388-408.
Smart, Alan, and Carolyn L. Hsu. 2007. "Corruption or Social Capital? Tact and the Performance of *Guanxi* in Market Socialist China." In *Corruption and the Secret of Law: A Legal Anthropological Perspective*, edited by Monique Nuijten and Gerhard Anders, 167-89. Aldershot, UK: Ashgate.
Sözen, Zeynep. 2019. "The Unofficial Gift in Cantemir's History of the Ottoman Empire: Forms and Functions." *Multidisciplinary Research Journal* 11 (2): 39-51.
Stanley, Tim. 2011. "Ottoman Gift Exchange: Royal Give and Take." In *Gifts of the Sultan: The Arts of Giving at the Islamic Courts*, edited by Linda Komaroff, 148-66. Los Angeles: Los Angeles County Museum of Art.
Stefini, Tommaso. 2020. "Justice and Commerce: Ottoman and Venetian Courts in Istanbul during the Seventeenth Century." PhD diss., Yale University.
Stilt, Kristen, and Roy Mottahadeh. 2003. "Public and Private as Viewed through the Work of the *Muhtasib*." *Social Research* 70 (3): 735-48.
Suhara, Manabu. 2004. "Corruption in Russia: A Historical Perspective." In *Democracy and Market Economics in Central and Eastern Europe: Are New Institutions Being Consolidated?*, edited by Tadayuki Hayashi, 383-403. Sapporo: Slavic Research Centre, Hokkaido University.
Sümer, Faruk. 2001. "Karamanoğulları." In *TDV İslâm Ansiklopedisi*, 24: 454-60. Istanbul: Türk Diyanet Vakfı.
Svensson, Jakob. 2005. "Eight Questions about Corruption." *Journal of Economic Perspectives* 19 (3): 19-42.
Sykes, Gresham M. and David Matza. 1957. "Techniques of Neutralization: A Theory of Delinquency." *American Sociological Review* 22: 664-70.
Tabakoğlu, Ahmet. 1986. *Gerileme Dönemine Girerken Osmanlı Maliyesi*. Istanbul: Dergah Yayınları.
Tabakoğlu, Ahmet. 2016. *Osmanlı Mali Tarihi*. Istanbul: Dergah Yayınları.
Taki, Victor. 2011. "Orientalism on the Margins: The Ottoman Empire under Russian Eyes." *Kritika: Explorations in Russian and Eurasian History* 12 (2): 321-51.
Talbot, Michael. 2017. *British Ottoman Relations, 1661-1807: Commerce and Diplomatic Practice in Eighteenth-Century Istanbul*. Woodbridge, UK: Boydell.
Taş, Hülya. 2007. "Osmanlıda 'Şikayet Hakkı'nın Kullanımı Üzerine Düşünceler." *Memleket, Siyaset, Yönetim* 2 (3): 187-204.
Terzioğlu, Derin. 2007. "Bir Tercüme ve bir İntihal Vakası: Ya da İbn Teymiyye'nin *Siyasetü's-şer'iyye*'sini Osmanlıcaya Kim(ler) Nasıl Aktardı?" *Türklük Bilgisi Araştırmaları Dergisi* 31 (2): 247-75.
Terzioğlu, Derin. 2010. "Sunna-Minded Sufi Preachers in Service of the Ottoman State: The *Naṣīḥatnāme* of Hasan Addressed to Murad IV." *Archivum Ottomanicum* 27: 241-312.
Terzioğlu, Derin. 2012-13. "How to Conceptualize Ottoman Sunnitization: A Historiographical Discussion." *Turcica* 44: 301-38.
Tezcan, Baki. 2009. "The Ottoman 'Mevali' as 'Lords of the Law.'" *Journal of Islamic Studies* 20 (3): 383-407.
Tezcan, Baki. 2010. *The Second Ottoman Empire: Political and Social Transformation in the Early Modern World*. Cambridge: Cambridge University Press.

Thornton, Patricia M. 2007. *Disciplining the State: Virtue, Violence, and State-Making in Modern China*. Harvard East Asian Monographs 283. Cambridge, MA: Harvard University Asia Center.

Tiihonen, Seppo, ed. 2003. *The History of Corruption in Central Government*. Amsterdam: IOS Press.

Tillier, Mathieu. 2009. "Qāḍīs and the Political Use of the *Maẓālim* Jurisdiction under the ʿAbbāsids." In *Public Violence in Islamic Societies: Power, Discipline, and the Construction of the Public Sphere, 7th–19th Centuries CE*, edited by Christian Lange and Maribel Fierro, 42–66. Edinburgh: Edinburgh University Press.

Tillier, Mathieu. 2017. "Qadis and Their Social Networks: Defining the Judge's Neutrality in Abbasid Iraq." *Journal of Abbasid Studies* 4 (2): 123–41.

Tillier, Mathieu. 2018. "The Mazalim in Historiography." In *The Oxford Handbook of Islamic Law*, edited by Anver M. Emon and Rumee Ahmed, 357–80. Oxford: Oxford University Press.

Tirole, Jean. 1986. "Hierarchies and Bureaucracies: On the Role of Collusion in Organizations." *Journal of Law, Economics, and Organization* 2 (2): 181–214.

Tor, D. G. 2011. "The Islamisation of Iranian Kingly Ideals in the Persianate Fürstenspiegel." *Iran* 49: 115–22.

Torsello, Davide, and Bertrand Venard. 2016. "The Anthropology of Corruption." *Journal of Management Inquiry* 25 (1): 34–54.

Tosun, Miraç. 2017. "18. Yüzyıl Trabzon'unda Namaz İbadetinin Önemi ve İmamlar." *Karadeniz İncelemeleri Dergisi* 22: 59–71.

Tuğ, Başak. 2017. *Politics of Honor in Ottoman Anatolia: Sexual Violence and Socio-Legal Surveillance in the Eighteenth Century*. Leiden: Brill.

Tuğluca, Murat. 2010. "Osmanlı'da Devlet—Toplum İlişkilerinin Açık Alanı: Şikayet Mekanizması ve İşleyiş Biçimi (1683–1699)." PhD diss., Hacettepe Üniversitesi, Ankara.

Turan, Ahmet Nezihi. 2002. "Bir Pîşkeş Defteri İçin." *Ankara Üniversitesi Osmanlı Tarihi Araştırma ve Uygulama Merkezi Dergisi* 13: 59–74.

Türek, Ahmed, and Fahri Çetin Derin. 1969. "Feyzullah Efendi'nin Kendi Kaleminden Hal Tercümesi." *Tarih Dergisi* 23, 205–18.

Türek, Ahmed, and Fahri Çetin Derin. 1970. "Feyzullah Efendi'nin Kendi Kaleminden Hal Tercümesi." *Tarih Dergisi* 24, 69–92.

Tyan, Emilé. 1960. "ʿAdl." In *Encyclopaedia of Islam*, 2nd ed., 1: 209–10. Leiden: Brill.

Tyan, Emilé, and Gyula Káldy-Nagy. 1978. "Ḳāḍī," In *Encyclopaedia of Islam*, 2nd ed. Leiden: Brill. http://dx.doi.org/10.1163/1573-3912_islam_COM_0410. Last accessed December 24, 2024.

Uludağ, Süleyman. 2010. "Takvâ." In *TDV İslâm Ansiklopedisi*, 39: 484–6. Istanbul: Türk Diyanet Vakfı.

Ünal, Uğur. 2015. *Osmanlı Arşivinde Şeyhülislam Fetvaları*. Istanbul: Başbakanlık Devlet Arşivleri Genel Müdürlüğü.

Ungureanu, Camil. 2013. "Bourdieu and Derrida on Gift: Beyond 'Double Truth' and Paradox." *Human Studies* 36 (3): 393–409.

Uzunçarşılı, İsmail Hakkı. 1988. *Osmanlı Devletinin İlmiye Teşkilâtı*. Ankara: Türk Tarih Kurumu Basımevi.

van Berkel, Maaike. 2007. "Ibn Khaldūn, a Critical Historian at Work: The *Muqaddima* on Secretaries and Secretarial Writing." In *O Ye Gentlemen: Arabic Studies on Science and Literary Culture in Honour of Remke Kruk*, edited by Arnoud Vrolijk and Jan P. Hogendijk, 247–61. Leiden: Brill.

van Berkel, Maaike, 2011. "Embezzlement and Reimbursement: Disciplining Officials in 'Abbāsid Baghdad (8th–10th Centuries A.D.)." *International Journal of Public Administration* 34 (11): 712–19.

van Berkel, Maaike. 2018. "Fighting Corruption between Theory and Practice." In *Anti-Corruption in History: From Antiquity to the Modern Era*, edited by Ronald Kroeze, André Vitória, and Guy Geltner, 65–76. Oxford: Oxford University Press.

van den Boogert, Maurits. 2003. "Consular Jurisdiction in the Ottoman Legal System in the Eighteenth Century." *Oriente Moderno* 22 (83): 613–34.

van den Boogert, Maurits. 2005. *The Capitulations and the Ottoman Legal System: Kadıs, Consuls and Beratlıs in the 18th Century*. Leiden: Brill.

van den Boogert, Maurits. 2007. "Freemasonry in Eighteenth-Century Izmir? A Critical Analysis of Alexander Drummond's Travels (1754)." In *Ottoman Izmir: Studies in Honour of Alexander H. de Groot*, edited by Maurits van den Boogert, 104–21. Leiden: Nederlands Instituut voor het Nabije Oosten.

van den Boogert, Maurits. 2010. "Provocative Wealth: Non-Muslim Elites in Eighteenth-Century Aleppo." *Journal of Early Modern History* 14: 219–37.

van Gelder, Geert. 2001. "Mirror for Princes or Vizor for Viziers: The Twelfth-Century Arabic Popular Encyclopedia '*Mufīd al-ʿulūm*' and Its Relationship with the Anonymous Persian '*Baḥr al-fawāʾid*'." *Bulletin of the School of Oriental and African Studies* 64 (3): 313–38.

van Prooijen, Jan W., and Paul A. M. van Lange, eds. 2016. *Cheating, Corruption, and Concealment: The Roots of Dishonesty*. Cambridge: Cambridge University Press.

van Steenbergen, Jo. 2006. *Order out of Chaos: Patronage, Conflict, and Mamluk Sociopolitical Culture 741–784/1341–1382*. Leiden: Brill.

van Steenbergen, Jo, Patrick Wing, and Kristof D'hulster. 2016a. "The Mamlukization of the Mamluk Sultanate? State Formation and the History of Fifteenth Century Egypt and Syria: Part I—Old Problems and New Trends." *History Compass* 14: 549–59.

van Steenbergen, Jo, Patrick Wing, and Kristof D'hulster. 2016b. "The Mamlukization of the Mamluk Sultanate? State Formation and the History of Fifteenth Century Egypt and Syria: Part II—Comparative Solutions and a New Research Agenda." *History Compass* 14: 560–9.

Valensi, Lucette. 1993. *The Birth of the Despot*. Translated by Arthur Denner. Ithaca: Cornell University Press.

Vanneste, Tjil. 2021. *Intra-European Litigation in Eighteenth-Century Izmir: The Role of the Merchants' Style*. Leiden: Brill.

Varlık, Mustafa Çetin. 1996. "Germiyanoğulları." In *TDV İslâm Ansiklopedisi*, 14: 33–5. Istanbul: Türk Diyanet Vakfı.

Varlık, Nükhet. 2015. *Plague and Empire in the Early Modern Mediterranean World: The Ottoman Experience, 1347–1600*. Cambridge: Cambridge University Press.

Vlami, Despina. 2015. *Trading with the Ottomans: The Levant Company in the Middle East*. London and New York: I. B. Tauris.

Vogel, Frank E. 2003. "The Public and Private in Saudi Arabia: Restrictions on the Powers of Committees for Ordering the Good and Forbidding Evil." *Social Research* 70 (3): 749–68.

Wang, Liping, and Julia Adams. 2011. "Interlocking Patrimonialisms and State Formation in Qing China and Early Modern Europe." *Annals of the American Academy of Political and Social Science* 636 (1): 164–81.

Wedel, Janine R. 2012. "Rethinking Corruption in an Age of Ambiguity." *The Annual Review of Law and Social Science* 8: 453–98.

Werner, Cynthia. 2000. "Gifts, Bribes, and Development in Post-Soviet Kazakstan." *Human Organization* 59 (1): 11–22.

White, Sam. 2011. *The Climate of Rebellion in the Early Modern Ottoman Empire.* Cambridge: Cambridge University Press.

Will, Pierre-Etienne. 2004. "Officials and Money in Late Imperial China: State Finances, Private Expectations and the Problem of Corruption in a Changing Environment." In *Corrupt Histories*, edited by Emmanuel Kreike and William C. Jordan, 29–82. Rochester: University of Rochester Press.

Wolf, Eric. 1982. *Europe and the People without History.* Berkeley: University of California Press.

Wolfinbarger, Mary Finley. 1990. "Motivations and Symbolism in Gift-Giving Behavior." In *NA—Advances in Consumer Research*, edited by Marvin E. Goldberg, Gerald Gorn, and Richard W. Pollay, 17: 699–706. Provo, UT: Association for Consumer Research.

Xin, Katherine R., and Jone L. Pearce. 1996. "*Guanxi*: Connections as Substitutes for Formal Institutional Support." *Academy of Management Journal* 39 (6): 1641–58.

Yan, Yunxiang. 2009. *The Individualization of Chinese Society.* Oxford: Berg.

Yan, Yunxiang. 2010. "The Chinese Path to Individualization." *The British Journal of Sociology* 61 (3): 489–512.

Yanagihashi, Hiroyuki. 1996. "The Judicial Functions of the *Sulṭān* in Civil Cases according to the Mālikīs up to the Sixth/Twelfth Century." *Islamic Law and Society* 3 (1): 41–74.

Yavuz, Yusuf Şevki. 1995. "Fâsık." In *TDV İslâm Ansiklopedisi*, 12: 202–5. Istanbul: Türk Diyanet Vakfı.

Yaycıoğlu, Ali. 2012. "Provincial Power-Holders and the Empire in the Late Ottoman World: Conflict or Partnership?" In *The Ottoman World*, edited by Christine Woodhead, 436–52. Abingdon, UK: Routledge.

Yaycıoğlu, Ali. 2016. *Partners of the Empire: The Crisis of the Ottoman Order in the Age of Revolutions.* Stanford, CA: Stanford University Press.

Yılmaz, Hüseyin. 2003. "Osmanlı Tarihçiliğinde Tanzimat Öncesi Siyaset Düşüncesine Yaklaşımlar." *Türkiye Araştırmaları Literatür Dergisi* 1 (2): 231–98.

Yüksel, Emrullah. 1992. "Birgivî." In *TDV İslâm Ansiklopedisi*, 6: 191–4. Istanbul: Türk Diyanet Vakfı.

Yun-Casalilla, Bartolomé. 2021. "Reflections of an Early Modern Historian on the Modern History of Corruption and Empire." In *Corruption, Empire and Colonialism in the Modern Era: A Global Perspective*, edited by Ronald Kroeze, Pol Dalmau, and Frédéric Monier, 23–43. Singapore: Palgrave Macmillan.

Yurdakul, İlhami. 2021. "II. Abdülhamid Devri'nde Ulemazadenin Dersiamlık ve İstanbul Müderrisliği Ruusu Sınavından Muafiyeti ve Kota İmtiyazı." In *Sahn-ı Semân'dan Dârülfünûn'a Osmanlı'da İlim ve Fikir Dünyası—XIX. Yüzyıl*, edited by Ahmet Hamdi Furat, 73–7. Istanbul: Zeytinburnu Belediyesi Yayınları.

Yurdakul, İlhami. 2022. *İktidarın Ruhu: Osmanlı'dan Cumhuriyet'e Kişizade İmtiyazları (Beşik Uleması, Siyaseten Katl, Müsadere).* Istanbul: İletişim.

Yurtseven, Yılmaz. 2018. "İslam-Osmanlı Muhakeme Hukukunda Şahitlik Müesssesi." *Yıldırım Beyazıt Hukuk Dergisi* 3 (2): 85–139.

Zaman, Muhammad Qasim. 2004. "The 'Ulama of Contemporary Islam and their Conceptions of the Common Good." In *Public Islam and the Common Good*, edited by Armando Salvatore and Dale Eickelman, 129–55. Leiden: Brill.

Zarinebaf, Fariba. 2010. *Crime and Punishment in Istanbul 1700–1800.* Berkeley: University of California Press.

Zarinebaf-Shahr, Fariba. 1996. "Women, Law, and Imperial Justice in Ottoman Istanbul in the Late Seventeenth Century." In *Women, the Family, and Divorce Laws in Islamic History*, edited by Amira El-Azhary Sonbol, 81–96. Syracuse, NY: Syracuse University Press.

Ze'evi, Dror. 2006. *Producing Desire: Changing Sexual Discourse in the Ottoman Middle East, 1500–1900*. Berkeley: University of California Press.

Zelin, Madeleine. 1984. *The Magistrate's Tael: Rationalizing Fiscal Reform in Eighteenth-Century Ch'ing China*. Berkeley: University of California Press.

Zilfi, Madeline. 1983. "Elite Circulation in the Ottoman Empire: Great Mollas of the Eighteenth Century." *Journal of the Economic and Social History of the Orient* 26 (3): 318–64.

Zilfi, Madeline. 1988. *The Politics of Piety: The Ottoman Ulema in the Postcolonial Age (1600–1800)*. Minneapolis: Bibliotheca Islamica.

Zilfi, Madeline. 2006. "The Ottoman *Ulema*." In *The Cambridge History of Turkey*, edited by Suraiya Faroqhi, 3: 209–25. Cambridge: Cambridge University Press.

Index

For the benefit of digital users, indexed terms that span two pages (e.g., 52–53) may, on occasion, appear on only one of those pages.

abuse of power/office
   crimes linked to provincial authorities 96–8
   introductory remarks 93–4
   modern conceptualizations of corruption 98–9
   Quran 32
   role of mazalim 45–6
   rough correspondence among crime categories 99
   state-generated documents 82–3, 93–4
   types mentioned between the fifteenth and seventeenth centuries 94–5
accounts for foreign audiences *see* foreign accounts of corruption
adaletnames 81, 95–6, 98–9, 132
administration of justice
   see also Circle of Justice/Equity; false witnessing; qadis
   degeneration due to prevalence of bribery 255
   favoritism in official documents
      judicial appointments 258
      need to control entry into ilmiye establishment 256–7
      training for and staffing ilmiye positions 259
   foreign accounts of corruption
      advice to protect against against potentially corrupt actors 221–4
      concluding remarks 224
      diverging articulations 224
      false witnessing 213–20
      focus on qadis 208
      litigation fees 210
      prioritization of revenue raising 211–12
      privileging written documentation 219
      gifts as bribes 226
   historiography of corruption 10
   kanunnames as handy guides 114–15
   Ottoman jurisprudence 70–1
   patronage
      degeneration of madrasa education and administration of justice 255
      judgeship appointments based on favoritism 252
   advice literature 27, 144, 156
   appeal to higher loyalties 265–6

Balizade Mustafa Efendi's nepotism 252–3, 266
Birgivi Mehmed Efendi 180–3
bribery
   association with patronage 251–2
   bribe categories according to Ibn Nujaym 58
   commentary between sixteenth and eighteenth centuries
      association of bribery with greed 175
      broader associations of bribery 163
      causal links in corruption 168
      focus on bribery 157–62
      role of ordinary people 162
   gifts as bribes
      ambiguities 225–7
      attempt to distinguish two types of giving 229–31
      concluding remarks 237–8
      distinction based on objectives 225
      economic role of gifts 229
      gift exchanges among the political elite 228–9
      implications of their shared functions 232
      legitimate expectations of reciprocity 225

bribery (*cont.*)
    litigants' offers to the qadis 234–5
    'macro patterns of economic organization' 232–4
    modern Ottoman scholarship 227–8
    reasons to resist strict functional distinctions between different types of gifts 231–2
    relevance of insights on guanxi relations 235–7
    information based on mühimme, şikayet, and kalebend registers 132–4
    Ottoman jurisprudence on qadis' bribes
        Ibn Abidin's views on bribe-induced verdicts 67–70
        Ibn Nujaym's exploration of bribery 52–67
    pre-Ottoman jurisprudential sources 34–6
    pre-sixteenth century texts 151–3
    rationalization of 'legality' 263–4

Circle of Justice/Equity
    complex sociopolitical order 83
    functional tasks and responsibilities according to the Circle 85
    intrinsic notion of justice 85–6
    numerous characterizations of the Circle 84–5
    relationship with Ottoman economics 88–93
    representation of social divisions 83–4
    ruler's inclination to protect the flock 87–90
    wealth generation and extraction 86–8
comparative perspectives 3, 5–6, 20, 239
contextualization 6–7, 15–16
controlling corruption
    conceptual model based on a few key variables
        greater the costs of control, the higher the level of corruption 102
        measurement 102–4
        monitoring 104–9
        sanctions 109–22
    information based on mühimme, şikayet, and kalebend registers
        actors involved in corruption 128
        acts of corruption in mühimme and şikayet registers 133
        broader patterns in the kalebend registers 136–7
        categorizations and classifications of complaints 126–9
        collusion by government functionaries 134
        devrs in mühimme and şikayet registers 143
        direct appeals to imperial center 129–30
        effectiveness of the imperial center's involvement 135
        punishments 135, 137–41
        references to distributive conflicts 131
        references to embezzlement 131–2
        relative preponderance of corruption crimes 130–1
        resolution of complaints 134–5
        targetting of waqf affiliates 130
    review of main arguments 269
corruption
    concluding remarks
        challenge of formulating systematic claims 262
        exploitation of other research disciplines 262–3
        review of main arguments 262, 269
        specific case of Ahmed, the voiceless qadi 261–2, 267–9
    controlling corruption *see* controlling corruption
    foreign accounts of corruption *see* foreign accounts of corruption
    government corruption *see* government corruption
    historiography
        non-Ottomanist scholarship 3–9
        Ottomanist scholarship 9–26
    jurisprudential sources *see* jurisprudential sources
    in jurisprudential works and state-generated texts 100
    justifications of corruption *see* rationalizations of corruption
    modern and premodern perceptions distinguished 1–3
    patronage *see* patronage
    political literature *see* political literature
    state-generated documents *see* state-generated documents

denial of injury 264–5
denial of responsibility 264
denial of victim 265
Derviş Mehmed Paşa as an entrepreneurial administrator 186–8
devr 130, 143, 261
discourses
    broader trends in corruption 183
    causal links among particular grievances 168–9
    classical judicial discourse on corruption 49
    concluding remarks 270–1
    jurisprudential discourses 80–3
    kanunnames, adaletnames, and yasaknames 83
    political discourses 252–3
    sharia- and siyasa-discourses 224
discursive fields 26–7, 79, 144, 225–6, 231–2, 270

Ebussuud Efendi on qadi appointments 60–5
embezzlement
    commentary between sixteenth and eighteenth centuries 163–6
    harmful behaviour in government according to political texts 164
    historiography of corruption 1–2
    information based on mühimme, şikayet, and kalebend registers 123, 125–6, 131–3, 142
    political literature 163–6
    pre-Ottoman jurisprudential sources 32–3, 38–41
    rough correspondence among crime categories 99
evidence
    see also false witnessing
    burden of proof 72–3
    mazalim tribunals 46
    privileging written documentation 219
    punishment of corruption crimes 101–2
    qadis 210–12
    testimonies by false witnesses 41–2, 72
extraction see wealth extraction

false witnessing
    controlling corruption 111
    foreign accounts of corruption 206–8, 213–20, 222–4
    harmful behaviour in government according to political texts 164
    information based on mühimme, şikayet, and kalebend registers 123, 127–9, 132–4, 138–9
    Ottoman jurisprudence 72–7
    pre-Ottoman jurisprudential sources 41–2
    punishments 138–9
    state-generated documents 95
fatwas
    appointments to judgeships based on bribes 250
    bribes offered to get appointed to the position of the qadi 54, 56–7
    bribing third-party interceders 57–60
    charging mahsul 68–9
    Ebussuud's opinion 60–2
    favoritism 71
    fees for fatwas 77
    foreign accounts of corruption 207, 212–13
    Ibn Nujaym's treatise 53–4, 60
    interactions with muftis 64
    legality of payments associated with intercessions 64–5
    seizure of monies and property that belonged to the public treasury 78
favoritism
    see also patronage
    articulations in Ottoman jurisprudence 70–2
    harmful behaviour in government according to political texts 164
    historiography of corruption 1–2, 7, 28
    jurisprudential considerations of favoritism
        concentration of privilege and income in the hands of specific families 247
        qadis 246–8
    in official documents
        approach of Ottoman polity 259
        concluding remarks 260
        judicial appointments 258
        mülazemet system's degeneration 257–8
        need to control entry into ilmiye establishment 256–7
        training for and staffing ilmiye positions 259
    patronage distinguished 239–40
    political literature 163–6

favoritism (*cont.*)
  pre-Ottoman jurisprudential sources 38–9
  rough correspondence among crime categories 99
  state-generated documents 98–9
Feyzullah Efendi's nepotism 253–4
foreign accounts of corruption
  contentious use of sources 192–3
  corruption in administration of justice
    advice to protect against potentially corrupt actors 221–4
    concluding remarks 224
    diverging articulations 224
    false witnessing 213–20
    focus on qadis 208
    litigation fees 210
    prioritization of revenue raising 211–12
    privileging written documentation 219
    two characterizations 205–8
  information about foreign accounts 196
  overview of key points 28
  review of main arguments 270
  systemic factors affecting corruption 195–205
  value of these sources 193–4

gifts
  as bribes
    ambiguities 225–7
    attempt to distinguish two types of giving 229–31
    concluding remarks 237–8
    distinction based on objectives 225
    economic role of gifts 229
    gift exchanges among the political elite 228–9
    implications of their shared functions 232
    legitimate expectations of reciprocity 225
    litigants' offers to the qadis 234–5
    'macro patterns of economic organization' 232–4
    modern Ottoman scholarship 227–8
    overview of key points 28
    reasons to resist strict functional distinctions between different types of gifts 231–2
    relevance of insights on guanxi relations 235–7
controlling corruption 106–7
foreign accounts of corruption 200–2, 210–11
historiography of corruption 5–6, 18–23
Ottoman jurisprudence 62–5, 70–1, 77, 79–80
political literature
  alternative articulations in sixteenth to eighteenth centuries 184
  commentary between sixteenth and eighteenth centuries 166
pre-Ottoman jurisprudential sources 33–4, 36–8
rationalization of 'legality' 263–4
government corruption
  see also controlling corruption
  harmful behaviour in government according to political texts 164
  nonjudicial government corruption in Ottoman jurisprudence 78–9
  state-generated documents
    Circle of Justice and its political economy 83–93
    irreconcilable elements of Ottoman society 82–3
    preamble of the Niğbolu District Kanunname 1516 81–2
    types of abuse of office 93–100
guanxi 235–6

Habermas, Jürgen 24
hadith
  articulations about qadis and their corruption 52–4
  as jurisprudential source
    anxiety regarding gifts 36–8
    bribe-givers and bribe-takers 34–6
    concern with potential conflicts of interest 36
    embezzlement and favoritism 38–9
    foundational source for Islamic law and ethics 34
    unsteady basis for defining acts now linked to corruption 39

INDEX   313

Hırzü'l-Mülük on favoritism 250-1
historiography of corruption
  non-Ottomanist scholarship
    challenges to Western- and market
      oriented development models 4
    Chinese historiography 8
    economic approaches 4-5
    engagement of anthropologists and
      historians 5-6
    focus on political and public office
      corruption 4
    Islamic and Middle Eastern
      settings 8-9
    multiple disciplines 3-4
    shifts in broader connotations of
      concept 7-8
    tension in recent literature 6-7
  Ottomanist scholarship
    division of history into rise, decline,
      and collapse 11-12
    fundamental aspects of premodern
      Ottoman society 9-11
    nineteenth century as era of reform
      and modernization 12
    scholarly literature on modern
      Ottoman history 20-6
    scholarly literature on premodern
      Ottoman history 12-20

Ibn Abidin
  application of fatwas 56-7
  bribe categories according to Ibn
    Nujaym 58
  bribery defined 52
  classification of corruption 56
  compensation for qadis 210-11
  corruption of nonjudicial government
    officials 78-80
  fate of a bribe-taking qadis 67-9
  favoritism 246-7, 252
  gifts and bribes for qadis 63-4
  gifts as bribes 231
  gifts for intercessors 64-5
  gifts to muftis 77
  impermissibility of gifts to other officials 64
  importance of local customs 51
  mahsul payments and subcontracting
    qadiships 69-70
  patronage 247

  qadis who accepted bribes deserve
    dismissal 66
  rationale for focus 52
  status of qadiships 61
  tax farming 68-9
  witness corruption 73-4
Ibn Kemal on qadi appointments 59-62, 65
Ibn Nujaym
  acquisition of amirship 56-7
  bribe categories according to Ibn
    Nujaym 58
  classification of corruption 56
  consequences of bribes to qadis 66-8
  false witnessing 76
  fate of bribe-taking qadis 67-8
  gifts and bribes distinguished 62-3, 65
  gifts and bribes for qadis 64
  gifts as bribes 225, 231
  gifts for intercessors 55, 57-9, 62, 64-5
  legitimate and illegitimate forms of
    reciprocity 79-80
  permissible bribes 57
  qadis who accepted bribes deserve
    dismissal 66
  threats to judge's impartiality 70-1
  treatise on bribery 52-4
ilmiye 245-6
  demand for government positions 173
  differentiation among different
    patronage networks 243-4
  family connections 244
  justifications for patronage 244-5
  relationships involving friends, associates,
    or potential clients 245-6
imperial council
  accusations directed at the qadi of
    Bozöyük 261-2
  appeals from court decisions 220
  gifts as bribes 226-7, 233-4
  petitions to 122-3
  top of the state's bureaucratic-
    administrative setup 10
intisab/intisap 14-15, 242

jurisprudence
  considerations of favoritism
    concentration of privilege and income
      in the hands of specific families 247
    qadis 246-8

jurisprudence (*cont.*)
  Ottoman jurisprudence
    articulations about qadis and their
      corruption 52–71
    corruption in jurisprudential works
      and state-generated texts 100
    corruption of nonjudicial
      government officials in Ibn Abidin's
      work 78–80
    introductory remarks 50–2
    mufti's corruption 77
    witness corruption 72–7
  pre-Ottoman jurisprudential sources
    see also Ottoman jurisprudence
    attempts by Muslim jurists to compile
      and define venality 40–4
    concluding remarks 49
    corruption in jurisprudential works
      and state-generated texts 100
    hadith 34–9
    introductory remarks 29
    policing corruption and need for
      institutional development 44–9
    Quran 29–34, 39
    review of main arguments 269
jurisprudential sources
  overview of key points 27
justifications of corruption *see*
  rationalizations of corruption

kalebend registers
  actors involved in corruption 128
  broader patterns in the kalebend
    registers 136–7
  categorizations and classifications of
    complaints 126–9
  collusion by government
    functionaries 134
  deterrence 142
  direct appeals to imperial center 129–30
  effectiveness of the imperial center's
    involvement 135
  exile, confinement, and imprisonment
    for specific corruption crimes 142
  punishments 135, 137–41
  references to distributive conflicts 131
  references to embezzlement 131–2
  resolution of complaints 134–5
  targetting of waqf affiliates 130

kanunnames
Koçi Bey on favoritism 250–2, 255
Krafft, Hans Ulrich 233–6, 238
  administration of justice 114–15
  broad lists of crimes 111–12
  characterizations of corruption 94–5
  Circle of Justice 83, 85
  government-issued legal
    documentation 81
  no punishments listed 112
  qadis' income 208
  references to zulüm and teaddi 95
  select crimes and punishments in the
    General Kanunname of Sultan
    Süleyman 113
  wealth extraction 92, 98

mazalim tribunals
  historical roots of jurisdiction 46–7
  policing corruption and need for
    institutional development 45–7
  references to corruption 8–9
measurement of corruption 102–4
metaphor of the ledger 266
monitoring corruption
  institutional arrangements 104
  non-financial costs of reporting 108
  petitioning for help against
    crime 104–9
  thresholds for reporting of abuse 107–8
mühimme registers 46–7, 122–4
  actors involved in corruption 128
  acts of corruption in 133
  categorizations and classifications of
    complaints 126–9
  collusion by government
    functionaries 134
  concluding remarks 261–2
  deterrence 142
  devrs in 143
  direct appeals to imperial center 129–30
  effectiveness of the imperial center's
    involvement 135
  punishments 135, 137–41
  references to distributive conflicts 131
  references to embezzlement 131–2
  relative preponderance of corruption
    crimes 130–1
  resolution of complaints 134–5

specific case of Ahmed, the voiceless qadi 267–9
targetting of waqf affiliates 130
Mustafa Ali on favoritism 248–2, 255

Naima
  entrepreneurial means to control corruption 183–8
  on favoritism 252–4
nepotism
  harmful behaviour in government according to political texts 164
  holistic approach 5–6
  morality of patronage 239–41, 249
  Ottoman political discourses 184
  premodern and modern notions 4, 7
  Quran and hadith traditions 29–30, 33, 38–9
  venality of the official establishment 163–6
Niğbolu Kanunname 81–3, 85, 92–3
nonjudicial government corruption in Ottoman jurisprudence 78–9

Ottoman jurisprudence *see also* pre-Ottoman jurisprudential sources
  articulations about qadis and their corruption
    Ibn Abidin's views on bribe-induced verdicts 67–70
    bribe categories according to Ibn Nujaym 58
    favoritism 70–1
    limited references to punishments 70
    Ibn Nujaym's exploration of bribery 52–67
  corruption in jurisprudential works and state-generated texts 100
  corruption of nonjudicial officials in Ibn Abidin's work 78–9
  introductory remarks 50–2
  mufti's corruption
    gifts 77
    minimum attention in premodern jurisprudential works 77
  review of main arguments 269
  witness corruption 72–7

Ottoman political literature *see* political literature
Ottoman polity
  see also political literature; state-generated documents
  controlling corruption
    conceptual model based on a few key variables 102–22
    information based on mühimme, şikayet, and kalebend registers 122–43
    measurement 102–4
    monitoring 104–9
    sanctions 109–22
  existence of numerous publics in the seventeenth century Ottoman polity 25
  favoritism in official documents 256–9
  financial pressures beginning in the late sixteenth century 19
  Islam as major building block 16
  judicial and administrative transformation 21–2
  official legal school 50–1
  origins 9
  political literature
    alternative articulations in sixteenth to eighteenth centuries 179–88
    commentary between sixteenth and eighteenth centuries 156–78
    pre-sixteenth century texts 144–56

patrimonialism
  bases of social relationships 242
  'class-based patrimonialism' 254
  differentiation among different patronage networks 243–4
  family connections 244
  justifications for patronage 244–5
  relationships involving friends, associates, or potential clients 245–6
patronage
  see also favoritism
  defined 239–40
  favoritism in official documents 256–9
  historiography of corruption 7, 22
  introductory remarks 239–40

patronage (cont.)
  jurisprudential considerations of favoritism
    concentration of privilege and income in the hands of specific families 247
    qadis 246-8
  overview of key points 28
  patrimonialism and patronage in the ilmiye
    bases of social relationships 242
    differentiation among different patronage networks 243-4
    family connections 244
    justifications for patronage 244-5
    relationships involving friends, associates, or potential clients 245-6
  political literature
    'class-based patrimonialism' 254
    degeneration of madrasa education and administration of justice 255
    free association with bribery 251-2
    high-ranking appointments 250
    infrequent critical takes 248-9
    insights on the morality of favoritism 253-4
    judgeship appointments based on favoritism 252
    not universally regarded as transgressions 255-6
    specific criticisms of Mustafa Ali 249-50
  well-developed European academic literature 240-2
payment-for-appointment schemes
  commentary between sixteenth and eighteenth centuries 167-71, 178
  foreign accounts of corruption 200-4
  Mumcu's main criticism 18
  patronage in political literature 248-9, 255-6
petitioning for help against crime 104-9
Polanyi, Karl 36-7
policing corruption see also punishments
  auditing of official activities 44-5
  displacement of local qadis from established networks and tribal affiliations 44
  matters pertaining to state-society relations 47-8
  mazalim tribunals 45-7

political literature
  see also state-generated documents
  alternative articulations in sixteenth to eighteenth centuries
    approaches to public office corruption 179
    Birgivi 180-1
    bribery as an issue 179-80
    dangers of corruption for religious establishment 181-2
    Derviş Mehmed's entrepreneurial talent 187
    numerous perspectives 188
    originality of Naima's treatment 183-8
    recognition of hegemonic presence of the state 188
    'turn towards piety' 182-3
  Circle of Justice and its political economy
    complex sociopolitical order 83
    functional tasks and responsibilities according to the Circle 85
    intrinsic notion of justice 85-6
    numerous characterizations of the Circle 84-5
    relationship with Ottoman economics 88-93
    representation of social divisions 83-4
    ruler's inclination to protect the flock 87-90
    wealth generation and extraction 86-8
  commentary between sixteenth and eighteenth centuries
    absence of systemic description of appointment processes 172
    anguish over premature dismissals from office 172-3
    association of bribery with greed 175
    broader associations of bribery 163
    causal relationship among various acts of corruption 166-8
    context as an aid to understanding concerns 169-71
    demand for government positions 173
    earlier literature distinguished 156-7
    focus on bribery 157-62
    harmful behaviour in government according to political texts 164
    inequality of supply- and demand-side factors 175

moralistic and systemic measures to
    fight corruption 178
moralistic explanations of
    corruption 162-3
pre-emptive measures 178
proliferation of political literature 156
punishments 175-8
recurring references to other
    illegality 163-6
well-developed centralized polity 156
withdrawals from the agrarian
    sector 173-5
overview of key points 27
patronage
    'class-based patrimonialism' 254
    degeneration of madrasa
        education and administration of
        justice 255
    free association with bribery 251-2
    high-ranking appointments 250
    infrequent critical takes 248-9
    insights on the morality of
        favoritism 253-4
    judgeship appointments based on
        favoritism 252
    not universally regarded as
        transgressions 255-6
    predominance of criticisms 252-3
    specific criticisms of Mustafa Ali
        249-50
perspectives on corruption 189
pre-sixteenth century texts
    anti-imperial tendencies 146-7
    compassionate rulers 144-6
    defence of qadis' actions 154-5
    general observations on bribery 151-3
    introduction of self-interested
        and ultimately immoral
        practices 147-51
    sporadic references to corruption by
        qadis 151
    two perspectives on corruption 155-6
    works reflecting pre-sixteenth century
        perspectives 148
review of main arguments 269-70
pre-emptive measures
    attempts by Muslim jurists to compile
        and define venality 43
    commentary between sixteenth and
        eighteenth centuries 178

pre-Ottoman jurisprudential
    sources see also Ottoman
    jurisprudence
    attempts by Muslim jurists to compile
        and define venality
    choosing the right person for the
        job 43-4
    consideration of pre-emptive
        measures 43
    focus on the office of office of the
        qadi 40-3
concluding remarks 49
corruption in jurisprudential
    works and state-generated
    texts 100
hadith
    anxiety regarding gifts 36-8
    bribe-givers and bribe-takers 34-6
    concern with potential conflicts of
        interest 36
    embezzlement and favoritism 38-9
    foundational source for Islamic law
        and ethics 34
    unsteady basis for defining acts now
        linked to corruption 39
introductory remarks 29
policing corruption and need for
    institutional development
    auditing of official activities 44-5
    development of 'public law' 48-9
    displacement of local qadis from
        established networks and tribal
        affiliations 44
    matters pertaining to state-society
        relations 47-8
    mazalim tribunals 45-7
Quran
    absence of systematic guidance
        33-4
    acts of abuse often linked with
        corruption 32-3
    condemnations of nepotism and
        embezzlement 33
    root words 29-31
    semantic links among F-s-d, Z-l-m,
        and F-s-q in the Quran 31
    terminology 29-30
    unsteady basis for defining acts now
        linked to corruption 39
review of main arguments 269

public office
  see also corruption
  historiography of corruption 6–7
  modern conceptualizations of
    corruption 98–9
public office corruption see corruption
public versus private sphere 24–6
publics 24–5, 201
punishments
  classical works of jurisprudence 47
  commentary between sixteenth and
    eighteenth centuries 175–8
  false witnessing 138–9
  hadith literature 38
  information based on mühimme, şikayet,
    and kalebend registers 135, 137–41
  measures to control corruption as proposed
    by Ottoman commentators 176
  Ottoman jurisprudence
    false witnessing 75–6
    limited references to punishments 70
    Ibn Nujaym's exploration of bribery
      53–4, 66
  qadi's corruption 41
  sanctions against corruption
    absence of punishment prescriptions
      in official sources 111–14
    effectiveness of negative sanctions 111
    fiqh and siyasa traditions
      distinguished 116–18
    function of kanunnames 114–15
    lack of references for extractive
      transgressions 116
    political consequences 119
    punishment scale for salaried persons
      in Qinq China 115
    relative effectiveness 118–19
    select crimes and punishments in the
      General Kanunname of Sultan
      Süleyman 113

qadis
  see also administration of justice
  articulations in Ottoman jurisprudence
    Ibn Abidin's views on bribe-induced
      verdicts 67–70
    bribe categories according to
      Ibn Nujaym 58
    favoritism 70–1

  limited references to punishments 70
  Ibn Nujaym's exploration of
    bribery 52–67
  errors 41–3
  foreign accounts of corruption
    advice to protect against against
      potentially corrupt actors 221–4
    corrupt qadis 212–13
    focus of literature 208
    gifts as bribes 234–5
    information based on mühimme, şikayet,
      and kalebend registers 129
    jurisprudential considerations of
      favoritism 246–8
  pre-Ottoman jurisprudential sources
    displacement of local qadis from
      established networks and tribal
      affiliations 44
    focus of premodern jurisprudential
      considerations 40–3
  pre-sixteenth century political texts 151–5
  specific case of Ahmed, the voiceless
    qadi 267–9
Quran
  articulations about qadis and their
    corruption 52–4
  emphasis on communal unity and
    wellbeing 29
  as jurisprudential source
    absence of systematic guidance 33–4
    acts of abuse often linked with
      corruption 32–3
    condemnations of nepotism and
      embezzlement 33
    root words 29–31
    semantic links among F-s-d, Z-l-m,
      and F-s-q in the Quran 31
    terminology 29–30
    unsteady basis for defining acts now
      linked to corruption 39

rationalizations of corruption
  'appeal to higher loyalties' 265–6
  defenses used by transgressing
    agents 267
  'denial of injury' 264–5
  'denial of responsibility' 264
  'denial of victim' 265
  'metaphor of the ledger' 266

'refocusing attention' 266
review of main arguments 270
'social weighting' 265
reciprocity
  ahadith 36–7
  concluding remarks 265–6
  gifts as bribes 225, 231–4, 236–8
  jurisprudential treatments of corruption 79–80
  monetary or in-kind outlays accompanied by office grants 19
  primary function of Islamic law 47
  ruler's relationship with the military 89–90
reform treaties 27, 144

sale of offices
  candidacies for judicial positions 166
  Ottoman political discourses 201
  poverty as cause 166
sanctions against corruption
  absence of punishments prescriptions in official sources 111–14
  effectiveness of negative sanctions 111
  fiqh and siyasa traditions distinguished 116–18
  function of kanunnames 114–15
  important influences on state's efforts to control corruption 120–2
  lack of references for extractive transgressions 116
  political consequences 119
  relative effectiveness 118–19
  select crimes and punishments in the General Kanunname of Sultan Süleyman 113
  use of positive and negative sanctions 109–10
shari'a courts 45–7
şikayet registers
  actors involved in corruption 128
  acts of corruption in 133
  categorizations and classifications of complaints 126–9
  collusion by government functionaries 134
  concluding remarks 261–2
  deterrence 142
  devrs in 143

direct appeals to imperial center 129–30
effectiveness of the imperial center's involvement 135
punishments 135, 137–41
references to distributive conflicts 131
references to embezzlement 131–2
relative preponderance of corruption crimes 130–1
resolution of complaints 134–5
targetting of waqf affiliates 130
siyaset
  art of staying in the saddle 48–9
  discretionary privileges 117
  extra-divine traditions of government 116
  foreign accounts of corruption 224
  rationales for punishment 116–17
  relationship between the ruler and his servants 116
social weighting 265
state-generated documents
  see also political literature
  Circle of Justice and its political economy
    functional tasks and responsibilities according to the Circle 85
    intrinsic notion of justice 85–6
    numerous characterizations of the Circle 84–5
    relationship with Ottoman economics 88–93
    representation of social divisions 83–4
    ruler's inclination to protect the flock 87–90
    wealth generation and extraction 86–8
  corruption in jurisprudential works and state-generated texts 100
  favoritism in official documents
    approach of Ottoman polity 259
    concluding remarks 260
    judicial appointments 258
    mülazemet system's degeneration 257–8
    need to control entry into ilmiye establishment 256–7
    training for and staffing ilmiye positions 259

state-generated documents (*cont.*)
  irreconcilable elements of Ottoman society 82-3
  overview of key points 27
  preamble of the Niğbolu District Kanunname 1516 81-2
  review of main arguments 269
  types of abuse of office
    crimes linked to provincial authorities 96-8
    introductory remarks 93-4
    modern conceptualizations of corruption 98-9
    rough correspondence among crime categories 99
    types mentioned between the fifteenth and seventeenth centuries 94-5

Tatarcık Abdullah Efendi on favoritism 255, 259
tributary state and conflicts 86-8, 100

wealth extraction
  acts of corruption in mühimme and şikayet registers 133
  commentary between sixteenth and eighteenth centuries
    causal links in corruption 168
    recurring references to other illegality 163-6
  concluding remarks 263-5, 267-71
  corruption in jurisprudential works and state-generated texts 100
  denial of responsibility 264
  devrs in mühimme and şikayet registers 143
  foreign accounts of corruption 203-4, 210-11
  gifts as bribes 229
  harmful behaviour in government according to political texts 164
  historiography of corruption 1-2, 10-11, 21-2
  information based on mühimme, şikayet, and kalebend registers 112, 116, 118-19, 121-3, 125, 130-4, 142
  measurement of corruption 102-4
  Ottoman jurisprudence 78-9
  perspectives on corruption 189
  political literature 145-50, 155-6, 170, 187
  pre-Ottoman jurisprudential sources 40-1
  rough correspondence among crime categories 99
  state-generated documents 81-4, 86-96, 98
witness corruption *see* false witnessing